The economics of multinational enterprise

The economics of multinational enterprise

Neil Hood
Stephen Young

Longman
London and New York

Longman Group Limited
Longman House, Burnt Mill, Harlow
Essex CM20 2JE, England
Associated companies throughout the world.

Published in the United States of America
by Longman Inc., New York

First published 1979
Second impression 1981
Third impression 1982
Fourth impression 1983
Fifth impression 1984

British Library Cataloguing in Publication Data

Hood, Neil
    The economics of multinational enterprise.
    1. International business enterprises
    I. Title II. Young, Stephen
    338.8'8   HD2755.5   78-40796

    ISBN 0-582-44388-1

Printed in Singapore by Selector Printing Co Pte Ltd.

Contents

Foreword

is now well documented. Though there are still some areas of their operations about which there is still a lacuna of

industrial and geographical structure of operations, their organisational pattern, their managerial strategies and their impact on trade, technology and employment has become generally well established and appreciated. Indeed, it is now recognised that to some extent at least, some of the broad economic questions such as those to do with the impact of multinational enterprises on the employment and balance of payments of home and host countries, is no longer (if it ever

This is a timely book. Although over the last decade and a half the multinational enterprise has been one of the most actively researched areas by business and academic economists, there have been few textbooks which have attempted to synthesise the main streams of thought about the economic rationale of this particular institution, its effects on international resource allocation and the economic welfare of the countries in which it operates, and policies pursued by Governments towards it. This, I believe, the present book does – and does to the considerable credit of the authors.

The book is timely for another reason. In retrospect, the second half of the 1970s may turn out to be a watershed in the development and study of multinational enterprises and of the reactions to them. Contrary to a widespread view held in the late 1960s, there is a growing opinion that the multinational enterprise – at least in its present form – may well have passed the peak of its influence in world affairs, and like the dinosaurs of old, will gradually give way to institutional forms more suited to the political and economic needs of the last decades of the century. Whether or not this is so – and the authors offer some speculations of their own in Chapter 9 – there can be little doubt that the traditional role cast for a multinational enterprise – *viz* a large US or European enterprise engaged primarily in capital intensive resource based ventures or high technology manufacturing activities, usually with 100 per cent ownership of its affiliates, is becoming less and less appropriate. Not only are new investing countries, notably Japan and some developing countries, entering the arena; but the joint venture and a host of contractual arrangements are taking over from the fully owned affiliate as the predominant modality of involvement; the sectors in which multinationals are active are widening all the time; and many medium sized companies are actively exploiting foreign markets.

Viewed from the perspective of the student of multinational enterprises, the 1970s saw the conclusion of the first stage of research and writings on the subject. Indeed, borrowing from the title of one of the books on the subject by a distinguished scholar in the field, research on the multinational enterprise is moving into its 'mature' stage.[1] Following the pioneering work of Raymond Vernon and his colleagues, the anatomy of multinational enterprises and its activities is now well documented. Though there are still several areas of their operations about which there is still a lacuna of facts, gradually, the industrial and geographical structure of operations, their organisational patterns, their managerial strategies and their impact on trade, technology and employment has become generally well established and appreciated. Indeed, it is now recognised that to seek general answers to some of the broad economic questions such as those to do with the impact of multinational enterprises on the employment and balance of payments of home and host countries, is no longer (if it ever was) a very rewarding exercise, and that attention would be more productively directed to more specific issues – e.g. those related to individual sectors or case studies of particular companies. At the same time, there are still many unexplored areas such as the impact of multinationals in service industries, state owned multinationals and multinationals from less developed countries demanding attention.

Then too, research on the theory of international production, i.e. production financed by foreign direct investment and undertaken by multinational enterprises has reached a consolidatory stage. From a host of explanations put forward in the 1960s from various interrelated strands, an eclectic or synthetic theory of international production has emerged, which treats international production as a particular vehicle of the international economic involvement of firms, and seeks to explain it in these terms. The authors of this book pay particular attention to the most recent contributions in this area which have their lineage traceable to the work of economists on the theory of the firm and international trade.

Finally, policy towards the multinational enterprise (or the transnational corporation as it is also known) has evolved to an extent that it is appropriate to pause, look back and take stock. The pendulum of opinions and policies towards foreign direct investment and the multinational enterprise has swung violently since the mid 1950s when foreign direct investment was universally acclaimed by both developed and developing countries for the capital, technology and management skills it brought with it. At that time, comparatively little attention was paid to the costs of such investment, and almost none to the effects of the control of decision-taking being in the hands of foreign companies.

But, gradually it was these issues that became the central point of discussion about the effects of international direct investment in the 1960s and early 1970s. First attention was concentrated on ensuring that any monopoly power of multinational enterprises was minimised; then, on the appropriateness of the decisions they took to allocate the resources of their foreign affiliates – particularly in cases where these latter were regarded as part of a global strategy. Finally the focus was widened to embrace the international economic order in which the multinationals operated, it being argued that whatever the beneficial effects of international direct investments as a means of resource transference across boundaries, it locked transferring and recipient countries into a relationship, which the latter did not always perceive to be in its long term political or economic interests. Attention in the 1970s has thus been directed to finding ways and means of minimising the extent of foreign control over the resources imported by countries, either by reducing the equity participation of multinational enterprises, or by ensuring that as far as possible, their activities advanced national goals and objectives.

Now, in the late 1970s, there are signs that the confrontation stage between multinational enterprises and governments may have reached its peak. Although as the authors describe, some countries remain actively hostile to foreign direct investment, and there is no doubt that all countries are increasing their surveillance of foreign firms in their midst, there are also definite signs of a more conciliatory approach towards multinational enterprises. Not only is this shown by the opening of the doors of Japan and East European countries to foreign direct investment; several developed countries, e.g. Australia and Canada, and developing nations like Argentina and Mexico have liberalised their policies towards foreign based companies in the last year or so. It seems out of confrontation may come a period of better understanding and one of a more constructive relationship, whereby a more balanced and conciliatory approach to the costs and benefits of multinational enterprises is taken.

The multinationals are themselves showing more awareness of the needs of countries in which they operate by engaging in new forms and more cooperation. To this extent, the 1980s may see a new phase of relationship being established; we may well have come through the honeymoon period of the 1950s and the reaction and hostility of the 1960s and 1970s to a (hopeful) maturing of relationships between multinationals and governments in the 1980s.

For all these reasons then, a textbook which takes stock of research and policy up to the mid 1970s is especially welcome. The task of course is a challenge, albeit a daunting one. Even in 400 pages, it is not possible to encompass, even superficially, all the major strands of a subject which embraces wide areas of economics and business studies; the authors are the first to admit that many important effects of multinational enterprises are not considered in any depth. But I believe they do give to readers a good sense of the present state of knowledge on the subject.

The format of the book I find particularly rewarding. First, it relates work on multinational enterprises to the main stream of economic doctrine; nowhere is this more clearly shown than in the chapters on the theory of the firm and international trade. Second, each chapter deals systematically both with the theory and empirical evidence on the particular issues under discussion. This, I believe, the reader – and particularly the student reader – will find helpful.

In short, this book presents a succinct description and evaluation of our state of knowledge about multinational enterprises and their role in the world economy of the late 1970s. It is a most worthwhile contribution to the literature. It will be equally valuable as a textbook to students and as a reference book to practitioners and to those who have any dealing with multinational enterprises. Finally, university and college teachers and researchers will find themselves grateful to the authors for providing, within the cover of this book, so much both to ease their work and to make it more pleasant.

John H. Dunning

1. **Mira Wilkins** (1974) *The Maturing of Multinational Enterprise: American Business Abroad from 1914–70*. Harvard Univ. Press.

Preface

The enormous growth in interest in the economics of multinationals over recent years has been reflected in a growing volume of literature on most dimensions of the subject. This expansion of material has not, however, resulted in many attempts to examine the multinational enterprise (MNE) from first principles. Neither has there been a commensurate development of texts which present the subject systematically and comprehensively to students at undergraduate and graduate level. This book has been designed to fill this gap and facilitate the more specific consideration of this topic within economics and related subjects.

The approach taken has been to select certain key issues in the operation of the multinational enterprise and examine the contribution which economics can make to their understanding. Thus Chapters 2 to 7 cover the determinants of foreign direct investment, the economic questions concerning the operation of the MNE, the MNE and international trade, the relationship between foreign direct investment and economic development, and finally the vital subject of control of the MNE from the perspective of both home and host nations. Chapter 8 moves away from orthodox economic theory to consider some of the radical views on the multinational enterprise. Finally, the introductory and concluding chapters are respectively concerned with the scope and direction of the MNE and with a review of the future. Wherever possible an attempt has been made to provide a balanced treatment of theory and available empirical evidence, with care being taken to note the areas where theory, evidence, or both, require further development.

We are inevitably indebted to many individuals for their help during the various stages of this project. We are particularly grateful to Professor John Dunning. He took an active interest in this book from its early stages, in spite of his own very heavy schedule of work. His advice, encouragement and wide knowledge of the subject enabled him to make a contribution which we regard as invaluable. Many others gave us constructive advice on draft chapters at various stages. These include Alan Rugman (University of Winnipeg); Vern Terpstra (University of Michigan); Dale Larson (then Katholieke Universiteit Te Leuven); George Yannopoulos (University of Reading) and Alastair Young (Paisley College). Our Paisley colleague John

Duignan gave us a most useful set of comments on the draft at a particularly important stage. None of these individuals is, however, in any way responsible for the book as it stands. The continued patience of our secretarial assistants, Jean Beggs, Ella Kininmonth and Margaret Jamieson has been truly remarkable, and they have our unreserved thanks for their work and their ability to remain pleasant throughout. And our very numerous library requests were competently handled by David Strachan and Rosanna McLennan. Finally, we acknowledge the long-suffering of our wives, Anna and Anne, and our children, Annette, Cameron, Nicolas and Juliette, who have received less attention than they deserve during this project.

Acknowledgements

We are grateful to the following for permission to reproduce copyright material:

George Allen and Unwin Publishers Ltd., for a table from *Economic Analysis and the Multinational Enterprise* by E. Mansfield; George Allen and Unwin Publishers Ltd., and Humanities Press Inc., for a table from *Studies in International Investment* by J. Dunning; American Economic Association and the author, Professor H. G. Grubel for a table from 'Internationally Diversified Portfolios: Welfare Gains and Capital Flows' from *American Economic Review* Vol 58, 1968; Ballinger Publishing Company for Tables 2.1.1, 3.4.1–2, 2.4.6 and 2.1.2 based on data from *Tracing the Multinationals: A Sourcebook on US Based Enterprises* by J. W. Curhan, W. H. Davidson and R. Suri, Copyright 1977, Ballinger Publishing Company; Bank of England for an adapted table 'Exchange Rates and Comparative Interest Rates' from the Statistical Annex to *Bank of England Quarterly Bulletin*; Basil Blackwell and Mott Ltd., for a table based on data from 'The Product Cycle and International Production: UK Pharmaceuticals' by T. G. Parry from *Journal of Industrial Economics* Vol XXIV September 1975–76; Cambridge University Press for an extract and a table based on data from 'Manufactured Exports from Less Developed Countries and Multinational Firms' by G. K. Helleiner from *Economic Journal* March 1973, and a table based on data from 'Transnational Corporations and Manufactured Exports from Poor Countries' by D. Nayyar from *Economic Journal* Vol 88, 1978; Columbia Graduate School of Business for a table from 'Choosing Foreign Locations: One Company's Experience' by E. S. Groo from *Columbia Journal of World Business* September–October 1972; Commission of the European Communities for tables based on data from *Survey of Multinational Enterprises* Vol 1, July 1978; The Economic Record, Journal of the Economic Society of Australia and New Zealand for two figures from 'The Benefits and Costs of Private Investment from Abroad: A Theoretical Approach' pp. 13–35 by G. D. A. Mac-Dougall from *Economic Records* Vol 36, 1960; General Agreement on Tariffs and Trade for two tables based on data from *International Trade*; Harcourt Brace Jovanovich Inc., for Fig 7.1 p. 54 from

Business Behaviour, Value and Growth Revised Edition by William J. Baumol © 1967 by Harcourt Brace Jovanovich Inc., Reproduced by permission of the publishers; Harvard Institute of Economic Research, Littauer Centre for two figures based on data from *American Exports and Foreign Direct Investment* by T. Horst, Discussion Paper No. 361, 1974; Harvard University Press for a table based on data from *The World's Multinational Enterprises: A Sourcebook of Tables* by J. W. Vaupel and J. Curhan; Journal of World Trade Law for a table from 'Technology Imports and Direct Foreign Investment in Japan' by T. Ozawa from *Journal of World Trade Law* Vol 7, No. 6, 1973; Lexington Books, D. C. Heath & Company for two tables and a fig pp. 149, 187, 122 from *Testing Theories of Economic Imperialism* edited by Steven J. Rosen and James R. Kurth © 1974 D. C. Heath & Company, reprinted by permission of the publishers; Longman Group Ltd., for two tables from *The Economics of Innovation* by Parker, 1974; M. C. B. (Management Decision) for a table from 'Some Aspects of International Pricing' by J. C. Baker and J. K. Ryan from *Management Decision* Vol II 1973; McGraw Hill Book Company for a table p. 77 from *Pentagon Capitalism* by S. Melman © 1970 McGraw-Hill Book Company. Used with permission of McGraw-Hill Book Company; Macmillan London and Basingstoke Ltd., for an adapted table from *The Gap Between Rich and Poor Nations* edited by G. Ranis, a table and extracts from *Foreign Investment Transnationals and Developing Countries* by S. Lall and P. Streeton; Macmillan, London and Basingstoke Ltd., and Harvard University Press for a figure from *The Corporate Economy* edited by R. L. Marris and A. Wood; Meerut University Economics Association for a table from 'A Macro-Economic Approach to Foreign Direct Investment' by Kojima from *Hitotsubashi Journal* 1973; The M.I.T. Press for Fig 2 p. 26 and an adapted Table 1 p. 99 from *The International Corporation* by Charles P. Kindleberger; Monthly Review Press for an extract and a table based on *The Age of Imperialism* by H. Magdoff Copyright © 1966, 1968 by Monthly Review Inc. Reprinted by permission of Monthly Review Press; National Industrial Conference Board for a table from 'Inter Company Transactions in the Multinational Firm' by J. Greene and M. G. Duerr *Managing International Business* No. 6, 1970; North-Holland Publishing Company for a figure from *Firm and Industry Determinants of the Decision to Invest Abroad: an empirical study* by T. Horst; Oxford University Press for two tables based on data from pp. 260–73 'The Extent and Significance of the Nationalization of Foreign Owned Assets in Developing Countries' by M. L. Williams *Oxford Economic Papers* Vol 27, No. 2 July 1975, four tables from 'Characteristics and Motivations of the US Corporations which Manufacture Abroad' by J. W. Vaupel from 'The Determinants of International Production' by J. H. Dunning, *Oxford Economic Papers* Vol 25 1973, a table from 'The Commodity

Composition of International Trade in Manufactures: An Empirical Analysis' by E. E. Leamer from *Oxford Economic Papers* Vol 26, 1974, and a table based on data from *Private Foreign Investment in Development* by G. Reuber et al, published by Clarendon Press 1973; Rutgers University and the author for an extract and a figure from 'The Neotechnology Account of International Trade: The case of Petrochemicals' by Robert B. Stobaugh from *Journal of International Business Studies* Fall 1971; the author, Professor T. W. Swan for a figure from 'Longer-run Problems of the Balance of Payments' from *The Australian Economy A Volume of Readings* edited by H. W. Arndt and W. M. Corden 1963; United Nations Institute for Training and Research for a table based on data from 'The Transfer of Technology Economics of Offshore Assembly: The Case of the Semiconductor Industry' by Y. S. Chang from *UNITAR* 1971; University of East Anglia and the author, for a table from 'Internation and Oligopoly and Dependent Industrialization in the Latin American Motor Industry' by R. Jenkins Discussion Paper No. 13 October 1976; The University of Chicago Press for a table from 'The Impact of Research and Development on US Trade' by D. B. Keesing from Journal of Political Economy 75, 1967.

Whilst every effort has been made, we are unable to trace the copyright owner of an adapted Table 1.1 p. 81 from *Industry in Britain* by J. H. Dunning 1976 and would appreciate any information which would enable us to do so.

The scope and direction
of multinational enterprise

Introduction

There are few modern economic institutions that have been the focus
of more contention than the multinational corporation. Alternatively
welcomed and spurned, praised and denigrated, controlled and
deemed uncontrollable, such enterprises have been at the centre of
wide-ranging debates both within their domestic base and in recipient
nations. Even a casual exploration of the literature will demonstrate
the strength of positive and negative feeling towards the multinational
firm. The US Tariff Commission, with visionary air, hailed it as a fact
'beyond dispute that the spread of multinational business ranks with
the development of the steam engine, electric power, and the
automobile as one of the major events of modern economic history'.[1]*
As a consequence of the international corporation, some would argue
that the world is in the process of becoming an integrated unit – 'a
global shopping centre'.[2] Others would stress sinister dimensions, and
emphasise the origins of the multinational company in the US. '. . .
military interventions in Greece, Iran, Lebanon, the Congo, Cuba
(etc.) . . .; military missions throughout most of the "free world" and
American economic dominance of countless Third-World countries
have combined to impress upon all but the most recalcitrant observer
the truth that in the post-war period the United States has been a
formidable imperialist power'.[3] This latter response views private
direct investment abroad as an inevitable part of a wider political
process within which there may be little harmony of interests between
the parties.

Analysis of multinational business is thus clouded by controversy,
variety of interpretation and numerous, frequently emotive, value
judgements. Nor are these debates static. What was once regarded as a
competitive environment where 'foreign investors acted as neutral
agents of capital and technological transfer is now seen as a highly
oligopolistic world of transnational corporations possessing great
commercial and economic power, and posing a challenge to national
policy and economic independence'.[4] Such a view is very prevalent
within Third-World nations striving for both national and economic

---

* Superior numerals indicate Notes and References on pp. 376–92.

identity. In addition labour groups in home countries, initially tolerant of the multinational company, have become increasingly restless over what is seen as the export of jobs by 'runaway' firms. As one American labour leader expressed the problem: 'Entire industries, growth industries . . . and many thousands of urgently needed jobs are exported. To many of us in the labor movement it portends a mass exodus.'[5]

It is to such problems that this book is devoted. The aim is to identify the theoretical framework which underlies the various facets of multinationality and to examine and weigh the matching empirical evidence, in an attempt to facilitate a greater understanding of the economics of the multinational enterprise.

Definition and terms

Many different attempts have been made to arrive at a concise definition of multinational enterprise. One of the principal reasons for the variety of definitions stems from different weightings attributed to the characteristics of companies which operate internationally.[6] 'Multinational' clearly is not an apt description of a corporation whose only international involvement takes the form of exporting either finished and intermediate goods or factor inputs (such as capital), or which has portfolio investments in some foreign distributors. The essential elements of MNE operations are direct (as distinct from portfolio) investment abroad giving a power of control over decision-making in a foreign enterprise; the collective transfer of resources, involving factor inputs such as knowledge and entre-preneurship as well as money capital; and finally the requirement that the income-generating assets acquired by this process be located in a number of countries. Minimum size of corporation might be added to this list, but there is little justification for such a restriction since the behavioural characteristics of MNEs as examined within this book are not necessarily a function of size as such. Within these basic elements, different commentators would place different emphases. For example, some consider that to be an MNE, a corporation must have 25 per cent or more 'foreign content', either in assets, employment or income source. Again, there is the view that multinationality requires income-generating assets to be owned in a minimum number of countries, usually five or six. Finally, on the meaning of 'direct' investment, the usual interpretation would require at least 25 per cent of the share capital of the foreign enterprise to be owned by the parent. This assumption of a required degree of ownership to permit operational control is an important one. It is reasonable to accept that where affiliates are wholly- or majority-owned, control will normally be held by the foreign investor. But even if only a small amount of equity capital is provided by the MNE, this does not necessarily mean loss of control for the multinational firm. The fact is that the corporation is providing a package which includes technology and management skills as well as money capital. Given that in many cases the MNE is uniquely in a position to organise and co-ordinate the operation of these separate resources, control may be effectively retained by the foreign firm, irrespective of the ownership arrangements. That there is no definitive relationship between ownership and control can be indicated by a different example. If a host country is able to negotiate and establish guidelines relating to the behaviour of MNEs operating within its boundaries, it may be able to reduce the control held by the foreign firm, even if the latter owns all or a majority of the equity.[7]

For the purpose of this book, the working definition is couched in inclusive rather than exclusive terms. A multinational enterprise is a corporation which owns (in whole or in part), controls and manages income-generating assets in more than one country. In so doing it engages in international production, namely production across national boundaries financed by foreign direct investment. The abbreviated form MNE is used throughout, in preference to what are effectively surrogate terms such as MNC (multinational corporation) and TNC (transnational corporation), the latter being the nomenclature employed by the United Nations. Within this broad definition there are a bewildering variety of types of operation and organisation. In operational terms, an MNE can be offering a service (e.g. airlines); be resource-oriented (e.g. oil and mining corporations); or be engaged in manufacturing activity. It is very common to find MNEs operating in a number of these areas, either directly or indirectly. Thus for example oil corporations like Exxon explore, refine, manufacture by-products, distribute and service appliances. From an organisational viewpoint, an MNE may not be solely privately owned. It may as a corporation be partially owned and managed by its home country government (as is, for example, British Leyland) or alternatively it may have within its subsidiaries a mixture of ownership patterns depending on regulations imposed by host governments, commercial expediency and so on.

There are of course a number of very different methods of internally managing MNEs which can 'change their appearance'. Some corporations (e.g. Johnson & Johnson) adopt a policy of allowing considerable autonomy in subsidiaries both in finance and product development. Others have tight central control of strategy, and allow the development of only the most routine managerial functions at subsidiary level. This is particularly the case where the MNE is highly dependent on intra-group trade between subsidiaries. Other corporations again operate on neither of these philosophies, but rather develop systems to suit individual managements, countries, technologies or product groups. Essentially, however, MNEs consist of a number of linked business establishments, which are planned and operated together to achieve established objectives. MNEs must be regarded as integrated business systems in order to analyse their behaviour.

A number of other terms are widely used throughout this book. In the first place the terms home and host nation occur frequently. The *home nation* is the country which has acted as the base for the expansion and initial development of the MNE. It may no longer be either the largest sales area or the locus of the majority of shareholders. It will, nevertheless, normally still be the base from which ultimate control is exercised. A *host nation* is one of the countries in which the MNE operates, irrespective of the relative size of that operation within the corporate whole and independent of the ownership mix. In addition a distinction is necessary between the *parent* company and its *subsidiaries* or *affiliates*. Essentially the parent MNE is taken to be the company which operates out of the home nation, while the subsidiaries and affiliates (the two terms being used interchangeably) are located in the host countries.[8]

Justification for study of the MNE

Perhaps the most basic justification for examining the economics of the MNE lies in its rapid emergence as a new widespread form of institution whose existence affects, and frequently challenges, the established institutional order. The influences of the MNE are both complex and comprehensive. For both home and host nations, they pose problems of sovereignty; of the effectiveness of macro-economic policy, when constituent units of MNEs are subject to external decision making; and of regulation, when social and economic policy objectives are not being attained. While such challenges to domestic autonomy exist most obviously in host nations, many states are by no means single-minded. In frequent instances they actively compete for the benefits brought by foreign direct investment, particularly where the domestic economy has long-run structural or development problems. Nor is the home country from which the MNE regulates its activities immune. There are, for example, both benefits in repatriated profits from abroad and potential costs in terms of employment creation in other economies. In reality the ambivalence of both home and host governments towards MNEs is characteristic of all institutional response to their activities. As far as domestic institutions such as indigenous industry and banks are concerned, MNEs are again both welcome and unwelcome. By transferring technology, and management skills, they increase competition (a cost) but may also improve the quality of the labour force (a benefit) for local corporations. For banks and financial institutions, they offer new business, although at the same time they may be criticised for using their home-country connections. The dilemma of international institutions, such as the United Nations and the World Bank, is no less real since MNEs simultaneously offer contributions to economic growth and development while posing major problems of regulation. From all these perspectives, the multinational corporation offers both benefits and costs.

MNEs are not unique in posing such evaluation problems. The degree of uniqueness stems from their size, contribution to world trade and extremely rapid expansion over the past 30 years. It is from issues of scale, resources and growth that the awareness of the true distinctiveness of the behaviour of MNEs emerges. This behaviour is reflected in the relative power of many MNEs to deploy resources and influence the distribution of output to a degree far beyond that achieved by any former business institution. At a micro level it is experienced when, for example, an MNE pursues a global rationalisation policy resulting in plant closures and unemployment with minimum consultation with host governments; or when investigations reveal pricing policies designed to maximise taxation liabilities in areas of low corporate taxation. The economic power of many MNEs is real and the scope for its exercise is extensive. That alone would justify further study of the phenomenon.

The MNE and its near relations

A corporation rarely becomes multinational overnight. While the process can be rapid if aided, for example, by merger and take-over of production facilities, it is more commonly the result of longer-term business planning. Other forms of international trading play their part in the formation of an MNE and frequently continue to play an important role thereafter. On taking the decision to expand and diversify, any corporation has several choices of method: develop domestic operations on a multi-plant basis; export (and import); initiate licensing and related technical agreements; develop portfolio investment overseas; or engage in overseas production.

It requires no more than casual observation to note that most large corporations employ all these methods and/or use combinations of the basic options according to circumstances. These alternatives can be usefully considered in two ways at this point in the analysis. They can be regarded as stages, in that some well-established MNEs have adopted each of them in sequence. Having found that further domestic market penetration was difficult even within a multi-plant, multi-product system, foreign markets were tested and products (developed initially for the home market) were subsequently exported. As overseas markets developed and required product development for their specific needs, the corporations licensed host country producers to expand the market. The licensees were frequently guaranteed minimum efficient scale of operations on the basis of the former imported product range. The end of this approach was invariably the establishment of owned and controlled manufacturing units abroad, i.e. international production in its true sense. Alternatively, the options outlined can be regarded as different ways of exploiting comparative advantage in domestic and particularly in foreign markets. In some ways this latter approach throws greater light on the behaviour of MNEs which are capable of adopting an infinite variety of modes of operation dependent on products, technology, market size, political constraints, taxation, local laws and so on. From whatever perspective, it is important to see these methods of approach as analytically distinct while collectively forming part of the integrated MNE system. They are briefly considered as such in the following section:

The multi-plant domestic operation

Although normal processes of expansion and market growth do result in corporations expanding their domestic and international operations simultaneously, the one commonly precedes the other. The reasons for the establishment of additional plant facilities within a domestic framework are very varied. Diversification associated with the development of the firm from a single product to a multi-product enterprise; the size of regional markets; economies of agglomeration with suppliers or buyers; restrictions on plant expansion in urban sites; and management philosophies of keeping individual plant size at a predetermined optimum are only a few of the variables. Corporation size, competition, technology and incentives to locate in particular areas can equally well explain this development. The net effect is normally to raise penetration in regional or sectoral markets and provide experience of controlling several plants. The limits to this method of expansion are set by market size, and, invariably, the level of competition, both of which factors will hinder the achievement of growth objectives. At this stage, the multi-plant domestic corporation resembles the MNE only in so far as spatial integration is involved in both instances, and a requirement exists to develop skills in monitoring and controlling at a distance. In addition, both types of operation have a range of options regarding the specialisation of products or particular processes, either vertically or horizontally, between plants.

Exporting (and importing)

A large number of corporations develop international interests as a means of opening up new markets and thereby overcoming domestic market constraints. By such action it is hoped to raise volume and preserve or raise profit margins. Preliminary overseas ventures derived from such motives may be limited to exporting from a home base. Not only is this likely to be the least-risk method of operating internationally, but it also has the advantage of involving a limited capital commitment.

There are, however, some serious limitations for many firms in employing exporting as the basis for long-term strategy. It is invariably difficult to find importers and agents who will both provide adequate market information and have the same expansion ambitions as a large corporation with extensive experience in its home market. The likelihood of such a match is further decreased when two different economic and technical environments are involved. While exporting may involve little expenditure, in that standardised products are supplied, substantial product development costs may in fact be required if a long-term position is to be established in the market. Direct exporting would not always reveal that need in time. Moreover, the type of service and customer liaison necessary for many technical products may not be available to the exporter, especially in markets in developing nations. Of equal importance are the difficulties associated with the policies employed by governments regarding imports. Trade, regulatory and administrative barriers combine to produce significant risks for many corporations, particularly where exports are a high and growing proportion of turnover and where dependence upon agents, etc. is increasing. Again, in the longer term both technologies and factor endowments change, thereby adjusting the relative costs of production between the exporting and importing countries. For these and many other reasons, total dependence on 'direct' export strategies for growth is relatively rare in large corporations. Other supporting strategies are normally required.

In comparison with international production, therefore, exporting lacks flexibility and development potential. An advantage which exporting may be presumed to share with foreign direct investment, namely close control, may also be illusory when the role of importers and agents is taken into consideration. The one similarity derives from the fact that in both cases products are sold outside national boundaries and the need exists to take account of legal, cultural and environmental differences in foreign markets.

It should be noted that a company may become involved internationally through importing rather than exporting. Vertical, as opposed to horizontal, expansion may take place to obtain supplies of raw materials. The object of such a strategy may be to cut production costs by obtaining inputs more cheaply or to provide security of supply. But once again the possibility of achieving these objectives may be severely constrained by lack of control, and pressures would exist in the long term for the company to become more operationally involved through direct investment.

Licensing and technical agreements

Corporations holding proprietary rights to technology and trade marks frequently engage in international operations by licensing foreign firms to develop particular markets abroad. There are a host of different types of licensing agreements. For example, licences may be exclusive or non-exclusive; that is the licensee may or may not be given exclusive rights within particular markets. Time scales covered by licensing agreements also vary, but contracts covering 5- or 10-year periods are usual. Furthermore, the way in which the licensor gains his return ranges from lump sum payments to percentage returns on sales over the agreed period. As licensors, corporations will try to ensure that they exert some form of control during the agreement ranging, for instance, from specific clauses within the contractual agreement regarding suppliers, marketing, etc. to equity participation in the licensee's operations. Some of the latter arrangements constitute the beginnings of foreign direct investment where, for example, the licensor begins to take a significant equity interest in the licensee. This may be a particularly appealing method of direct entry to a market since set-up costs and delays can be minimised and existing contacts utilised. Licensing nevertheless is by no means always undertaken by choice. In some countries with tight controls on direct investment (e.g. Japan) it was for a time virtually the only form of market entry available.

As with exporting, licensing agreements can often inhibit the longer term development of a market, as commonly licensees do not perform up to expectations. Among the more indeterminate costs of such agreements are those associated with policing. These arise because the licensor is effectively contracting out his products and his reputation in the market concerned. Quality, reliability and service standards are among the items out of the control of the licensor and in the hands of the local supplier. Problems in this sphere have resulted in corporations being induced into direct investment before they had planned to do so. Some control may be exercised in licensing agreements through the terms of contracts agreed with licensees; but increasingly, regulations are being introduced nationally and internationally to limit contract terms. These make licensing agreements more attractive to recipient governments but less attractive to foreign firms. Licensing agreements are often associated with contracts for technical and managerial assistance. Technical aid projects may, however, go beyond normal licensing arrangements. For example, corporations specialising in the construction and operation of major capital equipment projects (such as European consortia building chemical, textile and car plants in the Middle East and USSR) frequently not only design, arrange finance and construct plants abroad, but also engage staff and manage the total operation through an initial run-in period. With such 'turn-key' projects a developing nation aims to manage its own key industries and after a period of time, control as well as ownership passes to the host country. In other cases technical aid agreements and management contracts are employed as substitutes for licensing. This sometimes happens where governments are opposed to the lack of domestic control involved with licensing deals; but this strategy only increases control if and when the hired management are replaced by indigenous personnel. Overall, the volume of fees earned by large corporations through such sales of intangible assets has grown rapidly since the early 1960s and now represents an important source of income for many. On the other hand, from the viewpoint of the corporation, the key question is whether or not fees earned compensate for the profits which could have been obtained by other forms of involvement in the market, particularly given the relatively short-term nature of technical and managerial aid agreements.

Portfolio investment

Portfolio investment involves the acquisition of foreign securities by individuals or institutions without any control over or participation in the management of the companies concerned. There are a number of important strategic reasons for a corporation taking shares in foreign companies, either as a precursor to direct investment or as a part of long-run planning. Portfolio holdings may reinforce technical, licensing or distribution agreements or may be a way of spreading the corporation's interests in other countries. The latter has invariably underlying motivations such as establishing a base for longer-run acquisition or diversification or the collection of market information. In other instances portfolio investment may represent pre-emptive action to avoid a take-over by a domestic or foreign competitor; or the investment may be motivated by a desire to profit from a market or sector in which the corporation is not directly involved.

While these, and many other, motives may explain portfolio holdings abroad, few manufacturing corporations would base long-run planning on this form of investment. It has two basic weaknesses when compared with the direct approach. Firstly it rarely allows the opportunity to fully exploit the corporation's technical or product advantages and secondly it involves ownership but little or no management and control. The lack of ability to manage assets held in this way invariably precludes the corporation being able to completely integrate a foreign holding as it could by direct investment.

Foreign direct investment

Foreign direct investment is distinguished from portfolio investment in that it involves ownership (in part or whole) and management of a foreign operation; in addition, with direct investment abroad a package of resources is transferred, whereas with portfolio investment the resources are transmitted independently of each other. The most clear-cut example of foreign direct investment occurs where a firm sets up wholly-owned subsidiaries abroad. These subsidiaries may be established by the take-over of existing local firms or they may take the form of new greenfield ventures. But subsidiaries need not be wholly-owned: foreign direct investment may involve a joint venture agreement where a foreign-based firm has a majority share, an equal share or a minority share in the ownership of an enterprise abroad; the important requirement, as noted earlier, is that the foreign company has operating control.[9] This is the crucial point: a corporation with extensive portfolio interests may have much greater investment commitment overseas than one with a number of selling subsidiaries which it controls. Nevertheless only the latter represents foreign direct investment.

The *multinational enterprise* represents the outworking of this foreign direct investment process. How similar to or dissimilar from its near relations is the MNE?[10]

Firstly, as with the *multi-plant domestic operation*, the MNE owns and controls production units in more than one location. On the other hand the MNE's production units are operated in different nation states. Secondly, as with an *exporting firm*, the MNE sells goods across national boundaries. Conversely, unlike the exporting firm, the MNE also produces these goods outside its domestic location and moreover a large part of MNE exports may represent intragroup trade. Thirdly, like the *national firm licensing foreign manufacturers*, the MNE is involved in foreign production. But the multinational company owns and controls its manufacturing units located abroad, and this characteristic also clearly distinguishes the MNE from a basically national company with foreign portfolio holdings. These and other key distinguishing features of the multinational firm are considered further in later paragraphs.

Historical review of overseas investment

Foreign investment has played an important role in the international economy since the latter part of the nineteenth century. In the pre-1914 period, capital movements were associated with large-scale population movements out of Europe. The majority of these were fixed interest, portfolio investments, with the UK being the most important creditor nation, accounting for over half of the total international capital outstanding in 1914. Indeed in the half century up to 1914, the UK invested abroad an annual average of four per cent of its national income, and as much as seven per cent in the 10 years immediately preceding the First World War. These figures have probably never been equalled anywhere since and for such reasons the period up to the First World War has been regarded as the golden age of international capital movements. The UK was the major investor for a variety of reasons, including domestic prosperity; a desire to secure imports of primary products; and a highly developed institutional framework which successfully channelled available funds overseas. Geographically around 60 per cent of this investment was in the Americas and Australasia. Its sectoral distribution also reflected underlying motivations: 40 per cent of the investment was in railways, while 30 per cent was in government or municipal securities. Both the volume and direction of portfolio investment flows during this period were strongly influenced by the attractive interest rates obtainable in foreign locations.

The First World War and its aftermath had a dramatic effect on the relative wealth of the major European nations. As a result of loss or repudiation of investments, war debts and reconstruction costs, continental Europe had changed from net creditor to net debtor status by the 1920s, while the United States' position was reversed from that of a debtor to a creditor country. By 1929 the United Kingdom was still the principal creditor nation, but the US made considerable investment abroad in these years; and partly associated with the increasing importance of America, the pattern of investment was changing. Thus direct investment in overseas subsidiaries expanded to account for around 25 per cent of total overseas lending.

The more critical period had yet to come. Despite repeated attempts in international conferences, the major nations were unable to restore an equilibrium to the international economy. Economic depression in the US, and subsequently in Europe, created new interest in national economic self-sufficiency and domestic employment levels. The general recession conditions produced chronic problems for international capital flows. Exchange controls, competitive devaluations, tariff barriers, market-sharing and price-fixing cartels were all symptoms of the economic climate. Portfolio investment suffered most: the depression curtailed foreign investment and led to a significant volume of capital being repatriated; although, in fact, much of the portfolio capital proved unmarketable due to the conditions prevailing. Direct investment, especially from the US to Europe, continued to grow slowly, but in relation to total foreign investment its volume was still small. The period ended with the Second World War, bringing severe financial losses to the principal participating nations, and as a consequence the two leading creditor nations of 1938, the US and the UK, were debtors by 1945.

The years after the Second World War saw a crucial shift in the climate for international investment. This laid the basis for the present and probable future pattern of capital flows, where direct foreign investment is dominant. These post-war years contrast markedly with the era of high colonialism before 1914 when portfolio investment was pre-eminent. The origins of direct investment activity were present in the latter period, given the existence of a number of powerful trading companies. However, the scale, diversity of location and source country, penetration and type of comparative advantage in contemporary MNE operations differs sharply from these times.

There were many factors operating to produce a favourable climate after 1945. The period from the beginning of Marshall Aid in 1948 to the formation of the EEC in 1958 was one of heavy United States involvement in both European and international economic reconstruction through government loans and grants abroad. United States corporations were aided in their access to foreign countries by the Marshall Plan operations and subsequently by the gradual liberalisation of trade and payments; and they were in the unique position of having the capacity to export, and resources to expand, abroad. The convertibility of the dollar, the IMF, the formation of the GATT and so on were all part of this new situation. In addition, certain tax policies of the US Government favoured foreign operations; in particular the re-investment of foreign earnings was encouraged since tax was only payable on profits when they were repatriated to the US. Thus foreign direct investment became the major component of private capital flows, with the United States the principal source and Europe a major recipient. Most European countries were very short of foreign exchange after the war and were only too pleased to welcome inward direct investment at least initially; although by the 1960s several European states, notably France, had become less welcoming when faced with the massive inward flow.

It was not simply the economic climate which facilitated the growth of the MNE after 1945. A revolution in transport and communications, typified by the development of jet aircraft and the computer, removed many of the barriers to transnational production. More than that, however, markets in capital, knowledge and management failed to provide a mechanism for efficient resource transfer. During the nineteenth century, capital was the principal resource transferred between countries and the existence of adequate capital markets encouraged portfolio investment. But in the twentieth century and particularly after 1945, capital, technology and management skills came to represent a closely integrated package of resources to the firm. Because of the inadequacy of markets in knowledge, for example, and because the value of the resources combined was greater than the sum of the individual elements, direct investment became the principal means for resource transfer.

The general trends in *all* international capital movements between the end of the Second World War and the mid-1960s are shown in Table 1.1. The period was dominated by official investment, including investment from governments and international institutions, and covering reconstruction schemes such as the Marshall Plan.

The strength of the recovery of private investment is also indicated, the vast majority of which was direct rather than portfolio capital: between 1951 and 1964 for instance, around 90 per cent of the private total took the form of direct investment to establish overseas affiliates. Nearly three-quarters of all capital emanated from the US and this source dominated both private direct and official investment (the latter mainly taking the form of grants). The US dominance can be explained in terms of the investment climate discussed above, economic power and technological and managerial advantage. The

Table 1.1 Net flow of long-term capital and official donations from capital exporting countries (1946–64, $ million)

	Private		Official (Donations and capital)*		Private and official together	
	Total	Per annum	Total	Per annum	Total	Per annum
1946–50	9,145	1,829	n.a.	n.a.	n.a.	n.a.
1951–55	9,675	1,935	12,970	2,594	22,645	4,529
1956–59	14,760	3,690	16,416	4,104	31,176	7,794
1960–61	6,213	3,106	11,164	5,582	17,377	8,689
1961–64	5,310	1,770	17,427	5,809	22,737	7,579
1946–64	45,103	2,374	n.a.	n.a.	n.a.	n.a.
1951–64	35,958	2,568	57,977	4,141	93,935	6,710

* The capital component was repayable, the donations non-repayable.
(*Source:* Dunning, 1970, p. 24.)

UK continued to be an important source country, its importance as a financial centre and the historic portfolio investment connections with its former empire being contributory factors.

The rapid expansion of foreign direct investment continued into the 1970s, when world-wide economic circumstances began to change. Inflation, economic depression and fears of protectionism all had an impact on multinational firms. In addition the growing economic power of Western Europe and Japan, relative to the United States, was contributing to some change in the sources of direct investment. From the viewpoint of host countries, attitudes to inward direct investment were altering. While initially foreign investment may have been welcomed as a means of assisting economic growth, self-reliance and economic independence started to emerge as important themes. The majority of host nations began to introduce regulatory provisions in an attempt to increase the net benefits associated with MNE operations, and to direct MNE activities along lines consistent with development goals. Associated with these trends, the forms of international involvement by multinational companies have been changing. But whether this is only a passing phase or a true transition towards quite different arrangements for transferring resources internationally is as yet unknown.

Characteristics of MNEs

Although the underlying forces creating MNEs are varied and complex, the corporations which emerged from this historical process have several common dimensions and distinguishing features:

Table 1.2 Foreign content of the 25 largest industrial corporations (end 1976)

Corporation	Home country	Major industry	Sales ($ billion)*	Foreign assets as % of total assets	Foreign earnings as % of total earnings	Foreign sales as % of total consolidated sales	
						Exports from home country	Sales of overseas affiliates to 3rd parties
1. Exxon	US	Petroleum	48.6	54	n.a.		72
2. General Motors	US	Petroleum	47.2	12	18		24
3. Royal Dutch/Shell	Netherlands/UK	Petroleum	36.1	50	64		62
4. Ford	US	Motor Vehicles	28.8	40	45		31
5. Texaco	US	Petroleum	26.5	54	45	n.a.	n.a.
6. Mobil	US	Petroleum	26.1	49	38	n.a.	n.a.
7. National Iranian Oil	Iran	Petroleum	19.7	n.a.	n.a.	n.a.	
8. Standard Oil (Calif.)	US	Petroleum	19.4	43	48		59
9. British Petroleum	UK	Petroleum	19.1	n.a.	n.a.	5	78
10. Gulf Oil	US	Petroleum	16.5	43	46		55
11. IBM	US	Office Equipment	16.3	36	55	8	50
12. Unilever	UK/Netherlands	Food	15.8	36	51		40
13. General Electric	US	Electrical	15.7	27	37	12	26
14. Chrysler	US	Motor Vehicles	15.5	33	22		28
15. ITT	US	Electrical	11.8	36	39		49
16. Standard Oil (Indiana)	US	Petroleum	11.5	34	22		25
17. Philips	Netherlands	Electrical	11.5	26	n.a.		37
18. ENI	Italy	Petroleum	10.0	n.a.	n.a.	n.a.	
19. Françaises des Pétroles	France	Petroleum	9.9	65	n.a.		54
20. Renault	France	Motor Vehicles	9.4	n.a.	n.a.		45

21. Hoechst	Germany	Chemicals	9.3	n.a.	35	32
22. BASF	Germany	Chemicals	9.2	41	25	20
23. Petróleos de Venezuela	Venezuela	Petroleum	9.1	n.a.	n.a.	96
24. Daimler-Benz	Germany	Motor Vehicles	8.9	n.a.	39	21
25. United States Steel	US	Metal Refining	8.6	n.a.	3	n.a.

Note: GNP figures for OECD countries in $ billion were as follows: USA 1,706.5; Japan 552.9; Germany 437.0; France 304.3; Italy 133.0; Spain 102.6; Australia 94.2; Netherlands 86.5; Belgium 66.6; Sweden 64.2; Switzerland 59.0; Turkey 41.1; Austria 39.6; Denmark 37.5; Finland 27.6; Norway 25.8; Greece 22.6; New Zealand 12.7; Portugal 12.0; Ireland 8.0; Luxembourg 2.0; Iceland 1.4. Data refer to 1976, except for Italy, Luxembourg, Norway, Portugal and Sweden for which figures are for 1975. GNP data were converted from national currencies using mid-year exchange rates (Source: International Monetary Fund, 1978).

* 'Billion' means 'one thousand million' throughout this book.

(*Source:* UN Economic and Social Council, 1978, Table IV-I.)

Size

While it would be wrong to suggest that large firm size is a prerequisite for multinationality, nevertheless the truly *multi*-national firms are enormous corporations. Closely linked with this characteristic is the oligopolistic nature of MNEs and their operation in industries dominated by advanced technology, product differentiation and extensive advertising. Table 1.2 shows the scale of operations of the top 25 industrial corporations in the world in 1976, nearly all of which are multinational firms as indicated by the data on foreign assets, earnings and sales. The importance of petroleum and motor vehicle producers within the group is particularly evident, and in total the sales of the 25 corporations amounted to over $450 billion. It is difficult to assess the economic and political power which size brings to large MNEs. A large corporation may be relatively weak in any one country if its activities are widely diffused; conversely a small MNE may be able to exert considerable influence within a small economy if its foreign operations are concentrated geographically. Even so, aggregate size alone is indicative of the magnitude of MNEs' control over resources.

If size were the only criterion, many multinationals would rival nation states as economic entities. As the table indicates, the sales of Exxon and General Motors, for example, are greater than the gross national products of countries such as Austria, Denmark, New Zealand, Greece, etc. It is strictly invalid to make comparisons of this sort, and the figures can only be used to suggest orders of magnitude. What is more valuable is to compare the value products of companies with the GNPs of countries. Estimates made on this basis still show that some of these huge corporations have value products greater than certain of the small OECD countries and very much greater than many developing states.[11] Undoubtedly such companies have the potential to influence world affairs and the course of events in individual host countries in very significant ways. The involvement of ITT in Chile, the Lockheed bribes scandal and the activities of the international oil companies – the so-called 'Seven Sisters' – all bear witness to the relationship between size and power.

The size and ownership distribution of a larger sample of MNEs as at 1973, derived from data prepared by the EEC Commission, is shown in Table 1.3. In total these leading MNEs employed 25.1 million people in 1973, representing 12 per cent of total employment in that year in OECD countries. The dominance of US corporations is evident, with 126 of the 260 largest MNEs being American based. What is perhaps particularly interesting nevertheless is the importance of some of the smaller European countries as bases for giant multinational firms. Thus eight of the world's largest MNEs are based in Sweden, five in Switzerland and six in the Netherlands. Included within this group are well-known companies such as Unilever, Philips,

Table 1.3 Countries of origin and employment in the 260 largest* MNEs (1973)

	No. of companies	Total employees (million)	Average no. of employees
United States	126	11.8	93,806
EEC	105	11.5	109,373
of which			
UK	49	4.0	82,244
West Germany	21	2.8	134,078
France	19	2.1	108,309
Italy†	8	1.3	166,272
Netherlands‡	6	1.2	191,256
Belgium	2	0.1	51,496
Other Europe			
Sweden	8	0.4	52,648
Switzerland	5	0.4	74,360
Austria	1	0.1	79,734
Japan	9	0.6	65,717
Canada	4	0.2	61,325
Australia	2	0.1	50,000
Total	260	25.1	96,589

* In terms of number of employees.
† Includes Pirelli/Dunlop.
‡ Includes Unilever and Royal Dutch/Shell.

(*Source:* Commission of the European Communities, July 1976.)

Royal Dutch/Shell, Nestlé, SKF, and so on. In the case of Japan the major international companies include Mitsubishi Heavy Industries, Matsushita Electric, Mitsui and Hitachi. These firms, in common with other Japanese corporations, have been reluctant to invest in manufacturing facilities abroad, particularly in the Western industrialised countries. Although the major Japanese markets are in the advanced countries, companies based in Japan have preferred to export at a marginal rate of profit and make the domestic consumer bear the costs of initial capital outlay. Motor vehicle manufacturers such as Toyota and Nissan are good examples of firms still pursuing this type of strategy. But this is changing and likely to change much further as concern increases about the size of the Japanese trade surplus.

Ownership

Turning specifically to the ownership of MNEs, Table 1.4 presents data relating to the stock of direct investment abroad for the years up

18   *The scope and direction of multinational enterprise*

to 1976. The United States accounted for just under half of the total stock in the latest year. When the UK, West Germany, Japan and Switzerland are included, almost four-fifths of the direct investment stock is accounted for. As the figures in the previous section would suggest, within each of these sources foreign direct investment is concentrated in the hands of a limited number of corporations: in the US, around 300 firms are responsible for 70 per cent of investment; in the UK, 165 firms for 80 per cent; and 82 West German companies provide 70 per cent of that country's stock of direct investment abroad.[12]

Table 1.4 Stock of direct investment abroad of developed market economies by major country of origin

Country of origin	$ billion, end year				% of total, end year	
	1967	1971	1975	1976	1967	1976
USA	56.6	82.8	124.2	137.2	53.8	47.6
UK	17.5	23.7	30.8	32.1	16.6	11.2
W. Germany	3.0	7.3	16.0	19.9	2.8	6.9
Japan*	1.5	4.4	15.9	19.4	1.4	6.7
Switzerland	5.0	9.5	16.9	18.6	4.8	6.5
France	6.0	7.3	11.1	11.9	5.7	4.1
Canada	3.7	6.5	10.5	11.1	3.5	3.9
Netherlands	2.2	4.0	8.5	9.8	2.1	3.4
Sweden	1.7	2.4	4.4	5.0	1.6	1.7
Belgium/Luxembourg	2.0	2.4	3.2	3.6	1.9	1.2
Italy	2.1	3.0	3.3	2.9	2.0	1.0
Total†	101.3	153.3	243.8	270.4	96.2	94.2
All Other	4.0	5.1	15.1	16.8	3.8	5.8
Grand total	105.3	158.4	258.9	287.2	100.0	100.0

* Fiscal year beginning 1 April of year indicated.
† Totals do not always equal sum of individual column entries in source.

(*Source:* UN Economic and Social Council, 1978, Table III-32.)

Over time, the limited comparisons given in Table 1.4 reveal that the US dominance of foreign direct investment is being eroded somewhat; while the UK's share of the total stock has also shrunk significantly. By contrast, Japan, West Germany and Switzerland have shown rapid growth, the three countries together accounting for 20.1 per cent of total investment in 1976 as compared with 9.0 per cent ten years earlier.

What this table does not reveal is that ownership of direct investment abroad is becoming much more diffuse. It is certainly true that multinationality is, and will continue to be, dominated by the rich, industrialised countries. On the other hand, in recent years companies in the bigger and wealthier of the developing countries have begun to establish affiliates in the smaller and poorer states. Firms in Brazil, Mexico, India, Hong Kong, the Philippines and elsewhere now have significant direct investments abroad. In 1976, for instance, Hong Kong's investment stock in Indonesia was valued at $728 m.; conversely Thailand had $30 m. direct investment in Hong Kong. And within Latin America, Mexican direct investment in Brazil, Chile and Colombia totalled about $20 m.[13]

In addition, ownership is becoming more diffuse as a result of the entry of socialist countries into the multinational arena. By means of intergovernmental agreements with the developed countries, the USSR and Eastern European states have created a framework for economic cooperation in the fields of technology, science and industry. It has been estimated that by 1976 these socialist countries had more than 700 trading and manufacturing concerns in developed and developing countries in comparison with only 50 in 1962.[14]

Growth

The remarkable growth of the multinational firm can be dated quite precisely to the post-1945 period, facilitated by a technological revolution which has encompassed transportation, communications, data processing and management techniques. From the end of the Second World War until the mid-1960s, foreign investment was expanding more rapidly than the rate of GNP growth of national economies; and even in the period from 1967 to 1976 the stock of direct investment has increased at about the same rate as the GNP of developed countries.[15]

The post-war development of MNEs emerges particularly clearly from data relating to the numbers of new affiliates established. The nature of this expansion for UK, Continental European and Japanese, as well as US *manufacturing* multinationals is shown in Fig. 1.1 and Table 1.5. The relative expansion paths must be taken as indicative only, since the samples of firms are not strictly comparable and the periods covered by the data are different: the American data are derived from a major study at Harvard University relating to 180 (originally 187) of the largest industrial firms manufacturing in six or more countries in 1963; the original work provided data for the years 1914–67, but the more recent research relates to the period 1951–75. By contrast the data for the other source countries refers to the years up to 1970, incorporating information relating to the affiliates of 134 Continental European and UK parents and 75 Japanese parents.

As Fig. 1.1 reveals, the number of new manufacturing subsidiaries formed by the sample of American MNEs peaked in 1968 when an average of three affiliates were formed by each parent corporation (546 affiliates in total); by 1975 the number of new subsidiaries

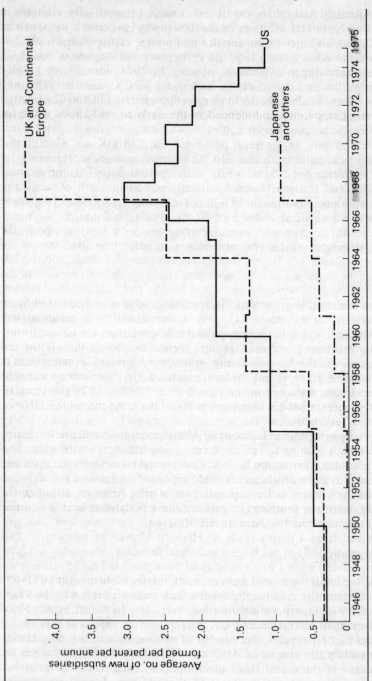

Fig. 1.1 Rate of new affiliate establishment per annum by a sample of US, European, Japanese and other MNEs (*Sources:* Vaupel and Curhan, 1973; Curhan, Davidson and Suri, 1977)

established had fallen to just over one per parent (204 affiliates in total). Not all the affiliates established in any year remain in existence, of course, as a consequence of liquidations, expropriations, etc. but over the whole period 1951–75 there was a net increase of 5,622 US manufacturing subsidiaries in the sample corporations. Figure 1.1 also shows that the take-off period for non-US MNEs was rather later than for US multinationals: the main growth period for UK and Continental European parents commenced in the early to mid-1960s while for Japanese parents, the build-up of new affiliates was only beginning late in the 1960s. In the years 1965–67, the 134 UK and Continental European parents formed 330 affiliates per annum, representing 2.4 subsidiaries per parent; while in the period 1968–70, the average number of affiliates formed annually was 586, a rate of subsidiary establishment per parent of 4.4. In these latter years, the 75 Japanese parents formed an average of 70 affiliates annually.

   Table 1.5 permits some observations to be made about the geographical spread of affiliates established by the sample of corporations. For US multinationals, continental Europe and the UK have been the major host countries. The geographical diversity of the investment is, however, indicated by the fact that South America, Canada, and the Far East (after 1960) have also been significant recipients. The United Kingdom has continued to be an important source country with former colonial links explaining the concentration of investment in Africa, Asia and the Pacific and conversely the low volume of investment in South America. Although UK investment in mainland Europe has become increasingly significant since the mid-1960s, intra-Europe investment is nowhere near as great for UK MNEs as for MNEs based on the Continent. As the table indicates, nearly one half of all the subsidiaries formed by Continental MNEs have been located in Europe itself, traditional links and the formation of the EEC and EFTA being contributory factors. Japanese investment, finally, has been strongly oriented towards the Asia and Pacific region. More recently MNEs based in Japan have shown a growing interest in Europe and, particularly, America, although the investments or proposed investments have not always been welcomed by the host countries concerned.[16]

Locational spread

Reflecting the size and growth of multinational firms from different source countries, some corporations have very widespread networks of affiliates. As will be discussed in later chapters, this geographical diversity of MNEs places them in a position of considerable flexibility because of the wide range of options which exist in decision areas such as sourcing, pricing, etc. And the more multinational a company is, the better it is able to take advantage of changes in the economic environment internationally. For 9,500 MNEs, Table 1.6 illustrates

Table 1.5 Average number of new manufacturing subsidiaries formed per annum by geographical area*

US PARENTS (1951-75)†

	1951-55	1956-60	1961-65	1966-67	1968-69	1970-71	1972-73	1974-75
Canada	18.4	22.8	33.4	44.0	70.5	48.0	43.0	20.5
Latin America	24.4	59.2	76.6	88.0	87.0	72.5	76.5	49.5
Europe	25.6	72.2	136.8	167.5	237.0	208.5	179.0	104.0
Africa and Middle East	1.4	4.2	10.4	15.0	18.0	12.0	8.5	13.5
Asia and Pacific	14.0	33.6	65.2	75.5	96.0	90.0	71.0	49.0
Total‡	83.8	192.0	322.4	390.0	508.5	431.0	378.0	236.5

NON-US PARENTS (1953-70)†

UK Parents	1953-55	1956-58	1959-61	1962-64	1965-67	1968-70
US and Canada	3.4	12.9	14.0	10.9	22.3	37.9
South America	2.6	2.4	7.7	4.1	6.7	10.7
Europe	2.3	3.4	32.3	29.8	44.1	73.4
Africa	4.7	4.4	24.0	27.1	34.3	57.1
Asia and Pacific	5.4	8.3	32.4	35.7	46.1	61.2
Total‡	18.3	31.3	111.0	106.3	153.0	243.0
Continental European Parents						
North and South America	13.3	15.7	26.8	21.1	45.9	91.3
Europe and UK	19.7	19.6	30.7	41.4	107.6	201.5
Africa, Asia and Pacific	6.0	7.5	19.9	13.8	23.2	51.5
Total‡	39.0	43.7	77.3	76.3	177.3	343.3
Japanese and Other Parents						
Asia and Pacific	1.0	1.0	11.0	19.0	22.3	53.0
Other	0.7	3.7	3.7	11.0	15.3	16.7
Total‡	1.7	4.7	14.7	30.0	37.7	69.7

* Data derived from a sample of 180 US-based MNEs and the 209 largest non-US industrial firms.
† For the period 1946-52 the average numbers of new manufacturing subsidiaries established annually were: UK parents 28.8; Continental European parents 18.4; Japanese and Other Parents 0.3; and for a slightly larger sample of 187 US parents 55.1.
‡ Totals do not always equal sum of individual column entries in source.

(*Sources*: Curhan, Davidson and Suri, 1977, Table 2.2.4; Vaupel and Curhan, 1973, Table 1.17.3-5.)

Table 1.6 Variations in international diversification of MNEs by nationality of parent (1973)

Country of origin	No. of parents	Percentage of parents with affiliates in				
		1 country	2–9 countries	10–19 countries	20 countries or more	
United States	2,567	44	39	12	5	
United Kingdom	1,588	36	50	8	6	
West Germany	1,222	39	53	5	3	
Switzerland	756	60	35	4	1	
France	565	34	51	10	5	
Netherlands	467	52	38	7	3	
Sweden	301	35	47	12	6	
Canada	268	57	39	3	1	
Belgium	252	44	44	8	4	
Australia	228	55	43	1	1	
Italy	213	52	40	1	7	
Japan	211	42	49	7	2	
Total*	9,481	45	44	7	4	

* Includes other countries such as Norway, Denmark, New Zealand, Luxembourg, Austria, etc. 29 countries in total.
(*Source:* Commission of the European Committees, July 1976.)

the size of affiliate networks. The data refer to all affiliates including non-manufacturing units and may therefore exaggerate the economic significance of MNEs. Even so the figures reveal that 11 per cent of multinationals have subsidiaries in at least 10 countries; and this rises to 18 per cent for Swedish MNEs, and 17 and 14 per cent respectively for US and UK multinationals. It is noteworthy, conversely, that nearly half (45 per cent) of all MNEs have links with only one foreign country and many of these may be domestic firms in little more than name. For example, 60 per cent of Swiss firms have affiliates in only one host country, a high proportion of which may be located just over the Swiss border within the Common Market, to take advantage of the tariff-free zone. Many of these companies with links in only one or a small number of foreign countries are inevitably small firms, which leads to an important conclusion, namely that multinationality is not the exclusive preserve of large corporations.

The existence of networks of foreign affiliates within multinational companies opens up the possibility of integrated production and marketing on a global basis. This, in turn, may give rise to extensive intra-firm trade as various stages in the production process are located in different countries or as affiliates specialise on a particular part of the total product line. This issue will be considered fully in Chapter 4, but intra-MNE transfers now constitute a very significant part of the total volume of international trade. And where such intra-company transfers take place, important questions arise over the prices (transfer prices) to be charged to members of the group.

Host country distribution of foreign direct investment

The breakdown of foreign direct investment by host country is given in Table 1.7. The earlier discussion indicated the dominance of the USA, UK, Germany and Japan as sources of direct investment, and Table 1.7 shows that, apart from Japan where special factors apply, these same countries are also important recipients of direct investment. In 1975, Canada together with the US, UK and Germany were hosts to 41 per cent of the total stock of direct investment from the developed countries. This proportion has, furthermore, increased from a figure of 38 per cent in 1967, indicating that direct investment is tending to become a two-way interchange between the developed countries themselves.

The importance of Canada as a host to US investment particularly is well known, and the United Kingdom has also obtained a high proportion of US direct investment. More recently the United States itself has become an important host country: in the decade up to 1973 the growth rate of foreign direct investment in the US averaged around 6 per cent per annum, whereas since 1973 it has been increasing at an average annual rate of about 20 per cent. Although the UK, Canada and the Netherlands account for four-fifths of the investment into the

Table 1.7 Stock of direct investment abroad of developed market economies by major host countries and host country groups

Host country and host country group	% of total, end year		
	1967	1971	1975
Developed market economies	69	72	74
of which:			
Canada	18	17	15
USA	9	9	11
UK	8	9	9
W. Germany	3	5	6
Other	30	32	33
Developing countries	31	28	26
of which:			
OPEC*	9	7	6
Tax havens†	2	3	3
Other	20	18	17
Total	100	100	100
Total value of stock ($ billion)	105	158	259

* Organisation of Petroleum Exporting Countries.
† Bahamas, Barbados, Bermuda, Cayman Islands, Netherlands Antilles and Panama.

(*Source*: UN Economic and Social Council, 1978, Table III–33.)

United States, there has also been a rapid expansion in investment from Japan, France and Germany. Volkswagen's decision to build a major plant to manufacture the Rabbit in the US, the purchase by Babcock & Wilcox of American Chain & Cable and the Honda investment in motorcycle manufacture in Ohio, are only some recent illustrations of this expansion. While there are many reasons for the trend, the large market, growing strength of non-US MNEs, trends in international exchange rates and labour costs and US 'open door' policies in some business sectors must all be contributory factors.

By contrast with these trends, the total stock of investment in developing countries has fallen from 31 per cent in 1967 to 26 per cent in 1975. A more detailed breakdown of the investment in the less developed countries (LDCs) is presented in Table 1.8. The investment stock in OPEC countries has fallen as a proportion of total investment in developing countries. While the wealth of the petroleum producing countries might be expected to attract MNEs like bees to a honeypot, nationalisation and similar policies in the petroleum industry have reduced the value of the stock and may have adversely affected confidence in other sectors. The table shows that Venezuela and Iran have been particularly affected, and it is no coincidence that both countries have national oil companies which rank among the top industrial corporations in the world (Table 1.2).

The investment stock residing in tax havens has been increasing, leaving all other developing countries with a fairly constant two-thirds

Table 1.8   Direct investment stock in developing countries

Host countries	1967		1971		1975	
	$ billion	%	$ billion	%	$ billion	%
Total stock	32.8	100.0	43.3	100.0	68.2	100.0
OPEC countries	9.1	27.7	11.6	26.8	15.6	22.9
of which:						
Venezuela	3.5	10.6	3.7	8.5	4.0	5.9
Indonesia	0.2	0.6	1.0	2.3	3.5	5.1
Nigeria	1.1	3.3	1.7	3.9	2.9	4.3
Iran	0.7	2.1	0.9	2.1	1.2	1.8
Tax havens	2.3	7.0	3.9	9.0	8.9	13.0
All other developing countries	21.4	65.3	27.8	64.2	43.7	64.1
of which:						
Brazil	3.7	11.3	5.1	11.8	9.1	13.3
Mexico	1.8	5.5	2.4	5.5	4.8	7.0
India	1.3	4.0	1.6	3.7	2.4	3.5
Malaysia	0.7	2.1	0.9	2.1	2.3	3.4
Argentina	1.8	5.5	2.2	5.1	2.0	2.9
Singapore	0.2	0.6	0.4	0.9	1.7	2.5
Peru	0.8	2.4	0.9	2.1	1.7	2.5
Hong Kong	0.3	0.9	0.6	1.4	1.3	1.9
Philippines	0.7	2.1	0.9	2.1	1.2	1.8
Trinidad and Tobago	0.7	2.1	1.0	2.3	1.2	1.8
Total above 10 countries	12.0	36.5	16.0	37.0	27.7	40.6

(*Source:* UN Economic and Social Council, 1978, Table III–47.)

share of investment in the period 1967–75. Brazil is the most important host nation within the latter group, accounting for 13.3 per cent of the stock of investment in 1975 in comparison with 11.3 per cent in 1967. Mexico, Hong Kong, Singapore and Malaysia have also obtained an increased share of investment. Some of this is intra-LDC investment as noted earlier, but the vast majority represents investment designed to take advantage of low labour costs and the attractive incentives offered by the host governments concerned. The pros and cons of this international division of labour type investment will be debated at various points in the chapters which follow. In comparison with these trends, India and Argentina are two countries in which the stock of direct investment has shown a relative decline over the period. At least partially this reflects host government regulation and a hostile economic climate.

More generally, multinational investment within the developing countries has focused heavily on those states with the highest level of incomes:

Table 1.9 Relationship between GNP and stock of foreign direct investment in developing countries (excluding OPEC countries and tax havens)

Countries with per capita income in 1975 of	Foreign direct investment stock (end 1975)	Foreign direct investment stock as % of GNP
$1,000 or more	22.3	9.5
$500–999	10.4	9.7
$200–499	5.8	6.8
$Under 200	6.5	3.3

(*Source:* UN Economic and Social Council, 1978, Table 5.)

To date, MNEs have found the least developed countries very unattractive locations for investment.

In concluding this discussion on the host country distribution of foreign direct investment, it should be pointed out that the operation of Western-based multinationals in the centrally planned economies is increasing. Although equity participation and manufacturing activity have both been on a limited scale, MNEs have shown considerable flexibility in their modes of operation in the socialist countries. These have included cooperative production ventures, turn-key projects, technical agreements and so on, and individually some of the projects involved are of immense size. Thus for example Fiat's agreement with the USSR has resulted in the production of around half of the Russian passenger car total in recent years.

Divestment

Previous comments have hinted at ways in which host countries may force changes in their relationships with MNEs through, for example, nationalisation or expropriation. But the MNEs for their part may respond by divestment (alternatively termed disinvestment) involving withdrawal from particular locations through the sale or liquidation of their assets.

From the perspective of the host nation the concerns over divestment policies do not merely relate to divestment as a counter strategy or bargaining weapon. Rather the principal fear is that since MNEs are attempting to maximise or optimise on a global scale, they may be prone to take extreme action on discovering that particular ventures, locations or investments are showing inadequate returns. Divestment is clearly a politically sensitive issue both within MNEs and in host nations. And sensitivity to changing locational decisions is particularly high in developing host states, for while the developed countries act as both home and host to the MNE, most LDCs are exclusively hosts. Moreover the impact of divestment on employment in developing countries is likely to be much more serious.

Data on the scale and impact of divestment are not plentiful. Table 1.10 summarises the results for the 180 US MNEs in the Harvard project. The figures must be considered in a tentative way, particularly since the data include expropriations as well as sales and liquidations. In any event, the figures indicate that exits (excluding mergers) have increased significantly in relation to the formation of new affiliates since the mid-1960s: the exit rate rose from between 10 and 12 per cent in the period 1951–65 to 26.3 per cent in the 1966–70 period and then to 42 per cent in the most recent years. Geographically, about two-fifths of the exits for the entire period involved US affiliates in Europe; and another 27 per cent were affiliates in Latin America. These figures are reasonably closely related to the proportion of new subsidiaries formed in the respective areas.

Table 1.10   Divestment patterns in 180 US MNEs

	1951–55	1956–60	1961–65	1966–70	1971–75	1951–75
(a) Overview						
No. of new affiliates established	989	1,957	3,225	4,385	3,239	13,795
No. of exits excluding mergers (EEMs)*	116	207	316	1,154	1,359	3,152
EEMs as % of new affiliates established	11.7	10.6	9.8	26.3	42.0	22.8
(b) Method of exit (%)						
Sold	34.5	22.7	25.9	53.2	53.9	48.1
Liquidated	44.8	38.6	49.7	44.1	39.8	42.5
Expropriated	0.9	26.1	7.6	0.9	5.9	5.3
Unknown	19.8	12.6	16.8	1.8	0.4	4.1
Total EEMs	100.0	100.0	100.0	100.0	100.0	100.0
(c) Geograhical distribution of EEMs (%)						
Europe	39.7	30.9	38.3	45.4	42.9	42.4
Latin America	20.7	46.4	26.9	27.1	24.6	27.0
Canada	22.4	13.5	17.4	12.6	12.9	13.6
Others	17.2	9.2	17.4	14.9	19.6	17.0
Total EEMs	100.0	100.0	100.0	100.0	100.0	100.0

* EEMs represent exits excluding mergers, thus incorporating liquidations, expropriations and the sale of foreign affiliates to independent parties.

(*Source:* Curhan, Davidson and Suri, 1977, Tables 2.1.1, 3.4.1–2 and 3.4.6.)

Although the results must be interpreted cautiously, they are confirmed by other evidence which again showed a sharp increase in the number of divestments in the 1970s. It appears, however, that the vast majority of the affected operations are small: a study covering the period 1967–71 revealed that almost 75 per cent of the exits involved affiliates with annual sales of under $10 million.[17] In spite of this it would be wrong to understress the implications of divestment for particular regions and host countries. Similarly, closures and redundancies in MNE affiliates must have an important influence upon the way in which governments view the behaviour of multinationals. This is so even if on balance MNEs bring more secure and stable employment than that provided by indigenous firms. From the MNE perspective, divestments will produce short-run financial loss and longer-term costs of disrupted relationships with host governments.

Methods of entry and ownership patterns

These two issues are pertinent to the debate over the impact of MNEs in host countries and to the changing forms of MNE involvement abroad. From the viewpoint of recipient states, the belief is that in general the establishment of greenfield ventures is preferable to entry through acquisition. Grass-roots entry at least increases the number of firms in the industry and may thereby increase competition. Hostility to entry via merger/take-over activity has been just as apparent in developed as in developing host states, because of the additional fear that MNEs may use acquisitions as a means of gaining access to host country technology.

Table 1.11 Methods of entry of affiliates of 180 US MNEs in host countries

Methods of entry	Percentage of affiliates					
	1951–55	1956–60	1961–65	1966–70	1971–75	1951–75
Newly formed	51.3	51.6	44.3	43.7	48.6	46.6
Acquired	30.4	33.0	40.8	49.1	46.3	42.9
Others and unknown	18.3	15.4	14.9	7.2	5.1	10.5
Total	100.0	100.0	100.0	100.0	100.0	100.0
Total no. of affiliates	989	1,957	3,225	4,385	3,239	13,795

(*Source:* Curhan, Davidson and Suri, 1977, Table 2.1.3.)

Table 1.11 shows that for US MNEs at least, the importance of the acquisition route has been increasing: between 1951 and 1960 less than one-third of new affiliates were formed by merger/take-overs, but this figure rose to almost one-half in the years 1966–70. The slight decline in the proportion of acquisitions in the most recent period may be indicative of greater host country concern over this method of entry; and as a consequence of policy initiatives by governments, MNEs may find themselves under increasing pressure in future to form completely new establishments.

Host government regulation of the multinational firm goes much wider than the method of entry only, and Table 1.12 considers another important question which is that of ownership of MNE affiliates. Historically, US firms have preferred to serve foreign markets by means of wholly-owned subsidiaries in order to retain control of key areas of decision-making and to preserve proprietary technology. MNEs based in other countries have traditionally been more flexible in their approach to markets abroad, with less insistence on the wholly-owned subsidiary form of organisation. The data in Table 1.12 bear out this point, but also show that increasingly in developing countries MNEs are being required to permit equity participation by host country investors. For US-based MNEs, the proportion of new wholly-owned subsidiaries established declined from 58 per cent in the period prior to 1951 to 44 per cent in the years 1971–75; comparing the years before 1951 with the period 1966–70, for European-based MNEs the proportion of new wholly-owned affiliates formed fell from 39 per cent to 19 per cent, and for other MNEs from 27 per cent to 6 per cent of the total. By contrast there was a sharp rise in the proportion of minority-owned subsidiaries being established.

These trends are clear evidence of changes in the form of MNE involvement internationally, arising from growing host country and international concern over the impact of the multinational corporation. By securing a degree of equity ownership, the aim is to increase national control of the MNE and eliminate some of the perceived abuses of these corporations. Joint venture agreements are not the only means by which host governments attempt to change the character of the MNE. Some governments may enter into non-equity deals, involving management and design contracts, marketing agreements and turn-key arrangements, similar to the agreements operated by MNEs in socialist countries.[18] Additionally recipient countries may legislate to control the behaviour of MNEs in areas such as the employment of local labour, repatriation of profits, transfer of technology, and levels of exports. And at the international level, bodies like the United Nations are pressing for greater global regulation of multinational corporations.

All of these moves are requiring greater adaptability from the MNEs, which may mean a quite different role for international firms in the future. It is not coincidental that, relatively speaking, Japanese and Western European MNEs are becoming more important in comparison with American firms, for the former have shown

Table 1.12 Distribution of ownership patterns* of manufacturing affiliates established in developing countries by 391 MNEs

Home country and type of ownership	Period of establishment (% of affiliates)				
	Before 1951	1951–60	1961–65	1966–70	1971–75
Affiliates of 180 United States-based corporations					
Wholly-owned	58.4	44.5	37.4	46.2	43.7
Majority-owned	12.2	21.4	19.2	17.8	17.3
Co-owned	5.6	7.9	11.4	11.2	10.4
Minority-owned	11.2	18.8	21.7	21.5	28.2
Unknown	12.6	7.4	10.3	3.3	0.4
Total	100.0	100.0	100.0	100.0	100.0
Total no. of affiliates	214	229	281	303	231
Affiliates of 135 Continental European and United Kingdom-based corporations					
Wholly-owned	39.1	31.6	20.9	18.9	
Majority-owned	15.4	20.1	15.6	16.4	
Co-owned	5.3	6.5	11.1	6.6	
Minority-owned	9.8	27.9	35.8	42.1	
Unknown	30.4	13.9	16.6	16.0	
Total	100.0	100.0	100.0	100.0	
Total no. of affiliates	266	244	416	694	
Affiliates of 76 other MNEs					
Wholly-owned	27.4	16.7	10.7	6.1	
Majority owned	8.2	26.2	12.5	8.3	
Co-owned	12.3	7.1	6.3	7.5	
Minority-owned	16.5	42.9	66.7	74.2	
Unknown	35.6	7.1	3.8	3.9	
Total	100.0	100.0	100.0	100.0	
Total no. of affiliates	73	42	159	279	

* Affiliates of which the parent firm owns 95 per cent or more are classified as wholly owned; 51–94 per cent as majority owned; 50 per cent as co-owned; 5–49 per cent as minority owned.

(*Source:* UN Economic and Social Council, 1978, Table III–25, derived from Vaupel and Curhan, 1973, and Curhan, Davidson and Suri, 1977.)

themselves to be particularly flexible when it comes to negotiating forms of international involvement other than the wholly or majority-owned affiliate. Conversely most of the most widely publicised disputes between MNEs and host governments over issues such as forms of involvement have concerned US multinationals.

Industry distribution

The early development of foreign direct investment was concentrated in the extractive and public utility fields, invariably in less developed economies. The period since 1945 has, however, seen the emergence of MNE activity which is typically concerned with manufacturing. As Table 1.13 indicates, manufacturing represented, on average, 47 per cent of the 1974 stock of foreign investment of five of the principal source countries. Extractive industries, including petroleum and mining and smelting, accounted for a further 25 per cent of the total stock, with services making up the remaining 28 per cent. The manufacturing sector continued to increase its share of total investment during the early 1970s, but the more interesting feature was the expansion of service industries. Advertising agencies, banks, insurance companies and management consulting firms have expanded their networks rapidly during the 1970s. In many cases the companies concerned were attracted abroad by the prior international expansion of their clients. Considering only banking firms, the 50 largest banks in the world increased their number of branches operating abroad by more than 60 per cent between 1971 and 1976, to total over 3,000 units in the latter year.[19]

The country pattern of investment differs quite markedly as Table 1.13 also reveals. The 1974 share of total foreign investment stock represented by manufacturing ranged from a low of 35 per cent in Japan to a high of 71 per cent in Germany, with the USA, UK and Canada varying between 45 and 50 per cent. Within the manufacturing sector itself, the types of commodities produced are fairly varied, particularly as between Japan and the European and N. American countries. In West Germany, high technology goods such as chemicals and electrical products dominate. Chemicals, machinery, electrical products and transport equipment account for nearly two-thirds of the overseas manufacturing investment of the US (and about half of that of the UK). The expansion of US owned affiliates has thus largely been in the manufacture of products with a high technology content, where research and development costs are a relatively high proportion of total costs (at least for the parent company) and where the skilled labour content in the final output is high. These are also industries in which oligopolistic market structures are common in home and, by competitive entry from overseas, in host nations.

In the case of Japanese overseas manufacturing activities by contrast, basically three types of investment are involved. In some areas, particularly in Asia and Latin America, operations have been established to produce and sell low-technology goods, e.g. textiles, in tariff-protected markets. Another reason for Japanese companies investing in developing countries is to export pollution-creating activities; environmental problems in Japan have led to suggestions that certain industrial operations should be undertaken abroad.[20] A

Table 1.13 Selected developed market economies: stock of direct investment abroad by major industrial sector

Sector	USA* $ million	%	UK $ million	%	Canada $ million	%	W. Germany† $ million	%	Japan $ million	%
1971 Total industry of which:	101,313	100.0	23,717	100.0	6,524	100.0	7,277	100.0	3,962	100.0
Extractive‡	30,989	30.6	8,051	33.9	938	14.4	350	4.8	892	22.5
Manufacturing	44,370	43.8	10,033	42.3	3,437	52.7	5,796	79.6	1,092	27.6
Services	25,954	25.6	5,633	23.8	2,149	32.9	1,131	15.6	1,978	49.9
(Banking and insurance)§	(9,726)	(9.6)	(1,212)	(5.1)	(405)	(6.2)	(494)	(6.8)	(843)	(21.3)
1974 Total industry of which:	137,244	100.0	31,277	100.0	9,390	100.0	19,915	100.0	10,620	100.0
Extractive	36,771	26.8	8,747	28.0	1,963	20.9	1,419	7.1	2,778	26.2
Manufacturing	61,062	44.5	14,131	45.2	4,729	50.4	14,032	70.5	3,723	35.0
Services	39,411	28.7	8,399	26.8	2,698	28.7	4,464	22.4	4,119	38.8
(Banking and insurance)	(16,392)	(11.9)	(1,410)	(4.5)	(622)	(6.8)	(1,941)	(9.7)	(2,376)	(22.4)

* Refers to the years 1973 and 1976.
† Refers to the years 1971 and 1976.
‡ In the case of the USA and Canada, extractive relates to mining, smelting and petroleum. In the case of Japan, it refers to mining, agriculture and fishing.
§ Banking and insurance figures given separately to show the importance of this sub-sector.

(*Source:* UN Economic and Social Council, 1978, Table III–38.)

further type of manufacturing investment in countries such as Taiwan, South Korea and Hong Kong, results from firms attempting to gain access to cheap foreign labour; some of these are the export platform type of investments where labour-intensive processes within high technology industries are located outside Japan. The final type of investment, which is relatively small to date, takes place in high technology products, e.g. colour TVs, in developed countries. Aside from manufacturing operations, it is noteworthy that Japanese investment in service industries is quite high, although declining as a proportion of the total. This relates to the establishment of local marketing and allied facilities in Japan's major export market, the US, as well as finance houses, insurance companies, etc. The other and growing sector of Japanese direct investment abroad relates to extractive industries: Japan is extremely short of most kinds of raw materials and various agricultural products and in the wake of feared global shortages, efforts are being made to reduce vulnerability through direct investments.

Diversification strategies

Instead of categorising MNE investment by industry sector, an alternative approach is to focus on the type of expansion strategy employed. Thus most MNEs have their origins in horizontal, vertical or conglomerate expansion strategies. Horizontal expansion for an MNE involves the manufacture of the same basic products in different countries. The manufacture of breakfast cereals in the UK by Kelloggs, the US food manufacturer, would be an example of this. Vertical expansion takes place where a corporation locates different stages in the production or marketing process in various countries: oil companies engaged in extraction, refining, retailing, etc. in different countries are an obvious example. More recently US electronics companies such as Texas Instruments and Motorola have located certain stages of the production sequence (particularly the assembly operation) in Hong Kong, Singapore, Mexico and so on; and Japanese and European electronics firms have also diversified vertically in a similar manner. Corporations such as Ford have expanded both horizontally and vertically because of the complexities of car production, which requires interests in steel production, components manufacture, distribution and finance. Nestlé provides another illustration of an MNE whose strategy has moved from vertical diversification (by interests for example in cocoa production) to horizontal diversification and the manufacture of other food products.

Conglomerate expansion takes place where a company manufactures internationally a diversified range of products. The giant US conglomerate corporation ITT is involved in electronics, telecommunications, pharmaceuticals, cosmetics, insurance (Abbey Life Assurance Co. Ltd. in the UK, for instance), food, lighting fixtures, sanitary fittings, hotels (Sheraton Group), etc. A number of Japanese MNEs have developed as conglomerates, including for example Mitsubishi and the other large trading corporations. Within such corporations individual activities such as steel or electronics may expand vertically or horizontally. Some MNEs, such as Lonrho, have their origins in resource-based activity such as mining and plantations, but have expanded to become conglomerates with wide interests covering retailing, engineering and so on.

It is difficult to distinguish empirically between types of diversification. Horizontal diversification seems to be more prevalent among US MNEs, whereas a significant proportion of Japanese and UK multinationals are probably vertically diversified. In the former case this reflects Japanese policy of investing abroad in industries where comparative advantage is being lost at home due to high labour costs. With respect to the UK, the emergence of many MNEs from companies with colonial links in plantations, mining, mineral extraction, etc. is one explanatory factor. There is also some evidence of a greater tendency towards vertical diversification in the more multinational firms. In such vertically integrated corporations, intra-company trade plays a crucial role in the operation, as an affiliate may receive its inputs from one branch of the MNE and supply its outputs to another division.

Penetration of MNEs in host country industries

Given the industry concentration of foreign direct investment and its concentration in a relatively small number of host countries, it would be expected that the penetration of multinational firms within key industrial sectors in recipient states would frequently be very high. Table 1.14 shows the overall shares of output, employment and plant and equipment expenditures of US affiliates in seven host nations. The importance of US firms in Canadian manufacturing industry is particularly striking, accounting for 52 per cent of output in 1970 and one-third of gross fixed domestic capital formation. In the UK, Belgium, Mexico and Brazil also, American companies are responsible for over 15 per cent of output and between 9 per cent (Mexico) and 21 per cent (UK) of gross investment. By these measures the countries concerned are fairly dependent on external decision-making, which raises potential problems for government domestic policies. The data are taken one step further in Table 1.15 which shows the penetration of US MNEs in six high technology industries alone. United States-based multinationals have a strong market position in all of these industries, but the instrument sector is particularly noteworthy. In the five developed countries, American MNEs accounted for 90 per cent of instrument output in Canada, about one-half of output in Belgium and the UK and 20–25 per cent of production in France and Germany. In the transport industry too, American companies are very

Table 1.14 Penetration of 300 US multinational corporations in the manufacturing industries of 7 host nations

Host country		Share of Output (%)	Plant and equipment expenditure (as % of gross fixed domestic capital formation)	Employment in US affiliates (000s)
UK	1966	10.5	16.3	566
	1970	16.4	20.9	715
Germany	1966	5.8	9.2	264
	1970	8.0	12.3	429
France	1966	5.9	4.3	114
	1970	6.1	5.8	196
Belgium*	1966	10.3	17.0	74
	1970	15.7	14.1	141
Canada	1966	48.5	42.7	554
	1970	51.8	32.2	551
Mexico	1966	16.1	6.7	106
	1970	24.8	9.3	184
Brazil	1966	11.6	12.4	128
	1970	17.8	18.3	176

* Includes Luxembourg.

(*Source:* US Tariff Commission, 1973.)

Table 1.15 Penetration of 300 US multinational corporations in six high technology industries in 1970

	Percentage share of output					
Host country	Chemicals	Electrical machinery	Instruments	Non-electrical machinery	Rubber	Transport equipment
UK	21	18	56	21	31	27
Germany	7	6	25	11	11	25
France	12	8	20	14	6	8
Belgium*	48	43	45	41	82	18
Canada	85	82	90	80	98	90
Mexico	20	52	n.a.	63	40	45
Brazil	19	24	n.a.	34	48	65

* Includes Luxembourg.

(*Source:* US Tariff Commission, 1973.)

powerful in all host countries except France. France is indeed an exceptional case overall, where the government has tried resolutely to minimise foreign investment. It was in fact the storm of protest that followed the Chrysler take-over of Simca in 1963 (via the purchase of dispersed shareholdings held in Switzerland and beyond the reach of French exchange controls) that established government attitudes towards inward direct investment in general.

Table 1.16 Estimated foreign controlled shares of selected industries in Canada, Mexico, Brazil, Turkey and India

Industry	Canada (1972) % of foreign owned assets	Mexico (1970) % of sales by foreign controlled enterprises	Brazil (1974)* % of foreign owned assets	Turkey (1974) % of foreign owned assets	India (1973) % of output by foreign controlled firms
Total manufacturing	58	28	29	41	13
of which:					
Textiles	n.a.	n.a.	n.a.	74	n.a.
Food	n.a.	n.a.	31	58}	n.a.
Tobacco	n.a.	80	99		n.a.
Paper	53	27	n.a.	56	n.a.
Chemicals	88	67	n.a.	n.a.	33
Rubber	99	84	61	59	52
Electrical machinery	74	79	61	54	n.a.
Non-electrical machinery	n.a.	62	n.a.	43	25
Transport equipment	58	49	68}	n.a.	10}
Motor vehicles	96	n.a.		38	

* Based on 5,113 non-financial enterprises.

n.a. = not available or negligible.

(*Source:* Adapted from UN Economic and Social Council, 1978, Tables III-59, III-60, and III-61.)

The data in Tables 1.14 and 1.15 are rather out of date and are restricted to US MNEs only. Table 1.16, therefore, presents further information relating to all foreign affiliate activities in a number of host states. The figures are not comparable as between countries since they refer to different years and different measures of penetration. Even so it is apparent that MNE control of industry in the countries concerned is such as to provide the firms with considerable economic and non-economic power. Since the structure of product markets in which MNEs operate is oligopolistic, then conduct which results in high prices, above-normal returns, high barriers to entry and so on might typically be expected. As a result, host country performance could be adversely affected.

The financing of MNE affiliate operations

In concluding this examination of the characteristics of multinational corporations, attention needs to be paid to one further feature of such firms, that is their ability to tap a wide variety of alternative sources of funds to finance their foreign operations. The affiliates of multinational corporations may obtain funds from:

 (i) *The parent firm's home country.* Here the finance may come from the parent itself either in the form of equity or loans. Alternatively the subsidiary may obtain funds from other sources in the home country. For example a US affiliate abroad may borrow directly from United States financial intermediaries or sell securities on the American capital market.

 (ii) *Undistributed profits and depreciation provisions.* Once the affiliate becomes established and begins to earn profits, expansion may be financed from this source. A certain proportion of profits are likely to be remitted to the parent company, but any undistributed profits are available for ploughing back into the business. Again depreciation provisions are a further source of internal finance.

(iii) *The host country or third countries.* A wide range of other sources exist within the host country itself and in third countries. In the host country, the affiliate may be able to raise equity capital, borrow from banks and other financial institutions and sell securities. Equally the subsidiary may raise finance in the capital markets of third countries or in the Euro-currency markets; and it may be able to borrow from other affiliates of the parent located in these third countries.

While all these alternatives exist in theory, realistically there will be a number of constraints on the flexibility of the MNE affiliate. Most obviously, in Third World countries capital markets are often undeveloped, and even in some European countries the full range of financial institutions and markets is not available. Moreover apparently similar financial institutions may have different functions and provide different types of finance, e.g. while the commercial banks in the UK are mainly sources of short-term funds, in Germany commercial banks provide, in addition, equity finance and long-term loans. More important constraints on the affiliate perhaps are the regulations of host countries, which may limit the raising of capital locally or restrict dividend remittances, and home country regulations concerning the permitted outflow of capital from the parent. When all this is said, however, the MNE affiliate has a much wider range of funding sources than the equivalent local firm, and this factor has been considered as providing a significant advantage to the foreign subsidiary. It is also a major point of criticism against MNEs that their multinationality allows investment independent of national control mechanisms. The possibility of affiliate growth through reinvested earnings and local borrowing is also claimed to reduce the balance of payments advantages derived from capital inflows from the parent and to restrict the finance available to local firms.

Some evidence on these issues, relating to a sample of US affiliates during the period 1966–72 is presented in Fig. 1.2. As indicated, during these years internal funds averaged 50 per cent of the total, nearly 16 per cent representing retained earnings and 34 per cent depreciation and similar charges. Forty-five per cent of funds were obtained externally, but of this figure just over 13 per cent came from US sources. Thus almost one-third of all finance was raised in the host country or in third countries (including funds raised from sister affiliates). The figures are taken one stage further in Table 1.17 which shows the sources of funds for US affiliates located in various regions and operating in various industries. A number of points stand out. Excluding the petroleum industry, only a very small proportion of total funds were obtained from US sources. Similarly affiliates located in Canada and Latin America received little finance from the United States. United States' affiliates in Canada are particularly significant in another way, namely in their reliance on internal funds: nearly two-thirds of funds came from undistributed profits and depreciation compared with 50 per cent for all affiliates. These figures are heavily influenced by the fact that controls over capital outflows from the US were in operation in one form or another throughout the period covered by the data. Nevertheless the figures show quite clearly that a substantial part of US 'foreign' direct investment is financed not from the home country at all but from the host nation and third countries.

Reviewing the information presented in this chapter, it is clear that the multinational enterprise is a phenomenon unlike that of any other business enterprise. Many of the characteristics of the MNE are common to other forms of business organisation, but no other institution exhibits the complete range of characteristics, and to such an extent, as the multinational firm. The size and geographical

Table 1.17 Per cent distribution of sources of funds for a sample of majority-owned foreign affiliates of US companies. 1966–72 average by industry and area

	Total sources	Internal funds			External funds			
		Total†	Undistributed profits	Depreciation and similar charges	Total†	From US sources	From foreign sources*	Other
All industries, all areas	100	50	16	34	45	13	32	5
By industry:								
Petroleum	100	44	9	35	51	23	28	5
Manufacturing	100	56	19	38	40	9	31	4
Other industries	100	43	20	23	50	6	44	7
By area:								
Canada	100	64	25	38	28	7	21	8
Europe	100	44	10	34	52	17	35	4
Other developed countries	100	43	16	26	54	16	38	3
Latin America	100	55	13	42	42	7	36	3
Other developing countries, international, and unallocated	100	50	22	28	45	14	31	5

* Sources outside the United States.
† Totals do not always equal sum of individual row entries because of rounding.

(*Source:* US Department of Commerce, July 1975.)

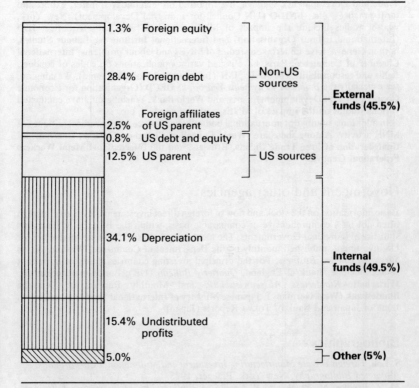

Fig. 1.2 Sources of funds for a sample of majority-owned foreign affiliates of US companies, 1966–72 (*Source*: US Department of Commerce, July 1975).

diversity of many multinationals; their concentration in high research and skill-intensive industries; their importance in world trade; their growth and profitability; and the dominance of the industrialised world as the base for MNEs are all factors of major economic significance. Such factors give the MNE its true distinctiveness and require careful consideration and analysis.

Sources

The sources listed in this section are cited for their general usefulness in the study of MNEs, though they only constitute a small selection from the large and growing range of material available. More specific information on further reading is given at the end of each of the subsequent chapters.

International organisations

UN Centre on Transnational Corporations, New York, whose wide range of excellent publications include *The CTC Reporter;* **UNCTAD** (United Nations Conference on

Trade and Development), Geneva, has reported on technology transfer, export and tariff practices, etc.; **UNIDO** (UN Council for Industrial Development), New York, whose studies include the impact of MNEs in Africa and Latin America; **ILO** (International Labour Organisation) and **International Institute for Labour Studies,** both in Geneva, have undertaken studies of MNEs and labour problems; **International Chamber of Commerce,** Paris, have issued various publications on codes of conduct, rights and responsibilities of MNEs; **IMF** (International Monetary Fund), Washington, see especially the *Balance of Payments Yearbook;* **OECD** (Organisation for Economic Cooperation and Development), Paris, and **World Bank,** Washington, have conducted various studies on the impact of MNEs, codes of conduct, etc.

In addition a number of international bodies have produced more radical critiques of MNE activity. Among these are: **World Council of Churches,** Geneva; **International Confederation of Free Trade Unions,** Brussels; and the **International Metal Workers Federation,** Geneva.

Government and other agencies

Basic information on the stock and flow of foreign direct investment is available, though often not on a comprehensive or comparable basis, within the Balance of Payments statistics of individual Governments. The most comprehensive figures available are for US investment, published monthly by the **Department of Commerce,** Washington, as *Survey of Current Business.* For the principal investing countries the most important sources include: **Bank of England,** *Quarterly Bulletin* (UK); **Bundesministerium für Wirtschaft,** *Runderlass Aussenwirtschaft;* and Monthly Reports of **Deutsche Bundesbank** (West Germany); **Japanese Ministry of International Trade and Industry,** Bank of Japan and Bank of Tokyo Reports (Japan).

Bibliographies

S. Lall, *Foreign Private Manufacturing Investment and Multinational Corporations: An Annotated Bibliography,* New York: Praeger, 1975.

M. Z. Brooke, M. Black and P. Neville, *A Bibliography of International Business,* London: Macmillan, 1976.

A useful bibliography of the more radical writings is that by H. Strharsky and M. Riesch (eds), *The Transnational Corporations and the Third World,* Washington: CODOC International Secretariat, 1975.

A publication which contains both a bibliography and a guide to company information sources is: J. O. Mekeirle (ed.), *Multinational Corporations: The ECSIM Guide to Information Sources,* European Centre for Study and Information on Multinational Corporations, Farnborough, Hants.: Saxon House, 1978.

Current information and research

Research findings on the economics of MNEs are published in a wide range of general economic journals and hence the best approach is to start with the *Journal of Economic Literature* as a guide to individual worldwide journals. Relevant material is also published in the more business-oriented journals, among the most useful of which are: *Journal of International Business Studies; Columbia Journal of World Business; Harvard Business Review; Management International Review.*

The collection of more current material on MNEs is always difficult but is aided by regular study of publications such as: *Fortune; Wall Street Journal; Financial Times; New York Times; Business Week; Economist; Business International;* and *Vision.*

The most complete record of current research on MNEs is now being maintained by the **UN Centre on Transnational Corporations.** The first directory of research has been issued as *Survey of Research on Transnational Corporations,* E.77 II.A.16, New York: United Nations Centre on Transnational Corporations, 1977.

Performance and ownership

J. W. Vaupel and **J. Curhan,** *The World's Multinational Enterprises: A Sourcebook of Tables,* Boston: Division of Research, Harvard Business School, 1973, contains an extensive collection of material relating to the affiliates of US, UK, Continental European, Japanese and other MNEs for the period up to 1970. More up-to-date information relating to US-based enterprises is contained in **J. P. Curhan, W. H. Davidson** and **R. Suri,** *Tracing the Multinationals: A Sourcebook on US-based Enterprises,* Cambridge, Mass.: Ballinger Publishing Company, 1977.

There are also an ever increasing number of directories on ownership. *Who Owns Whom* in its various country versions, *Moodies* and *Dun and Bradstreet* remain basic sources. Collections of performance data constitute a growth industry and among these are: *Jane's Major Companies of Europe; Europe's 500 Largest Companies;* and *Fortune 500* and *2nd 500* data.

Questions for discussion

1. In a study prepared by the UN Secretariat, the term MNE was used 'to cover all enterprises which control assets – factories, mines, sales offices and the like – in two or more countries'. The Group of Eminent Persons, on the other hand, defined MNEs as 'enterprises which own or control production or service facilities outside the country in which they are based. Such enterprises are not always incorporated or private; they can also be cooperatives or state-owned entities.' (Definitions quoted in UN Economic and Social Council (1978), p. 158). Discuss the similarities and differences between these two definitions.

2. What are the differences between foreign direct investment and (*a*) the multiplant domestic operation; (*b*) exporting (and importing); (*c*) licensing and technical agreements, and (*d*) portfolio investment?

3. What are the principal causes of the rapid growth in MNE activity since the Second World War?

4. How can the recent expansion of Japanese and German foreign direct investment be explained?

5. 'MNEs are simply oligopolists on a grand scale. As such there is no difficulty in understanding where they have been, what they do or where they are going.' Discuss.

6. 'The declining popularity of US investors in Europe is nothing compared with the vilification they and their European counterparts are subjected to in some developing countries.' Why? Is there any possible harmony of interests in such cases?

7. Has the MNE a future beyond AD 2000?

8. What are the *essential* features of an MNE?

Chapter 2

The determinants
of foreign direct investment

Summary

1. Foreign direct investment is a product of imperfections in goods and factor markets throughout the world. In a perfect market situation no advantage could accrue to the prospective multinational company. But normally some advantage is required to enable the MNE to produce and compete successfully in an unfamiliar foreign environment.

2. Numerous ownership-specific advantages have been suggested by MNE theorists, deriving from: technology and marketing skills; oligopolistic market structure and behaviour; excess managerial capacity; financial and monetary factors, including access to cheap capital and diversification of investments; access to raw materials.

3. The possession of ownership-specific advantages alone would not explain why a firm should engage in foreign production, since it could exploit its unique advantages by, say, licensing a foreign producer. To clarify this, theorists have turned to the ideas of Coase, who introduced the concept of internalisation. Since the market is costly and inefficient for undertaking certain types of transactions, companies may reject the market and organise these transactions within the firm itself. For example, because of difficulties in placing a value on the knowledge obtained from long term R & D, firms may internalise the knowledge and engage in foreign direct investment to exploit it.

4. Even then, ownership-specific advantages represent only a necessary and not a sufficient condition for foreign direct investment. To explain the preference for investment abroad over exporting from the home country, another group of location-specific factors needs to be taken into account. These factors include trade barriers, host government policies, relative labour costs, and market size and growth. One or a combination of these factors may tip the balance and encourage the firm to locate production facilities abroad. In addition, the influence of these various factors may depend upon the stage of the product's life cycle, as between a new, mature or standardised commodity.

5. The theory of foreign direct investment provides certain pointers to the efficiency of MNEs in resource allocation but it cannot predict unambiguously. Considerable scope therefore exists for further

developments, particularly to differentiate between the sources of market imperfections which MNEs are claimed to internalise. Furthermore the theory is more satisfactory in explaining horizontal direct investments than in providing an explanation for resource-based and export-platform type investments. The inter-relationships between ownership-specific and country-specific advantages also require clarification. Finally, attention is only beginning to be given to an overall theory of international production in which foreign investment is considered as merely one method of servicing markets abroad (see Chapter 4).

6. Empirical studies of direct investment abroad have been handicapped by data limitations, and sometimes by unsatisfactory methodology. The most valuable regression studies have indicated that size of firm and a measure of technological intensity are the most important determinants of investment abroad. There are some difficulties in interpreting the meaning of these results. Size, for example, may represent a proxy for all or most of the possible ownership-specific advantages and/or it may describe sheer oligopolistic market power. Technological intensity on the other hand – in the form of R & D and advertising expenditures or the employment of technical and professional staff – is a proxy variable for the firm's ability to create knowledge. Surveys of businessmen have indicated that the host government's attitude to inward foreign investment, political stability and the prospects of market growth are the most important factors in determining the location of manufacturing facilities.

Attention has been focused on the role of the multinational enterprise within the world economy, stressing the distinguishing characteristics of this unique phenomenon. Progressing from this, the aim of the present chapter is to identify and summarise recent attempts to explain the growth and development of such multinational companies, highlighting both theoretical and empirical contributions.

Contributions to the theory of the multinational enterprise

In this chapter, the theory of foreign direct investment is viewed from an economic perspective. But it is important to accept that a number of other approaches could be developed. Political considerations, for example, are inevitably of some importance in the process of MNE development overseas and could be incorporated into the theory as in the neo-imperialist explanations for the growth of the international firm. Alternatively a socio-psychological approach might be taken in which the aspirations of individuals and groups within the firm provided the motive for direct investment abroad. Or again foreign investment might be viewed as a historical process allied to twentieth-century developments in transport and communications including air services, telephone and telex links etc.

Within the economics discipline itself many areas of analysis, including the theory of the firm, the theory of monopolistic competition, capital theory, location theory and international trade theory are potentially relevant to the topic of multinationality. However, traditional explanations of international economic involvement derived from such theories fail to explain certain crucial features of foreign direct investment, and particularly the aspect of ownership control. Thus inter-country differences in the supply of capital might explain why investment would flow from countries where capital was abundant to countries where it was scarce; but not why these flows would take the form of direct investment. Similarly, differences between various countries in terms of wages, taxes, tariffs and so on might help to explain in which country production activities were to be located, but not why production was undertaken by a foreign rather than an indigenous firm.

It may be assumed that a multinational firm operating in a foreign country is faced with certain additional costs in comparison with a local competitor. These arise from cultural, legal, institutional and linguistic differences, lack of knowledge of local market conditions, and the increased expense in terms of communications and misunderstandings of operating at a distance. For MNE investment to prove profitable, therefore, the firm entering from abroad must have some advantages not shared by its local competitors. This is the starting point for all theories of foreign direct investment and the MNE.[1] To be exploitable, these advantages must be, at least in part, specific to the firm and readily transferable within the firm and across distance. *The existence of such ownership-specific advantages represents a necessary but not a sufficient condition for foreign direct investment.* The fact that a foreign firm possesses some monopolistic or oligopolistic advantage over indigenous competitors gives the MNE its unique character but would not explain why the production process need be located abroad. The foreign firm could exploit its advantage through producing at home and exporting or by licensing a foreign producer. *To explain the choice of foreign direct investment over the alternatives of exporting and licensing, it is necessary to take into account (at least in some cases) location-specific factors such as relative costs of production, trade barriers, market characteristics and the like.*

It is important to be clear on the distinction between ownership- and location-specific factors. All companies operating within a particular country, whether at home or abroad, will have access to the resources of labour, capital, management, etc. available within that country.

Similarly all firms will be operating within the same economic environment, as influenced by government policies and so on. These *location-specific characteristics* of a country will influence the operations of all firms, domestic or foreign, operating within the country. Some companies, however, will also possess certain kinds of knowledge which are not available to all the other firms. These *ownership-specific factors,* which are internal to a particular firm, are capable of being combined with other resources either in the home country or in a foreign country. It is the association of ownership- and locational-specific factors which determines whether, firstly, a particular firm has an advantage over other firms, and secondly, whether the firm will exploit that advantage by producing abroad, by exporting or by licensing. Together the two sets of factors, therefore, represent the essential conditions for multinationality, and form the basis for the theories of foreign direct investment evolving in the literature.[2] The main contributions to the locational question derive from international trade and location theory, while the theory of the firm and the theory of monopolistic competition are chiefly relevant to the issue of ownership-specific advantages.

The market imperfections approach

The 'pure' orthodox theory of the firm cannot be applied to foreign direct investment. With perfect competition, firms do not possess market power; they produce homogeneous products and have equal access to all productive factors. In such a world there would be no such thing as direct foreign investment since no advantage could accrue to the prospective multinational firm. Foreign direct investment is therefore a by-product of imperfect markets. As Kindleberger (1969) has stated: 'For direct investment to thrive there must be some imperfection in markets for goods or factors including among the latter technology, or some interference in competition by government or by firms, which separates markets.'[3] Thus national and international market imperfections both permit the multinational firm to acquire its monopoly advantage in its domestic environment and to exploit this through foreign production. These departures from perfect competition may occur, firstly, in goods markets and include product differentiation, brand names, special marketing skills or collusion in pricing. Secondly, there may be departures from competition in factor markets, taking the form of special managerial skills, differences in access to capital markets and technology protected by patents. Thirdly, imperfect competition may be reflected in the existence of internal or external economies of scale. And finally, government policies in respect of taxes, tariffs, interest rates, exchange rates and so forth may also create imperfect markets.

Early theorists of foreign direct investment therefore focused on one or a number of ownership advantages which MNEs were believed to have acquired within this imperfectly competitive environment. The names initially associated with this approach were Hymer and Kindleberger who noted numerous potential advantages including patented or unavailable technology, special access to capital or markets, economies of scale, economies of vertical integration, differentiated products, etc.[4] Subsequently the theory has been both refined and extended to cover other sources of oligopolistic and monopolistic advantage. These ownership advantages deriving from imperfect markets are considered in the next section.

The sources of advantage to multinational firms

(a) Technological advantages

The central role played by this factor, variously described as technology, information, knowledge, intangible capital and know-how has been emphasised by all writers on the MNE. The technology contribution of MNEs is, moreover, not only their major source of advantage, but it is also probably their most desirable attribute from the viewpoint of host countries. Reflecting the definitions given, technological advantage is seen in a fairly broad sense to include production secrets, management organisational techniques and marketing skills. Therefore technology does not merely include the discovery of *new products and new production processes*, although much of the research and development effort of multinational firms will clearly have this end in view. Associated with this role in developing new products and processes, MNEs take out patents or adopt other means to keep their innovations secret or unusable by other firms.

New products and processes are the most tangible component of MNEs' technological advantage, but there are other aspects which may be at least as important. In particular, the *ability to differentiate products* may be highly significant particularly where technology becomes standardised. By means of 'minor physical variations, "brand name" and subjective distinctions created by advertising, or differences in the ancillary terms and conditions of sale',[5] the product may be protected from exact imitation.

Production differentiation in turn is a reflection of more *general marketing skills*. The functions of marketing research, selling, advertising and promotions are all necessary to the attainment of customer loyalty. The success of American firms such as Kellogg, Coca-Cola, Heinz, Proctor and Gamble, is based to a much greater extent on marketing expertise than on laboratory R & D.

A third source of technological advantage may lie in the *superior organisational skills and management techniques* of MNEs as compared with local competitors. The advantage may arise from better trained or educated, or more experienced managers. Alternatively superior organisational structure may facilitate more rapid and more efficient decision-taking. Or again management techniques, in areas such as finance, may be more sophisticated. Such factors may help explain, for example, the growth of international hotel chains such as the Hilton, Intercontinental, Sheraton, etc.

Certain characteristics of knowledge have been stressed by various authors as being particularly pertinent to an explanation of why MNEs choose international production rather than exporting or licensing. H.G. Johnson has suggested that knowledge has the characteristic of a public good to the firm.[6] That is, once the know-how has been achieved, foreign subsidiaries can draw on it, e.g. R & D results, knowledge of markets, access to cheaper inputs, without any additional cost to the parent company. The know-how might thus be made available to the subsidiary at a low cost whereas the competitive domestic firm would have to bear the full cost of obtaining the information. For this to be important in promoting direct investment, however, there must either be no other potential buyers of the know-how or alternatively the MNE must be able to earn a higher return by retaining the knowledge within the firm itself.

An additional point suggested in relation to knowledge about product differentiation is that it cannot easily be separated from the production process or the marketing activity of the firm. Thus licensing would not be feasible since the information relating to differentiating the product could not be transferred independently of the firm and its management. More generally, a knowledge advantage must be easily transferable within the firm and across national boundaries, but less easily transferable between different firms whether in the same or in different countries.

(b) Industrial organisation

Another source of advantage to multinational firms is seen as deriving from oligopolistic market structure and behaviour. This is closely linked in the literature with technological advantage, for several reasons.[7] In the first place, large size is an important attribute for successful innovation given the increasingly high costs of R & D and the economies of scale available in R & D work. Secondly, the profitable exploitation of technology requires some degree of monopoly, if secrets are not to be lost to competitors. Moreover, large firms are most protected by the patent system because of the high costs of taking out and defending patents internationally. Finally product differentiation is frequently associated with oligopolistic market structures.

However, the industrial organisation feature which is particularly emphasised is that of economies of scale, since this produces an important source of market power to large firms. It may appear on first consideration that scale economies favour the centralisation of production and the servicing of markets via exports rather than overseas direct investment. But when trade barriers in foreign markets, and the exhaustion of existing scale economies or anti-trust provisions in home markets are taken into account, then direct investment may be necessary. In these cases the possibility of exploiting economies of scale within the overseas market becomes relevant. It is important to distinguish between plant and firm economies of scale, the former involving production processes and the latter non-production activities. Increasing concentration has not generally been accompanied by a trend towards ever-increasing plant size and it is the non-production economies which are particularly important. These include advantages derived from the centralisation of R & D, marketing, finance and other management functions which will not be available to smaller local competitors. The ability to establish large scale distribution networks may also produce major economies for the large, multi-plant firm.

F. T. Knickerbocker[8] has gone furthest in developing an oligopoly model of MNEs, suggesting that oligopolists follow each other into new foreign markets as a defensive strategy. Once one firm establishes manufacturing facilities, the others follow suit in order to negate any advantage that the former might gain. While it may be argued that such a 'bunching' of foreign investment could be a response to simultaneous profit opportunity rather than market structure, the framework may well help to explain the volume of investment in Europe during the 1960s, and the presence of numerous MNEs in certain less developed countries. This approach, however, does not indicate the nature of the advantage which the multinational oligopolists possess over indigenous firms nor how the investment behaviour of the initiating firm is to be interpreted.

(c) Managerial and entrepreneurial capacity

Management skills and organisational ability have already been considered as a source of advantage to international firms. It may not only be the possession of this superior ability which stimulates multinationality, but also the fact that managerial capacity may be under-utilised at certain stages of the firm's development.[9] Resources such as management have to be purchased in discrete quantities, but the services of such highly specialised management personnel may not be fully utilised without some expansion in the scale of the firm's operations. Entry into foreign markets or an increase in the scale of foreign operations may permit further utilisation of the internationally mobile resource of management. Better utilisation of management capacity could, of course, come about by domestic industrial diversification, by exporting or by licensing foreign firms, as well as by foreign production itself.

It is noteworthy that once this expansion has occurred, or even to achieve the expansion, it may be necessary to employ other types of indivisible factors, which in turn may generate a further incentive to expand at home or abroad.

(d) Financial and monetary

This covers a diverse range of factors associated with capital market imperfections. These consider, for example, the impact of interest rate variations, exchange rate fluctuations and the varying structures and efficiencies of international capital markets on foreign direct investment.

(i) The influence of currency variations. It has been suggested by R. Z. Aliber that the pattern of foreign direct investment reflects the fact that source country firms (multinationals) capitalise the same stream of expected earnings at a higher rate than host country firms.[10] The MNEs are able to do this because of the relative hardness of the currencies of capital exporting countries and thus the existence of a currency premium. In essence when borrowings are made in the international capital market, the rate of interest charged on such loans will carry a premium which reflects the risks of possible depreciation of the currency concerned. It was assumed that there was a tendency for portfolio investors to take no account of the fact that a multinational company operates in different currency areas. The assumption is therefore that the MNE has to charge interest on borrowings as if its total operation was in a domestic base. However, suppose that for a US MNE operating in the UK, for example, the currency premium on sterling is higher than that on dollars (assuming that dollars were the preferred currency).[11] Then the effective rate of interest on borrowings for the US affiliate in the UK may be lower than for local UK companies. In general this may result in the MNE often being able to borrow at a lower rate of interest than an indigenous firm to finance capital expenditures in the host country, and achieve potential gain (or loss) through fluctuating currency values. The Aliber model is shown diagrammatically in the Appendix on pages 84–5.

Relating Aliber's model to the observed facts, the rapid growth of US direct investment during the 1950s and 1960s could be associated with the strength of the dollar during this period and the existence of a currency premium. Conversely the strength of the Japanese yen and certain European currencies could provide interesting pointers for the future; but US and UK MNEs have continued to grow despite the weaknesses of their respective currencies in recent years. Indeed arguments are sometimes put forward that UK MNEs, for instance, have an added incentive to invest abroad at a time of weakness of sterling in order to benefit from the exchange rate gains when converting, say deutsch-mark earnings into £ sterling. More generally the approach could not explain the widespread cross-investment between Europe and the US. Nor could it account for either the investment of US firms within the dollar area, or multinational investment in LDCs where capital markets may be nonexistent and foreign exchanges highly regulated.

(ii) Cheaper capital.   The view that MNEs can exploit exchange risk and thereby gain an advantage over local competitors is part of a more general hypothesis that multinationals may enjoy a cheaper supply of capital than indigenous firms. The financial strength of the parent company and its established credit rating may permit the MNE subsidiaries to obtain favourable terms when raising capital locally. Moreover certain capital markets in developed countries, e.g. Euro-currency markets, may not be open to local competitors. However, neither cheaper nor more favoured access to capital would explain why investment should take the form of direct as opposed to portfolio investment. Nor is it likely that this factor *per se* would provide sufficient advantage to offset the additional costs associated with operating across national boundaries.

(iii) Portfolio diversification.   One of the main theoretical strands in the study of international investment stems from the theory of portfolio choice, i.e. where the investor develops an 'efficient' portfolio of investment in which risk-aversion and expected value of returns are balanced. The net effect of this process is the diversification of the portfolio over a range of assets, so as to balance risk, liquidity preference, national conditions, and so on. Much of this work is concerned with portfolio behaviour by individual investors studying foreign equity markets and may not be so appropriate to a corporate direct investor such as an MNE.[12] Indeed it may be argued that if such a process was applied by an MNE, the end result would be a range of minority holdings abroad, rather than direct, controlling investments. But this is only so if a fairly substantial proportion of the portfolio is tied up in a single holding, which may not be the case. The individual shareholder in the MNE could achieve his own optimum by a diffusion of holdings, without requiring any one of his holdings to pursue such a strategy. In an international setting, on the other hand, institutional or other barriers to the free flow of financial capital may prevent investors from achieving portfolio diversification themselves.

Thus a line of approach which seems promising is that which views foreign direct investment and international diversification as a means of reducing risk.[13] The multinational firm may enjoy a more stable stream of profits over time if it has direct investments in foreign countries where the economies are less than perfectly positively correlated with economic fluctuations in the home country. Furthermore, the divorce of ownership from control may be important in applying the portfolio choice model of expansion, since diversification via foreign direct investment may increase managerial discretion by reducing risk.

In general, while financial and monetary factors may provide MNEs with some exploitable ownership specific advantages, they do not seem to be sufficiently important to be other than permissive factors in foreign investment. Thus, there has not been any substantial modification of existing theories of corporate financial behaviour emerging from MNE study, although the various developments noted have been among those posing potentially interesting hypotheses for explaining the role of finance in the foreign investment process. There is no doubt, however, that the area of financial management has become increasingly important since the collapse of the fixed exchange rate system, the world-wide acceleration in inflation rates, and the growing divergence between the relative strengths and weaknesses of various economies. Effective currency and financial management may now have become as important in determining the profitability of MNE affiliates as the production and marketing performance of the firms themselves.

(e) Access to raw materials

A requirement for particular raw materials may clearly be a *country*-specific factor influencing the location of foreign extractive, processing or production activities. But if multinational firms have privileged access to raw materials or minerals, then this becomes a *firm*-specific advantage. Such privileged access may arise from control over production of the material (as in mining and plantations); from control over processing (as in vertically integrated mineral and food processing); or from control over the final markets for agricultural products or over the transportation of such products.[14] Of course the source of an MNE's unique access to raw materials is not explained; this must be deemed to have emerged from other factors such as, for instance, a technological, marketing or financial advantage in the mining and processing industries. And this would be perfectly feasible, since a firm with an established marketing system could earn more from the development of foreign raw materials than a local firm with no marketing outlets in the industrialised countries. In any event, once acquired the MNE concerned is in a powerful monopolistic or oligopolistic position which it may exploit either in domestic or other foreign markets. Under such circumstances an industry would shift from a situation with numerous small competitive firms to one with a few large, vertically integrated concerns, seeking security with assured access to sources of inputs and outlets for products.[15] The oil industry with its seven multinationals dominating the world scene is a classic example of this.

These various explanations for the possession of ownership-specific advantages all derive from the existence of less than perfect product and factor markets, and represent orthodox economic opinion. While the issue will not be pursued further until Chapter 8, it should be noted that radical economists would tend to reject these explanations for the growth of multinational firms. To radicals the MNE's advantage derives from neo-imperialism, with the home country government playing a crucial role through the supply of 'aid' and military equipment and associated political and diplomatic pressure. Examples can undoubtedly be given of home government involvement, particularly where nationalisation or expropriation threats exist. But in general, as later evidence will indicate, such factors could not be considered as representing a normal or permanent source of advantage to MNEs.

Towards a theory of foreign direct investment

Regarding the conventional explanations considered, the importance to be attached to the various attributes of MNEs differs significantly. The technology factor (including marketing skills) is of paramount importance, with the other variables merely supplementing or reinforcing this key characteristic. Even then, there are still difficulties in making the step from outlining the sources of advantage possessed by MNEs to incorporating these into a theory of foreign direct investment. Thus to decide to produce abroad, the firm requires more than just identifiable advantages. The economic rent obtainable from the possession of these advantages must be increased by production in a foreign location, otherwise the firm could exploit its unique advantage by licensing or by producing at home and exporting. Kindleberger, for example, points out that: 'Where the license fee fails to capture the full rent interest in technical superiority, the advantage lies in direct investment.'[16] However, the key question as to why the full rent is not obtainable through the market is left unanswered. Caves argues (with respect to his favoured explanation of product differentiation advantages) that direct investment was preferable to licensing since the know-how could not be transferred independently of the firm and its management. The view was that licensing a foreign producer would be as profitable as direct investment in specific cases only, such as where the advantage of the parent firm lies in some once-for-all innovation. Alternatively a small firm might settle for licensing, since the extra control and communication costs of operating abroad might prove prohibitive at the company's scale of output.

This view that some of the advantages possessed by the firm might not prove marketable is closer to the true explanation for multinationality, but does not provide a comprehensive, systematic theory. In seeking this explanation theorists have in recent years resurrected the ideas of Ronald Coase, who in 1937 produced a workable explanation of the origins and equilibrium size of firms.[17] The basic idea is that the market is costly and inefficient for undertaking certain types of transactions. These transactions' costs of using the market are: the cost of finding a relevant price; the cost of defining the obligations of both parties to a contract; the risk associated with accepting such contracts; and, the taxes to be paid on market transactions. The existence of these various costs means that whenever transactions can be organised and carried out at a lower cost *within the firm* than *through the market,* they will be internalised and undertaken by the firm itself. The Coase theorem was originally developed to apply to the multi-plant indigenous firm, but the internalisation concept is equally applicable to multinational firms. Thus MNEs appear where it is less costly to allocate international resources internally than to use the market. In this way the MNE is able to capitalise on the possession of its unique advantage. The general market imperfections framework still applies, of course, since it is the imperfections in the external means of resource allocation which provide the incentive for internalisation; where markets are perfectly competitive, internalisation could not improve upon the external market allocation.

This approach can be best understood by reference to specific examples:[18] Singer was the first US MNE, investing initially in Scotland in 1867. While the company produced a good quality sewing machine, its particular advantage related to the services associated with its machine. Thus the company provided instructors, demonstrators and credit, and thereby made it possible for the average housewife to buy and use sewing machines. Singer's experience in the USA was that licensing was unsatisfactory because of difficulties in devising and enforcing contracts between itself and licensees (which can be expressed in terms of imperfections in external markets). Consequently the company moved to wholly owned retail outlets in its domestic expansion, and thereafter to direct investment in its overseas growth. In the same way other US firms held on to important parts of their total operation in foreign markets, such as Kodak with processing or Heinz with their sales force. Again, it is possible to see why a new type of steelmaking plant might be built under licence but not a new computer system, where adaptation to customer requirements, after-sales service and software are important parts of the package. As a final example, companies such as Kentucky Fried Chicken, Holiday Inns, and McDonalds are able to operate abroad with licensees because it is possible to clearly specify the obligations of the parties involved and arrive at a mutually agreeable price.

The theory of foreign direct investment

A systematic attempt to incorporate these ideas into a theory of the multinational enterprise was first undertaken by P. J. Buckley and M. Casson (1976).[19] The authors criticise previous work on MNEs as lacking a comprehensive theoretical base, especially in failing to take full account of the many activities of the firm outside production. These activities, e.g. research and development, marketing, the training of labour, the building of a management team, etc. are considered to be interdependent and connected by flows of intermediate products. These intermediate products are not just semi-processed materials, but more often are types of knowledge incorporated in patents, human capital and so on. Imperfect competition in these markets is as important as in final markets, and the profit maximising firm facing such imperfections will attempt to internalise the intermediate products within its own organisation. A number of such imperfections are considered to be particularly important in stimulating internalisation. For example, government intervention in the form of tariff, taxation, dividend remittance and exchange rate policies provides a rationale for internalisation, since in this way the firm has the opportunity, through transfer pricing, to minimise tax payments, etc. Again, imperfections may arise from inequalities between buyer and seller with respect to knowledge concerning the nature or value of the product. When the seller is better informed than the buyer but is unable to convince the latter that the price quoted is reasonable, there is an incentive for the seller to undertake the buyer's activities (processing, selling, etc.) himself. Where the internalisation process occurs across national boundaries, MNEs are claimed to be generated.

It is suggested that the incentive to internalise depends on the relationship between four groups of factors: (i) *industry-specific factors,* e.g. nature of the product, external market structure and economies of scale; (ii) *region-specific factors,* e.g. geographical distance, and cultural differences; (iii) *nation-specific factors,* e.g. political and fiscal factors; (iv) *firm-specific factors,* e.g. management expertise. The main emphasis is on industry-specific factors, and within the group the *knowledge factor* is considered to be of major importance, for several reasons. In the first place, knowledge provides a monopoly advantage which can best be exploited through discriminatory pricing by the firm itself, rather than, for example, by licensing. Secondly, the production of knowledge requires long-term research and development, and at any stage before project completion the value of the knowledge obtained may be difficult to establish, if the firm were contemplating selling. Again, simply because of valuation difficulties, flows of knowledge are a useful area for transfer pricing.

There are, inevitably, costs involved in internalisation. Increased accounting and control information is required; communication costs rise; and, with a general dislike of MNEs in many host countries, there are also the costs of political discrimination to be taken into account. For net benefits to result to the firm from internalisation, therefore, these costs must be more than offset by the advantages accruing from the process.

How does this internalisation approach differ from the theories of technological advantage, industrial organisation, etc. presented earlier? The difference is that it is not the possession of a unique asset *per se* which gives a firm its advantage. Rather it is the process of internalising that asset as opposed to selling it to a foreign producer which gives the MNE its unique advantage. As Buckley and Casson see it the MNE's advantages are 'the rewards for past investment in (i) R & D facilities which create an advantage in technological fields, (ii) the creation of an integrated team of skills, the rent from which is greater than the sum of the rewards to individuals . . . (iii) *the creation of an information transmission network which allows the benefits of (i) and (ii) to be transmitted at low cost within the organisation, but also protects such information, including knowledge of market conditions, from outsiders'.*[20] Relating the internalisation approach to another theory noted earlier, namely that of excess managerial capacity, it is not the surplus managerial resources *per se* which leads to direct investment abroad. Rather it is the ability of firms to combine these resources with others to exploit economies in the production of joint products.

It could be argued that under this model, internalisation would be as much a characteristic of a multi-plant uninational firm as of a multinational firm, and this is accepted. But with internalisation of the knowledge market, and assuming profit maximisation as an objective for the firm, multinationality would be logical to exploit the knowledge advantage possessed. In this sense the approach has strong links with theories in the Hymer-Kindleberger tradition (see note 4). However, the framework is more comprehensively expressed than most others, and the model would seem to have fairly general applicability in oligopolistic markets such as typify MNE operations. The major difficulty (as the next section will show) comes in trying to validate the internalisation hypothesis empirically. Moreover the important question is whether or not the theory can be extended to the long run, even on present knowledge of the MNE expansion process: for example, whether the political or other costs of internalisation will ultimately become prohibitive if nations adopt discriminatory policies towards MNEs, as in the area of transfer pricing. Certainly some parts of the process seem eminently suitable for the application of codes of conduct.

A second theory which has a number of similarities to that of Buckley and Casson has been developed by Magee[21]. This is discussed more fully in Chapter 3 (pp. 104–5) in the context of the theory of information but in essence the argument is that the MNE's advantage derives from its ability to ensure full appropriability of the returns to its investment in the production of new technology. This appropriability theory again draws upon the internalisation concept, since it is the MNE's ability to internalise technology which is one of the factors facilitating appropriability. In addition, however, the international patent system will provide protection for certain types of technology. The problems of replicating complex technologies will also give some protection; and the multinational firm may try to disguise the new technology incorporated into its products by various means. Where Magee differs from Buckley and Casson is in the emphasis on the appropriability of returns from technology creation: the appropriability problem arises in private markets because of the public good nature of technology. The differences are not fundamental, nevertheless, and the appropriability theory is again related to the work of Coase, Hymer, Caves, Johnson, etc.

The role of locational factors in the foreign direct investment decision

The theory is not yet complete. It has been shown that in imperfect market situations firms have an incentive to internalise certain activities within their own organisation. By this means they may exploit ownership-specific advantages which will enable them to compete with local firms, given that the latter have inherent benefits in terms of knowledge of local markets, and of the legal and institutional framework within the country, etc. The internalisation/appropriability model provides an adequate basis for explaining some of the preference for foreign direct investment over licensing: firms whose uniqueness is related to marketing skill, production co-ordination, or secret technology, are most likely to favour direct investment. On the other hand, conditions within the host country itself will also influence the choice between direct investment and licensing. To take only one obvious example the possibility of licensing advanced technology may not exist in many LDCs because of the unavailability of the necessary skills among indigenous firms.

The existence of ownership advantages, moreover, will not solely explain why direct investment is preferred over exporting. Given some unique advantage the firm might simply produce at home and serve third country markets through exports. Once again, therefore, it is necessary to introduce locational factors relating to the host country to fully explain why a firm will take the trouble and accept the risks of organising manufacturing operations abroad. A number of locational factors are pertinent to this situation:

(a)   Labour costs[22]
Imperfections in international markets for labour, such as immigration controls which reduce labour mobility between countries, may lead to differences in real wage costs. In this way, particularly as technology becomes standardised, production may be transferred to the source of labour inputs. The transfer of certain assembly operations within vertically integrated firms to LDC locations is an example of this type of foreign direct investment. The assembly of electronics components in offshore locations such as Korea, Singapore, Taiwan or Hong Kong, represent a case in point, where MNEs operate a world-wide sourcing policy for manufacture and assembly with the aim of minimising total production costs. Similarly, the production of low technology products (e.g. toys, clothing and sports equipment) in these and other low wage areas, may be cited as a further illustration. While this type of direct investment has been growing rapidly it is relatively unimportant quantitatively. As will be indicated, nevertheless, wage cost

differences appear to have also had some influence on decisions by US firms relating to direct investment in Europe and Canada.

(b) Marketing factors

Characteristics of host countries such as market size, market growth, stage of development and the presence of local competition, will influence decisions on direct investment. Particularly if trade barriers exist in the host country, factors such as size of market are clearly relevant to the possibility of exploiting economies of scale in production and marketing. Similarly where host country competition is strong, a 'made locally' label may assist in obtaining sales. And production and marketing adaptation to cater for differences in tastes and requirements (e.g. contrast the size and design of cars made by Ford, General Motors and Chrysler in the USA with those made by the same companies in their European locations) may only be economic if the host country market is sufficiently large. These types of factors will be particularly important in respect of direct investment in developed countries, but the formation of free trade areas or customs unions within groups of LDCs may offer similar potential.

(c) Trade barriers

The existence of tariff and non-tariff barriers will also affect the choice between direct investment and exporting. Some host countries have deliberately used tariffs, quotas, local standards, etc. to encourage direct investment. In the LDCs the import substitution strategies pursued by some countries were designed to induce foreign firms, which had previously exported, to set up local manufacturing facilities. And in Canada, high tariffs have been used to attract US direct investment when, in terms of proximity, exporting might have been logical and feasible. Even if host countries choose to use tariffs and so on for reasons unassociated with foreign direct investment, e.g. to protect the balance of payments, this may still have the effect of inducing foreign firms to change the way in which they supply the host country market. As a final point, transport costs should also be considered as a trade barrier influencing decisions on exporting and foreign production.[23]

(d) Government policy

Apart from government policy relating to tariffs and other forms of protectionism, host governments may have other direct or indirect influences upon the way in which foreign firms approach host country markets. The general political, social and economic environment (the so-called 'investment climate') will affect firms' perceptions of risk and thus influence the location of their manufacturing operations. Similarly, policies relating to acquisitions, local participation in manufacturing operations, profit remittances, etc. will affect the method of market servicing.

The product cycle

The relative importance of these location-specific characteristics of host countries will change over time as the product itself moves through its life cycle. As a consequence the company's choice between exports, foreign subsidiary production, and licensing could also change. It was to incorporate such dynamic elements that the product cycle model was developed by S. Hirsch and R. Vernon.[24]

From the date of its introduction on the market, the life of a product can be divided into three stages, progressing from the 'new' to the 'mature' and ultimately the 'standardised' commodity. The product cycle thesis relates these stages to the locational decisions made by firms and to the choice between exports and overseas production. Because of high per capita incomes in the USA and the converse, high unit labour costs, it was argued that a particular incentive existed in America to develop new products which were labour-saving or were designed to satisfy high-income wants. Even if a greater propensity existed in the USA to develop new products, this did not necessarily imply that production would be located in America. However in the first stage of the product cycle, it was considered that there were inherent tendencies for firms to choose a domestic production location. At this early stage the price elasticity of demand might be fairly low because of product differentiation or monopoly advantages possessed by the innovating firm, thus reducing the importance of cost differences between locations. Close contact with customers and suppliers was also necessary at this stage to iron out teething problems with the product, or change product specifications.

The second stage is that of the maturing product. Some element of standardisation has been introduced in design and production. In general there is less need for the flexibility that goes with experimentation and product development, and long-run production with established technology becomes possible. There is thus more concern about the costs of production particularly since competitors may by now have appeared on the scene. Furthermore the dimensions of the market may be changing as opportunities appear abroad, particularly in relatively advanced countries such as in Western Europe. Both of these points affect the production location decision. On the profit maximising premise, it was concluded that as long as the marginal production costs plus the transport costs of the goods exported from the USA were lower than the average costs of prospective production in the importing market, the US investor would export and avoid direct investment. When it eventually became economic to invest, Western Europe would be the preferred choice of location since demand patterns were close to those in the US but at the time the thesis was formulated, in the mid 1960s, labour costs were relatively low. In the final stage in this model, namely the standardised product, the priority is for the lowest cost supply point. Market knowledge and information flows are now less important; competition is primarily on price grounds. The net effect is that production or assembly might be transferred to developing countries with low labour costs. Ultimately imitation abroad could result in imports into the innovation-initiating country from foreign subsidiaries.

The process is represented diagrammatically in Fig. 2.1 as between the US and Europe.[25] The critical time periods are t_1 where US exports begin, t_2 where European production begins, and t_3 where US imports begin. From t_2 onwards, a significant proportion of European output can be assumed to be produced by US MNE-affiliates in Europe, and similarly when the US begins to import, American affiliates will also be involved.

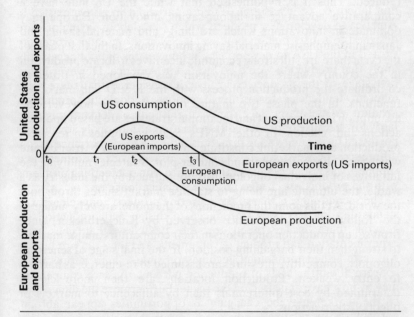

Fig. 2.1 The product cycle concept.

The product life cycle theory mainly provides a framework within which early post-war expansion of US investment into Europe can be interpreted. However, the sequential development process assumed may still have some applicability for firms which are expanding abroad for the first time and for MNE activity associated with final product type. It may be less applicable now for established MNEs: the model of planning products for one market before selling these abroad does not adequately describe the complex activity of market segmentation in different countries which underlies much MNE practice. Vernon himself has accepted that the approach is less satisfactory in explaining behaviour where the MNE employs a developed global strategy towards its interests. The model is principally useful in focusing on the interaction between the factors which influence the location of production but it does not *per se* explain the source of multinationals' ownership-specific advantages. The thesis thus needs to be considered in association with the firm-specific advantages discussed in the earlier section.

Subsequent work by Vernon has led to modifications of his initial theory to emphasise the oligopolistic behaviour of MNEs.[26] The three phases of the cycle are thus viewed respectively as those of *innovation-based oligopoly, mature oligopoly* and *senescent oligopoly*. Innovations continue to be developed in line with domestic market conditions, but the emphasis on the USA as a source of new products is reduced. Thus it is hypothesised that while the US may have a comparative advantage in labour-saving innovation, Europe may dominate in innovations which are land– and material–saving and Japan may emphasise material-saving innovations. In the first phase of the cycle there are still strong economic incentives to locate production in the country where the innovation was developed in order to co-ordinate the production process with the R & D and marketing functions. In the phase two mature oligopoly stage however, the assumption is that product and locational strategies are based upon the actions and reactions of other MNEs. Scale economies in research, production and marketing constitute an effective entry barrier behind which rival oligopolists plot and counter-plot. Strategies nullifying the initiatives of individual oligolopolists are pursued by the industry as a whole, the ultimate aim being to stabilise market shares throughout the world. At this point the predictions of the model are very similar to the 'follow-the-leader' practice observed by Knickerbocker, since firms set up production operations in their competitors' major markets to strengthen their bargaining position. In the final stage of senescent oligopoly, competitive pressures are assumed to re-emerge, as barriers to entry weaken. Production locations are then more closely determined by cost differentials than by adjacency to markets or oligopolistic reactions.

In this formulation the product cycle model has close links with some Marxist theories of international capitalism which stress the emergence of oligopolistic equilibrium between giant multinational firms. Stability would exist when each of the rival oligopolists produces in the various major world markets. It has been suggested that the end result would be a tendency towards a spatial hierarchy of economic activity. As routine activities in both production and distribution were dispersed according to cost minimisation criteria (as in senescent oligopoly), this would be countered by an increasing trend towards centralisation of key functions in the developed home countries, thus creating spatial interdependence on a global scale.[27]

Some or all of these *locational factors,* therefore, need to be associated with the *ownership advantages of firms* to determine whether or not a company will engage in international operations through direct investment abroad. Where these locational attributes favour a foreign country rather than the home country, then it is hypothesised that a home country firm possessing certain ownership advantages will choose to set up its manufacturing operations abroad rather than in its domestic location. Conversely if costs of production are lower in its home country and/or if the major markets exist at home, etc. then the firm may simply manufacture at home and exploit its ownership advantages through exports.

Summary and critique of the theory

Drawing together the discussion on the foregoing it is possible to point out a number of conclusions and weaknesses of the theory developing in the literature:

(i) The existence of ownership-specific assets, and the internalisation of these assets within the firm, provides the MNE with its particular uniqueness. Secret technology and marketing skills are thought to be the most important components of this uniqueness; but financial and monetary variables, spare managerial capacity and oligopolistic market structures are considered in different circumstances to provide reinforcement. It is possible in fact that the internalisation model pays inadequate attention to oligopolistic competition and sheer market power as a determinant of foreign direct investment, and also to dynamic factors such as those emphasised by Vernon in the product cycle thesis.

(ii) It is the incentive to internalise which partially explains why direct investment is preferred over licensing. Where there are problems in making and enforcing contracts, where the marketing skills of the managers and employees are significant attributes of the firm, or where production coordination is important, there are likely to be few licensing deals.

(iii) The choice between direct investment and exporting and also between foreign investment and licensing, will not only depend on ownership-specific advantages. The latter represent a necessary but not a sufficient condition for foreign direct investment. The decision to locate the production process abroad rather than produce at home and export will be determined by country characteristics, such as labour costs, trade barriers, government policy, etc. Furthermore the choice between direct investment abroad and licensing will also be dependent upon locational factors. For example, where the host country market is small licensing may be preferred; or where the host country market is large but domestic firms have a strong market position, barriers to entry may preclude direct investment by foreign firms.

(iv) Although the ownership- and location-specific factors have been considered separately, it is clear that they are interconnected. Firm-specific endowments must inevitably reflect to some extent country-specific factors. This point emerges implicitly in the product cycle theory, where Vernon assumed that characteristics of the *United States' economy,* viz. high incomes and high labour costs, gave *US firms* an advantage in the development of new products. It could also be argued that because a country such as America is well endowed with skilled labour, this provides US firms supplying high technology goods with a comparative advantage. On the other hand, as between companies in the same industry, which have equal access to these country-specific endowments, performance will still vary considerably, dependent principally upon relative managerial expertise in the companies. It is the managerial factor therefore which is the true firm-specific resource and which encompasses factors such as cheaper capital, technological advantages, etc. which were identified earlier as ownership-specific endowments. Some consideration is being given to establishing a clearer distinction between firm- and country-specific factors, but the theory as it stands is weak in this regard, and similarly the interrelationships between the variables create problems for empirical research.[28]

(v) The theory of direct foreign investment would predict that there are certain industry types in which multinational firms would tend to predominate. Research-intensive industries, for example, might be strongly oriented towards multinationality because of the opportunities which are presented for internalisation. Moreover research would be concentrated on sophisticated technologies because appropriability will be higher for complex than for simple ideas. Similarly marketing-intensive industries, where product differentiation, advertising, distribution networks, and after-sales advice and service are important, could provide many MNEs; and within this group, consumer goods' firms would predominate. Other industries could include those involved with perishable agricultural commodities and with intermediate products in capital-intensive manufacturing processes. Also the geographical concentration of raw materials in foreign countries may encourage internalisation to assure access, as in industries such as aluminium, copper and oil. Finally, outside the manufacturing sector, operations such as insurance, banking, airlines and hotels seem to provide conditions favourable for MNEs, namely the requirements of skill intensity, capital availability and coordination and integration of inputs.[29]

(vi) The theory would also suggest that multinationality would be more common among large firms. This arises from the fact that the costs of internalisation would be lower in the large firm. Conversely, the gains from internalising transactions would be higher because of, for instance, economies of scale in the application of new technology across a number of products, greater potential for appropriating the returns from technology creation and greater management skills. The greater financial resources and easier access to capital would also be factors assisting the large firm; while the small company could be hampered by an inability to identify profitable investment opportunities abroad given the costs of undertaking search procedures. In spite of these predictions, many firms with overseas operations are not large. The flexibility of the small company may be an important ownership-specific advantage. Additionally, as in the domestic market, the small firm multinational may succeed by identifying a niche in the market, which large companies have ignored because the products concerned constituted only a small proportion of their output.

(vii) What does the theory say about the impact of MNEs on the efficiency of resource allocation internationally?[30] The starting point for this discussion was that MNEs exist because of imperfect markets. The ability of these firms to internalise such imperfections provides MNEs with their ability to produce and compete successfully across national boundaries. But the important question is whether in the process MNEs do or do not themselves create further imperfections. It is a major defect in the theory that it is unable to predict unambiguously on this issue. The reason for this is that the theory still does not adequately differentiate between the sources of market imperfections, as, for example, between: government policy-induced imperfections; imperfections arising from the absence of external markets; or imperfections of competition. To take an example, if the imperfection takes the form of tariffs or other barriers to trade, then the fact that MNEs are able to overcome these might be deemed to promote a more efficient distribution of resources. But suppose that an MNE locates manufacturing facilities behind a tariff wall and proceeds to use its market power to erect barriers to entry, operate restrictive practices and in this way obtain monopoly profits – then it is adversely affecting the efficiency of resource allocation. Alternatively, if tariff barriers induce a number of MNEs to set up operations of inefficient scale on the follow-the-leader oligopoly model, then once again economic efficiency is impaired.

Moreover a second problem in making predictions relating to the efficiency of resource allocation derives from the fact that the source of the MNE's uniqueness has yet to be completely clarified in the theory. If the advantage derives from the internalisation of knowledge created through past investment in R & D, there may be a presumption of benefit to both source and host countries. Direct investment abroad has allowed MNEs to overcome imperfect markets for knowledge and thereby reduced barriers to the production and diffusion of technology. On the other hand, if the advantage derives from brand name and product differentiation attributes (arising from heavy advertising), this may be a means of erecting entry barriers in foreign markets to inhibit competition.

As a result of these factors, there are two quite different viewpoints on the role of the MNE. On the one hand, it may be considered that MNEs produce a more efficient distribution of resources by internalising market imperfections. This may be a consequence of the replacement of non-existent or inefficient external markets by internal ones as in the case of the market for technology. Alternatively it may derive from the MNE's ability to overcome imperfections produced by government policies relating to tariff and non-tariff barriers, taxes, exchange rates, etc. Thus through their role in the development and diffusion of technology; through their ability to take a global perspective and engage in worldwide scanning; and through rational locational decision-making based on underlying factor costs, MNEs represent an integrating force in the world economy, and improve the international allocation of resources. Whether or not the welfare of the home or host countries benefits is a different issue, which will be considered in Chapter 4.

The alternative view is that MNEs themselves create market imperfections and thereby distort resource allocation. Since they generally operate in oligopolistic markets, MNEs may exploit patent protection, raise entry barriers and operate restrictive practices. Furthermore they may be able to by-pass government regulations designed to stimulate competition and efficiency and circumvent market mechanisms. This crucial issue is taken further in Chapter 3 where some consideration is given to the efficiency of MNEs in the production and diffusion of technology. For example, do oligopolistic market structures lead to wasteful duplication of research and development? Again in Chapter 4 the problem is viewed from the different standpoint of international trade theory. Free trade in association with perfect competition is deemed to maximise the value of world output as countries specialise according to comparative advantage. Therefore does foreign direct investment, which may be trade replacing, enhance or detract from comparative advantage?

(viii) The theory concentrates on horizontal investments, where the aim is to produce abroad some or all of the goods which are manufactured domestically. This is to some extent an inevitable consequence of the focus on American investment and on investment trends in the period up to the mid-1960s. Arising from this, however, less attention has been paid to direct investments which are made to secure natural resources; and to 'export-platform' type investments in low wage countries, where certain stages of the production sequence are located abroad or labour-intensive products are manufactured in foreign countries. As Chapter 1 revealed, much of Japanese investment is of these types and an increasing, although still small, volume of US investment is designed to exploit cheap labour in the Far East and elsewhere.

This has important implications for the theory. Indeed the initial premise of all theories of foreign direct investment – namely an MNE needs some advantage to enable it to compete successfully with a local competitor in an unfamiliar environment – is open to question.[31] In the case of Japanese ventures in developing countries, for example, there may be few if any local competitors. Furthermore the host country may discourage local competition to ensure that maximum economies of scale are obtained. On the other hand, for some products such as steel, motor vehicles and chemicals, the market in which Japanese MNEs compete is a world market. Therefore it is the international competitive position which is relevant rather than the local competitive situation, and Japanese firms still require firm-specific advantages to enable them to compete. It has been suggested that the principal advantages possessed by such Japanese companies are their worldwide marketing networks which were set up initially to handle exports, but are now used to market goods manufactured in offshore production bases.

The product cycle theory of Vernon also has some relevance to Japanese direct investment abroad. Vernon considered the sequential approach to foreign direct investment from the viewpoint of the US, as the principal innovator of new products. Japan, in the main, has been an imitator rather than an innovator, but it is not inconceivable for the former to also opt for overseas production in the mature stage of the product cycle. In particular, Japan may succeed in making substantial physical improvements to the products concerned and/or it may successfully differentiate its products through brand names and advertising. Japanese firms may then decide to produce abroad in order to combine these firm-specific advantages with the ownership advantages (in the form of low wages) of foreign countries.

Some types of Japanese direct investment, nevertheless, cannot be explained by the theory presented in this chapter.[32] Overseas investment in extractive industries, which is designed to alleviate Japan's resource dependency, is a case in point. Here, direct investment is based on factors such as a desire to reduce external vulnerability. From an individual firm viewpoint, this is quite compatible with the internalisation model but in Japan, government policy has a key role to play. Thus the government–business relationship in Japan means that overseas investment is seen as a part of national policy and is in relative harmony with the national interest. As a result, as one commentator has observed: '. . . the trend of Japan's DFI (direct foreign investment) . . . reflects more the adaptive behaviour of the entire Japanese economy to changing world economic conditions than the random market behaviour of its individual firms'.[33] Some of these points are considered again in Chapter 4 when consideration is given to the impact of US and Japanese direct investment on international trade flows.

Empirical evidence on the determinants of foreign direct investment

A selection of the research studies undertaken to test various theories of the growth and development of the MNE are examined within this section. The classification system presented previously is used as far as possible, although it is not always possible to provide a complete match between theory and empiricism. Much of the knowledge available on the MNE is derived from surveys of MNE practice and performance, which make no claims to verifying theory as such. In spite of this, survey material has a valuable contribution to make in assisting an understanding of the foreign investment process, and some of the research is presented below.

The sources of advantage to multinational firms

In the attempt to identify the special characteristics of multinational firms a number of studies have focused on the differences between multinational and domestic corporations in terms of their size, growth and performance or their relative expenditures in areas such as research and development. The results of one of these studies are summarised in Table 2.1.[34]

This work by Vaupel also produced evidence that MNEs were more diversified in their product structure and paid higher annual wages in the US. The major research study undertaken by Vernon and his colleagues at Harvard University confirmed the broad findings, namely that MNEs tend to be larger, more profitable, more advertising- and research-oriented and more diversified than other firms.[35] Furthermore, more recent work by Parker has verified that the technological bias in much of US MNE activity also applied to non-US

Table 2.1 Characteristics of the largest US companies (1964)

Company type	National enterprise*	Transnational enterprise*	Multinational enterprise*
Number in sample	125	194	172
R & D expenditure as % of sales	0.6	1.6	2.6
Advertising expenditure as % of sales	1.7	1.9	2.5
Net profits on invested capital 1960–64 (%)	6.7	7.3	8.9
Average sales ($m)	160	200	460

* NEs manufacture in US only; TNEs manufacture in 1–5 foreign countries; MNEs manufacture in at least 6 foreign countries.

(*Source:* Vaupel, 1971.)

MNEs except for Japan.[36] The data for the European companies are given in Table 2.2: about one-half of all multinational firms were considered to be research-intensive in comparison with only about 15 per cent of other companies (with lower foreign involvement). Japanese firms represent a major exception in that there was virtually no difference in the relative research intensity of MNEs as compared with TNEs or NEs, but the reasons for this will become apparent later.

The converse of the studies comparing MNEs to domestic industry in their home country is the comparison of the characteristics of MNE affiliates and indigenous industry in the host country. The frequently observed syndrome of greater capital and skill intensity, larger size and

Table 2.2 European companies, by research intensity and multinationality (1971)

	Per cent of companies			Per cent of sales		
	MNE*	TNE*	NE*	MNE*	TNE*	NE*
Research intensive	48.8	12.5	17.4	54.6	13.7	9.5
Not research intensive	51.2	87.5	82.6	45.4	86.3	90.5
Total	100.0	100.0	100.0	100.0	100.0	100.0
Number of companies and value of sales in $ m.	123	24	23	$164,396	$13,932	$16,102

* MNEs have more than 5 manufacturing affiliates in different countries or over 15% of group sales accounted for by affiliates; for TNEs the equivalent figures are 3–5 affiliates or 5–15% of sales; and for national enterprises (NEs), 2 or fewer affiliates or less than 5% of sales.

(*Source:* Parker, 1974.)

higher exports than host nation companies does not always hold, although the extensive work by Dunning on US investment in UK manufacturing industry does lend support to the general hypotheses. Some of the results of this are presented in Table 2.3.[37]

Table 2.3   Characteristics of all UK firms and US affiliates*

Average figures for	UK firms	US affiliates in the UK
Supply characteristics		
1. Net capital expenditure per employee (£)	191.0	221.2§
2. Non operative/total workers (%)	26.2	30.3§
3. R & D expenditure as a % of sales	1.08	1.60§
4. Economies of scale†	1.09**	1.09**
5. Advertising expenditure as a % of sales	1.18	1.33§
Marketing characteristics		
6. Output growth/GNP growth	1.02**	1.14**
7. Exports/imports ratio	1.23**	1.66**
8. Concentration ratio‡	70.9**	74.7**

* Data refer to following years/periods: 1. Average of 1963 and 1970 figures.
  2. 1970. 3. R & D annual average 1967/69; Sales 1968. 4. 1963. 5. 1963.
  6. 1958–1970. 7. 1967. 8. 1963.
† Labour productivity of largest 10% of establishments divided by labour
  productivity of other 90%, as an index of the extent to which large firms enjoy
  economies of scale.
‡ Output of 5 largest firms as proportion of total output.
§ Weighted by distribution of US sales/employment.
** Weighted by distribution of UK and US sales respectively.

(*Source:* Dunning, 1973a.)

Although the findings need to be interpreted with caution, this study highlights some of the contributory factors in MNE penetration in the UK. Once again the R & D and advertising intensity of the multinational firms sets them apart from UK companies. In addition, however, the table shows that the US affiliates employed a higher proportion of non-operative workers, were more capital-intensive, were found in more concentrated sectors, and were faster growing than local firms. The essential problem in all of such work remains one of distinguishing cause and effect, having identified salient differences in characteristics. In order to do this it is necessary to focus on research which is explanatory rather than descriptive in nature, and on research which is designed to test specific theories of foreign direct investment.

(a) Technology, economies of scale and under-utilised resources
Reflecting the development of the theory, empirical studies have attempted to explain the pattern of foreign direct investment in terms of one or a number of the ownership advantages of MNEs. The contribution of one of the earliest writers, Stephen Hymer, was mainly

on the theoretical side, and Caves's original work on the product differentiation advantages of MNEs was also more concerned with the formulation than with the testing of hypotheses.[38] However, the latter indicated that a high correlation existed between the extent of product differentiation and the proportion of firms in an industry having foreign subsidiaries. For example, firms in industries such as cars, consumer durables, scientific instruments, etc. had numerous foreign affiliates, while firms in paper, primary metals and textile industries had few. Caves contended that the same pattern emerged when countries which were major importers of capital, such as Canada and the UK, were considered. In both countries, MNE affiliates accounted for a high proportion of production in certain industry categories.

Caves accepted that product differentiation might not be the only industrial attribute explaining the incidence of direct investment, and some of his later work introduced other ownership advantages which were hypothesised to be possessed by foreign affiliates in comparison with their indigenous competitors. In an analysis of the causes of foreign direct investment in Canadian and UK manufacturing industry, three potential advantages were tested: (a) the possession of intangible assets, e.g. product differentiation, (b) economies accruing to the multi-plant firm beyond the technical economies of efficient scale plant (e.g. in marketing, research, etc.) and (c) the availability of under-utilised entrepreneurial resources in the firm.[39] The results of the regression analysis showed that the intangible assets variable – chiefly an industry's R & D and advertising expenditure as a per cent of sales – was a significant determinant of all foreign firms' shares of both Canadian and UK manufacturing industries. The multi-plant hypothesis appeared to hold for Canada but not for the UK, presumably due to the geographical proximity of Canada to the US, while the entrepreneurial resources variable gained only weak empirical support.

This research broadly verified the results obtained by Orr who constructed a regression model to relate foreign control (and import market shares) in Canadian manufacturing industry to a number of ownership variables.[40] Both US and total foreign control were found to be significantly higher in industries characterised by high advertising intensity, high capital requirements and intensive research and development. Caves and Orr also introduced various location specific variables into their models, specifically the rate of effective tariff protection, and a measure of relative production/payroll costs between the home and host country. However, contrary perhaps to expectations, neither of the variables seemed to have much influence on the choice between foreign direct investment and other methods of market servicing such as exports.

The problem in such studies comes in interpreting the results obtained and particularly in relating the empiricism to the theory. To Caves, R & D and advertising intensity represented a proxy for intangible assets possessed by the firm. But there need not necessarily be any relationship between expenditure on R & D or advertising and the resulting output. Moreover new or differentiated products derived from these expenditures could be marketed in the domestic economy. It has been suggested alternatively that R & D intensity provides some indication of the economies of scale and under-utilised resources available to the firm. Thus because of the lumpiness of R & D expenditures, products or processes may be developed which cannot be utilised at the particular stage of the firm's development; R & D too may be an area where significant economies of scale exist for the firm. It has been argued finally that since the incentive and the opportunity to internalise is particularly great in the case of knowledge, and since internalisation of markets is believed to lead to internationalisation of firms, then companies with the most intensive R & D programmes will have the highest incidence of multinationality. This latter point is essentially the justification given by Buckley and Casson for employing R & D intensity in testing their theory of the MNE.[41] Thus while the Buckley and Casson model is much extended from that of earlier writers, the empirical research ends up fairly close to similar work of Caves and Orr above. The results too are relatively similar indicating that on average the degree of multinationality is higher in R & D-intensive industries and for capital-intensive firms. The methodology used was however quite different: based on a sample of 170 non-US firms and over 250 US firms, the degree of multinationality of the companies (represented by the estimated proportion of the value of sales attributable to production abroad) was related to variables indicating R & D-intensity and capital-intensity. The influence of industry type and nationality of parent company on the degree of multinationality was also estimated.

The impact of variables such as R & D-, advertising- and capital-intensity on multinationality is thus clearly established. In another important piece of work relating to US investment in Canada, however, Horst has indicated that such factors were either industry-specific or could be captured in size of firm.[42] The initial stage of the research aimed at explaining the determinants of an industry's propensity to establish affiliates in Canada. Product differentiation – represented by R & D effort – was shown to have a significant influence; conversely, industries in which economies of scale at the plant level were important were seen to have fewer foreign investors. In the second stage Horst also investigated why some firms in a given industry invested abroad while others did not. The regression results revealed a close relationship between firm size and the propensity to invest abroad. As Fig. 2.2 indicates, the probability that a firm will be either multinational (defined as a corporation with at least six foreign affiliates, in addition to an affiliate in Canada) or, at least, establish an affiliate in Canada, increased steadily with firm size. That is , the most important ownership advantage explaining foreign production (and also trade) was size of firm.

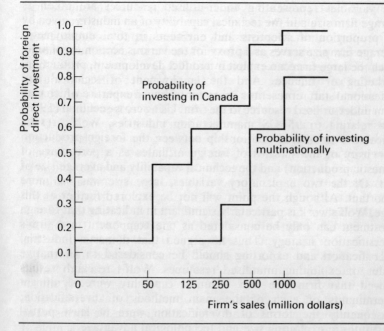

Fig. 2.2 Relationship between firm size and the probability of foreign direct investment (*Source*: Horst, 1972a).

The Horst finding is not unexpected in terms of the theory presented earlier, and particularly the oligopolistic theory of foreign direct investment. Foreign production may require a threshold level of operation before fixed costs can be covered and a reasonable level of profits earned. Associated with this, there may be diminishing costs of entering new markets after some point, with increasing knowledge, bargaining power, confidence and the spreading of risks. Again there may be financial and technological advantages arising from the integration of activities over several countries, which facilitate the rapid transfer of funds and know-how, and the avoidance of taxes and restrictions. Finally, it has been pointed out that the internal resources of a firm are just as important to its growth as external ones. Therefore a company which has expanded rapidly in its domestic location may possess the necessary attributes in terms of management, experience, etc. which will also enable it to develop abroad. On this interpretation the size variable may incorporate all or most of the other ownership-specific advantages, thereby producing a cumulative and dynamic effect on the expansion of MNEs.[43]

One study which links size of firm and technological intensity is that of B. M. Wolf.[44] The hypothesis is that in the course of its development a firm may find that some of its resources are not being fully utilised, and as a result it proceeds to diversify either in its domestic market or via internationalisation (exporting, foreign investment or licensing).

The variables representing under-utilised resources are taken as average firm size and the technical capability of an industry, given by the proportion of scientists and engineers in total employment. Average firm size serves as a proxy for the various economies of scale which the large firm can exploit in product development, production, marketing or finance. And the employment of technical and professional staff represents a proxy for technical expertise which may be an under-utilised resource to the firm. Using cross-sectional (1963) data relating to 95 US manufacturing industries, Wolf's results indicated a significant relationship between the foreign production propensity of firms (sales of foreign affiliates as a percentage of domestic production) and the technical capability and average size of firm. Of the two explanatory variables, large size was the more important. Although the point will not be explored further at this stage, Wolf's work is particularly significant in indicating that foreign investment can only be considered as one component in a firm's diversification strategy. Thus he argued that domestic industrial diversification and exporting should be considered as alternative means of exploiting unutilised resources. Wolf's research results showed that firm size and technical capability were significant determinants of each of the main methods of diversification; consequently the forms of diversification were at least partial substitutes in exploiting size and technological advantage.

Before concluding this section some mention of Knickerbocker's theory of oligopolistic reaction is necessary.[45] Knickerbocker himself tested the theory on a sample of 187 US-based MNEs, the same firms which formed the basis of the Harvard research directed by Vernon.[46] Using the four-firm concentration ratio as an index of the presence of oligopoly, it was demonstrated that the bunching of investment in foreign markets was positively correlated with the existence of oligopoly. However the data also revealed that this 'bunching' was strongly correlated with other variables, including the profitability of foreign investment in the particular industry, and an index of environmental stability in the MNE's domestic market. Knickerbocker's own results thus appear to be open to various interpretations; and this would be logical since it was suggested earlier that bunching might only be one feature of oligopolistic behaviour among MNEs. However, the results should not be ignored and what seems to be required is the incorporation of the Knickerbocker model within a wider empirical framework. This has yet to be done.

Attention has been focused on only a few of the studies which have appeared in the last few years. Recent work by Horst at the Brookings Institution and by Buckley and Dunning might also be noted, particularly in so far as they tend to validate the results of other research.[47] It is, of course, difficult to exactly compare various sets of results, for a number of reasons, including differences in viewpoint as between home and host countries. To take only selected examples,

Caves's (1974a) dependent variable was the share of foreign owned firms in Canadian and UK manufacturing industries, whereas Horst (1972b) was concerned with identifying both industry and enterprise characteristics of the involvement by US firms in Canada. In the first case host country data were being used, in the latter instance home country data. Even so, there appear to be encouraging similarities in the results obtained. The provisos which need to be considered are as follows: firstly, it is not always obvious that the direction of causality is correctly specified. In the case of the size variable it may be postulated that large firm size stimulates diversification and multinationality. But, equally plausibly, it could be argued that size may be the by-product of expansion rather than the stimulus. Furthermore, rather than R & D intensity encouraging multinationality, it could be considered that the greater the firm's existing foreign involvement the greater the prospective return to R & D, since the results could be spread over more markets. Therefore, increased foreign investment could encourage increased R & D. Secondly, on an associated point, the relationship between size and other ownership advantages is not completely clear. Does size, for example, represent a composite measure of ownership-specific advantages or is its influence separate, say, from that of technology? As the theoretical section revealed, the separate influences may be difficult to disentangle. Thirdly, while the theory has evolved in the direction of explaining MNEs' advantages in terms of their greater propensity to internalise certain activities, this has barely influenced empirical work. Most of the variables used in research are fairly traditional. This partly reflects the fact that other data are unavailable, but it also reveals that a specific test of the internalisation theory will be difficult to devise. Finally, it should be noted that almost all the empirical studies have related to US MNEs, and much more work is therefore required on multinationals of European and Japanese parentage.

(b) Financial and monetary studies

While most empirical research has concentrated on the assumed technology and oligopoly advantages of MNEs, work on the role of financial and monetary factors in foreign investment has also been continuing. Early studies related to the *cheap capital* argument compared foreign and domestic earnings in seeking an explanation for investment abroad. Domestic returns were equated with the cost of capital, with cost being viewed in an opportunity sense. Then returns abroad were directly compared with returns at home, the expectation being that the latter would be lower because of capital abundance in the home country. During the 1950s this explanation seemed to fit the facts since the after-tax rate of return obtained by US manufacturing affiliates in Europe was consistently three or four percentage points greater than the returns on US domestic manufacturing. In the 1960s, however, the US capital stake in European manufacturing continued its strong growth in spite of the fact that in the first half of the decade earnings were no higher than in America, and between 1965 and 1970 higher returns could generally be obtained in domestic US manufacturing. In general, therefore, the differential returns argument for foreign direct investment has received little support. It would indeed be unlikely to find differences in profit rates corresponding to flows of foreign investment: published earnings figures say nothing about transfer pricing in response to differences in tax rates, exchange controls, etc. and moreover, differences in profit rates partly correspond to risk differentials; and in industries characterised by oligopolistic competition, returns on new projects may differ substantially from earnings on existing operations.[48]

A number of empirical studies have attempted to interpret various aspects of the foreign investment decision from research on *portfolio diversification*. Grubel, for example, set out to explain long-term asset holdings, examining potential rates of return in the stock markets of 11 countries.[49] Some of the results are presented in Table 2.4.

Table 2.4   Rates of return from investing in foreign capital markets (average 1959–66)

Country	Rate of return per cent per annum	Standard deviation	Value of $100 at end of period	Correlation with USA
USA	7.54	47.26	178.92	1.0000
Canada	5.95	41.19	158.82	0.7025*
United Kingdom	9.59	65.28	208.00	0.2414*
West Germany	7.32	94.69	175.95	0.3008*
France	4.27	49.60	139.69	0.1938*
Italy	8.12	103.33	186.74	0.1465
Japan	16.54	92.52	340.21	0.1149

* Statistically significant at the 5 per cent level.

(*Source:* Grubel, 1968.)

From this, a model was developed incorporating rates of return and variances of portfolios, which could be employed to arrive at efficiently diversified portfolios. While acknowledging the limitations of the model, Grubel claimed that it did provide an explanation of the real world phenomenon of two-way flows of portfolio investment between the US and Europe. Although his favoured explanation of direct investment was that it results from cost conditions in oligopolistic industries, it was suggested that the portfolio model might also have relevance to direct investment. Grubel claimed that the approach led to the hypothesis that large-scale US direct investment in Europe was part of a stock adjustment process which started when European currencies became legally convertible after 1958. While not directly transferable to MNE investment, this type of study does identify variables and processes which changed attitudes on overall investment abroad.

Various attempts have been made to apply the portfolio approach to the geographical distribution of direct foreign investment. As a case in point, Stevens used the portfolio model to explain the proportion of US direct investment directed to Latin America and Canada.[50] More recently, Paxson used a stock adjustment version of the model to explain the geographical distribution of assets for US and British MNEs.[51] The optimal geographical distribution of assets was first calculated, based on historical earnings experience and the standard deviation and covariance of returns. The difference between actual and optimal shares of the total portfolio held in various areas was then estimated. Finally these differences were compared with the percentage increase in assets in each region between 1964 and 1970. As the stock adjustment model would indicate, asset growth was positively correlated with the difference between actual and optimal portfolios. On the other hand, when Paxson applied the same methodology to two companies – British American Tobacco and Unilever – it was found that regional differences between actual and optimal portfolio shares were uncorrelated with investment behaviour.

A related portfolio argument is that diversification reduces risk. Work, for example, by Cohen and Rugman has shown that for US corporations an increase in the number of countries in which a firm operates and/or an increase in the ratio of foreign to total activities, reduces profit variance (where variance is a proxy for risk).[52] The valuation of a company's shares is dependent not only on the level but also on the stability of profits. Therefore since international diversification increases stability the firm is better off. Domestic expansion and diversification does not offer the same opportunities: with product diversification in the domestic market, the firm is still subject to the fluctuations of the home economy; while domestic expansion of firms with operations concentrated in a single industry may attract the attention of the antitrust authorities. At the very least international diversification will reinforce other ownership advantages possessed by MNEs.

The Aliber hypothesis that earnings are capitalised at a higher rate in the leading home countries than in host countries has attracted considerable interest. But it is not an approach which lends itself to empirical verification. Surveys undertaken on the initial location decisions of MNEs in host nations have indicated that the level and potential variability of the exchange rate influence choice. Similarly short-term movements of resources are often influenced by monetary variables. However these are location-specific rather than ownership-specific factors. If the Aliber theory was interpreted slightly differently – to mean that earnings are capitalised at a higher rate for large MNEs than for small uninational firms – then it becomes identical to the argument of the previous paragraph. Stability of earnings may bid up the MNE's shares to a higher price/earnings ratio, enabling it to buy out small national firms.[53]

From this brief review of the literature, it is clear that most of the research has only been able to contribute indirectly to the study of foreign direct investment. Research relating to risk diversification is, however, promising, particularly given the greater interest in the role of foreign investment as only one of the possible avenues open to the firm in its expansion strategy. Efforts to integrate such factors into wider studies of foreign investment may thus prove a fruitful area for further work. Moreover, as the next section will show, financial and monetary factors are important in locational decisions, with businessmen considering the 'investment climate' to be a major influence on their investment plans.

The role of locational factors in foreign direct investment

In the earlier theoretical section it was indicated that ownership-specific advantages were only a necessary condition for foreign direct investment. Other location-specific factors had to be introduced to show why the method of foreign involvement chosen was direct investment as opposed to exporting or licensing. In some of the empirical work already reported, attention was paid to the mode of foreign involvement: Caves and Orr, in studying foreign investment in Canada, both introduced location-specific variables into their models, although the results were fairly limited.[54] Caves in fact concluded that only the variable measuring differences in payroll costs between parent company and affiliates appeared to be of any significance in influencing the choice between investment and licensing. Again Wolf showed that the same ownership variables, viz. size and technical manpower, explained both trade and foreign production.[55] But he did not introduce any locational variables, which would have helped to indicate the circumstances under which the two methods of foreign involvement would have been used. Generally therefore most of the studies focused on explaining why certain industries were more internationally oriented than others; or why foreign affiliates were more important in some industries than others.

Numerous studies have been undertaken incorporating locational variables to attempt to explain the actual method of servicing foreign markets (usually concentrating on the choice between exports and direct investment). However the major contributions to the locational question have been derived from work in the field of international trade, and therefore the detailed discussion of these studies will be left until Chapter 4. The most recent theoretical and empirical developments will also be considered in the same chapter. This latter work aims to integrate both international investment and international trade in order to derive an overall explanation for international production. In the present section, therefore, only limited attention is paid to the role of locational factors in the foreign direct investment decision process.

Most of the early work on direct investment abroad, which took the form of surveys of businessmen, had an implicit locational bias. Table 2.5 summarises the results of a number of these surveys, when companies themselves have been asked to indicate their reasons for investing abroad at all or for establishing affiliates in particular countries. Regrettably almost all refer to US foreign direct investment. Nevertheless, the conclusions are clear: market size and growth emerge as the most important determinants of overseas investment, together with political stability and host government attitudes. 'Defensive' reasons come next in importance, particularly fears of losing existing markets and barriers to trade; and other 'investment climate' variables associated with exchange rate stability and tax structures are also significant. Reviewing these and other studies, aimed at assessing the importance of specific factors in the foreign direct investment decision, Dunning concludes that the size and growth of markets is the most significant variable.[56] In order to provide a complete explanation for direct foreign investment, of course, these location-specific factors need to be considered in association with the ownership-specific advantages possessed by firms (particularly size and technological intensity). Even then survey results are of limited value because generally they do not permit an evaluation to be made of the importance of particular goals or determinants.

The kinds of reasons put forward by businessmen become more relevant when expansionary investment is considered, or when a definite decision has been made to set up in a particular Continent without a commitment to any country. In these circumstances, the comparative costs of establishing or expanding on one site, rather than another, will be looked at carefully. Included in the calculation will be the relative financial inducements available from governments, labour and raw material supplies and costs, size of markets and so on. In addition, for expansionary investment, political and 'climatic' variables become important: a manufacturing presence in a number of countries can provide significant protection against cost and exchange rate movements; and politically a dispersal policy may be advantageous to the MNE since its visibility in any single country is minimised, and the likelihood of government interference thereby reduced. Such issues reflect the different balance in the reasons given in Table 2.5 as between Australia and New Zealand, and Scotland and Ireland. Given that a US firm has decided to invest in Europe, it still has a large number of country options open to it. Understandably, therefore, relative cost factors and regional policy incentives are much more important in decisions within Europe. The Scottish example is particularly interesting in this regard: one-half of the US firms locating manufacturing plants in Scotland mentioned central government regional policy (and specifically Industrial Development Certificate policy) as their main reason.[57]

Table 2.5 Determinants of US* foreign direct investment – summary of selected surveys

Number of times factors mentioned	(a) Foreign investment in general		(b) Investment in specific countries			
			Australia	New Zealand	Scotland	Ireland
Marketing factors						
1. Size of market	262}		–	21}	14	28
2. Market growth	19	141 / 158	89 / 7 / 82			
3. To maintain share of market	130	126	35 / 12	30	6	1
4. To advance exports of parent company	–	1	2	–	1	–
5. Need to maintain close customer contact	–	7	–	–	9	–
6. Dissatisfaction with existing market arrangements	–	–	5	15	–	–
7. Export base	104	3 / 3	25	–	–	39
	496	425	124 / 119	66	30	57
	33	44				
Barriers to trade						
1. Barriers to trade	130	14}	28 / 21	78 / 76	–	11
2. Preference of local customers for local products	–		1	24	–	–
	130	14	29 / 21	102 / 76		11
Cost factors						
1. To be near source of supply	–	3	14	–	2	–
2. Availability of labour	209	–	–	–	53	–
3. Availability of raw materials	12	114	7	–	–	–
4. Availability of capital/technology	–	78	–	–	11 / 18	40}
5. Lower labour costs	79	103	–	–		
6. Lower other production costs	–	–	11 / 22	–	–	–
7. Lower transport costs	7	20	–	–	18	–
8. Financial (*et al.*) inducements by government	–	1	13	–	52	45
9. More favourable cost levels	50	134	14	–	–	–
	338	429	46 / 20 / 4	35	154	85
	19					

	Robinson† (1961)	Behrman (1962)	Basi‡ (1966)	Brash (1966)	Forsyth§ (1972)	Kolde (1968)	Deane (1970)	Forsyth• (1972)	Andrews (1972)
Investment climate									
1. General attitude to foreign investment	–¶	–	145	–	–	6	–	10	–
2. Political stability	115	–	159	–	–	–	–	–	–
3. Limitation on ownership	20	–	–	–	–	–	–	–	–
4. Currency exchange regulations	105 }	–	–	–	–	–	–	–	–
5. Stability of foreign exchange		–	151	–	–	4	–	–	–
6. Tax structure	–	–	131	–	–	–	–	–	–
7. Familiarity with country	–	–	100	–	–	–	–	–	–
	240	–	686	–	–	10	–	10	–
General									
1. Expected higher profits	182	20	144	37	14	5	39	43	50
2. Other	252	14	112	–	–	–	–	–	–
	434	34	256	37	14	5	39	43	50
Total	1,638	97	1,796	304	171	100	226	227	203
Number of firms in sample	205	72	214	100	105	104	139	105	80

* Studies refer to US direct investment, except Deane which relates to all foreign investment in New Zealand.
† Number of times factors are ranked 1–3 in a 6-point scale.
‡ Listed as 'crucially' or 'fairly important' in Basi's 3-point scale.
§ Reasons given by firms for investing outside the US.
• Reasons for locating in Scotland.
¶ Dealt with separately but regarded as crucially important.
** Totals do not always equal sum of individual column entries in source.

(*Source*: Dunning, 1973a.)

The other empirical studies on location which are relevant to MNEs have mainly used econometric methods. These have tended to confirm that size and growth of markets was the single most important demand variable influencing foreign investment. But, of course, cost factors, trade barriers and government policy measures will also influence the choice between direct investment abroad and other forms of international involvement, such as exporting. To consider the impact of these various locational variables within a general framework, it is useful to focus on some of the studies which have been undertaken into the product cycle thesis.

Product cycle studies

There have been numerous attempts to test the product life cycle theory, using broadly similar methodologies. Essentially it would be expected that firms in the innovating country would supply foreign markets by exports during the early stages of the product life cycle. As manufacturers in other countries initiated production, exports from the innovating country (as a percentage of total output) would decline. Firms in the innovating state might then switch to foreign direct investment to take advantage of locational factors in these foreign countries.

Most of the empirical studies have concentrated on explaining the dynamics of exports from the innovating country. The evidence of Stobaugh's research on nine products in the petrochemical industry is highlighted in Fig. 2.3.[58] Exports begin some years after production and peak about 25 years after the commencement of output. As new

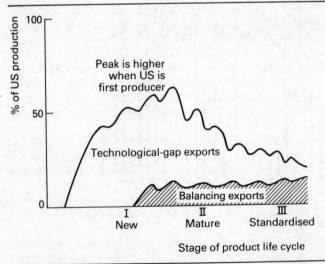

Fig. 2.3 Typical pattern of United States exports of petrochemicals relative to US production (*Source*: Stobaugh, 1971a).

plants are constructed abroad then US exports as a percentage of total output begin to decline. Exports still, however, continue both to non-producing countries ('technological-gap' exports) and to producing countries (balancing exports). The latter are the more interesting and occur for three reasons: firstly, there may be only one source of supply in the foreign country but the local customers might wish to have several supply sources. Secondly, new capacity can only be added in large lumps, so producing periodic shortages in any given country. Thirdly, and most important in this context, MNEs will have established affiliates abroad and exports may continue from the parent to affiliates. It would be anticipated that late in the life of the product LDCs, with lower production costs, would become the major sources of supply and export back to the USA and other developed countries; but few such developments have occurred in petrochemicals. As Stobaugh notes: 'Only one of the 350 plants in the world that manufacture any one of the nine petrochemicals in this study was built in a less developed country without a large domestic market for the consumption of the product'.[59] Petrochemicals may not be typical, however. Klein, for example, found that comparative advantage eventually shifted to lower wage countries in the case of the four pharmaceutical companies he studied.[60] Other evidence has shown that the exports of manufactured goods from Greece and Central America tended to be standardised products developed elsewhere; and generally LDC exports of manufactures are from mature industries, excluding, of course, exports of electronics, etc. from LDC locations.[61]

Other interesting industry examples can be quoted. After the Second World War the USA was a major exporter of radio receivers. As the technology became known abroad (and particularly in Japan), the US imported large quantities of radios. The trade flow began to favour the US again with the development of transistors. Eventually the US began to import transistors, but exports commenced a third time with the development of printed circuitry. In the electronic components industry, the transition from vacuum tubes to transistors, and then to integrated and miniaturised circuits resulted in similar trade patterns.

It is more relevant to assess the role of MNEs in the product life cycle, but there has been less research on this. One notable exception is Parry's study of UK pharmaceutical firms.[62] Table 2.6 presents, in a simplified form, some of the results obtained. As indicated, the importance of international production varies systematically with product age, a conclusion which is at least indicative of a product cycle effect.

While these and other results support the product cycle approach, caution must be exercised in claiming that this is an immediate explanation of MNE expansion paths. As has been pointed out, the product cycle model is essentially concerned with the innovation, trade

Table 2.6 Exports and affiliate sales of ethical pharmaceutical products (1972)

	'Age' of products (years)*			
	Under 5	5–10	11–15	Over 15
Export sales ($000's)	25,477	34,488	2,348	135
Affiliate sales ($000's)†	5,336	87,859	13,060	15,568
Ratio of affiliate sales to total foreign sales	0.173	0.718	0.848	0.991

* Years since commercial innovation in the UK. There were 4 products within each age-group.
† Includes joint ventures and sales under licence.

(*Source:* Parry, 1975–76.)

and investment of nationally-based firms, rather than with international production by a true multinational company of world-wide operation. The MNE requires to be in a position to innovate in products and processes in any of its markets, and indeed initiate the development phase of the product cycle from any of these markets. Having said this the industry studies show that many MNEs commenced international production via a product cycle type of expansion from their home base.

Inevitably the concluding comments to this section must be interim comments only, given that the studies which focus specifically on the mode of foreign involvement will not be considered until later. It is nevertheless clear that location-specific factors may have an important bearing on the choice between foreign direct investment and other forms of international involvement. More than this, however, the evidence already provided reveals that decisions to produce abroad do not necessarily entail cessation of exports from the parent company. The complementarity or substitutability between exports and foreign production again requires much closer consideration.

Appendix 2.1 The Aliber model: alternative methods of exploiting a foreign market

The significance of currency area considerations is illustrated in Fig. App. 2.1 below. The Fig. shows how an MNE might exploit a monopolistic advantage in a foreign market, the notations referring to the following:

1. Y_M shows the profit on export sales from the source country; K_M in turn indicates the capitalised value of this income to the *source country firm*.
2. Assuming that the advantage was exploited by a *host country firm*, its income stream is represented by Y_D; the capitalised value of the income stream to that firm is K_D.

3. Finally, assuming production in the host country by the *source country firm,* Y_F shows the income stream and K_F its capitalised value. Y_F is smaller than Y_D, because in operating away from its domestic base the multinational faces extra control and communication costs. In spite of this, however, because of the impact of a currency premium, the capitalised value of the MNE affiliate's earnings rise above those of the host country firm after some point.

The relationship between market size and the alternative methods of exploiting a foreign market can be explored from this model. Below a market of OA, the source country firm will export. If over OB, direct investment in foreign production will occur, since the capitalised earnings from the affiliate's output rise above those of its indigenous competitor. Between OA and OB licensing would be the best alternative.

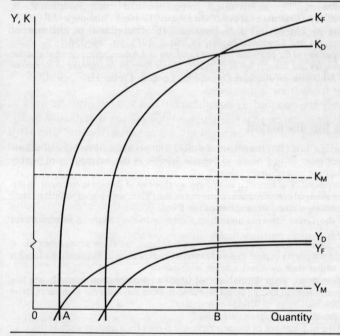

Fig. (App.) 2.1 The Aliber model: alternative methods of exploiting a foreign market (*Source*: Aliber, 1970).

Further reading

1. For a good, brief summary of some of the earlier theories of the MNE see: **P. J. Buckley and M. Casson,** *The Future of the Multinational Enterprise,* London: Macmillan, 1976, Ch. 3, 'Alternative theories of the multinational enterprise', pp. 66–84.

2. Some of these earlier theories are worth reading in the original, particularly: (i) **R. E. Caves,** 'International corporations: the industrial economics of foreign investment', 1971, reprinted in J. H. Dunning (ed.), *International Investment,* Harmondsworth: Penguin Books, 1972, pp. 265–301; (ii) **R. Vernon,** 'International investment and international trade in the product cycle', 1966, reprinted on pp. 305–25 in the same volume; (iii) **R. Z. Aliber,**'A theory of direct foreign investment' in C. P. Kindleberger (ed.), *The International Corporation,* Cambridge, Mass: MIT Press, 1970, pp. 17–34.

3. For a statement of the Buckley-Casson model itself, see Buckley and Casson op. cit. Ch. 2, pp. 52–65. See also **S. P. Magee,** 'Information and the multinational corporation: an appropriability theory of direct foreign investment', in J. N. Bhagwati (ed.), *The New International Economic Order,* Cambridge, Mass.: MIT Press, 1977, pp. 317–40.

4. A general statement of the internalisation model, integrating earlier theories and attempting to formulate a theory of international production is in: **J. H. Dunning,** 'Trade, location of economic activity and the multinational enterprise: a search for an eclectic approach', in B. Ohlin (ed.), *The International Allocation of Economic Activity,* London: Macmillan, 1977.

5. Excellent summaries of theory and empirical evidence are provided by: (i) **G. C. Hufbauer,** 'The multinational corporation and direct investment', in P. B. Kenen (ed.), *International Trade and Finance,* London: Cambridge U.P., 1975, particularly pp. 258–82; (ii) **J. H. Dunning,** 'The determinants of international production', *Oxford Economic Papers,* **25,** No. 3, 1973, pp. 289–336.

6. For a comparison of the characteristics of Japanese and American investment and the implications for the theory, see K. Kojima, *Direct Foreign Investment: A Japanese Model of Multinational Business Operations,* London: Croom Helm, 1978.

Questions for discussion

1. Why is foreign direct investment incompatible with perfect markets? Consider how direct investment abroad begins to become feasible as the assumptions of perfect competition are progressively relaxed.

2. Assess the relevance of financial and monetary theories of foreign investment, in the light of the changed economic circumstances of the 1970s, with higher inflation rates, floating exchange rates, weaknesses of the $ etc.

3. Appraise the Coase theorem and its applicability to the theory of foreign direct investment.

4. Given the possession of ownership-specific advantages, are there any reasons why a firm should not simply exploit these advantages by exporting or by licensing a foreign producer rather than by direct foreign investment?

5. Empirical evidence suggests that size of firm and technological intensity are the major determinants of foreign direct investment. Does this evidence provide support for the evolving theory of foreign investment?

6. Is the multinational enterprise 'efficient'?

7. What are the implications of the product cycle theory for a country such as the UK, which is both a major home and host country for multinational firms? Is there any evidence of product cycle predictions being fulfilled?

8. Is it possible to explain the emergence of Japanese multinational firms in terms of the theory of foreign direct investment presented in this chapter?

Further reading

1. For a good, brief, non-technical review of the earlier theories, the MNE, P. J. Buckley and M. Casson, *The Future of the Multinational Enterprise,* London: Macmillan, 1976, Ch. 3, 'Alternative theories of the multinational enterprise', pp. 66–84.

The economics
of the multinational firm

Summary

1. The review of the managerial, behavioural and modern profit maximising theories of the firm indicates that each of these have a part to play in understanding MNE behaviour. In the case of large MNEs operating in a variety of environments with extensive affiliate networks and varying ownership patterns, it may be necessary to employ aspects of all of the theories to explain behaviour. This will be the case even if it is accepted that profit maximisation is the overall long-run *corporate* objective.

2. The operating principles of MNEs may be viewed as those of international oligopolists and their behaviour analysed within an oligopoly framework. Two aspects of MNE behaviour are particularly important, firstly, their role in the production of new information (technology) and secondly, their pricing practices. The theory of information points to welfare maximisation in a situation where a single (governmental information-creating body develops and diffuses information as a public good. In reality, private firms are responsible for much of the investment in information creation and MNEs have a particularly important role to play. Through internalisation processes, MNEs are able to ensure greater appropriability of the returns to investment in new information; and therefore a greater incentive exists within multinationals than in other firms to invest in information-creation.

3. The pricing strategies open to MNEs assist the process of appropriating the returns to investment in information-creation. Price discrimination and market segmentation policies are thus necessary for appropriability and in this sense are compatible with economic efficiency. But it is difficult to distinguish between such pricing policies and those which are oligopolistic and are aimed at maintaining a market position and at earning excess profits. Manipulative transfer pricing designed to switch profits between locations, entry-limit pricing aimed at discouraging entry, and predatory dumping designed to gain market access and drive out competition are all examples of restrictive pricing practices which MNEs may employ in their various locations. These pricing tactics in turn may be linked to cartel agreements, tying contracts and exclusive dealing arrangements.

4. Many of the theoretical contributions considered are difficult to test conclusively. The weight of empirical evidence suggests that MNE behaviour accords with the predictions of profit maximising theories. Furthermore, it is clear that MNEs have been important creators of information in many industrial sectors. However, although R & D intensity and degree of multinationality are significantly related, cause and effect are not easily separated. The most problematic area relates to pricing practices in multinational firms, since many of the interview studies which have been undertaken with corporation executives are open to varying interpretations. Even so, the research confirms the range of price alternatives and policies open to MNEs; the importance of price in the management strategies of MNEs; and the situations in which manipulative transfer pricing may be employed. Studies on the locational behaviour of MNEs point to many of the classical tenets of location theory holding for international corporations, including market size, labour costs and the size and quality of the labour pool. Evidence on the role of Government fiscal incentives in influencing investment decisions is mixed.

5. Studies of profitability reveal higher rates of return in MNE affiliates as compared with indigenous corporations; similarly, productivity is usually higher in MNE affiliates. More recent (albeit limited) evidence, nevertheless, does not indicate strongly that MNE affiliates are allocatively efficient; and, when special factors are removed, it is not always clear that multinational affiliates are technically more efficient than indigenous firms.

The MNE and modern microeconomic theory

The growth in the importance of the MNE has resulted in various attempts being made to analyse and predict its behaviour patterns. The contributions by economists in this field have been largely based on the existing body of standard neo-classical theory concerning the goals and behaviour of the firm. The aim of this chapter is to consider how applicable these existing theories of the firm are to the MNE, given the distinctive characteristics of multinational companies. Beginning with an analysis of the objectives of MNEs, the theory section examines modern developments in the theory of the firm and the way in which these aid understanding of multinational corporations. Thereafter MNE behaviour is analysed in terms of international oligopoly, thus enabling the reader to maintain the framework of market imperfections as a basic point of reference for the study of multinationality.

An important linking theme emerging from Chapter 2 is the

motivation to internalise. The drive to minimise transaction costs, as outlined by Coase, is motivated by a desire for long-run profit maximisation. However, the internalisation process developed by models in the Coase tradition could well provide a series of objective functions which the firm would seek to maximise; and these might, in the short term at least, override the more familiar objectives such as profit or sales maximisation. For example, using discriminatory pricing to exploit a monopoly advantage in knowledge may produce widely differing short-term returns on capital in different markets. A similar situation could emerge where an MNE is gradually positioning itself through internalisation for a particular offensive on a market. It is important to note that the internalisation process and the other explanations of the dynamics of the MNE which were considered in the last chapter are only separated from this chapter for purposes of exposition. Thus, while the economics of the expansion process and the economics of the internal operation of the MNE appear in different chapters, they are inextricably linked together and must be seen as such.

It must be pointed out initially that the study of the MNE has tended to be empirical and that objectives and motivation have received less attention than they merit. A reflection on some of the theoretical contributions reviewed in the former chapter will illustrate this point. Several make implicit assumptions about the MNE's objectives, while few investigate them in detail.

The MNE and modern theories of the firm

Recent contributions to the theory of the firm have stemmed from claims that the classical assumption of profit maximisation is too restrictive as a basis for understanding the behaviour of large corporations in complex, contemporary environments. Oligopolistic market structures and the absence of competitive pressures, government legislation in fields such as pricing, managerial discretion, and market entry strategies are among a host of factors which may inhibit profit maximisation at least in the short run. Observations of firm behaviour have therefore generated a number of alternative theories of motivation.

Certain of these newer theories of the firm appear immediately applicable to the MNE. They are concerned with large corporations with a degree of monopoly power in their markets. Such corporations are deemed to be sufficiently large for managers to be able to resist profit maximising pressures from widely diffused groups of shareholders whose individual equity holdings may be small. The separation of ownership from control is thus generally assumed. The theories also imply competition based on extensive market segmentation and related product differentiation as befits oligopolistic activity. Complex, divisionalised structures are the normal organisational pattern. In all these aspects they appear ideally suited to analysing MNE behaviour. On the other hand, some of the distinguishing characteristics of the MNE pose problems for any theory of the firm. For example, the motives of the parent corporation may differ from those of its affiliates at any one point in time. The degree to which this is so will depend on the particular MNE. One of the basic skills of the MNE is flexibility of both objective and organisation. It is possible to observe that MNEs do establish affiliates overseas in order to achieve greater profits, sales or growth than would have been possible in their domestic market. But it would be naïve to approach the next section in search of a single theory or group of theories which provide a universal description of MNE behaviour. Neither can the models be exhaustively examined since there has been very little testing of theories of the firm with respect to MNEs.

For the purposes of this brief review, the theories are classified in broad groupings, namely managerial, behavioural, and contemporary profit maximisation. Inevitably, it has been necessary to be selective in the coverage given in what is a rapidly expanding field.

(a) Managerial theories

Baumol's own experience of the importance which oligopolistic industries attach to the value of their sales is expressed in his *sales revenue maximisation* model.[1] At output $0Q_1$ (Fig. 3.1) the firm will maximise sales revenue but may not be earning sufficient profit to either satisfy its shareholders' demand for dividends or the demands of the capital market should it require to raise additional funds. On the other hand, the profit maximising output, $0Q_2$, requires the firm to operate below full capacity. In practice, Baumol contended, neither of these two output quantities may in fact be pursued. The firm lives in the real world and there are several constraints pushing it towards the attainment of a minimum level of profits. This acceptable level might be a reflection of shareholders' interests; of the expectations of both creditors and potential lenders; industry norms and so on. This profit constraint is fixed at π_M in Fig. 3.1. Only after this has been achieved will profits become secondary to sales as an objective. The sales maximising firm will thus produce an output of $0Q_3$.

It is quite possible that this analysis could be applied to multinational firms. An MNE could readily sell at a lower price to obtain extra output (Q_2Q_3), so as perhaps to raise market share in a particular region. As regards the profit constraint, the MNE is largely responsible to shareholders in the home country, although much of its borrowing may be in host countries. π_M could therefore vary considerably in different locations although it will tend to be standardised by the application of corporate performance norms throughout the MNE.

Williamson, like Baumol, places considerable stress on the motivation of management in his theory of managerial discretion.[2] His basic contention is that in running their business operation, managers

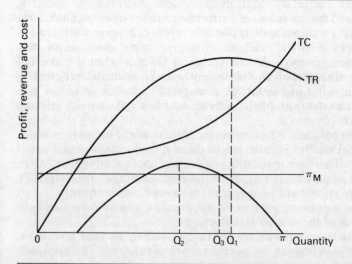

Fig. 3.1 W. J. Baumol: Sales revenue maximisation model.

are required to have an unusual form of rationality. They are required to be able to distinguish between their individual interests and the decisions they make as managers *per se*. Williamson argues that managers will run the firm in their own best interests. They will attempt to maximise their own utility functions, and therefore their power and prestige, in terms of three critical variables: expenditure on staff (the number and quality of staff employed); expenditure on emoluments (expense accounts, high quality offices etc.); and discretionary investment spending (namely investment beyond that required for strictly economic reasons, which reflects the power and preferences of management).

Simplifying Williamson's approach, the utility function of management can be viewed as -

$$U = \int (S, M, Id)$$

where   S = expenditure on staff

       M = managerial emoluments

       Id = discretionary investment (formally defined as reported profits less minimum acceptable profits, less taxation)

Although this model could be relevant in assessing the behaviour of MNEs at corporate level there are problems at affiliate level. Consider, for example, discretionary investment. The concept of reported profits presumes that local management can manipulate performance returns and report results which give them funds to disburse. Some MNE control systems would allow this, others would not. Tight budgetary controls, very low discretionary spending ceilings, and special in-house performance ratios often preclude such behaviour. This is not to deny that other types of managerial discretion are present in MNE affiliates. There is ample evidence of new management teams (with different utility functions) being appointed to ailing affiliates which subsequently make dramatic progress in profitability. In some instances, managerial discretion increases with the size and maturity of the affiliate and is a reflection of growing autonomy.

Both Baumol and Williamson give prominence to the ways in which managerial control is reflected in the static allocation of the firm's resources. There are inevitably problems of applicability to the MNE, therefore, since longer-run, more dynamic considerations frequently appear to dominate managerial behaviour. Consequently, it is necessary to examine some of the major contributions to the theory of the *growth* of the firm in recent years.

Penrose lays emphasis on the role played by *optimal investment strategy* in determining the overall growth of the firm.[3] This approach provides an unusual explanation for profit maximising behaviour through the following process. Management will endeavour to select the most profitable investments in any planning programme in order to generate funds for future investment from current earnings. Such a solution in time t will ensure new investment in period t + 1 which, given a limited dividend policy, will finance expansion in t + 2 and so on. Growth in this model is assured by the profit retention policies of the controlling managers. The role of management is crucial in another respect. The growth process is not only constrained by finance but also by the resources in the managerial team. To Penrose, the coherence, skill and experience of that team are crucial in planning and financing an optimal investment path.

The stress laid on internal human resources is important in relating this approach to the MNE. Large corporations do possess, and lay much store by, acquired managerial experience through which profit opportunities are diagnosed. Such experience is an important dimension of an MNE's comparative advantage. An optimal investment strategy may, however, be difficult to define in the terms used by Penrose. For example, an MNE with a global strategy can operate on a longer time horizon and in suboptimal investments in order to open a market to one of its products in an early stage of R & D. Nevertheless, the implicit suggestion in Penrose that progressive expansion is conditional on the existence of a management team able to identify and plan profitable investment at each crucial review stage, could explain the process and perhaps some of the direction of MNE growth.

The growth model presented by Marris is a 'steady-state' model, i.e. the firm makes a once-for-all choice of a constant rate of growth which is pursued thereafter in perpetuity.[4] Marris acknowledges that in *managerial capitalism* the primary aim of management will be growth in the size of the corporation, subject to a strong influence from shareholders with whom they share some important common interests. Both parties have an interest in high stock-market prices to aid new capital issues and asset values, avoid cheap take-overs and so on. In Fig. 3.2, the managers' and shareholders' interests are represented by different positions on the transformation curve relating present value of shares (V) to steady growth rate (G). Assuming that V is the main determinant of shareholders' welfare, then point Y is their preferred strategy. From say, X to Y growth and valuation are both increased and there is therefore little conflict of interests; from Y, higher growth can only be financed from lower dividends. The range Y to Z encompasses the strategies preferred by the managers. Market opinion, risk of take-over and other common interests may, in practice, determine that there is a 'safe' operating range between points such as M and N in the diagram.

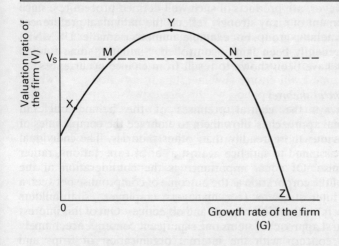

Fig. 3.2 The trade-off between share valuation and growth rate.

It is obviously possible to relate some aspects of Marris to MNEs, although not necessarily to multinationality as such. Persuading shareholders to forego dividends over a period to allow rapid foreign expansion is, in theory, a possible factor in maximising management utility. The major problem is one of applying steady state analysis such as that of Marris to the foreign investment process. The complexities of timing and directional patterns, domestic market pressures, and differential rates of foreign market expansion all preclude simple theorising.

Before concluding on managerial theories, it is worth noting that several of the less formal models on the direction of the growth of the firm may be of some relevance in explaining MNE behaviour. In this context Ansoff's work is interesting.[5] The core of the hypothesis is that implicitly or explicitly, firms should have a 'corporate strategy' to provide a unifying theme for all of their activities. And this strategy should be formulated so as to maximise the *synergy* (joint effects) potential between various industries and various operations within the firm. Such a strategy would require a firm to pursue investment opportunities in areas which are complementary to existing business so as to maximise sales, operating, investment and management synergy. Sales synergy occurs, for example, where products use common distribution channels, common warehousing, common advertising etc; investment synergy can result from joint use of plant, common tooling, the transfer of R & D from one product to another and so forth. This type of approach may well be useful in explaining the rapid expansion of some large MNEs, simply because of the implied advantages to be gained by planned, integrated and clearly specified action. It would also tie in with the theory presented in the previous chapter. Not all MNEs, however, are products of such well defined procedures, since the development of many strongly reflects the individual preferences of a tight ownership group. For example, numerous smaller US MNEs have until recently been family controlled. Similarly, some foreign investments have been shown to result from chance occurrences.

(b) Behavioural theories

In some ways the central premises of the behavioural and organisational approaches allow them to embrace the complexities of MNE behaviour more readily than other theories. The individual manager is assumed to satisfice against a set of expectations, rather than maximise. Of equal importance is the consideration of the behaviour of the corporation as the outcome of compromise between a number of interest groups (e.g. managers, employees, shareholders and customers) with different goals and objectives. Out of this interest in behavioural approaches stems one significant consequence, namely a renewed concern with the internal organisation of firms and especially with the existence of internal inefficiency (X-inefficiency). Comment in this section is restricted to examining only the principal developments in this area and linking them to the MNE.

Simon, as one of the earliest writers, argued that managerial knowledge must always be imperfect; decisions uncertain and complex.[6] This being so, the businessman does not know whether he is maximising or not and hence aims at 'satisfactory' profits. Both past experience and future uncertainty will define this profit level. It will be adjusted, but the costs of collecting information preclude all alternatives being explored. As a consequence, the 'satisfactory' profits point will probably not, Simon postulates, be the maximising level. Some of the essential characteristics of the MNE may alter the process which Simon describes. For example, MNEs often derive internal performance measures to define satisfactory behaviour within different parts of the organisation and also have access to extensive business intelligence. The end result, in terms of behaviour, may nevertheless differ fairly little from that of uninational companies. On the other hand, the higher risk involved in foreign operations may lead to an MNE's definition of satisfactory profit being significantly above the norm for a comparable domestic firm.

To Cyert and March, the behaviour of the firm had to be viewed through its decision-making processes.[7] Firms in the model are viewed as being operated by groups who come together in an 'organisational coalition'. The groups include trade unions, management, shareholders and so on whose individual interests may differ. For example, unions may place emphasis on higher wages, management on higher productivity and shareholders on overall rates of return on capital employed. The firm survives because, although individual and group objectives differ, the members accept the need to co-exist, and come closer to their objectives than would be possible if they were not involved in the firm. The final set of goals of the firm is a compromise which will almost always result in efficiency being below maximum, i.e. 'organisational slack' will exist. The coalition is held together because the slack results in excess 'payments' being distributed between members, with the acceptance of the inefficiency which this involves. These payments may be in cash, kind or in the right to contribute to policy. The bargaining process involved is under constant review and hence goals vary. While there are an indeterminate number of such goals possible, Cyert and March emphasise five: production, inventory, sales, market share and profit, each of which is the particular interest of some members of the coalition.

There are some interesting ways in which an MNE may behave as a Cyert and March firm. It is not unusual to find rapid expansion in foreign investment following a change in the balance of power between coalition members in the parent company. For instance, a change in the composition of a parent company board could lead to the pursuit of policies of investment abroad, in situations where home country unions had convinced former management that such action would be damaging to domestic employment. Again, if an MNE has affiliates in various locations, there are grounds for anticipating that numerous types of organisational slack will exist depending on the required compromises in these different locations. In some ways the ever-present 'centralisation v. decentralisation' dilemma of headquarters management in an MNE is a reflection of the need to balance the interests of the corporate coalition. Different sets of compromises will reflect different power structures at affiliate level and so, for example, a large well established and highly profitable MNE affiliate might conceivably have considerable autonomy. The trend towards concerted action by employees through international unionisation may raise yet further interesting applications of the Cyert and March approach. Such action by unions could, for instance, lead to more standard working conditions or payments' systems in MNE coalitions.

An example of a behavioural theory which refers specifically to the MNE is that developed by Aharoni.[8] He hypothesised that firms do not scan the environment in search of profit opportunities as suggested by the profit maximising model. The decision process is regarded rather as a series of steps, namely: the decision to look abroad; the investigation process; the commitment to invest; and finally follow-up reviews and refinements. In this process the strength of commitment to proceed consistently depends less on market growth and profit prospects than on the strength of the initiating stimulus. Externally, such a stimulus might be action taken by a foreign government against existing export operations; internally, the fact that a project has particular backing from a senior executive might provide a strong stimulus to multinationality. Aharoni considered that once the investigation process had been initiated, there was a tendency to discover that risks had been overestimated and returns underestimated. The long-run effect of such study of overseas investment prospects, assuming the continued strength of the initial or new stimuli, was to raise confidence and commitment and lead to international production.

The process which Aharoni describes may in fact be consistent with the profit maximisation hypothesis; and there has been extensive discussion in the literature as to whether in general such behavioural principles are incompatible with rational choice in profit maximisation. One illustration of this is given by Day, who developed a learning model from behavioural principles, which converges on the traditional marginalist position.[9] In this model the decision maker does not know his profit function but does know his past two decisions and the profits which resulted from them. By correcting for successful and unsuccessful decisions, the decision maker attains goal fulfilment at a point which may be close to that of profit maximisation. It may indeed be the case that existing theories can only be applied to the MNE in this spirit. The MNE by satisficing and suboptimising in particular products, plants and locations, hopes to converge efficiently (i.e. with minimum slack) on profit maximisation overall.

(c) Contemporary profit maximisation theories

Alongside the continuing controversy as to whether managerial and behavioural theories do, or can, encompass types of profit maximising behaviour, there are several pieces of work which explicitly assume profit maximising motivation. Two of these are summarised below.

In his later work, Williamson has postulated some important relationships between organisational form and performance.[10] He contends that 'managerial discretion' is applicable in the unitary form (U-form) organisation (see Appendix 3.1) but that developments in organisational structures towards multidivisional form (M-form) have effectively reduced discretion, sharpened central control and increased the applicability of the profit maximising hypothesis. As the firm grows, there are some central problems which emerge within the U-form organisation. For example, in a multi-product corporation, many coordinating decisions are required in order to link manufacturing, sales, engineering, etc. in each product area. U-form organisations find the chief executive faced with a range of coordinating decisions of widely varying degrees of importance. In the M-form organisation some of these are screened out at the operating division level, allowing the central control to be concerned with strategy. Such are the supposed benefits of M-form in more efficient control and planning that Williamson concludes: 'The organisation and operation of the large enterprise along the lines of M-form favours goal-pursuit and least cost behaviour more nearly associated with the neo-classical profit maximisation hypothesis than does the U-form organisational alternative.'[11]

It is not easy to generalise with respect to organisation form in MNEs, as there are many variations within any one type.[12] Within an M-form organisation, for example, operating divisions can be split by product group, geographical area and customer type or process. Where an MNE is organised on a geographical basis, for example, this means that foreign operations are being controlled by managers with geographical responsibilities for all or part of the world outside the home country. It is possible, alternatively, for foreign operations to be handled by an international division with overall functional responsibilities. Irrespective of the relative merits of these organisational variations, it might be expected in general that M-form organisation would improve operating efficiency in MNEs. A U-form organisation could not cope with the spatial diversity of multinational corporations. On the other hand, there is evidence of problems arising in M-form companies which derive from lack of long-range planning at affiliate level, suggesting that no organisation structure *per se* can guarantee success. Indeed, the frequent and high-level organisational changes in MNEs support the view that multinationality is not readily controllable and that corporations gravitate towards a satisfactory organisational form which takes account of their own individual circumstances in terms of products, marketing, technology and so on. What is clear with respect to organisational form in MNEs is that several factors are working to produce greater centralisation, including improved communications and refinements in systems of financial control. Some centralisation can even develop outwith the intention of the corporation, where key individuals take action which limits discretion and initiative in an affiliate. But it is easier to observe the trends to centralisation than it is to work out their consequences for resource allocation and there is no reason to associate moves towards M-form types of organisation in MNEs with greater centralisation.

The X-theory of the firm, first introduced by Leibenstein, constitutes a further attempt to reincarnate profit maximisation.[13] The maximisation of profits is assumed to be the goal of both the stock holders and fund managers, but may not be the goal of those employed within the organisation. For example, employees may in fact be maximising a different and conflicting utility function such as short-term salary gains. As a result, profit maximisation can only be achieved by some form of policing or tight monitoring without which X-inefficiency will be present. The organisation might thus operate well below its production possibility limits, involving significant under-utilisation of resources. This may reveal itself in many ways including labour non-cooperation, and productivity rates which differ sharply in operations where similar technology is employed.

Although developed to apply in monopoly, many aspects of this theory have relevance to oligopoly, since a number of Leibenstein's assumptions can hold equally well in that market condition. Incomplete and vague labour contracts; supervisory problems; vaguely defined measures of performance; the degree of scope which managers have in defining their own roles, and so forth, are all potential causes of X-inefficiency. This concept is again helpful in discussing the MNE. Clearly the scope for inefficiency in MNEs is heightened by the policing costs associated with different cultures, languages, degrees of unionisation and work ethics. Similarly, varying monetary incentives will be required in different locations to ensure employee cooperation with equity interests. An MNE would accept that monitoring costs are part of policing, but many would acknowledge that the achievement of absolute cooperation is both unlikely and too costly. For example, the shareholders of a corporation might consider that the management team of a particular affiliate are generally competent, but display weaknesses in, say, their sourcing policy for certain components. It would be possible to remove such decisions from their discretion, or require approval for every single sourcing decision. Neither alternative would reflect the general competence of the group or their overall performance record, and so marginal inefficiency is tolerated by allowing continued local autonomy.

Viewed collectively, therefore, modern theories of the firm have a contribution to make in understanding MNE behaviour, even though they have been subject to little formal testing in relation to multinationals. The greater problem is, however, that the predictions of the theories themselves are so diverse as to be compatible with numerous types of behaviour. Multinationality simply adds another dimension to the characteristics of modern industry considered by the models, such as the separation of ownership from control and oligopolistic competition; as well as involving the relaxation of some basic assumptions and the introduction of new ones. There is one basic problem even so, deriving from the fact that a multinational corporation may be composed of a large number of geographically diverse operating units. Existing theories are more able to explain overall MNE behaviour than that of individual affiliates. For example, a corporation may pursue profit maximisation, while having one affiliate which seems to accept X-inefficiency (in order to encourage a young management team); another affiliate attempting to maximise sales with a very low minimum profit constraint (to ensure market share in a market with long-run growth); while a third affiliate in a Third World location is given extensive managerial discretion for political reasons to preserve raw material supplies. Further, intra-company product allocation and pricing strategies may be important in explaining affiliate behaviour. The assessment of motivation is also complicated by both the type and degree of risk faced by the MNE. Oligopolistic interdependence and different political and cultural environments may make MNE activities abroad significantly more risky than their domestic operations. This could, for instance, lead to an MNE pursuing a short-run profit maximising strategy in an affiliate for fear of expropriation occurring through a change of government. Perhaps the most persistent problems in explaining behaviour arise from the complexities of organisational relationships in MNEs. Since these are dynamic, behavioural patterns are likely to change even with agreed overall objectives. For these reasons, the empirical section later in the chapter is concerned solely with the objective function of the MNE as a whole.

The economics of operating an MNE

MNEs can readily be characterised as international oligopolists. But this does not simplify analysis of their behaviour since there is no single accepted theory of oligopoly, given the diverse number of forms which it may take (and the accuracy of the statement is subject to provisos as will be indicated). There is agreement that oligopoly at national or international level implies an interdependence of policies and decisions among the competing firms. Therefore, any decision one firm makes in respect of product, price or promotions will affect the market position of competitors and result in counter-moves. However, these actions and reactions of competing oligopolists may be varied, thereby making prediction difficult. The nature of oligopoly requires the firms concerned to attempt to reduce the uncertainties of interdependence by lowering the cross-price elasticity of demand between their own products and those of their rivals through product differentiation (often backed by heavy advertising) and oligopoly pricing. Multinationality provides the oligopolist with a further set of markets within which to apply these classic principles of oligopoly behaviour; with different tax regimes across countries, the opportunities to profit from a variety of pricing policies are particularly apparent. Moreover, within an international framework, MNEs are able to utilise their various kinds of technological advantage as additional weapons to aid market segmentation and product differentiation. For these reasons, the emphasis in this section is on the economics of information and pricing in MNEs, with only limited treatment of other considerations.

(a) The economics of information and the MNE

Technology and multinationality are inseparable. As Johnson put it 'the transference of knowledge . . . is the crux of the direct investment process'.[14] For the purposes of this discussion, the many different types of knowledge created and transferred are grouped under the general heading of 'information'. They include the discovery and development of new products; the initiation of appropriate production functions; and the skills involved both in the creation and servicing of markets and in the effective use of product differentiation. Within this section, three important issues are developed. Firstly, the theoretical framework relating to the economics of information is outlined. Secondly, the relative role of competitive and monopolistic firms in the production of information is analysed; and finally, some aspects of the MNE's role are assessed.

The economic theory of information.[15]   Information is a durable, if intangible, good. Extensive resources may be required to produce it, but on creation and application the information generates a time stream of future benefits. These benefits will be distributed privately (to the information creator) and socially (to society). As a product, information is indivisible and thus has many characteristics of a public good. Once created by A, it can be used by B without A's continued use being precluded. A's private return on his investment may, of course, be affected significantly by the dissemination of this information. In other words A's ability to retain the information as his private property (i.e. his appropriability), will be impaired. The hypothesis that private appropriability is low for many of the types of information described, has led some economists to contend that private markets will tend to under-invest in the creation of new information, especially that involving fundamental technical research.

These properties of information immediately pose a dilemma from the viewpoint of welfare maximisation. As a public good, the conditions for optimality would require information to be openly available without charge (apart perhaps for covering the costs of circulating it). Clearly to do so would discourage new investment in information creation. In practice, either the legal system permits private firms to internalise the returns to parts of their stock of information (e.g. by temporary monopoly via patents) and thereby supports the creator's property rights; or alternatively, governments create the information and offer it free.

Pursuing these theoretical aspects of welfare maximisation, the potential for economic inefficiency emerging from the granting of a temporary monopoly through the patent system is readily illustrated in Fig. 3.3. DD_1 is the assumed demand curve for a product incorporating a new technology, DD_2 is the equivalent marginal revenue curve and SS_1 represents costs of production (assumed to be constant for simplicity). A policy designed to maximise social welfare would require the product to be sold at its production costs resulting in output $0Q_w$ and producing consumer surplus of DSP. Suppose instead that a temporary monopoly is allowed by legislation: this would enable the producer to charge a price of $0P_m$. Monopoly profits are thus shown by rectangle Y with the social gain being reduced by the amount of the triangle Z. Because the private return is less than the social return, the implication is that there will be under-investment in the creation of new information. Moreover, reflecting the monopoly price, output $0Q_m$ is well below the socially optimum output level, indicating that existing information will be used to a sub-optimal degree. Johnson went on to argue that because of the monopoly profits obtainable from successful information creation, there would be a waste of resources as rival firms replicated R & D in the attempt to be first to register patents.

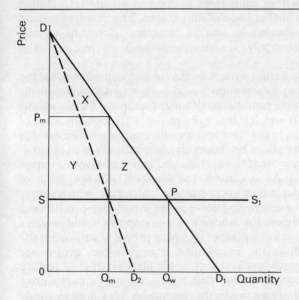

Fig. 3.3 Optimal and monopoly pricing of a new product.

The view that government creation of information is preferable to private market creation from a welfare viewpoint has, however, been queried. Suppose, for instance, that government undertakes the R & D, and makes the results freely available. The problem would inevitably arise on the selection of the R & D projects. Political pressures and the utility functions of bureaucrats might be more important in determining the projects to be undertaken than social rates of return. An alternative approach would be for the government to allow private firms to create the information, with government then purchasing the discovery and providing the information freely to all producers. Referring again to Fig. 3.3, the government would pay the private producer the monopoly profits shown by rectangle Y; then, by providing the information freely, welfare would rise by the amount of triangle Z. But this raises several difficulties: sellers of information might attempt to obtain the entire social value of the information (Y+Z) which would create redistributional problems; and because markets in information are imperfect, problems would be created in trying to establish the value of the new information. In these ways, it is possible that an inferior public allocation of R & D, the costs of establishing the value of new information etc., might more than offset any welfare losses associated with under-investment in new information by private firms.

Private firms and the production of information.   Leaving aside the debate over the welfare gains from public and private information creation, there is a further issue of importance. This revolves around the question of whether a market structure closer to perfect competition or monopoly is more conducive to research and information creation.

Arrow, one of the earlier writers on the subject, considered that the incentive to invest in information would be less under monopolistic than under competitive conditions; although (accepting the arguments expressed above), it was felt that even in the latter case the level of investment would be lower than was socially desirable.[16] The essence of the Arrow argument can be shown diagrammatically as in Fig. 3.4, where D and MR represent the average and marginal revenue curves for a product and AC indicates the constant average costs of production. Consider now a cost-reducing innovation, which simply lowers the constant average cost curve for an established product to a level such as AC_1. Before the innovation, a monopolist would produce an output of 0e and sell at a price of 0j, giving profits of anlj. After the innovation, for which the monopolist is responsible, profits are represented by the area cpmk, reflecting the higher output 0f and the lower price 0k. Suppose instead that a single firm in a competitive industry is involved, then prior to the innovation this company would be producing only a small quantity and earning zero economic profit. If this competitive firm discovers and implements the cost-reducing innovation, it cannot exploit its position by setting a monopoly price since this would attract entrants and cause it to lose sales. However, by setting a price just below 0a, the innovating firm will be able to win all the sales from its fellow competitors; and since the innovator is operating along cost curve AC_1, it will obtain profits of abqc.

Maintaining the assumption of linear demand and constant average costs, it can be shown that the competitor has the greater incentive to innovate since the competitor's gain (represented by abdc) will be greater than the monopolist's (which is the difference between anlj and cpmk)[17].

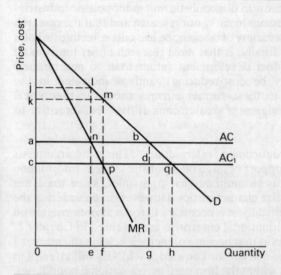

Fig. 3.4 Gains to a competitive and a monopolistic firm from innovation.

The case of a new product innovation may be rather different, because in these circumstances the same rewards are obtainable by both the competitor and the monopolist. This is so because neither firm has to give up anything to profit from the new product. Indeed, if the new product has a complementary relationship with existing products, the monopolist might profit even more from its introduction than a competitive firm would. With a substitutive relationship between new and existing products, on the other hand, the monopolist's incentive to offer new goods would be reduced.[18]

Even if it is true that, for a cost-reducing innovation with patent protection, the competitive industry will have the greatest incentive to innovate, this does not mean that more competitive market structures will necessarily result in greater information creation. In the first place, there may be imperfections in the patent system which inhibit a competitor with many potential rivals. The monopolist need not be deterred in this way, because control of the entire market could enable such a firm to appropriate the gains from the information even without patent protection. Secondly, firms in competitive industries may lack the resources to finance research and development. This latter argument, that large dominant firms are needed to bear the high costs of modern innovation, is widely accepted. It was articulated persuasively by Schumpeter and subsequently other arguments have been put forward to support the case.[19] It has been pointed out, for instance, that large firms can take a longer view and therefore wait longer for the pay-off, and that monopolistic companies are better able to bear the risks involved in large R & D projects. Against this, it has been suggested that firms in oligopolistic and monopolistic industries may be under less pressure to carry out research and that the research undertaken may, for a variety of reasons, be less cost-effective. What it is important to note, finally, is that most research effort tends to be devoted to new product development rather than to new process research (which may be cost-reducing), and as indicated in the previous paragraph, in these former circumstances the theoretical conclusion does not suggest a greater competitive firm incentive to innovate.

The MNE and the production of information.   The same arguments presented above in support of large oligopolistic firms as information creators, apply equally to multinational companies, since the latter generally exhibit similar characteristics. However, in considering the role of the MNE specifically, it is necessary to focus attention again on the theory of the multinational enterprise as presented in Chapter 2. The basis of the theory is that because of inefficiencies in the market – and particularly in the market for knowledge – MNEs will attempt to organise transactions within the firm itself across national boundaries. By this means the multinational firm can ensure greater appropriability of the private returns to its investment in new information. It has been argued by Magee that the patent system is only truly effective in protecting the appropriability of private returns to *product creation*.[20] However, the creation of new products is seen as only one of a number of distinct types of information, the others being information relating to *product development, production functions and markets*. Research and development spending by firms chiefly relates to product development, where the information generated by producing one good can be applied, through learning by doing, to other new products. An appropriability problem arises with respect to new product development, because the patent system only safeguards the initial prototypes of the commodity developed. Rival firms can utilise the information incorporated into the product development, if they are able to make an apparently significant though inexpensive change in the product's characteristics. But, through internalising the information created, MNEs are in a better position to ensure adequate appropriability. Moreover, as Magee argues, the MNE will also invest to protect appropriability, as, for example, computer companies invest to disguise the technology incorporated into new models of their computers and thereby prevent imitation by rival firms. Such operations are again more efficiently undertaken within the firm than through the market.

The theory would thus indicate that MNEs are likely to invest more heavily in information-creation than other firms because the possibilities for appropriation are greater. Similarly, theory suggests that investment in information is likely to be biased towards sophisticated information because internalisation and appropriation possibilities are greater for complex than for simple ideas. But nothing can be said about the efficiency of MNE research effort, that is the effectiveness of creating information from a given amount of spending. While not relating to the MNE, there is some evidence, for example, that the productivity of R & D may decline as the size of firm increases. Furthermore, no account is taken of the practices which MNEs may follow in order to facilitate appropriability of the returns from information creation. Greater appropriability may indeed encourage greater investment in information; but this desirable objective may be offset by the undesirable patterns of behaviour required to achieve such appropriability. Practices such as price discrimination, for instance, are an integral component of the internalisation model. This and other aspects of behaviour are considered in their own right in following paragraphs, and at this stage it is simply the link between price discrimination and information creation that is pursued.

It may be argued that since information has the character of a public good, it would be expected that a firm possessing it would behave like a discriminating monopolist. As Johnson expresses the position: 'since any additional earnings obtained by applying the knowledge in an additional market will be a net addition to its profits from the initial investment in creating the knowledge, the firm will have an incentive to extend its operations to any market that offers a positive profit and to fix the price it charges for the use of its knowledge, so as to maximise profit in each market'.[21] On this view, price discrimination and associated practices, such as product differentiation between countries and export restrictions on subsidiaries, are necessary to ensure the appropriation of returns and therefore to long-run investment in information creation. On the other hand, as will be indicated following, it is usually difficult to distinguish between pricing practices which can be said to be necessary to encourage the creation of information, and those which are merely oligopolistic, in the sense of being designed to maintain or reinforce a market position and are aimed at earning excess profits.

(b) The economics of MNE pricing
Since it is widely recognised that an understanding of the behaviour of oligopolists comes through observation of their pricing policies, this section examines certain aspects of the theory of oligopolistic pricing as it relates to the MNE. As oligopolists, MNEs could be expected to emphasise price stability, especially in their domestic market, being conscious of the possibilities and effects of retaliatory action. Overseas, MNEs will sometimes be in competition with other

oligopolists or they may have a technological advantage giving them a monopoly position which can be exploited through pricing. While stability may still therefore be a guiding principle, the method of determining prices for each of the foreign markets within which an MNE operates is obviously highly complex. Some of the major considerations include variations in exchange rates, differing degrees of market stability, the cost structures and transfer pricing policies of competitors, the volume of R & D expenditures to be recovered, price leadership and so on. Some of the most important forms of pricing behaviour are considered in the following paragraphs.[22]

Price discrimination becomes possible when the monopolistic firm is faced with two or more markets which are separated from each other in some way and within which elasticities of demand differ. By charging different prices in these circumstances (with the highest price in the market with the most inelastic demand), the firm can usually raise profits. The separate markets may be segments of a single national market, where buyer characteristics and hence demand elasticities vary, or different national markets. In the latter case, where sales abroad are made at a lower price than at home, the term 'dumping' is applied; similarly 'reverse dumping' operates where a firm sells abroad at a higher price than in the domestic market in order to exploit the inelasticity of demand of the foreign market. For price discrimination to be successful, 'leakage' between the markets must be minimal, e.g. because of transport costs internationally, otherwise buyers will be able to purchase in the cheaper market and sell in the dearer.

Figure 3.5 illustrates the theory of discriminatory pricing with a simple model assuming two markets (A and B), and a single

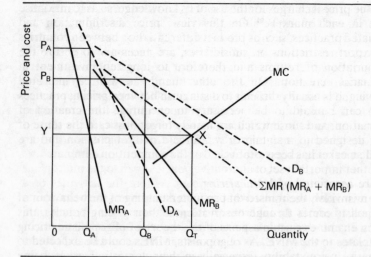

Fig. 3.5 Price discrimination between two markets.

homogeneous good (although the same analysis could apply to more markets and more goods). MR_A and D_A are the marginal revenue and average revenue curves for market A, and MR_B and D_B the equivalent curves for market B. MC is the firm's marginal cost curve, assuming output from one plant location. For profit maximisation, two conditions must be met. Marginal revenue and marginal cost should be equal and, secondly, marginal revenue in markets A and B should be equal. Summing MR_A and MR_B gives an aggregate marginal revenue schedule $\sum MR$. Point X marks the intersection of the MC and $\sum MR$ schedules, with $0Q_T$ being the total output to be produced. Where the horizontal line through X (XY) intersects with the marginal revenue schedules in each market, this determines the output which the firm should sell in the two segments – respectively $0Q_A$ and $0Q_B$. The prices to be charged in these two markets are $0P_A$ and $0P_B$, with the different prices reflecting the varying elasticities of demand in segments A and B. As noted, these markets could be a domestic and foreign market or two segments of a single national market.

It is not readily possible to illustrate all the alternatives for price discrimination which exist within an MNE. The parent MNE and its affiliates can practice both international and domestic price discrimination. In the latter instance, practice may be similar to that of a domestic firm operating in different regional markets or in industrial market sectors where elasticities of demand differ (as for example in the segments of the market for car components). Where an MNE practices international price discrimination, then it may be operating in a similar manner to a national firm which varies its domestic and export prices. In either case, price discrimination will normally be accompanied by general market segmentation policies, through, for example, product differentiation or export restrictions on affiliates. The MNE will usually be able to discriminate over a wider range of price and output because of the existence of an integrated system of manufacturing, distribution and service and because of its relative bargaining power in different markets. But actual practice may be very varied, and may not be linked very directly to profit goals. For example, the MNE may sell at a loss in a certain market in order to gain access to the market, to drive out competition or for some other short-run purpose. In international trade terms, this tactic is termed predatory dumping and is usually followed by an increase in prices after the market has been established or the competition eliminated.[23]

Another important set of alternative policies open to the multi-plant firm are associated with *transfer pricing*. Where the activities of a company involve the transfer of products and services between plants or offices, there is an inherent problem of arriving at appropriate charges. In the absence of external markets, the unfinished goods or in-house services involved in these exchange processes must be subject to agreed shadow prices. Even in cases where external markets do exist, managerial discretion is required to determine how appropriate such market prices are to intra-company transactions. The MNE has areas of discretion beyond those of the domestic multi-plant firm. Oligopoly and international operations combine to widen the scope. While there are constraints from customs and taxation authorities when pricing goods and services across international boundaries, the MNE can frequently determine prices on a purely accounting basis in order to maximise overall profits. An important part of income which parent companies receive from their foreign affiliates consists of compensation (largely in the form of royalties and licence fees) for technology transferred overseas. This area offers considerable scope for price discretion. In addition, there are many circumstances where the MNE may require to transmit profits from host country to parent or between host countries by pricing. For instance, where limits are imposed by a host government on income remittances, profits can be withdrawn by high management fees being charged for supervision and advice from the parent company. Again, political pressures may require that a loss-making subsidiary be shown to be in profit by reducing the cost of parts bought in from other affiliates of the same parent. Significant international differences in tax rates and tariffs and expectations of exchange rate variations can both play a part in the adjustment of internal pricing policies.

Some of the earliest theoretical work on transfer pricing was that undertaken by Hirshleifer.[24] Figure 3.6 illustrates the basic principles in two market situations, firstly, where a competitive external market exists, and secondly, where there is no external market. The model assumes a corporation with two divisions (which may be taken as a parent MNE and one of its affiliates or two MNE affiliates): I, the input division; and O, the output division, which manufactures the transferred product before selling to the final market. In Fig. 3.6(a) which assumes a *perfectly competitive market* for the transferred product, D_1 is the demand curve for this transferred product; MC_1 is the marginal cost curve of division I; D_O and MR_O are the demand and marginal revenue curves for division O. NMR_O is the net marginal revenue curve of division O, which is obtained by subtracting the marginal costs of processing and distribution of division O from the marginal revenue curve of that division. (Essentially therefore NMR_O represents the marginal costs involved in purchasing the transferred product.) Group profit maximisation requires both divisions to operate at the point where $MR = MC$. Given the transfer price rule that products should be transferred at the market price, profit maximisation for division O is at $0Q_O$ since at this output NMR_O equals the marginal cost of purchasing the transferred product, that is equals the marginal cost of purchasing the transferred product, that is D_1. In this situation there is an output shortfall (Q_O-Q_1) which is made up by the firm purchasing the transferred goods on the open market at the ruling price.

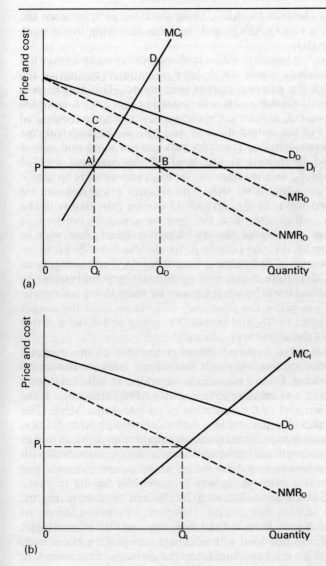

Fig. 3.6 Transfer pricing. (a) Product with a competitive external market: transfer price rule = market price (b) Product with no external market: transfer price rule = marginal cost of production.

Only this strategy maximises group profit since if division I has to raise output by Q_1Q_o, costs additional to making a purchase from the open market would have to be incurred. These extra costs are represented by the triangle ABD, being the difference between the costs to division I of Q_1ADQ_0 and the costs of buying in the open market of Q_1ABQ_0.

In practice, many transfers within multinational companies take the form of intermediate goods which have no external market or are goods for which the external market is imperfect. This former case where no external market exists is illustrated in Fig. 3.6(b). Here D_0 and NMR_0 represent, as before, the average revenue and net marginal revenue curves of the output division, and MC_1 is the marginal cost curve of the input division. Transfers between the input and output division should be priced at the level of the marginal cost of production, which, as the diagram shows, produces group profit maximisation at output level $0Q_1$. The transfer price rule can be operated in two ways: firstly, division O can be provided with the schedule MC_1, which can then be used as a supply function in establishing the quantity of the transferred product they wish to purchase. Secondly, division I can be given the schedule NMR_0 to use as a demand curve in determining output levels. The managers of division I will thus have a range of price/quantity combinations to operate against and it will be advantageous for them to expand output so long as MC_1 is below the price they will obtain from the output division. At a price of $0P_1$ and output $0Q_1$ group and division profit maximisation is simultaneously attained.

These models serve to direct attention to some of the practical problems of price, output and profit maximising decisions connected with transfer pricing. From a managerial viewpoint an efficient system of transfer pricing is a necessary concomitant to divisionalisation in the large corporation and to the operation of an integrated MNE. The transfer price rules incorporated into the models would permit division or affiliate managers to profit maximise as autonomous units, as well as facilitating group profit maximisation. Thus problems associated with management motivation in divisions or affiliates are reduced. For example, a transfer price policy which continually results in paper losses in an affiliate which is known to be efficient by other measures, could act as a serious disincentive. However, alternative means of budgetary control have been devised to ensure that affiliate managers within an MNE are provided with adequate non-profit goals in such circumstances. This is a key issue, for as the earlier section indicated, even if the overall objective of the MNE is the maximisation of group profits, at the individual affiliate level numerous alternative goals may be specified by the parent corporation. In this sense the models presented are over-simplistic not only because of the assumption of both group and division profit maximisation, but because they fail to consider any of the inter-country factors which may encourage manipulative transfer pricing. Variations in tax rates, tariffs, exchange rates, legislation etc. are the crucial factors in determining transfer pricing policies in multinational companies.

Although price discrimination and transfer pricing are at the centre of MNE operations, other widely practised aspects of oligopoly pricing behaviour may be observed. For example, *entry-limit pricing* can be an important weapon for the MNE, particularly in a market where technological advantage is receding and indigenous investment increasing. Behind the hypothesis of a limit price is the assumption that, in the long run, earnings will be greater under a price low enough to discourage entry than under a higher price that induces entry. The entry-limiting price will be higher the greater the barriers to entry, whether these consist of economies of scale, product differentiation advantages, patents or preferential access to raw materials. By following such a price policy, even if competitors are not completely excluded from an industry, they may be prevented from earning a satisfactory level of profits. Therefore, the promotional effort necessary to gain a significant market share may not be sustainable. Futhermore, *tying contracts* and *exclusive dealing agreements* (as for example where a computer hardware company insists that buyers purchase their software) can allow an MNE to gain economies of scale, discriminate in pricing, and again restrict entry. *Cartelisation* (both globally and in particular markets), involving agreements over price, output, market areas, productive capacity and advertising expenditures, is a further area where multinationality automatically increases the scope and pay-off. In all these cases being multinational merely increases the number of variations which can be introduced on well understood themes. But because of ambiguities in the anti-trust laws of different countries and other reasons, controls over *international* oligopolies are often not readily implemented.

In spite of the justification presented earlier for certain pricing policies, as for example price discrimination, it is obvious that many of the price strategies operated in the markets in which MNEs compete are inimical to efficiency and cannot be reconciled with the need to increase the private market appropriability of the returns from investment in new information.

(c) The efficiency of the MNE

The final measurement of MNE efficiency can only be determined by a considered weighing of costs and benefits. Inevitably the outcome of such analysis will depend on the valuation preferences of the viewer, whether home country, host country or the MNE itself. However, within the immediate context of this chapter the concern is with the private efficiency of the MNE as a business unit.

At this stage, it is necessary to focus on two of the central concepts which underly the economic measurement of efficiency and apply them to the MNE. One measure is to examine how closely the firms in an industry approximate to the lowest attainable costs for the actual outputs which they produce and distribute. This *technical efficiency* (X-efficiency) of an industry has two main determinants. The first is the efficiency of its market organisation. This is shown, for example, when existing plant size is compared with the size at which lowest unit costs are possible and when long-run capacity utilisation is compared to the most economical rate of utilisation. The second aspect concerns the internal efficiency of the individual member firms, especially in operating along cost minimising production functions. The degree of oligopoly makes it difficult to measure the efficiency of many markets in which MNEs operate. Regarding internal efficiency, an MNE may act as a catalyst by inducing a response from indigenous firms who compete with it or who are suppliers or customers. Differences in productivity, plant utilisation, and managerial skills might be indicators of technical efficiency within the MNE, but care should be taken in interpretation of these measures. Taking plant utilisation, for instance, some surplus might be necessary in order to allow high demand to be sustained over a longer period, and thus the output and employment gain might exceed the increase in unit costs from having lower loads at other times.

The second concept of efficiency is that of *allocative efficiency*. This measure concentrates on the size of a firm's output as judged by the relationship between its long-run selling price and its long-run marginal costs of production. In practice, measures evolved from this relationship are usually ratios such as the ratio of selling price to long-run average costs or average profits to investment stock and so forth. There are recurring problems in any inter-firm or inter-industry price/cost margin or profit rate comparisons. It will already be clear that these are heightened by MNE pricing policies. Evaluating profit rates is no less problematic. Even if a direct basis for comparison were possible and for example 'excess' MNE profits were identified, there would remain issues such as risk and innovation rewards to be considered.

Concluding comments

As the foregoing has indicated, many of the characteristics of MNEs seem to be those of international oligopolists and it would therefore appear that their behaviour patterns could be analysed within an oligopoly framework. Hence some of the newer theories of the firm which take specific account of characteristics of modern industry such as oligopoly, seem to be readily applicable to the MNE (although the wide differences between possible objectives at parent company and affiliate level cannot be handled easily by the theories). Similarly the well-known pricing practices of MNEs may apparently be assessed within an oligopolistic model. But it would be incorrect to take this interpretation too far, and reference to the theory of information is particularly important in facilitating a more plausible explanation of certain aspects of MNE behaviour, while maintaining the link with the theory of foreign direct investment as presented in Chapter 2.

Because of the public goods nature of new information its private market appropriability is low and consequently private markets will underinvest in information creation. In comparison with other private firms, however, multinational enterprises are better placed to appropriate the full value of new information. MNEs are able to do this by internalising activities within the firm itself across national frontiers, thereby protecting the new information from outsiders, and by the operation of practices such as price discrimination. Price discrimination in this sense is necessary for social efficiency, for without it, appropriability of the returns from creating new information would be low, and in the longer term, investment in the creation of new information would be reduced. Equally important points emerging from the links between the theory of information and the theory of foreign direct investment are, firstly, that firm size will tend to increase as MNEs seek to appropriate the returns from their investments in new information; and, secondly, that MNEs emphasise sophisticated technologies because appropriability is higher than for simple technologies.

Therefore, some of the activities which are casually labelled oligopolistic and exploitive may be necessary to ensure an adequate return from investment in information. But not all MNE practices may be viewed in this light: the operation of restrictive pricing practices to raise entry barriers etc. are undoubtedly efficiency inhibiting. What the theory presented in the present chapter has done is perhaps to strengthen the arguments provided by the internalisation model of Chapter 2 in highlighting the compatibility of multinationality with economic efficiency, at least under certain circumstances. It should be noted in conclusion that even if MNEs have a greater incentive than other private firms to invest in new information, this says nothing about their effectiveness in creating this information. As was pointed out, smaller firms seem to be more effective in translating investment in information into actual new products and processes.

The economics of the MNE: some empirical evidence

The objectives of the MNE

The theory section has already drawn attention to the problems of distinguishing between parent and affiliate behaviour in the MNE and to the general complexity of identifying motivation from the actions of corporations. These problems are heightened by the serious difficulties in obtaining suitable statistical data to permit effective testing of the various hypotheses relating to the objective function of the MNE. Further, much of the 'evidence' emerges from studies which concentrate on the corporations as a whole, and from research which has not been directly designed to study objectives as such.

Some work has been undertaken to test non-profit maximising theories. Studies, for example by Behrman and Stubenitsky, indicate that output growth alone or growth and sales maximisation (subject to a profit constraint) are the principal stimuli to foreign direct investment.[25] Some of the interview evidence presented to support these conclusions is open to various interpretations. Thus growth and profits are readily confused by executives, or, in some instances, are a surrogate for each other. Even in cases where executives claim that only a (minimum) profit constraint operates when deciding on investment abroad, it could be that the required percentage return is equal to the cost of capital, in which case this decision rule is consistent with profit maximisation.

The principles of the behavioural theories of the firm underly the work of Aharoni, and Miller and Weigel.[26] Aharoni emphasises various characteristics of the foreign direct investment process which he concludes are contrary to profit maximisation. These include the dependence on external stimuli to motivate serious search for overseas opportunities, and the goals of individual executives leading to 'undesirable projects' being pushed. Again some of these could readily be interpreted otherwise. For example, where the expected returns from extensive search of opportunities, markets, locations, etc. are low, then the firm (especially if it is relatively small) could be justified in rejecting a costly reconnaissance exercise. Therefore, such Aharoni-type behaviour *may* be profit maximising. However, if project opportunities offering returns significantly above the cost of capital were not being identified, then clearly behaviour could not be reconciled with profit maximisation. It is certainly not possible to explain away all of Aharoni's results as disguised profit maximisation, particularly the evidence that management's expectations of both risks and returns *before* search is biased against investment.

A high proportion of the investment functions which have been estimated for the MNE have their origins in neo-classical profit maximisation theory. One area where strong indications of profit-oriented behaviour have been identified is in the determination of plant and equipment expenditures of foreign subsidiaries and in the flow of direct investment. Various authors have shown conclusively that both foreign plant and equipment expenditures by US subsidiaries and the flow of direct investment are highly correlated with either affiliate sales or some measure of total output for the industry, economy or region concerned.[27] These findings are broadly consistent with forms of profit maximising behaviour. Similarly Knickerbocker's work on oligopolistic interdependence showed that 'bunching' of entry was significantly correlated with both US industry concentration indices and with the profitability of investment abroad in the relevant industry; a profit motive could again be construed from these results.[28] It would not be expected, of course, that the action of oligopolists in simultaneously entering a foreign market would itself lead to profit maximisation in each venture.

Taking an overview of the weight of evidence and the interpretation placed upon it by researchers, it is reasonable to conclude that profit maximisation theories are broadly supported by MNE behaviour, taking the corporation as a whole.[29] Thus MNE strategies and investment plans are primarily based on expectations of return and on risk calculations. Even so, a straightforward conclusion is not possible. Different researchers have operated under different assumptions and inevitably emphasise different variables. To be on safest ground it is probably wise to view MNE behaviour as a form of constrained profit maximisation, where financial, structural, environmental and general resource variables limit pursuit of maximum profits. Moreover while constrained profit maximisation may be the parent company goal, widely differing objectives will be pursued at affiliate level in order to achieve this corporate objective in the long run.

The dynamics of the MNE

(a) Research and development in MNEs

Large firms (many of which are multinational) operating in oligopolistic market structures, have undoubtedly played an important role in producing information. This information in turn has both caused, and been sustained by, the rapid growth of such corporations. It has been contended by Galbraith and others that a market structure in which a few large firms compete in an industry is an almost perfect one for inducing technical change. However, there is conflicting evidence on the relationship between firm size, market structure and R & D. For example, Mansfield concludes that as far as expenditures on R &D are concerned, the indications are that there is usually no tendency for the ratio of R & D expenditures to sales to be higher among the large companies than among their smaller competitors.[30] Nor is it clear that the speed of commercial introduction of new products and processes is more rapid in oligopoly. In fact greater concentration might produce slower rates of diffusion. This latter view is also supported, in relation to multinational firms, by Baran and Sweezy, who stress that the important feature of MNEs is their ability to control the rate at which new technologies are adopted.[31] In doing this, it is suggested that they are guided more by the overall impact which the new knowledge will have on corporate profitability than on the immediate return from its introduction in a particular project. Bearing these reservations in mind, large and multinational companies have been shown to be major producers of new technology. For example, OECD studies published in 1968 indicated that in the US, 47 per cent of all companies employing over 5,000 people (most of whom are multinational) undertook basic research.[32] It must also be observed, nevertheless, that 91 per cent of firms in this size category had government contracts, which clearly helps to explain the research output.

There have been various attempts to quantify the importance of the innovative role of the MNE specifically, although these require careful interpretation. The actual commercial introduction of new products clearly requires considerable resources and is thus a fruitful sphere for the multinational, and some of Mansfield's data on this issue are summarised in Table 3.1.[33] The figures suggest a link between multinationality and innovative behaviour, with between one half and all innovations being introduced by MNEs during the time-periods considered. But since MNEs dominate these industries in terms of sales and assets, it might be expected that they would be responsible for most innovations; and the link between size and multinationality cannot be ignored when considering the factors influencing innovative behaviour.

Table 3.1 Percentage of innovations introduced in the US by firms with productive facilities outside the US

Industry	Time Interval	%
Iron and Steel	1950–58	51
Petroleum	1950–58	85
Pharmaceuticals*	1950–62	94
Chemicals	1960–69	100

* Only the 20 most important innovations included.

(*Source:* Mansfield, 1974, p. 169.)

As was indicated in the previous chapter, Parker is among those who have tried to quantify the relationship between research intensive activities and multinational status.[34] Due to data and definitional problems, the conclusions are necessarily tentative, but Table 3.2 presents some of the results for the US part of the sample. It would appear that there are relatively few research intensive companies which are not multinational: out of a total of 136 research intensive firms only 17 were basically uninational corporations (defined as having two or fewer foreign subsidiaries or under 5 per cent of group sales accounted for by overseas activities). To some degree this is determined by the product area in which a company operates as this affects production locations and may require multinationality to exploit technological advantage and ensure market penetration. Even with this caution, Parker's data do suggest statistically significant relationships between the intensity of research and the degree of multinationality.

The nature and distribution of R & D operations in affiliates is one aspect of the innovative activity of MNEs which has attracted attention in recent years. In part this stems from welfare and sovereignty considerations regarding affiliate status. Researchers have been fairly evenly divided on the desirability of encouraging the decentralisation of R & D to affiliates. Even where the perspective has been that of the

Table 3.2 US companies by research intensity and multinationality

	MNE*		NE*		TNE*		MNE*		NE*		TNE*	
	Nos	%	Nos	%	Nos	%	Value of sales $mill	%	Value of sales $mill	%	Value of sales $mill	%
Research intensive	108	51.4	17	26.8	11	51.4	186,809	54.6	25,168	28.2	9,240	31.2
Not research intensive	102	48.6	84	73.2	30	48.6	155,341	45.4	64,225	71.8	20,354	68.8
Total	210	100.0	101	100.0	41	100.0	342,150	100.0	89,393	100.0	29,594	100.0

* MNEs have more than 5 manufacturing affiliates in different countries or over 15% of group sales accounted for by affiliates; for TNEs the equivalent figures are 3–5 affiliates or 5–15% of sales; and for national enterprises (NEs), 2 or fewer affiliates or less than 5% of sales.

(*Source:* Parker, 1974, p. 159.)

host country it has been acknowledged that research comparative advantage should be pursued like any other comparative advantage. A good case would seem to exist for strong central R & D in multinational companies. Problems associated with financial control of R & D budgets, costs of communication and policing and potential divergence from central product policies are all reasons behind centralisation. In addition the prevention of information leakages will be easier where R & D is centralised, a major factor when appropriability of returns from investment in information creation is so important. And cultural differences among countries which may create problems for the coordination of R & D can also be overcome by centralisation.

There are, on the other hand, various reasons why MNEs may decide to establish R & D operations abroad. In the first place, it is often advantageous to maintain close links with the local market when products are being developed. Secondly, certain environmental conditions (e.g. climate) in foreign locations cannot easily be reproduced at home. Thirdly, the salaries of scientists and engineers may be lower in host countries and/or particular skills may be more readily available abroad. And finally, by maintaining overseas R & D it is easier to monitor the activities of rival firms, and developments in scientific and technical fields.

Although information is scanty, R & D abroad by US MNEs represents only 5 per cent of R & D spending in the American domestic market. Moreover, when R & D spending is related to sales, it appears that the rate of expenditure at the affiliate level is only about half the rate of private US R & D.[35] There is a limited amount of case study material relating to the international R & D operations of MNEs. Until 1961 IBM, for example, only used its overseas R & D departments to support the local market. But in the 1960s the corporation began to develop a line of computers by coordinating R & D teams in various locations in the USA and Europe, thus responding to specific market requirements and maximising design skills. This 360 line of computers consisted of six basic models; and each R & D lab was allocated one of the models so that, for instance, the medium size machine was designed in England and the smaller machine in Germany. Another study has highlighted the ways in which an MNE's product can affect the type of R & D undertaken at affiliate level. At Eastman Kodak, because the product modifications required for different markets were minimal and the technology common, the corporation adopted an integrated system of R & D labs throughout affiliates; while in a case such as Chemetron, where technical advantage consisted of market related product developments, the R & D units were largely autonomous.

In total the available data on the production of new technology by multinational firms is very inadequate, and it is easy to exaggerate the significance of MNEs by considering only R & D spending. There is evidence that large firms in general are principally important in minor improvement inventions and that small firms and independent inventors are a principal source of fundamental inventions. On the other hand technological change in many industries seems to be due primarily to a succession of minor improvements rather than to these major breakthroughs. Thus, in spite of the fact that the technology factor is probably the key to multinational operations, little can be said about the MNE's role as a creator of new information.

(b) Pricing practices in MNEs

While it is relatively easy to identify some of the theoretical principles underlying pricing in international oligopoly, there is a scarcity of empirical work on pricing practice. Indeed the role of price within the marketing mix is not clearly understood. One study set out to examine pricing decisions in 51 US multinational companies in the consumer goods field, whose size placed them within the Fortune 500.[36] Senior marketing executives were asked to rate the factors they regarded as important when pricing in overseas markets. It was found that production costs and the prices of international competitors (usually other MNEs) received equally high mean ratings, and domestic competitors' prices were also seen as an important consideration (see Table 3.3). These results emphasise the cost orientation of the executives in the sample of MNEs, while the findings on domestic and international competitors' prices are broadly consistent with international product differentiation policies.

Table 3.3 International marketing managers' ratings of potential price considerations

Overall ranking (based on mean rating)	Price consideration	Mean rating score (0–6 scale)*	No. of firms ranking item as very important
1	Production costs	4.92	22
1	International competitors' prices	4.92	20
3	Domestic competitors' prices	4.30	15
4	Consumer demand	4.24	12
5	Transportation costs	3.58	7
6	Mark-up required by middlemen (both domestic and international)	3.17	4
7	Tariffs and various taxes	3.10	4
8	Volume of advertising and promotions	1.97	1

* Where 6 means 'very important' and 0 means 'unimportant'.

(*Source:* Baker and Ryans, 1973, p. 179.)

The limitations of such interview data are clear when any attempt is made to analyse the framework within which MNE prices are established. It has been shown that a very wide, complex range of variables may affect pricing behaviour.[37] Exogenous factors, especially those such as the degree of competition and taxation levels which would influence the effectiveness of transfer pricing, were shown to be important. Similarly endogenous variables (such as the determinants of performance in different affiliates in an integrated manufacturing system), scale of operations, government policies and so on were of equal note. Faced with this enormous range of possible influencing factors, it is clear that interview results on the lines of those presented in Table 3.3 will tend to be much oversimplified.

As observed earlier, one of the most interesting (and indeterminate) areas of internal MNE operations relates to transfer pricing. In the context of this section comment is restricted to the micro aspects of corporate behaviour. Fully documented evidence on transfer pricing practices is not readily available, which is inevitable given the growing number of external bodies with a vested interest in the internal pricing activities of MNEs. Thus for example in the US the basis for internal pricing practices has to be justified to the Internal Revenue Services; and in many developing countries customs authorities frequently query, if not actually specify, the ruling price. The probing interest of unions and anti-trust investigators raises further problems. For these and other reasons which complicate individual corporate behaviour, perhaps one of the most enlightening ways to examine practice is by a case-study approach.

This method was adopted in a qualitative study of 130 companies.[38] In broad terms, a distinction was made between companies establishing transfer prices on a 'cost-plus' basis and those operating 'negotiated prices' between selling and buying units. In the former the price was clearly linked to internal costs, while in the latter, broader strategic constraints dominated. The crucial factor in deciding which approach was used in international transactions was the availability of the product to the buying unit from external sources: where external markets did not exist the 'cost-plus' formula prevailed. Negotiated transfer prices were claimed to be based on some concept of a 'competitive' price, resting between minimum supplying and maximum purchasing price. The transfer pricing system in operation had to be related to budget or profit attainment in individual affiliates so as to ensure that management motivation was maintained: as was noted previously if the method of transfer pricing had the effect of lowering profits in a particular affiliate, then clearly other criteria than profits had to be used as performance goals.

Perhaps the complexities and variety of practices on 'cost-plus' formulae are most readily understood by the representative comments from executives as reproduced in Table 3.4. None of the comments give any indication of the ways in which companies may manipulate transfer prices in response to different national conditions; but this is hardly surprising since it is unlikely that executives would admit to the use of manipulative transfer pricing. In this study most corporations claimed to establish guiding principles and apply them in a routine manner to dealings between affiliates and between affiliates and

Table 3.4 Cost formulae for transfer pricing in MNEs: selected cases

Case 1

In the exchange of goods and services between our parent company and subsidiaries or between the subsidiaries themselves, we have arrived at a formula which covers the prices of the various products of components which are exchanged. This formula does not provide the same margin of profit for the producing company as we would normally expect to receive from regular customers. It does, however, provide enough profit so that there is an incentive to the producing companies to want to provide the services and products to other companies.

(electrical manufacturing company)

Case 2

One of our principles is that the company supplying the goods and services must make a reasonable profit on the transaction – most governments will accept 10% as 'reasonable'. It would be hard to support a thesis that an independent supplier would knowingly sell to an overseas customer at a known loss, unless there were obvious long-term benefits.

Another principle is that where the economics of the market place make it impractical to maintain normal percentage of profit at both ends of the line, transfer prices will be established so that both parties (exporter and importer) can share in a reduced profit level.

(machinery and equipment manufacturer)

Case 3

We sell products to and buy products from our overseas subsidiaries at cost plus 15%. Exceptions to the foregoing are sales to our Australian and Canadian subsidiaries where the customs regulations of these two countries require that sales be effected at domestic prices in effect in country of origin.

(petroleum company)

Case 4

Basically, our intercompany pricing policies are determined at the corporate level based on information furnished by the subsidiary. The prices established cover the cost of ingredients, containers, labour, a reasonable allocation of overhead, and a fixed percentage for profit and administrative expense. At the same time the landed price to the receiving company must be competitive with their other sources of supply, i.e. we do not subsidize the manufacturing company.

(food processing firm)

Case 5

We do not negotiate prices for items purchased from the parent but, rather, charge each subsidiary the cost of producing the item plus enough to cover administrative expenses. Purchases between subsidiaries are handled similarly. Nonrelated companies wishing to purchase our products are, of course, handled through our sales organization in a normal manner.

(rubber company)

Case 6

Finished goods prices are based on an established formula, i.e. standard costs plus certain related expenses. This same formula is also used in commercial relations between one overseas unit and another overseas unit.

(rubber company)

Case 7

When we ship products from our US operations to overseas units we expect a modest profit, 5% to 10%, sufficient to satisfy IRS* requirements. This covers handling charges but overlooks, of course, top administrative overhead.

(cleaning product manufacturer)

---

* IRS is the Internal Revenue Service of the USA.

(Source: Greene and Duerr, 1970.)

parent. And indeed many of the corporations claimed that similar formulae were applied in dealings with independent buyers. It is clearly difficult to verify either the application or the stability of these practices. One of the inherent strengths of the MNE is its flexibility in deciding on the intra-firm prices for some vital inputs (e.g. costs of transferred technology) and it is not easy to conceive of static formulae being rigidly applied.

In spite of the difficulties of obtaining information on manipulative transfer pricing, interview studies have shed some light on the types of situation where transfer price adjustments are particularly applicable. For example low transfer prices might be used to offset high import duties. Again, transfer price adjustments may be required to deal with situations where goods are transferred to a highly inflationary economy and where management must decide whether prices should reflect costs as expressed in the currency of the country of origin or in the currency of the receiving country. Similarly, political instability or high levels of taxation in a host economy may induce low prices on transfers out of such a country in order to repatriate profit. Adjustments in transfer prices can also be used to raise (or lower) an affiliate's credit status, modify balance sheets, and in the US case, where tax laws have tightened since the early 1960s, provide a substitute for a tax haven. The potential applications might therefore seem to be very numerous, but the extent to which multinationals actually use manipulative transfer pricing in these ways remains in some doubt. At the one extreme Stobaugh has argued that the use of financial tools such as transfer pricing to avoid taxes is much less than imagined.[39] Supporting this view is the evidence of Reddaway, who in considering the impact of UK investment abroad, concluded that 'with one or two exceptions companies participating in the enquiry *reported* that goods are transferred from subsidiary to parent on the basis of arms-length transactions so that the bulk of imports are valued on that basis'.[40] Moreover a survey of foreign affiliates – 90 American and 25 European – operating in the UK suggested that transfer pricing 'is less useful than is often believed as a means to avoid taxes'.[41] At the other extreme, some research work reports widespread use of profit-switching transfer pricing: one empirical study of US MNEs, for instance, indicated extensive operation of transfer pricing in Latin America due to a greater exposure to exchange rate risk; and Penrose has argued that an 'integrated firm always has an incentive to adjust the international transfer prices of its subsidiaries to take advantage of corporate organisation to maximise its consolidated profit after tax'.[42] Perhaps the fairest conclusion that can be reached is that most MNEs use transfer prices to switch profits at one time or another, depending on the particular investment involved and the particular host country. But it is doubtful if many companies consistently and comprehensively operate a transfer pricing system which is designed to switch profits for the long-term benefit of the parent corporation. There are many reasons for such a conclusion, not least of which are the external constraints in the form of inquisitive customs authorities etc. Moreover, at the internal level, there are further constraints. Even if the de-motivation of affiliate management is not a problem, too frequent adjustments in transfer prices will adversely influence the effectiveness of corporate control systems for affiliates and make planning exceedingly difficult.

(c) Locational choice

The previous discussions on knowledge and pricing covered important elements relating to the efficiency of the MNE. In this section a slightly wider view is taken by considering the factors underlying the locational behaviour of MNEs, although this again may exert a major influence on performance.

Most of the major investment decisions made by MNEs have locational dimensions. Even where, for example, an expansion decision does not involve choosing a new location, the dynamics of technological advantage and plant integration will affect existing affiliates. MNEs must remain flexible in all aspects of policy, including affiliate location. Although it is reasonable to stress the importance of locational strategy in MNEs, relatively little is known of the decision making process. Studies are of two types, *ex ante* and *ex post*. Comprehensive *ex ante* data are difficult to find although many of the standard procedures employed in locational search at the domestic level may hold. On a very limited basis, some case material does exist. In IBM an interesting weighting system was found to be employed to screen locational proposals which were submitted by local executives for the siting of foreign affiliates (Table 3.5).[43] The corporate head office assigned scores on each of the criteria and those locations with the highest scores were later investigated in detail. Truly multinational companies are likely to engage in this type of dialogue between local and parent company staff, and local knowledge could be an important element in choice of site.

Table 3.5 IBM location screening process

Factor	Points
Living conditions	100
Accessibility	75
Industrialisation	60
Labour availability	35
Economics (inc. construction costs and taxation)	35
Prestige effect on company reputation	35
Community capability and attitude	30
Total	370

(*Source:* Groo, 1972.)

There are a considerable number of *ex post* studies, exploring the factors influencing choice, taking either a macro or a micro approach. Of the latter type, Blackbourn's study of US firms in Western Europe shows the importance of market size in selecting a country for operations, with labour costs the second most important factor. The importance of market size also emerged clearly from the summary of research prepared by Dunning – see Chapter 2, Table 2.5 – but most studies do not suggest such a high weighting of 'amenity' factors (as the IBM model implies). Blackbourn's results on the selection of a location *within* a chosen country lay considerable stress on the labour pool, labour costs and access to markets.[44] As in some other research, grants from all government sources were shown to have limited significance. But evidence on this latter aspect is conflicting: Schöllhammer found that tax considerations ranked third in a list of nine locational determinants for the 140 MNEs which he studied;[45] also research relating to Ireland and Scotland found that fiscal incentives were important in attracting multinational firms.[46] At the other extreme, Aharoni concludes from a study of American firms investing in South American countries that 'tax incentives are not much more than a very costly and non-selective advertising device'.[47]

There have been some recent attempts to formally incorporate political factors into location models and apply these to MNEs. One study points to political considerations playing a negative role in the decision process.[48] Thus instability may deter an investment but a stable political environment might not in itself encourage foreign direct investment.

It is not possible to claim that all MNE locational behaviour is readily predictable, because of the political and social as well as economic elements in the choice. Long-run dynamics are also vital: there is already some evidence that US MNEs, as primarily market centred organisations, will tend to concentrate their European investment in locations closer to the centre of Europe as the EEC develops.[49] Similarly, some corporations have already changed the emphasis of their investment allocation from Europe to Third World countries. It is clear that some of the effects of such policy changes have significant political and social implications. Indeed the impact, or prospect, of these influences underlie many proposals for control of MNEs. It would be wrong to over-dramatise this point, nevertheless. In reality MNEs may only be slightly less subject to locational inertia than other companies. Moreover not all MNEs are in 'footloose' industries; indeed many have high fixed capital investment on each site. Even so, the fact that they have more flexibility than the single plant or national company should be a further factor making for improved performance.

(d) Assessing the efficiency of the MNE
There is widespread belief that MNEs by definition must be more efficient (from both technical and allocative viewpoints) than

indigenous industry. High capital investment, advanced technology, innovatory management and the concentration of investment in high growth sectors all support such predictions. The empirical evidence reviewed in this section, however, shows the need for a more balanced view.

Table 3.6 Profitability* of US affiliates and leading UK companies in manufacturing industry (1950–73).

Period (5-year averages)	UK quoted companies	US affiliates in the UK	US profitability as % of UK profitability
1950–54	9.5	18.2	192
1955–59	8.8	16.2	184
1960–64	7.7	11.6	151
1965–69	6.8	10.2	150
1970–73†	8.8	10.6	120

* Rate of return on capital, here defined as trading profits less depreciation less taxation divided by total net assets.
† 4 year period.

(*Source:* Dunning, 1976, p. 81.)

The evidence presented in Table 3.6 points to higher profitability in US affiliates as compared with quoted companies in the UK, although in this case a relative decline in US profitability is indicated: the rate of return in US affiliates was almost double that of UK quoted companies during the 1950s, about 50 per cent higher in the 1960s and 20 per cent greater in the early 1970s. In general profitability evidence tends to favour MNE affiliates in most host countries. Similarly, where productivity measures (for capital and labour) are used as indicators of efficiency, they suggest better performance in MNEs. Data problems again pose serious problems for most studies. Thus, for example, it has been shown that productivity in the North American operations of international companies is higher than in their European operations and that productivity in Germany and France is higher than in UK affiliates.[50] It is however very difficult to distinguish between corporation-specific factors and country-specific factors in explaining such differences. Indeed such an exercise is often difficult for the MNE itself.

In an attempt to undertake more objective tests of the effect of MNE competition on the efficiency of host country firms, Caves examined the operation of MNE affiliates in Australia and Canada.[51] It was hypothesised that the impact of MNE subsidiaries on allocative efficiency within host countries could be discerned from an inverse relationship between the profit rates of domestic firms and the competitive pressure supplied by foreign firms, as represented by the share of an industry's sales controlled by subsidiaries. The assumption behind this was that by reducing the excess profits earned by domestic competitors, allocative efficiency would be improved. Foreign investment may also compel higher technical efficiency in competing domestic firms and to test this the relationship between productivity levels and the MNEs' share of an industry's sales was estimated. Although the data were limited, the profits in Canadian industry did show a weak tendency to vary inversely with the foreign share, so giving slight support to the allocative efficiency hypothesis. With regard to technical efficiency it was found that subsidiary shares were unrelated to productivity levels in Canada (a result which Caves felt was due to the impact of Canadian tariffs); but a positive relationship was identified between subsidiary shares and the level of productivity in competing domestic firms in Australia. While these results are of considerable interest, conclusions can only be drawn very tentatively given data deficiencies.

One of the most interesting recent studies in this area is that by Solomon and Ingham.[52] They set out to compare MNE affiliates and indigenous companies in the mechanical engineering industry in the UK. It may be hypothesised that the tendency for MNEs to concentrate in sectors which were technically sophisticated, and had high profits and rapid growth, might be largely responsible for the profitability and expansion record of these companies and for their higher labour productivity and better export performance; further, more efficient location policies than were found in British industry might account for part of the improved performance of US affiliates. On analysing relative performance characteristics in the study sector, it was concluded that the apparent differences between MNE subsidiaries and indigenous companies were indeed significantly biased by a failure to take account of the industrial and regional distribution of direct foreign investment. For the mechanical engineering industry it was shown that when this bias was removed, indigenous firms had higher labour productivity and exported more than the American affiliates; also the MNE affiliates did not earn significantly larger profits or grow more quickly. This does not undermine the case for encouraging foreign direct investment as a means of improving industrial efficiency; rather, it suggests that the characteristics of MNE advantage have been incorrectly specified. The authors argue from the results that the claim that multinational industry introduces qualities of technological innovation and superior management to host countries is undermined: that is, MNEs may not increase technical efficiency. Even so, the fact that executives within the MNE are able to choose areas of activity which are profitable, rapidly expanding etc. also indicates a managerial skill which is not present within indigenous industry.

Some of these issues will be dealt with further in Chapter 5 when the impact of multinational firms on host countries is dealt with specifically. Summarising the available evidence, however, Parry concludes that on balance MNEs probably increase technical efficiency in host countries both through their own superior production efficiency and by inducing greater efficiency in indigenous firms.[53] But the gains may only be once-for-all gains following new entry by MNE affiliates and these benefits 'may be eroded by inefficient industrial structure; inappropriate plant; and, perhaps, excessive product differentiation by the established MNE over time'.[54] With respect to allocative efficiency, the argument is that entry of multinational firms into host countries will break down existing barriers to entry and increase competitive pressures. Conversely, there is evidence of multiple MNE entry into some host countries (on the 'follow-the-leader' model) which inevitably creates excess capacity and represents allocative, resource-use inefficiency. Similarly, manipulative transfer pricing may distort the allocative mechanism so that factor use reflects incorrect price signals.

The empirical evidence presented in this section can be seen to have contributed a certain amount to an understanding of the internal operations of multinational enterprises. Inevitably, however, because of the need to rely upon case study and interview data the results are neither comprehensive nor particularly satisfactory. Much of the empirical research, moreover, has not been designed to test the theory. As a consequence little more can be said about the important inter-relationships between firm size, multinationality, pricing practices and information creation. Cause and effect is still no more clearly evident. Thus, for instance, it is still not possible to judge whether oligopolists are more likely than other firms to invest in information because their position enables them to appropriate the returns, *or* whether causation runs the other way with firms which invest in information expanding in order to fully appropriate the returns through internalisation. Furthermore because of the reliance on interview data there remains a great deal of uncertainty over the extent to which firms do or do not use manipulative, profit-switching transfer prices.

Fortunately, most of the topics which have been covered in this chapter are developed again later in the book: the information/technology issue arises in the context of technology transfer in Chapter 5 and in the context of host country control of the MNE in Chapter 6. The subject of transfer pricing arises in these and in other chapters; and the impact of the MNE on the efficiency of host country firms also comes up again. The discussion within the previous pages does not, therefore, represent the final remarks on the topics concerned.

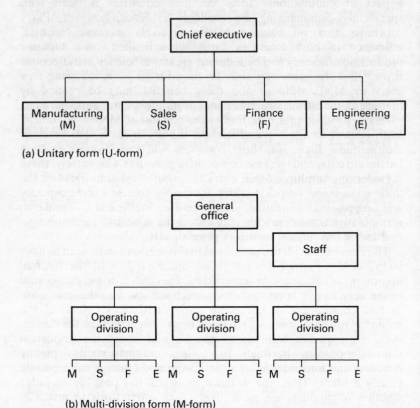

Fig. (App.) 3.1 Organisational form in corporations (unitary form and multi-division form) (*Source*: Williamson, 1970).

Further reading

1. For a thorough review of the applicability of theories of the firm to the MNE see:
   T. Horst, 'The theory of the firm' in J. H. Dunning (ed.), *Economic Analysis and the Multinational Enterprise,* London: George Allen & Unwin, 1974, pp. 31–46.
2. For readers who wish to revise their knowledge of theories of the firm as a background to the chapter there are a wide range of suitable texts. Among those most helpful for this purpose are: **W. D. Reekie,** *Managerial Economics,* London: Philip Allen, 1975, Ch. 2, pp. 30–54; **D. C. Hague,** *Managerial Economics,* London: Longman, 1974, Ch. 2, pp. 28–46; **J. R. Wildsmith,** *Managerial Theories of the Firm,* London: Martin Robertson, 1973.
3. Reekie is also useful for a review of pricing behaviour in oligopolistic markets (Reekie, *op. cit.* Ch. 7, pp. 159–207). For a specific application in the international field, see **C. P. Kindleberger,** *International Economics,* Homewood, Illinois: Irwin (5th ed.), 1973, Ch. 9.

4. The public-goods aspect of new information is considered in H. G. Johnson, 'The efficiency and welfare implications of the international corporation', 1970, reprinted in J. H. Dunning (ed.), *International Investment*, Harmondsworth: Penguin Books, 1972, pp. 455–75. An excellent article which develops an appropriability theory of foreign investment from this basic characteristic of information is: **S. P. Magee**, 'Information and the multinational corporation: an appropriability theory of direct foreign investment' in J. N. Bhagwati (ed.). *The New International Economic Order*, Cambridge, Mass.: MIT Press, 1977, pp. 317–40.

5. In order to consider a broader view of the economics of operating MNEs, such as that normally associated with international business programmes, see for example: **R. H. Mason, R. R. Miller** and **D. R. Weigel**, *The Economics of International Business*, New York: Wiley, 1975, particularly Ch. 10–15 inclusive, pp. 225–389; and **M. Z. Brooke** & **H. L. Remmers**, *The International Firm*, London: Pitman, 1977, particularly Parts 1 and 2.

Questions for discussion

1. Evaluate the contention that MNEs operate under a form of constrained profit maximisation.

2. Illustrate the ways in which an MNE operating on the organisational coalition model of Cyert and March would be subject to changes in strategy over time and in different locations.

3. To what extent does the X-theory of the firm contribute towards an understanding of the differences between parent intentions and affiliate behaviour?

4. In the light of the theory of information, can the multinational enterprise ever produce and diffuse knowledge in a way which will meet the demands of social welfare?

5. Indicate the links between the theory of information and the theory of foreign direct investment.

6. Why is price discrimination so important as a marketing weapon for the MNE?

7. 'Research and development requires size for its funding and multinationality for its exploitation.' Discuss in the light of the different patterns of foreign direct investment from the US and Japan.

8. Are the data on transfer pricing rules in Table 3.4 compatible with 'arm's length' price relationships between parent and affiliate?

9. Examine some of the reasons why it could be expected that productivity (of labour and capital) would be higher in MNEs than in indigenous companies.

Chapter 4

Multinationals and international trade

Summary

1. Neither classical Ricardian trade theory nor neo-classical Heckscher-Ohlin (H-O) theory can explain foreign direct investment. The reason is that both theories assume factors of production to be completely mobile within individual countries, but completely immobile between countries.

2. The more recent neo-factor trade theories (which extend the basic H-O model) and neo-technology theories (which develop the Ricardian approach) are more relevant to foreign direct investment and the MNE. The neo-factor theories introduce additional factors of production, specifically human capital and natural resources; while the neo-technology theories introduce technology, economies of scale, product differentiation etc. as explanations of trade flows.

3. Independently, similar explanations for foreign production were emerging from theorists of international investment; and the theories of trade and direct investment began to converge and overlap. For example, neo-technology theories were paralleled by the ownership-specific variables in theories of foreign investment (see Chapter 2).

4. Efforts are now being made to develop a generalised theory of international production drawing together trade and investment theory. This is necessary since decisions to export, to produce abroad or to license a foreign manufacturer are often alternative options for the same firm.

5. This approach is important because it indicates the circumstances under which neo-factor and neo-technology trade theories may or may not be adequate *per se* to explain MNE-generated trade. For example, Taiwan's comparative advantage may be derived from the availability of unskilled labour (neo-factor basis for trade); but MNEs may set up production activities in order to combine their ownership advantages (neo-technology factors) with the locational advantages of Taiwan. Exports may therefore appear to be based on neo-technology, or neo-factor plus neo-technology components. Also it may not be possible to explain intra-MNE trade in terms of trade theory if transfer prices do not reflect the value of factor inputs used.

6. Strong empirical support exists for the neo-factor and neo-technology theories as determinants of international trade flows, and similar explanatory variables also broadly account for foreign investment.

7. On the choice between the various forms of international involvement, the larger the size of firm the greater seems to be the propensity to produce abroad rather than to export. When the servicing of particular foreign markets is considered, high tariff barriers and large host country market size seem to be important factors encouraging direct investment rather than exporting. Models aiming to incorporate both these ownership- and location-specific variables and thereby test the theory of international production have had only limited empirical success.

8. Multinational firms are major traders: in 1970 exports of US MNEs represented almost one quarter of total world exports, and nearly two-thirds of American exports. On an intra-firm basis, it has been shown that 30 per cent of UK exports in 1973, 29 per cent and 59 per cent respectively of Swedish and Canadian exports in 1975, and about 50 per cent of US exports in 1974 took the form of intra-company transactions. Numerous studies have been undertaken to test the interaction between MNE trade and investment. The results indicate that for US MNEs significant complementarities exist between foreign affiliate production and parent company exports. These additional exports take the form of materials and components for further processing, finished products for resale etc. Evidence relating to the trade performance of the foreign affiliates themselves is much more mixed. Overall there is little evidence to indicate how aggregate MNE-generated trade influences the growth of world trade as a whole or nations' comparative advantage.

World trade flows

In the two decades following the early post-war reconstruction of the European economies, world trade expanded at an unprecedented rate. Between 1960 and 1970 alone the volume of trade more than doubled, and in spite of world-wide recession, rose by a further 30 per cent from 1970 to 1975. The expansion in value terms appears even more dramatic: the value of world exports rose from $78 billion in 1953 to $880 billion in 1975. Even allowing for the distorting impact of the higher rates of price inflation experienced in the 1970s – partly a consequence of the huge rise in oil prices at the end of 1973 – the growth is still impressive. It is only in very recent years that the expansion of world trade has slackened perceptibly. With gloomy macro-economic conditions and particularly high unemployment, protectionist pressures have been increasing in many states. The European countries and the United States have focused their complaints on Japan and low-wage Third World nations, and the outcome has been schemes such as the multi-fibre agreement to control the flow of imports from the less developed countries.[1] It is doubtful therefore if world trade will resume its pre-1970 rate of growth in the foreseeable future.

The major component of the expansion in trade until the early 1970s was the growth of exports of manufactured goods (Table 4.1). From the last quarter of the nineteenth century until the end of the 1930s, primary products accounted for a fairly stable 60 per cent of world exports by value. After 1945, on the other hand, the share of primary goods in total exports declined almost continuously to a low point of 30 per cent in 1972, before recovering somewhat in the wake of the oil crisis and world shortages of some key primary commodities.

Table 4.1 World trade* by commodity group

	1960	1965	1970	1975
Value ($ billion f.o.b.)				
Manufactures	65	103	192	500
Agricultural Products	40	50	64	150
Minerals and Fuels†	22	31	52	208
Total‡	129	187	313	878
Unit Value (1960 = 100)				
Manufactures	100	103	114	217
Agricultural Products	100	101	107	228
Minerals and Fuels†	100	109	123	489
Total‡	100	103	113	244
Volume (1960 = 100)				
Manufactures	100	155	260	360
Agricultural Products	100	123	150	165
Minerals and Fuels†	100	133	195	199
Total‡	100	141	215	283

* Exports
† Includes non-ferrous metals
‡ Totals include residual and unclassified items

(*Source:* GATT, 1977.)

A number of reasons have been suggested for the turnaround in the positions of primary and manufactured goods: the income elasticity of demand for many agricultural products is low; man-made and synthetic materials have been substituted for natural raw materials; economies have been achieved by the more efficient use of primary materials; protectionism, in the form, for example, of the EEC's common agricultural policy, has adversely affected primary goods exports; and structural factors in the importing countries, e.g. the increased importance of the service sector and of industries where the raw material content is low, have had a similar effect. As Table 4.1 shows, until 1970 there was also some decline in the terms of trade, at least for agricultural products.[2]

Reflecting the marked changes in the commodity composition of trade, the direction of trade flows has altered dramatically (Table 4.2).

Table 4.2   World trade by areas (per cent of total world exports by value)

Origin	Year	Destination				
		Industrial areas†	Developing areas	Eastern trading area	Total world*	
					%	$ billion f.o.b.
Industrial areas	1953	37.2	17.5	1.1	58.7	45.99
	1960	42.4	16.4	2.3	63.8	81.89
	1965	46.9	13.8	2.5	65.9	123.26
	1970	51.4	12.6	2.8	69.2	216.45
	1975	43.3	14.7	3.9	63.8	560.05
Developing areas	1953	19.3	6.7	0.4	27.0	21.08
	1960	15.0	4.9	1.0	21.4	27.49
	1965	13.6	4.1	1.3	19.5	36.51
	1970	12.8	3.5	1.0	17.7	55.45
	1975	17.2	5.5	1.1	24.2	213.40
Eastern trading area	1953	1.5	0.6	8.0	10.1	7.91
	1960	2.2	1.0	8.5	11.7	15.02
	1965	2.5	1.7	7.4	11.6	21.73
	1970	2.6	1.6	6.4	10.6	33.35
	1975	2.8	1.5	5.5	9.7	85.50
Total world*	1953	61.4	25.4	9.6	100.0	78.34
	1960	61.9	22.8	11.8	100.0	128.30
	1965	65.1	20.1	11.4	100.0	186.90
	1970	68.7	18.3	10.3	100.0	313.10
	1975	64.7	22.3	10.6	100.0	878.00

* Including Australia, New Zealand and South Africa.
† Value of trade between the industrial areas was as follows ($ billion):

1953	1960	1965	1970	1975
29.14	54.41	87.57	160.90	380.55

By comparison, the value of intra-Western Europe trade ($ billion) was:

1953	1960	1965	1970	1975
15.35	29.49	51.14	92.79	237.66

(*Source:* GATT, 1977 and earlier editions.)

In 1953 exports from the industrial areas were valued at $45 billion, 59 per cent of the world total; by 1970, the industrial areas' exports had increased fivefold and accounted for 69 per cent of the world total. Much of this growth was represented by exchanges between the industrial countries themselves. A pattern of world trade dominated by flows of manufactured goods between the developed countries was thus emerging. More than this, however, the exchange of imports and exports between the developed countries was increasingly taking the form of intra-industry trade in differentiated products.

The rapid expansion of trade in the post-war years is closely related to the sustained growth of output and incomes experienced by the developed countries, although other factors have played an important part. Firstly, multilateral tariff reductions, negotiated under the auspices of the General Agreement on Tariffs and Trade (GATT) from 1947, have had a major liberalising effect.[3] The formation of EFTA, and both the establishment and the enlargement of the EEC, also provided a major boost to trade (see the footnote to Table 4.2). Secondly, transportation costs have declined in relation to the value of the exported goods, as a result of changing methods of haulage and handling and the changed commodity composition of trade. Thirdly, and of prime importance within the context of this chapter, the growth of trade is in some way related to the rise of the multinational enterprise.

In 1970, the exports of US multinational firms were worth an estimated $72.8 billion, almost a quarter of total world exports in that year (Fig. 4.1).[4] The growth rate of US MNE exports has also exceeded the world average, rising by 69 per cent in the five years up to 1970, in comparison with an increase of 53 per cent for total world exports.[5] A significant proportion of these exports represent intra-MNE trade or what might be termed 'administered trade': in 1970 the US parent companies exported $13 billion of commodities to their affiliates abroad; exports from the affiliates back to the parent companies were valued at $8.1 billion; and intra-affiliate exports totalled $16.1 billion. In total, trade between US MNEs represented 12 per cent of world exports; or, expressing the figures in another way, intra-MNE trade represented about half of all multinational trade. A similar pattern is shown by other studies: for example, an investigation of German-based MNEs and German subsidiaries of non-German MNEs revealed that 43 per cent of exports and 55 per cent of imports were internalised in 1972.[6] More up-to-date figures on intra-firm trade are presented later in the chapter.

Concurrently, therefore, with the rapid growth of foreign-based production, which at first glance can be considered as export-substituting, multinational firms have also recorded large increases in trade. Much of this trade is taking place between the MNEs themselves as complex, sometimes world-wide, patterns of product and component manufacture and assembly are developed. It was always

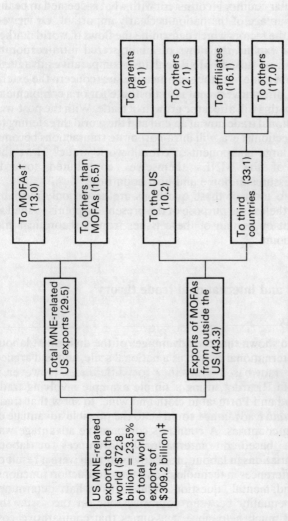

(Figures in brackets are estimated values in billions of dollars)

Fig. 4.1 The structure of US MNE-related trade* in 1970. (*Source*: US Tariff Commission, 1973.)

* Excludes imports by MNEs and their MOFAs from unaffiliated foreigners. US parents' imports from unaffiliated foreigners totalled 6.1 billion dollars.
† Majority-owned foreign affiliates.
‡ The figure for total world exports is slightly different from that given by the GATT.

the case that foreign direct investment and primary goods exports were complementary rather than competitive. From the nineteenth century onwards, firms in Europe and North America provided the capital and know-how to exploit natural resources abroad. Without this, trade in oil, rubber, timber, copper etc. would have been much reduced. The indications are, however, that foreign direct investment in manufacturing goods is also trade stimulating, and thus the key to a significant and growing portion of international trade is to be found in the development of the MNE.

The issues raised by the growth in administered trade are numerous and far-reaching. The question of whether or not MNE generated trade in a particular country is consistent with what is deemed to be the comparative advantage of the nation is clearly important. Or viewed another way, do the factors which determine the flows of world market transactions also explain the flows of administered intra-corporate trade? Deriving from this, do MNEs enhance comparative advantage and the gains from trade? Further significant issues concern the extent to which foreign direct investment is a substitute for or a complement to trade, and how this will affect the growth of trade. With the post-war boom in international trade now at an end and the world threatening to enter a new protectionist era, will intra-corporate transactions become an increasingly large component of overall world trade? Have the trade policies of the MNEs themselves contributed towards protectionist pressures in home and host countries?

The answers to most of these questions are as yet only partially available. Nevertheless the purpose of the present chapter is to shed at least a little light on certain of these issues from a theoretical and empirical standpoint.

Multinationals and international trade theory[7]

Classical theory

Adam Smith had shown that the advantages of the division of labour applied on an international as well as a national scale, and had argued the case for free trade based on *absolute* cost differences. However, it was left to David Ricardo[8], using a simple example involving trade between England and Portugal in cloth and wine, to show that trade based on *comparative* advantage could be to the possible advantage of the participating countries. A country's comparative advantage was deemed to be based on international differences in labour productivity. Variations in labour productivity in turn were a result of international differences in technology and thus production functions. The more fundamental question relates to what determines technological inequality between countries, but on this issue the theory is not of much help since it assumes that comparative cost differences are a fact of life. The reasons for international differences in technology are not therefore considered. The Ricardian model goes some way to explaining why trade occurs and the volume and commodity composition of trade flows. But the pattern of trade is considered to be virtually insensitive to demand differences and relative factor endowments. Any explanation for foreign direct investment, as opposed to trade, is ruled out by the explicit assumption of the classical theory of complete international immobility of factors of production. If this assumption is relaxed, the fact that differences in technology exist between countries is of some significance to international investment. Suppose that technological differences result in variations in the productivity of both labour and capital.[9] Then divergences in factor productivity could be exploited either by movement of goods or of factors of production. While this does not provide a sufficient explanation for foreign direct investment, the theory does at least indicate certain possible links between trade and investment through international differences in technology and productivity.

Neo-classical theory

It was in an attempt to explain *why* individual countries possess a comparative advantage in the export of given products that the factor-endowment theorem was developed by the Swedish economists Heckscher and Ohlin.[10] The Heckscher-Ohlin (H-O) theory explains a country's trade in terms of its endowment of factors of production, particularly capital and labour. In the terms used earlier, capital and labour represented the location specific endowments of countries. A country will have a comparative advantage and therefore will export those products in which its most abundant factor is used relatively intensively; conversely it will import the commodities which incorporate factors with which the country is poorly endowed. So a country which has relatively more capital than its trading partners will have a comparative advantage in and will export goods which require a high capital–labour ratio. The reason for this is that capital abundance will be reflected in a relatively lower price of capital, and of goods which utilise capital intensively. In the standard H-O theory, there can be no international direct investment since once again it is explicitly assumed that whereas factors of production are completely mobile domestically, capital and labour are completely immobile internationally. Unlike Ricardian theory, it was also assumed that production functions were the same everywhere, with information about technology being freely and instantly available in all countries.

While the fundamental ideas of Heckscher stretch back as far as 1919, what is now known as the H-O theory was not formalised fully until the 1950s in the hands of modern trade theorists such as Stolper, Samuelson, Johnson, and Jones.[11] One important development connected with the H-O model concerns the issue of factor price equalisation. Since free trade was at least a partial substitute for free factor movement, there would be a tendency for trade to contribute towards the equalisation of factor prices internationally. A country relatively well-endowed with labour will have low wages and will tend to export labour-intensive goods. Trade will raise incomes in the exporting country, and will thereby reduce or eliminate the wage differential between exporting and importing countries. The theory becomes more relevant to international investment when this assumption of factor immobility between countries is relaxed. If restrictions on trade exist between countries, then factors of production would be transferred internationally in response to differences in factor prices. In a capital abundant country, for example, capital would be exported to take advantage of higher returns available abroad; this would raise the price of capital in the capital exporting country and contribute to the equalisation of factor prices. However, there is no reason why capital should be transferred between countries in the form of direct rather than portfolio investment. Firms in the capital deficient country could borrow the cheaper capital abroad for injection into their own enterprises. In transferring and subsequently utilising the capital, the firms in this capital-deficient country are at no competitive disadvantage compared with companies in the capital-abundant area. This is so because all relevant knowledge is instantaneously and costlessly available to firms in all countries.

In spite of some evolution and refinement in the H-O model, it was not until the publication of Leontief's empirical study of the theory that major developments began to occur in the positive theory of international trade.[12] Applying input-output analysis to US data for 1947, Leontief examined how much capital and labour was required to produce $1 million of exports and import-competing goods. The findings indicated that the manufacture of US exports required a higher proportion of labour to capital than the production of import-competing goods. That is, the United States was (apparently) a capital-deficient country and specialised in labour intensive production. In the discussion which followed, there was a searching re-examination of the assumptions of the H-O theory, and a number of explanations for the 'Leontief Paradox' emerged:[13]

(i) The H-O theory assumed similar consumption patterns at different income levels. In fact, it was suggested, the US demand for capital intensive goods was much stronger than that in other countries, meaning higher prices in the US in spite of the relative capital abundance.

(ii) The H-O theory also assumed the non-reversibility of factor intensities in production. That is, the production function was such that if two commodities were being produced, one would always be labour intensive and the other capital intensive whatever the relative supply of factors and the ratio of factor prices. If this assumption is invalid then the possibility exists for the same goods to be produced by different methods in the US as compared with elsewhere. In these circumstances Leontief should not have been comparing export- and import-competing goods – with both being produced in the US; but rather with regard to imports the capital and labour requirements in each of the countries of origin concerned should have been calculated.

(iii) Leontief (as with the H-O theory) assumed only two factors of production, omitting to take natural resources into consideration.

(iv) Leontief himself suggested that US labour is sufficiently superior in quality to foreign labour for the USA to be a labour-abundant economy relative to the rest of the world. This could reflect superior technology, economies of scale or greater skill acquired by the investment in education and training.

As Tables 4.1 and 4.2 showed, by the date of the publication of Leontief's results in 1953, world trade was beginning to be dominated by intra-industry trade in manufactured goods between the advanced industrialised nations. Moreover, stimulated by the enormous post-war growth in direct foreign investment, intra-MNE trade was becoming increasingly important. Perhaps Leontief's prime contribution was to reveal that the Heckscher-Ohlin model abstracted from many of the factors which explained these increasingly important sectors of world trade. Thus more recent contributions, incorporating some of the factors noted above, have attempted to bring greater realism into the H-O model. Two broad strands of thought may be identified, termed, respectively, neo-factor and neo-technology theories of trade. These extensions to trade theory, aiming as they do to explain the observed pattern of trade in manufactured goods, inevitably also come closer to the phenomenon of foreign direct investment and the MNE. The neo-technology theories focus on the role of technological advantage and economies of scale in determining comparative advantage and international trade. Neo-factor theories, on the other hand, concentrate on the role of factors of production such as natural resources and human capital in influencing comparative advantage.

Neo-factor theories of trade

One group of neo-factor trade theories emphasises the role of 'human capital' as an influence on comparative advantage independent of the usual capital and labour measures.[14] The crucial point is that labour cannot be categorised as a single factor of production. Investment in 'human capital', e.g. managerial, professional and highly skilled labour, may produce for the country concerned an advantage in the output of skill-intensive goods. Therefore either labour skills should be incorporated as a separate third factor of production or capital measures should be adjusted to take account of labour skills (producing one factor of production incorporating both physical and human capital). This human capital theory is pertinent to trade, licensing and international investment: the latter may include or be based upon the transfer of human capital between countries, while trade may be based on the export of skill-intensive goods. Similarly the licensing of processes could be derived from advantages created by human capital in one country as compared with another. The human capital theory could, of course, be reversed to take account of relative endowments of unskilled labour. In this case an abundance of unskilled labour would promote the export of goods requiring few skills.

A further extension to the two factor (capital and labour) H-O theory involves the incorporation of natural resources as a factor of production. Natural resources have been considered to be complementary to capital and labour in determining comparative advantage. Indeed when the Leontief study was reworked to include natural resources as a factor of production, the 'Paradox' of American trade patterns disappeared.[15] Apart from trade, natural resource endowments are important in explaining certain of the more traditional types of direct foreign investment. In particular, backward vertical integration by foreign firms to gain access to raw material supplies is a common phenomenon.

These neo-factor theories represent extensions to the basic H-O theory of international trade, which focused on relative endowments of labour and capital. The introduction of other tangible factors of production undoubtedly increases the relevancy of the theory. Equally, the links between trade and international investment became clearer. However, the economic environment assumed by the neo-factor theories is still basically that of a competitive world economy. The neo-technology theories, on the other hand, take imperfect competition as their starting point and concentrate on differences in the production functions of enterprises.

Neo-technology theories of trade

While the neo-factor theories extend the H-O model, the neo-technology trade theories develop the classical Ricardian approach in assuming that comparative advantage derives from international differences in technology. The theory of *'technological gap'* exports originated from an article by Posner in 1961, who argued that trade will take place during the time lag while the rest of the world imitated the innovation of a firm or industry in a particular country.[16] The ability to innovate and create a quasi-monopoly position is attributable to a greater capacity to undertake research and development. Unlike the Ricardian approach, therefore, which based comparative advantage on unspecified technology factors, the technology gap theory introduces R & D as the means of creating innovations. The dynamic technological advantage obtained will gradually be eliminated as technology becomes standardised internationally. At this stage when production functions between countries again become similar, the pattern of output and trade will be determined by the static Heckscher-Ohlin conditions of relative factor endowments. This means that comparative advantage will favour locations with low labour costs.

The role of R & D in trade performance is well recognised, but the technological gap theory does not indicate why innovations occur in some countries rather than others. One explanation for this is provided by Vernon's *product cycle theory,* which indeed has many features in common with the technological gap concept. The product cycle theory sees market characteristics as the motivating force behind innovations. In the case of the United States this meant stress would be laid on innovations which were labour-saving or were designed to satisfy high income demands. The major importance of the product cycle approach lies in its appreciation of the close links between trade, foreign direct investment and the growth of the firm. While the product is 'new', costs of production are relatively unimportant; at the 'standardisation' stage, on the other hand, with competitive, probably cut-price products on the market, output costs become highly significant. At this point the innovator may look abroad for lower-cost production-locations and new markets.

Within this neo-technology group, various other theories of trade have been postulated. These may be linked under the general heading of 'monopolistically competitive theories'. One of these stresses the influence of *economies of scale* on nations' comparative advantage. A country with a large home market may be considered to have an advantage in the manufacture and export of goods produced under increasing returns to scale. Conversely a small home market may lead to the export of goods not subject to these conditions. Economies of scale are also important to Linder's *'preference similarity'* view of trade in manufactured goods.[17] According to this approach, industries expand initially to satisfy home market demand, and export once the domestic market is large enough to enable the industry to achieve economies of scale and competitive unit costs. Because the goods were designed for the preferences and income levels of the home market, exports will be directed to countries with a similar standard of living, where preferences may also be presumed to be fairly similar. Finally, in a similar manner, it has been argued that comparative advantage may be linked to *product differentiation* associated with national tastes.[18] Product differentiation to cater for particular home market tastes will create a comparative advantage in trade with countries where similar tastes exist. Minority tastes in the home country will be satisfied by imports from a country where such tastes are those of the majority.

This theory is particularly important in its relevance to intra-industry trade in industrialised products.

All of these neo-technology theories (with the exception of the product cycle model) were developed to explain flows of international trade rather than international investment. Yet independently, as Chapter 2, pp. 48–54, has indicated, models incorporating very similar variables were being formulated by theorists in the area of foreign direct investment: technology, product differentiation and economies of scale were all suggested as explanations for the growth of the multinational firm. The particular significance of Vernon's product cycle theory is that it attempted to integrate both trade and investment. Otherwise the links between the explanations for the various forms of international involvement were not investigated.

Trade barriers

Apart from the developments associated with the neo-factor and neo-technology theories, international trade theory was evolving in another direction in the late 1960s. Thus in the attempt to formulate a dynamic theory of comparative advantage, which represented a closer approximation to the real world, Johnson argued that trade barriers and trade interventions should be integrated into the theory.[19] Three such barriers have been identified:

(i) Transport costs. In classical and neo-classical trade theory, transport costs are only exceptionally taken into account. While for some products transport costs are no longer important in relation to the value of the commodity, for others geographical distance still represents a hindrance to exports. For trade to take place between two countries, price differences before trade must be wider than the costs of transfer.

(ii) Protectionism, represented by tariff and non-tariff barriers, exchange rate and taxation policies, goverment purchasing, state trading etc. The pure theory of international trade has traditionally taken these factors as exogenous for purposes of analysis, but in reality their impact is very considerable.

(iii) Cultural, political and environmental differences between countries, which influence tastes and preferences. For foreigners as compared with national citizens, these differences represent the additional costs of acquiring information about the markets for outputs and inputs.

In terms of dynamic comparative advantage, the first two groups of factors encourage the location of manufacturing facilities close to the market. The impact of the third group of factors is more complex: they are trade inhibiting in so far as exporters are affected by these inter-country differences (although the impact depends partly on the methods of distribution used in overseas markets). But they also inhibit the transfer of production because of the extra costs involved in dealing with foreign laws, tax systems and so on.

Once again, therefore, as trade theory moved closer to the realities and dynamics of international trade, so, implicitly or explicitly, the theories of trade and direct investment began to converge and overlap. The neo-factor theories had many similarities with what the international investment theorists termed the location-specific endowments of countries (see Chapter 2, pp. 58–63). The recognition of the role of barriers to trade was a further point of resemblance between trade and investment theory. The neo-technology theories again were paralleled by the ownership-specific variables incorporated into theories of foreign direct investment (Chapter 2, pp. 48–58).

Theory of international production

It was inevitable that attempts would be made to integrate the theories of trade and investment, particularly as it became clear that decisions to export or to manufacture abroad were often alternative options for the same firm. Trade represents one form of servicing a foreign market, but equally the market could be serviced by non-trade methods, i.e. by producing abroad or by licensing a foreign manufacturer. Beginning with Dunning (1973a), efforts have thus focused on drawing together the neo-factor and neo-technology theories of trade and the various theories of direct investment.[20] The aim is to develop a comprehensive theory of international production, where international production is defined so as to include both trade and non-trade servicing of foreign markets. While this seems to be the most promising approach, it would be incorrect to suggest that it is the only one. Corden, for example, has shown how overseas direct investment can be analysed within the framework of neo-classical trade theory, as various assumptions of the Heckscher-Ohlin model are dropped. Both of these approaches are considered in the following paragraphs.

(a) Neo-classical trade theory and the MNE[21]

In analysing the factors which influence the locational decisions of multinational firms, Corden takes the case of a corporation which manufactures a number of different commodities, which could be produced in any country. The following assumptions are then made:

1. In each country, production functions allow for at least three factor inputs. Two of these – physical capital goods and knowledge (human capital) – are mobile, while labour is immobile.
2. Capital and knowledge are perfectly mobile within the corporation.
3. The production functions and factor endowments facing the firm do not change over time.
4. Returns to scale are constant.
5. Trade barriers and government taxation and exchange rate policies etc. are either non-existent or do not affect locational decisions.

6. No transport costs.
7. For any given product, identical production functions in all locations.
8. Labour is homogeneous, but immobile between countries.

At this stage, the model developed differs from H-O only in so far as a third factor of production is introduced and the mobility of capital and knowledge is allowed for. In such a situation costs of production would tend to be the same in all locations and trade could cease. The mobility of capital and knowledge would equalise the returns to these factors as between the countries in which the firm operates.[22] The implications of progressively removing the assumptions of the model are then as follows:

(i) Two immobile factors (e.g. skilled and unskilled labour) and varying endowments of these factors between countries.   This involves the removal of assumption 8. With varying factor endowments, countries will specialise according to their relative abundance or scarcity of skilled and unskilled labour, as in the H-O model. Thus skilled labour-intensive products will be manufactured in the countries relatively well endowed with skilled labour.

(ii) Production functions vary.   This relaxes assumption 7. Since knowledge is mobile, production functions are assumed to vary because of the different physical infrastructures provided by governments or different political conditions etc. These influences may mean that one country is more efficient in producing most or all products. In this case the country concerned will attract the mobile factors and thus will tend to produce and export products intensive in capital and/or knowledge. However there is no reason why the transfer of capital etc. should take the form of direct investment.

(iii) Transport costs exist.   This removes assumption 6. Transport costs are trade inhibiting. At the extreme, there would be no trade and the firm would supply each country from local production; apart from this, there would be a tendency for production to be near markets.

(iv) Tariffs, import restrictions and differences in taxation exist.   This removes assumption 5. As with the existence of transport costs, tariffs and other import restrictions are trade inhibiting and provide a stimulus for local production. Differences in taxation will also influence location decisions.

(v) Returns to scale are increasing rather than constant.   The existence of economies of scale, together with different production functions and immobile factor endowment ratios will produce a tendency to centralise output of any product in only one or at least relatively few locations. Taking transport costs and protectionism

together with increasing returns, could reduce the trade inhibiting effects of the former. Countries with large domestic markets would have a comparative advantage in commodities which are economy-of-scale intensive, and enable them to export such products.

(vi) Production functions and factor endowments change over time. To the extent that such changes occur (e.g. because of increases in expenditure on education which raises the endowment of human capital), the firm will require to reallocate its resources.

(vii) Knowledge is imperfectly mobile. Knowledge and managerial know-how may only be transmitted to other countries at a cost and with lags. As knowledge abroad improves, comparative advantage may change along the lines of the product cycle theory. The static advantages possessed by a foreign country, perhaps in terms of low wages, may then outweigh the former knowledge advantage of the corporation's home country.

It is possible, therefore, to use some aspects of orthodox trade theory to derive predictions on the locational decisions of MNEs and their effects on trade flows. The proviso is that the assumption of complete factor immobility internationally, and certain other H-O assumptions, must be relaxed. The Corden approach considers only locational aspects of foreign investment decisions, derived basically, but not exclusively, from the neo-factor extensions to the H-O model. The more crucial neo-technology theories which relate to the exclusive possession of certain assets by firms are not handled adequately. As a result it is questionable how much more progress can be made within neo-classical theory. Within the variables considered above a wide range of predictions are possible. If the aim is a more comprehensive description of the real world, then an alternative approach must be sought.

(b) Trade and investment theory and foreign direct investment
Typical perhaps of the alternative approach to the problem is the work of Seev Hirsch.[23] Hirsch categorises the variables which influence international direct investment into three groups: comparative input costs; firm-specific revenue producing factors; information, communication and transaction costs, which increase with economic distance. The firm-specific factors are associated with the neo-technology trade theories, while the cost variables are inevitably affected by relative factor endowments, including those incorporated in the neo-factor theories.

Consider the case of a company located in country A which is planning to build a plant to supply a single product to a world consisting of two countries, A and B. The decision will depend upon the relationships between the following variables:

(i) P_a and P_b which represent production costs in countries A and B respectively. They include outlays on physical capital and purchases of current inputs such as labour and raw materials.

(ii) K represents firm-specific revenue producing know-how and intangible assets. Such assets have been created by investment in R & D, in advertising and promotions and in management techniques. K constitutes a form of temporary quasi-monopoly available to firms until rival companies are able to acquire the necessary skills.

(iii) M represents the cost differential by which export marketing costs exceed domestic marketing costs. The differential is made up of transport, packaging, handling and insurance costs; additional communication costs consequent on linguistic differences; and any tariffs imposed by the importing country. Formally $M = M_x - M_d$, where M_x represents export marketing costs per unit of sales and M_d represents domestic marketing costs per unit sale.

(iv) C represents the extra costs involved in controlling and coordinating foreign operations. Extra control costs are incurred when a firm establishes a plant abroad with foreign laws, taxation, language personnel procedures etc. Formally $C = C_x - C_d$, where C_x and C_d represent the costs of control and coordination in foreign and domestic operations respectively.

The conditions under which a firm located in country A will supply country B through exports or foreign direct investment can be expressed as:

Export to B if: 1. $P_a + M < P_b + K$
          and 2. $P_a + M < P_b + C$

Invest in B if: 1. $P_b + C < P_b + K$
          and 2. $P_b + C < P_a + M$

Suppose A is a high cost product manufacturer but has some advantage in the production of K. Direct investment abroad will take place if the technological and managerial advantages derived from the possession of K outweigh the extra control costs C associated with subsidiary operations. Omitting K, direct investment will be profitable if the costs of production (P_b) and control (C) in country B are less than production costs in A (P_a) plus export costs (M). (A similar relationship could also be shown diagrammatically as in Appendix 4.1). This provides an argument for locating abroad in a country as similar culturally and environmentally as the home country, thereby minimising C. Such a point has been put forward frequently to help explain why the UK obtained such a high proportion of US direct investment initially.

The variables K, M and C have a crucial role in this model. If they are zero, the most important conditions of the H-O theory are satisfied, and location of manufacture and direction of trade are determined by relative factor endowments. Since capital is mobile, portfolio investment may take place. But foreign firms do not possess any advantage over domestic firms which would enable them to profit from foreign direct investment.[24] The considerable significance of the variable K is particularly evident. The model would suggest that direct investment will be most important in technology-based industries, and this is confirmed by the evidence from US, European and Japanese multinational firms. In addition, K could represent a body of management techniques, and managerial expertise in fields such as marketing. When defined in this way, K and direct investment could be important in industries, e.g. automobiles, where the scale of production is large, thus making greater demands on organisational management ability. Similarly, direct investment could be found in industries, e.g. drugs, cosmetics, where marketing expertise is at a premium.

This discussion of the model developed by Hirsch essentially refers to an initial investment decision made by a firm with respect to a single product. The investment decision in these circumstances necessarily involves a decision to stop exporting the single 'final' good (although the parent company may still export components to its affiliate). As Hirsch states, however: 'once intermediate production and/or more goods are considered, it is no more possible to state on *a priori* grounds whether international direct investment is export-enhancing or export-replacing, from the point of view of the home country'.[25] By the process of establishing an affiliate abroad a corporation may replace exports by foreign production for some products in the line; other products which were not exported previously may then become potential exports since their competitive position has improved with the reduction in M, the export marketing cost differential. Therefore, on the key point of whether or not overseas production by MNEs substitutes for exports or increases exports, the theory, as it stands, cannot provide a straightforward answer.

This model is important for its integrative role, both in showing the conditions under which markets will be serviced by trade or direct foreign investment and in encompassing many of the individual theories of investment which were discussed in Chapter 2. It can, for example, help to explain the theory of foreign investment as an oligopolistic reaction, whereby the establishment of overseas affiliates in a given market occurs in clusters. So long as all firms are exporting they compete on equal terms, but as soon as one of the oligopolists establishes an affiliate, it eliminates M and obtains a marketing advantage abroad. To prevent this firm increasing its market share, the other companies are also required to set up subsidiaries abroad. By introducing a time element finally, and allowing for changes in relative production costs, as well as in M, C, and particularly K, the product cycle theory can be fitted into this same framework. Of course, the model requires considerable development. The nature of the advantages possessed by MNEs has not been identified carefully enough. The question of whether or not direct investment abroad is trade creating or trade inhibiting cannot be handled in a general fashion, and intra-firm trade, much involving intermediate goods, is dealt with crudely. The difficulties arise largely because multinational firms are typically multi-product companies. Once the analysis is extended beyond the single product situation, the possible alternative courses of action open to existing or aspiring MNEs increase very considerably.

Additionally the model does not clearly reveal the way in which trade and investment theory have been integrated to produce a theory of international production. And on this issue it is more valuable to refer to another attempt to produce an integrated theory of trade and investment, namely that of Dunning (1976).[26] This 'eclectic approach' distinguishes between the necessary and sufficient conditions for foreign direct investment in terms of *ownership* (the equivalent of the variable K in the model just outlined) and *location* effects, as in Chapter 2. A number of types of trade may be identified:

(i) For certain kinds of exports, it will be sufficient for the country concerned to possess a location advantage over the importing country. Trade based on relative factor endowments – capital, skilled and unskilled labour, natural resources – between the developed and less developed countries might be of this kind. This is the conventional factor and neo-factor proportions type of trade.

(ii) With respect to trade between the developed countries in differentiated consumer goods, or skill-intensive products, on the other hand, the exports may be primarily determined by the ownership advantages of the firms. For this type of trade neo-technology theory will be more relevant.

(iii) If, however, the locational endowments favour the importing country or a third country, then foreign production may replace exports. That is, the MNE uses its ownership advantages in the country where locational factors are most favourable. The firm may or may not thereafter export back to the home country from this foreign base. This explains why neither the neo-factor nor the neo-technology theories *per se* may be an adequate basis for explaining trade in which multinational firms are involved. The comparative advantage of a country such as Taiwan may lie in the production of unskilled labour-intensive goods, i.e. trade based on neo-factor theories. But these locational advantages of Taiwan may make it an attractive base for MNEs to exploit their ownership-specific advantages. The exports of Taiwan may therefore appear to be based on neo-technology factors or some combination of neo-factor and neo-technology components.

(iv) For trade between MNE affiliates and/or between the affiliates and the parent company, both groups of trade theories may be inadequate for a different reason. This derives from the fact that transfer prices may bear little resemblance to arm's length prices. As a result prices may not reflect the value of factor inputs used, and attempts to explain trade on the basis of neo-factor and neo-technology factors may be unsatisfactory or misleading.

(v) What is not indicated is why, within a particular industry, some firms become multinationals and produce abroad, while others remain in their home base and export overseas. Clearly some ownership advantages must be more important than others, and one possible distinguishing feature might be the size of firm. All other things being equal, the larger firm would have a greater ability to bear the risks associated with the movement of production facilities abroad.

The eclectic approach to the theory of international production has much to recommend it, although the theory has yet to be formalised. Until this is done many of the implications of MNEs for international trade will remain unexplored. For example, the issue of whether or not direct foreign investment substitutes for or complements trade remains teasingly unresolved. Nevertheless the integration of trade and investment theory has added at least a little to the debate over the impact of MNEs on resource allocation, and it is this issue which is now considered.

MNEs and the 'gains from trade'

With free trade and assuming perfect competition, resources will be employed so as to maximise the value of world output. Restrictions on trade however are a fact of economic life, meaning that such a first-best allocation of resources is not possible. In the sub-optimal world of second-best solutions it cannot always be postulated with certainty that a particular course of action will produce a gain. This complicates any assessment of the effects of MNEs. International firms are concerned with resource allocation between countries. Thus the establishment of a plant in a foreign country affects potential trade and the maximum value of world output. But trade policy instruments will be affecting resource allocation in any event. Therefore it is not possible to state positively whether or not the reallocation brought about by the MNEs will increase or decrease output and incomes in a particular situation.

Nevertheless, various observations can be made:

(i) When MNEs operate world-wide, they are able to take a global view and so can expand output or establish manufacturing facilities in least-cost locations. Where this happens, the MNE extends the international division of labour and enhances comparative advantage. Even if its operations are not world-wide, where the MNE transfers capital and technology (from a country well endowed with these resources) and combines these with immobile resources of labour or raw materials (in a country rich in such resources), then comparative advantage is being enhanced.

(ii) Kojima has distinguished between this 'trade-oriented' foreign direct investment which, it is argued, reinforces comparative advantage, and 'anti-trade-oriented' investment which has the reverse effect.[27] The view is that Japanese investment abroad is of the trade-oriented type, aimed at complementing the country's comparative advantage position. This includes investments in natural resource development; in traditional industries such as textiles, clothing and processing of steel; and in motor vehicle assembly, and the production of electronic components. Such investments exploit the comparative advantage of the recipient countries as represented by their endowments of natural resources and labour, and equally assist the labour and resource-scarce Japanese economy. The comparison is made with most US direct foreign investment, which is suggested as being anti-trade-oriented since it is made to protect an oligopolistic position or in response to trade barriers. Although this is not made clear, the types of investment involved would be those made by the USA in Canada and Western Europe. It is asserted that these investments came from industries which rank at the top of American comparative advantage, and therefore in the long run the competitive position of the industries concerned and of the whole American economy will be adversely affected.

What is therefore being contrasted is trade and investment between developed countries and LDCs, which is considered to be beneficial for comparative advantage and resource allocation; and trade and investment between the developed countries themselves, which is detrimental. And yet trade in manufactured goods and intra-industry trade in differentiated products between the developed countries has been the main engine behind the growth of world trade. It could not be argued that this has had other than beneficial effects for the world economy, and moreover, it has grown alongside foreign direct investment. The Kojima argument is the equivalent of saying that neo-factor based trade and investment is beneficial but not trade and investment associated with neo-technology factors and the ownership-specific advantages of firms. The product cycle model would in any event suggest that even if MNEs initially established manufacturing facilities in other developed countries, over time production would eventually be transferred to low wage LDCs for possible export back to the home country.

(A different perspective is taken on these issues in the discussion in Chapter 2, pp. 66–8).

There are still, however, other types of investment which could have adverse effects on the efficiency of resource allocation: one of these is investment, particularly in Third World countries, which utilises capital-intensive techniques and therefore fails to capitalise on the comparative advantage of such countries. Secondly, investment attracted by trade barriers may result in some waste of resources, unless the industry established develops from import substitution towards export orientation.

(iii) In interpreting his model of trade and investment, Hirsch has argued that 'international investment facilitates specialisation to a greater extent than trade, since pure exporters must incur differential export-marketing costs (M) from some of which the multinationals are exempt'.[28] Of course foreign production entails higher control costs (C), but presumably many of these would be once-for-all costs, e.g. the costs involved in understanding foreign laws and taxation systems.

(iv) Finally, to repeat the earlier comment, the impact of MNEs on the gains from trade depends on whether or not transfer prices in intra-MNE transactions differ markedly from arm's length prices.

The theory does not therefore provide an unambiguous answer to the issue of whether or not MNE's enhance the gains from trade. Investment by the industrialised countries in the LDCs, which is aimed at utilising the labour and natural resource endowments of the latter countries, is the most obviously beneficial type. But this represents a small proportion of total direct foreign investment. Cross-investment between the developed countries may or may not increase specialisation and enhance comparative advantage. There is, nevertheless, a presumption, aside from the adverse effects of transfer pricing and excluding investment of the 'oligopolistic band-wagon' type, that foreign direct investment has improved the international division of labour.

To sum up this question as a whole, international trade theory has undoubtedly made a contribution to understanding the process by which firms become multinational, and particularly to comprehending the locational policies of MNEs. In this way trade theory is also of considerable significance to the recently evolving, but still incomplete, theory of international production. The criticisms of the theory of foreign direct investment developed in Chapter 2 apply equally to international production theories, and in fact, the two are now indistinguishable, following the work of Dunning. For the future too, exporting, licensing and foreign investment need to be considered as part of a coordinated strategy of firms, and as different means of exploiting ownership-specific and locational-specific comparative advantage.

A note on tariff and customs union theory

Some comment has already been made on the impact of tariffs on the trade versus investment decision. The aim of this section is to expand the discussion so as to incorporate customs union theory. This is important given the oft-quoted argument that the formation of the European Economic Community and, to a lesser extent, the European Free Trade Area caused a very rapid upsurge in direct investment from the United States.

Suppose a firm is exporting abroad before the imposition of tariff barriers in its foreign markets. It may then decide to establish production facilities in the country or countries concerned so as to avoid the tariffs and protect its market position. If the exporting firm had built up its trade on the basis of low production costs in its home country (neo-factor trade), then the establishment of a foreign subsidiary may be a very imperfect substitute for exporting; the end-result may be lower profits. On the other hand if success had been based on technological and managerial advantages (neo-technology trade), these could be transferred intact to the foreign country. Even in this case it is arguable that the end result could be a reduction in profitability, at least in the short run. If it had been desirable the firm would presumably have established an affiliate before the tariff was introduced.

From the viewpoint of the host country, tariffs may be designed either for protection or to encourage direct investment by MNEs. In the former case, the host country is seeking to replace imports by production from domestic manufacturers. As outlined above such a policy could be circumvented by the MNE. In the latter instance the tariff is designed to encourage direct investment, so as to introduce technology-based industries into the economy, to stimulate competition and so on. But as has been shown by several writers, there is no guarantee that tariff policy will in fact encourage local production by the MNE, and there are, in addition, indirect effects to be taken into account, especially on export industries.[29]

A customs union combines elements of free trade with elements of greater protection. Because of this, it does not necessarily represent a movement towards a free trade optimum position.[30] The internal elimination of tariffs and the establishment of common external tariffs produces two conflicting *static effects:* trade creation which raises economic welfare and trade diversion which leads to a welfare loss. The positive trade creation effect is derived from the displacement of home production by imports from a lower cost partner country within the union. Trade diversion conversely involves a shift in imports from a country outside the union to a higher cost country within the union.

With regard to the role of MNEs in the customs union, attention also needs to be given to the so-called *dynamic effects*. In contrast to the once-for-all static changes produced by tariff elimination and realignment, the dynamic advantages include increased specialisation and economies of scale, the effects of increased competition and opportunities for faster economic growth.

It has been suggested that the massive volume of US direct investment in Europe after about 1955 is attributable to the combined influence of static and dynamic effects. On the one hand the trade diverting influence of the EEC had a significant adverse effect on US exports, thereby stimulating direct investment as a means of jumping the tariff wall. On the other hand, the increased market size and potential economic growth was a positive dynamic stimulus to foreign direct investment. This will be dealt with in more detail within the empirical section of this chapter.

Empirical evidence on international trade and foreign direct investment

Empirical studies of the determinants of international trade flows

A number of attempts have been made to test the Ricardian theory of comparative costs, but these were fairly simplistic.[31] In tracing the development of empirical research into trade in manufactures, therefore, it is convenient to begin with W. W. Leontief's test of the H-O theorem.[32] As was noted in the previous section, the apparently paradoxical results obtained set off a vigorous debate conducted at both the theoretical and empirical levels, which continued into the 1970s. The empirical studies undertaken revealed beyond doubt that a straightforward application of a two-factor (capital and labour) factor-proportions model along H-O lines was inadequate for understanding the pattern of United States trade, or indeed trade in manufactured goods in general.[33] To quote only one example, as part of a study of the determinants of the commodity structure of US trade in 1962, R. E. Baldwin repeated Leontief's test of the simple Heckscher-Ohlin theory.[34] Using capital and labour data alone, it was found that the Leontief Paradox still held. But on the basis of more detailed investigation (for example, taking capital to mean both physical and human capital) the Leontief results were reversed. Baldwin concluded that it was necessary to discard simple trade theories based on capital and labour alone in favour of multi-factor trade models. Such models would have to take into account relative differences in the skills of the labour force, natural resource conditions, technological differences, transportation costs and commercial policies.

In essence post-Leontief studies have followed the lines of development of the theory set out earlier. The initial research tended to concentrate on testing the validity or otherwise of one or a limited number of possible neo-factor or neo-technology trade determinants; whereas most recently the studies have been comprehensive in their approach, reflecting the emergence of a more general theoretical framework.

(a) Testing of neo-factor theories

Leontief himself reworked his original study of US trade to include natural resources as a third, quite separate factor of production. The fact that the 'paradox' was eliminated when this was done lends support for the role of natural resources in determining trade patterns; and other more recent evidence has confirmed this conclusion.[35] Similar empirical support has been obtained for another neo-factor theory, namely that of 'human capital', which attempts to explain trade patterns in terms of countries' relative labour skill availabilities. In one such study, Keesing calculated the skill requirements for the production of 1957 US manufactured exports and imports, based on five skill classes.[36] The coefficients obtained were then applied to the commodity composition of trade of various developed countries, with results as shown in Table 4.3.

Table 4.3 Export and import skill ratios*

Country	Exports	Imports
United States	.8170	.4740
West Germany	.6808	.4661
United Kingdom	.6251	.5377
France	.4896	.8182
Italy	.4609	.7127
Japan	.3129	.8372

* Requirements for classes I and II skills (skilled and professional workers) divided by requirements for classes IV and V (semi-skilled and unskilled workers).

(*Source:* Keesing, 1965.)

These results strongly supported the hypothesis that the United States had a comparative advantage in the export of skill-intensive commodities.

(b) Testing of neo-technology theories

Beginning with Posner in 1961, a stream of studies have appeared relating to the technological gap, imitation gap and product cycle theories. All of these theories have important features in common, and their importance lies in the specific links which are indicated between trade and foreign direct investment. Gruber, Mehta and Vernon found a strong positive correlation between R & D expenditures as a percentage of sales in nineteen US industries and the export/sales ratio for these same industries in 1962.[37] The five industries with the strongest research effort (transportation, electrical and non-electrical machinery, instruments and chemicals) accounted for 72 per cent of US exports and were responsible for 74 per cent of company-financed R & D expenditures. The results thus confirmed the hypothesis that R & D expenditures are an indicator of comparative cost advantages provided by the development of new products and productive methods. The research of Gruber *et al.* also revealed that the propensity for US industry to establish manufacturing facilities abroad was higher in the research-oriented than in other industries: in 1964 direct foreign investment by research-intensive industries totalled $9.7 billion; foreign direct investment by 14 other industries amounted to only $6.9 billion. The work, finally, touched upon the relationship between US exports and sales by US subsidiaries abroad, suggesting that the latter could conceivably (but need not necessarily) be export substituting from the US viewpoint. Such findings, particularly the former, are by now well established, but they were viewed as highly significant at the time when they appeared in 1967. The theme was developed further in tests of the product cycle hypothesis (Chapter 2, pp. 82–4). Otherwise, empirical research into trade determinants generally attempted to explain the export or import performance of particular countries or industries *in isolation,* i.e. ignoring the extent to which markets were serviced via subsidiary production rather than, or in addition to, trade.

A further neo-technology theory which has been subjected to extensive testing is the scale economy model. Beginning with Hufbauer, considerable support has been provided for the role of economies of scale in the determinants of trade structure.[38] It has been shown that large countries have relatively large exports from industries subject to greater scale economies, and vice-versa for smaller countries.

(c) General studies of trade determinants
The recent empirical studies of trade determinants have tended to be more comprehensive in their approach, aiming to incorporate both neo-factor and neo-technology variables into the models. The work of Hufbauer is particularly noteworthy as a pioneering attempt to test a range of theories across a large number of countries.[39] Hufbauer correlated national attributes calculated for 24 countries with the characteristics of *exports* for these countries. The country attributes included: fixed capital per manufacturing employee and skilled employees as a percentage of total employment to approximate factor endowments; total manufacturing output to represent the possible realisation of scale economies; and GDP per capita to represent technological sophistication. The characteristics of the exports included: capital per man, skill ratios, wages per man, scale economies, consumer goods ratio, first trade date and product differentiation. Capital per man, wage differentials and skill ratios

were designed to reflect the factor endowments theory; economies of scale arising from specialisation in the home market were associated with the scale economy model; the first trade date represented the introduction of new products according to the technological gap theory; product differentiation represented a stage of specialisation in the product cycle; and finally the ratio of consumer goods to total industry sales was designed to capture the stage of economic development. These indices were then used to test empirically the various trade models. The results indicated that the data were consistent with virtually all the models, with neo-factor and neo-technology theories performing equally well. To quote Hufbauer: 'it must be conceded that many different characteristics express themselves in export patterns. No one theory monopolizes the explanations of manufactures trade.'[40]

Because of the methodology used (rank correlations), no real attempt could be made by Hufbauer to say which of several closely competing theories was 'best'. Thus more recent work, for example by Leamer, which permitted the multiple testing of competing theories is of considerable importance.[41] Leamer's analysis sought to explain the factors determining the commodity *imports* of 28 manufactures for 12 industrialised Atlantic area countries in 1958. Three groups of variables were incorporated into the model: 1. Resistance group – tariff levels and distance to markets. The inclusion of these factors was necessitated by the use of imports as the dependent variable. 2. Stage-of-development group – levels of GNP and population, representing both technological sophistication and possible economies of scale. 3.   Resource group – capital per employee, expenditure on education as a percentage of national income, R & D spending as a percentage of GNP, installed electricity capacity. The conclusion was that trade dependence ratios (imports as a percentage of GNP) were best explained by the development variables, GNP and population. These variables, it was suggested, were most closely linked with scale economy theories but could also be associated with the product cycle. The distance and tariff variables offered the next best predictions, while the resource variables were, as a group, non-significant. While the major thrust of Leamer's work involved cross-country analysis, some interesting results were also produced on the determinants of individual countries' trade (Table 4.4). As would be expected, the coefficients for the US are large and positive in nearly all cases, meaning that America has a large GNP, abundant capital, substantial R & D expenditures etc. Relatively, however, the most important determining factors appear to be GNP and R & D. At the opposite end of the spectrum is Portugal with low R & D expenditures and low educational spending, and comparative advantage derived from (presumably) an unskilled, low-wage labour force and proximity to European markets. The UK, France and West Germany occupy an intermediate position between these extremes.

Table 4.4 Factors* determining the trade of selected countries

Country	Distance	GNP	Population	R & D	Capital/labour ratio	Electricity	Education
United States	+5.1	+32.8	+10.1	+26.6	+4.5	+1.7	+ 6.0
West Germany	-0.4	+ 3.4	+ 2.1	+ 0.2	–	-0.2	–
United Kingdom	-0.1	+ 4.6	+ 2.0	+ 2.2	-0.1	–	+ 0.2
Italy	–	+ 0.5	+ 1.8	– 3.1	-1.5	–1.0	– 1.5
Portugal	+0.5	-16.9	– 1.3	–23.6	-5.7	-5.4	–10.3

– = Less than 0.05

* The signs indicate whether the country exceeds (+) or falls short of (–) the average of the other countries' variables. Tariff variables excluded.

(*Source:* Leamer, 1974.)

Leamer's results, which emphasise the importance of stage-of-development and resistance factors, are influenced strongly by the choice of dependent variable (import/GNP ratio). When the data were recalculated with the *import/export ratio* as the dependent variable, the resource factors performed much better than the resistance and development groups, with the R & D measure being particularly important. This result has been confirmed by other work which has been designed to explain import/export ratios: Baldwin found that the numbers of engineers and scientists in different industries were positively correlated with net exports and that US exports were R & D intensive. These findings were interpreted as reflecting the importance of both skill factors and the activities of export industries that result in new and improved products.[42]

Because the various studies reviewed differ in focus, in methodology, in the data used and so on, it is not yet possible to generalise with any certainty as to the relative importance of the various trade theories. Certainly it is clear that neither the simple Ricardian nor the Heckscher-Ohlin model provides a satisfactory explanation of the direction and commodity composition of trade. Conversely the newer neo-factor and neo-technology theories have received powerful empirical support separately and in combination. And in particular the importance of technological influences is abundantly clear. Even so, since the variables employed are highly collinear in many instances, it is difficult to discriminate among the theories as a means of choosing the 'best' explanation. Perhaps alternatively what is required is some 'composite variable' which is based on both factor proportions and technology trade theories.[43]

What is plain is that although empirical studies of trade have largely developed in isolation from studies of foreign direct investment, many of the same variables have been used in the models formulated. Therefore the potential, although unexplored until very recently, existed for integrating empirical work on trade and investment in just the same way that an overall theory of international production is presently evolving. As an introduction to this work, it is useful to focus on one attempt to indicate the interactions between the determinants of trade and direct foreign investment. Using trade data for 1962, 1964 and 1966 Katrak analysed comparative US/UK exports of major industries in terms of the human skills, technological gap and scale economy theories.[44] The results of the rank correlations and regression analysis indicated that the scale economy explanation performed best, but the results for the human skills theory were also favourable. And, equally importantly, the results did seem to suggest that the two theories were independent of each other. That is labour skills and economies of scale exerted a separate influence on US/UK exports. On the other hand, the R & D intensity variable (representing the technological gap) was almost always non-significant. It can be argued that the reason for this result was that since UK incomes were fairly high and the country placed a relatively heavy stress on industrial innovation and product development, its export strength was derived from roughly the same characteristics that governed US export performance. In any event Dunning and Buckley extended and updated this work in an attempt to investigate the extent to which the three theories were able to explain not only comparative US/UK trade but also foreign production, that is, both the trade and non-trade involvement of the two countries.[45] In Katrak's original article the results on US/UK exports did not support the technological gap theory. Buckley and Dunning's results on US/UK overall international involvement (exports plus foreign production) on the other hand, lent least support to the scale economy theory. Their conclusion was that investment in knowledge through R & D was more important as a determinant of international production than of trade; while investment in human capital was important both for exports and for foreign production. The fact that scale factors, which were vital in explaining domestic exports, were unimportant in explaining international production seems reasonable. Where scale effects are significant, the comparative costs of exporting are thereby reduced, thus militating against overseas manufacture.

Empirical studies of the interaction between trade and foreign direct investment

Aside from the research just noted, numerous studies have now appeared, which implicitly or explicitly concern the interaction between trade and foreign direct investment. Such studies have aimed at answering widely differing questions. At the risk of over-simplification, empirical studies have been directed at four main issues: (a) the mode of foreign involvement; (b) the testing of a theory of international production; (c) does trade substitute for or complement foreign direct investment? (d) MNE trade and nations' comparative advantage.

(a) The mode of foreign involvement
Here some of the important questions to be answered include: Why produce abroad rather than service the foreign market through exports from the home country? What advantages lie in non-trade servicing? What barriers exist to trade servicing? How far are trade theories relevant to decisions relating to the mode of foreign involvement?

The influence of firm size. Ample evidence now exists to show that trade and foreign investment are different ways of exploiting the ownership advantages of firms: Wolf, for example, found that two ownership variables, the size of the firm and the employment of technical manpower, explained not only domestic diversification, but also exporting and foreign production by US firms (see Chapter 2, pp. 73–4 for further details).[46] Average firm size was more strongly associated with the foreign production propensity and domestic industrial diversification than with the export propensity. This suggests that foreign production and domestic diversification require a greater capital outlay and entail greater risk than does exporting, difficulties which the large firm is better able to overcome.

Other results, which indicate that the influence of size of firm on the method of sourcing does not apply solely to US MNEs, have been presented by Buckley and Pearce.[47] The work related to 156 of the world's largest enterprises in 1972. The importance of affiliate production as a method of foreign involvement to these firms is shown in Table 4.5, together with an industry breakdown. As indicated, Swiss and 'Joint and Other' firms operate abroad almost wholly through foreign production. Conversely only 12 per cent of Japanese foreign involvement takes the form of production overseas, the remaining 88 per cent representing exports from the parent companies in Japan itself. Looking at the industry breakdown, the striking feature is the complete reliance of aircraft firms on exporting as a method of marketing abroad; the heavy reliance of iron and steel companies and to a lesser extent vehicle manufacturers on exports is also noteworthy. These industries are characterised by substantial economies of scale which inhibit foreign production. In addition both the aircraft and iron and steel industries are politically and strategically sensitive which introduces constraints on locational policies. Regression analysis was undertaken, relating the sourcing ratios of companies to three groups of independent variables: size of firm, and dummy variables representing nationality of firm and industry type. Firm size emerged as a very significant explanatory variable, indicating that large companies are more likely to service an overseas market by affiliate production than are smaller firms. Certain of the nationality and industry variables were also significant, reflecting the wide variations in sourcing ratios indicated in Table 4.5.

The influence of locational factors.   This model just considered did not introduce any specific locational variables which would have facilitated an explanation of other conditions under which foreign production might have been chosen rather than exporting. To consider this it is necessary to turn to other research, which is oriented towards an explanation of the method of servicing *particular* host country markets. In a 1972 paper, Horst examined the relationship between US exports to the Canadian market and the sales of US affiliates in Canada.[48] The conclusion was that the most important factor influencing the decision whether or not to invest in Canada was the height of Canadian tariffs – the higher the tariff, the smaller the share of US exports and the larger the share of US subsidiary production in Canada. The sales of US exports to total US sales in Canada (exports plus foreign manufacture) was also negatively related to the size of the

Table 4.5 Sourcing ratios* by country and industry

Home country	No. of firms	Production of foreign affiliates / Production of foreign affiliates + parent company exports	Industry	Production of foreign affiliates / Production of foreign affiliates + parent company exports
UK	28	63.5%	Oil and Petroleum Products	89.4%
Japan	17	12.4%	Motor Vehicles	30.5%
France	3	20.8%	Tobacco	94.6%
Germany	11	50.7%	Paper Products	62.8%
Benelux	3	80.0%	Chemicals and Pharmaceuticals	70.6%
Italy	3	53.5%	Aircraft	0
Switzerland	3	94.4%	Iron and Steel	9.0%
Canada	3	35.0%	Food Products and Beverages	96.2%
Sweden	5	38.9%	Packaging Products and Containers	88.1%
Joint and Other	5	95.2%	Textiles, Clothing and Footwear	58.2%
US	75	88.2%	Electronics and Electrical Engineering	56.3%
			Mechanical Engineering	66.9%
			Other Metals	73.7%
Total	156	74.4%	Total	74.4%

* Production of foreign affiliates

Production of foreign affiliates + parent company exports (weighted by sales)

(*Source*: Buckley and Pearce, 1977.)

Canadian market, a result which ties in with the demand side of the product cycle thesis. Jud extended this work on Canada and found that in addition to tariffs and market size, a higher degree of industrial concentration was also important in encouraging a shift from exports to affiliate production in Canada.[49] Similar studies have been undertaken in relation to US investment in the EEC and EFTA, and again it has been found that the ratios of US exports to US affiliate sales in the UK and the EEC were negatively influenced by tariff levels.[50] The results of these regression studies thus tend to bear out the conclusions of surveys of businessmen, where market size and growth and trade barriers were seen as important locational determinants.

An industry study which further confirms, but also extends, these types of conclusions was that undertaken by Parry on pharmaceuticals.[51] The study aimed to establish the factors explaining variations in the ratio of non-trade (licensing and foreign investment) to trade sales. For UK pharmaceutical firms in 15 foreign countries, it was found that the most important variables influencing the ratio were the size of the local market and the growth of that market; a tariff variable was statistically significant but explained only a small amount of the variability in the non-trade/trade ratio. At the second stage of the research Parry was more concerned with explaining the split between licensing and foreign affiliate production, i.e. the non-trade element of foreign involvement. Again the market variables were significant, indicating that the larger the market the greater the licensing commitment. In this case the market size variable seemed to be capturing some effects associated with barriers to entry, as for example the operation of direct investment restrictions in Mexico and Japan. Moreover, a variable representing non-tariff barriers to trade was particularly related to the commitment to licensing. Parry explained this in terms of special factors within the pharmaceutical industry. Thus regulations over the registration of new drugs and quality control could favour the domestic manufacturer and act as an effective deterrent to direct investment. The tariff variable, conversely, was negatively associated with the licensing commitment, suggesting that the downward trend in tariff barriers encourages increased licensing. These results are extremely interesting, particularly in indicating for the first time the types of factors which influence the choice between foreign direct investment and licensing. This consideration had previously been ignored because of lack of data.

(b) The testing of a theory of international production

Summarising the empirical results obtained on mode of foreign involvement, it has been shown that both ownership-specific variables (particularly size of firm) and location-specific variables (such as tariff and non-tariff barriers, and host country market size and growth) influence the choice between exporting, foreign production and licensing. Such results bring the empirical research closer to the evolving theory of international production, but are much less than a comprehensive test of this theory. However, both Dunning and Hirsch, who have made significant contributions to this evolving theory, have also made attempts to test their models empirically, incorporating such ownership- and location-specific variables. This work, which is a further extension of the empirical research considered above, is therefore now discussed.

It will be recalled that the Hirsch model distinguishes between four sets of variables which are believed to influence a country's dependence on foreign production:[52]

(i) Relative production costs at home and abroad. This is represented in the empirical study by relative average hourly wage rates and capital/labour ratio.

(ii) Firm-specific revenue producing know-how and intangible assets, proxied by the ratio of non-production to all workers in an industry.

(iii) Cost differential by which export marketing costs exceed domestic marketing costs. The proxy used here was the advertising/sales ratio.

(iv) Extra costs involved in controlling and coordinating foreign production operations – represented by the average number of employees per manufacturing establishment.

In addition, various market size factors were introduced as explanatory factors. Regrettably, the proxies used for (iii) and (iv) do not seem in any way adequate. Effectively, ownership-specific proxies appear to be used when the variables required are location-specific. For example, tariff and distance variables would give a better indication of the differential between export and domestic marketing costs.

Hirsch uses these explanatory variables to try to explain the share of eight host country markets accounted for by: sales of US foreign affiliates; imports from the US by MNEs; imports from the US by non-MNEs; imports from countries other than the US; and sales by domestic firms. The results are very mixed, and except for the equation relating to US foreign affiliate sales, explain only a small proportion of the variability in market shares. This would tie in with the point noted above that some of the variables have been incorrectly specified and/or that important variables have been omitted.

The wage cost variable is significant and positive in the equations relating to US company activity; and the knowledge variable is also positive and significant, particularly in the equations relating to multinational activity. The plant size variable was positive for US suppliers but negative for non-US suppliers. Other explanatory variables performed poorly. Hirsch interpreted these results as indicating that 'the shares of foreign affiliates vary more with hourly wage rate, skill intensity and average plant size than do the share of both multinational and non-multinational US based suppliers. . . . The data are . . . consistent with the hypothesis that US firms enjoy a competitive edge in knowledge intensive industries, and, furthermore, that this advantage is more pronounced in subsidiary production than in exports. The advantages of production over trade presumably derive from the absence of trade-retarding effects of export marketing cost differentials which do not apply to MNE sales.' In this last sentence Hirsch is accepting that he has not in fact identified the location-specific factors which are of primary importance in the trade v. invest decision. The model as a whole does not therefore represent much of a step forward from an empirical viewpoint.

Dunning, using the same 1970 US Tariff Commission data, sought to test two basic hypotheses.[53] The first was that the competitive advantage of a country's enterprises in servicing foreign markets was determined by the *ownership* advantages of the enterprises and the *location* advantages of countries in which they produced. And secondly, that the *form* of the involvement would depend chiefly on the relative attractiveness of different locations. Using a series of variables suggested by neo-factor and neo-technology trade theories and location theory, Dunning tested these hypotheses for a group of five industrialised host countries (Canada, Benelux, France, West Germany and the UK) over fourteen industry groups.

To test the first hypothesis, regression equations were calculated using three different dependent variables: the ratio of affiliate sales plus exports to total industry sales in the host country; the ratio of affiliate sales to total industry sales; and the export/total industry sales ratio. In each case, three explanatory factors were consistently significant. These were host country market size, average hourly compensation in the host country and the skilled employment ratio. The latter variable may be interpreted as a measure of technological advantage which MNEs could exploit either through exporting or foreign production. But it is not so clear why the other variables should encourage exporting as well as foreign production. A number of other explanatory factors were significant in certain of the equations, the tariff variable being especially noteworthy. This was highly significant in the equation relating to affiliate sales/total industry sales, and corroborates earlier evidence on the influence of tariffs on foreign direct investment.

To test the second hypothesis relating to the form of foreign involvement, the dependent variable used was the ratio of exports to affiliate sales. The two explanatory factors which emerged as significant and positive were: growth in sales per man in the host country between 1966 and 1970; and the average ratio of net income to sales of all firms in different industries and countries for 1966 and 1970. The total explanatory power of the equations estimated was quite good, but once again there are severe problems in interpreting the results. For example it is not obvious why higher sales per man should be associated with a greater export propensity.

In general, the same kinds of empirical problems which have been noted previously have cropped up again with this work. Essentially many of these difficulties stem from data deficiencies, which mean that the proxy variables incorporated in the models may be interpreted in different ways or indeed that proxies are unavailable. The problem is even greater than this, however, since in some cases the factors which might adequately reflect the advantages of internalisation and the incentives to internalise have not yet been satisfactorily specified. Finally, statistical problems deriving, for example, from collinearity between the various independent variables are also a source of concern. A satisfactory test of the theory of international production is thus still to be devised.

(c) Does trade substitute for or complement foreign direct investment?
The topic which has attracted most attention from an empirical viewpoint is undoubtedly that of the effect of foreign direct investment on home country exports. And yet it is not *per se* of overwhelming importance to issues such as the effect of direct investment on world-wide economic efficiency, comparative advantage and the gains from trade. Even if investment substitutes for trade this matters little if the investment complements the comparative advantage of home and host countries, since resource allocation is thereby being improved. In reality the reason for the emphasis on this topic is related to the policy question of the impact of multinational firms on the balance of payments; and more specifically to the impact of US MNEs on the United States balance of payments (a topic which is considered in detail in Chapter 7). Nevertheless it has been shown that world trade and intra-MNE trade has expanded alongside the growth of direct foreign investment. Since this has significant implications in world terms, then the topic is worthy of consideration in this context.

It is possible to specify certain trade effects that could be associated with the operations of multinational firms:

(i) Export generating effects, resulting from additional sales of finished goods, components, raw materials or capital equipment. These exports may come from the parent company or the subsidiary; or they may consist of additional exports from independent suppliers in the home country to the subsidiary. After a period of time, domestic manufacturers in the foreign country may themselves begin to produce and export the products introduced initially by the MNE. Similarly the foreign subsidiary may begin to export components or finished products back to the market of the parent company (as predicted by the product cycle theory), or to third countries. Particularly if the affiliate is allowed autonomy, it may itself develop new products quite independently of its parent's product line, which then represent potential exports.

(ii) Export displacement effects.　These effects occur if output from an overseas subsidiary replaces exports from the parent company; if subsidiary production replaces exports from a competitor in the home country; if subsidiary manufacture replaces exports from another affiliate in either the local or third country markets; or if subsidiary manufacture replaces exports previously made by a third country supplier to the host country.

The net effect of export generation and export replacement determines whether or not trade is increased or diminished for the world as a whole as a result of foreign direct investment. The range of possible outcomes is very wide, particularly in the normal multi-product firm, depending on the complementarity or substitutability of different products in manufacture and in marketing. Such complexities in the real world situation, of course, create major problems for empirical research.

Home country exports.　Most research in fact has not attempted to answer this question, but rather has had the much more limited aim of assessing whether or not outward direct investment substitutes for or complements home country exports. Some of the research studies which had the primary aim of establishing the determinants of exports and foreign production also provided indirect evidence that the two modes of foreign involvement were substitutes for each other. More substantive evidence relating to the dynamics of the export/investment relationship, however, emerged from work by Horst in 1974.[54] Regression analysis was applied to 1966 data relating to 23 manufacturing industries and 8 countries or areas. The method was to relate US exports and US subsidiary sales separately to variables aimed at determining the origins of US comparative advantage (e.g. R & D, advertising expenditures, plant size etc.). The equations were then recalculated to derive the relationship between exports and subsidiary sales, all other variables being held constant. The estimated relationship is shown in Fig. 4.2. As indicated, as long as foreign subsidiary net sales (as a percentage of domestic shipments) were small, an increase in sales was accompanied by a rise in US exports (as a percentage of domestic shipments). After some point a further rise in subsidiary sales was accompanied by a fall-off in exports. The implication was that over most of the range the complementarities existing between exports and subsidiary sales have tended to outweigh any substitutional effects. These complementarities could derive either from the complementarity of goods in use or from joint marketing efforts (as regards distribution, advertising, market research, etc.).

In two other important studies, Lipsey and Weiss examined the interrelationships between the exports and direct foreign investment of the US and 13 other major exporting countries, firstly for the pharmaceutical industry and then for manufacturing industry in

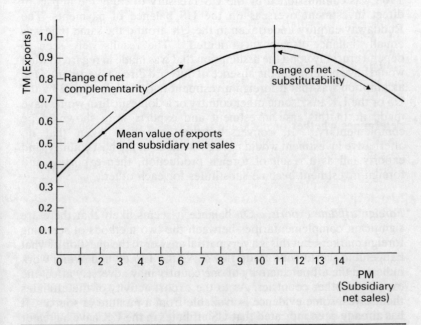

Note: Maximum value of TM equal to 0.97% achieved when PM equal to 10.6%

Fig. 4.2 Estimated relationship between US parent exports as percentage of domestic shipments (TM) and subsidiary net sales as percentage of domestic shipments (PM) (*Source*: Horst, 1974a).

general.[55] The results of the regression analyses for the wider study showed that the level of activity of US manufacturing affiliates was positively related to US exports. Similarly, the number of foreign-owned manufacturing affiliates was also positively related to exports by foreign countries. The size of the regression coefficients indicated that every $1 of affiliate sales was associated with exports worth about 10 cents. The additions to exports were deemed to take the form of materials and components for further processing, finished products for resale by affiliates, and exports by parents to unaffiliated foreign firms. Interestingly, US manufacturing affiliate activity was negatively related to exports by the 13 other countries and, in certain cases at least, foreign affiliate operations were negatively related to US exports. These results therefore suggest complementarity between the form of supply (exports or affiliate manufacture), whether US or non-US MNEs were involved, but substitutability between the nationalities of supplying firms.

The earliest studies relating to the complementarity or substitutability of exports and foreign affiliate activity were very definitely policy-oriented. For example, the Hufbauer/Adler study published in

1968 was commissioned by the US Treasury to study the impact of direct investment overseas on the US balance of payments. The Reddaway enquiry undertaken in the UK around the same time was equally balance-of-payments-oriented.[56] The results were seen to depend crucially upon the assumption that was made in regard to what would have occurred in the absence of outward direct investment. One assumption was that if foreign investment had not been made by the US or the UK first, some other country or a domestic firm would have made it. In this case investment and exports were shown to be complementary.[57] If, conversely, the view was taken that no alternative investment would have been made in the host country, and exports fall as a result of foreign production, then exporting and foreign investment become substitutes for each other.

Foreign affiliate exports.   On balance it seems likely that there are significant complementarities between the two methods of servicing foreign markets, but this is a very partial answer to the question of what happens to world-wide trade flows. As the Lipsey and Weiss work indicated the affiliate activity of one country may adversely affect the exports of other countries. As to the export activity of the affiliates themselves, some evidence is available from a mixture of sources. It has already been indicated that US affiliates in the UK have a greater export propensity than indigenous firms. On the other hand Lall and Streeten in their work on six less developed countries concluded that 'foreign control does not generally seem to promote exports and may even inhibit it'.[58] Of the 46 foreign controlled firms in their sample, 35 per cent exported nothing at all; and for a further 49 per cent of firms, exports accounted for less than 9 per cent of sales. The best export performances came from firms in the Kenyan and Jamaican samples. The leading Kenyan exporters were located in industries such as soaps, detergents, shoes, cement and petroleum products, and aimed chiefly at the neighbouring East African countries. The major exporting firms in Jamaica were involved in the manufacture of food products, clothing and paint. The sample therefore contained no examples of LDC affiliates engaged in the manufacture or assembly of, say, electronic components for export to the industrialised countries. As will be indicated, countries engaged in these activities have been able to experience very rapid rates of export growth on the basis of MNE operations.

These points, which suggest an association between the types of investment and the export performance of affiliates, relate to the distinction made by Kojima between trade- and anti-trade-oriented direct investment. Forecasts of Japanese direct overseas investment indicate an increase from $2.7 m. in 1969 to $27.3 m. in 1980 with a breakdown by industry type as follows:

Table 4.6 Japanese direct overseas investment by industry

	1969 (%)	1980 (%)
Resource-oriented	40.7	50.8
Labour- and market-oriented	23.1	26.2
Finance and services	36.2	23.0
Total	100.0	100.0

(*Source:* Kojima, 1973.)

The resource-oriented investment will obviously generate exports from the affiliates, and similarly the labour-oriented investment aims at establishing an export base for exporting back to the investing country as well as to third country markets. In terms of the debate as to whether or not foreign direct investment substitutes for exports from the home country, Japanese investment in textiles, clothing etc. probably does substantially replace Japanese exports. But in aggregate terms trade may be increased with the transfer of production to lower cost manufacturers in Taiwan, Korea, Singapore and Hong Kong. The industry balance of US direct investment is quite different to that of Japan. There is a much stronger emphasis on operations in other developed countries and on market-oriented investment in the LDCs. As a result the exports from US affiliates on average could be expected to be lower than from Japanese affiliates. However this does not reveal how the aggregate trade effects compare as between the two sets of multinational firms. And even the latter would not indicate whether or not one type of investment has a more beneficial effect on the pattern of comparative advantage than the other. Much more work remains to be undertaken on this issue. Further data on the links between foreign investment and trade flows are presented in Chapter 5 in the context of the discussion on host country balance of payments.

(d) MNE trade and nations' comparative advantage

Aside from the issue of how foreign direct investment affects the level of trade, there is a related question of some importance. This refers to whether or not the pattern of MNE-generated trade conforms to the patterns which are consistent with the competitiveness of a country's industries. In other words do the same factors which explain the aggregate level of trade also explain MNE-generated trade? If the answer is 'no', then it may be assumed that traditional sources of a nation's competitiveness are being eroded.

One study directed to answering this question was that undertaken by Cornell, once again using data from the US Tariff Commission.[59] For aggregate and MNE exports and imports and for domestic shipments, Cornell calculated the attributes of these commodity flows in terms of capital per worker, labour intensity, human skills, scale economies, product differentiation etc. The conclusion in relation to 1970 trade figures was that 'In general . . . the patterns of MNC trade reflect the patterns of US comparative advantage as measured by the characteristic contents of traded goods.' Cornell also calculated the characteristic content of 'new' trade generated between 1966 and 1970. In this case there was some suggestion that MNE exports 'embodied significantly fewer of the characteristics that appear to govern the basic elements of comparative advantage of aggregate new US exports in international trade.' This might be indicative of an erosion of comparative advantage, but Cornell considers another possible explanation. This is that MNEs' trade reflects the establishment of foreign operations by firms which are not well-endowed with attributes that would produce strong performance in import and export markets. However, considerable evidence has already been quoted to show that basically the same ownership advantages explain both exports and foreign production, and therefore the 'erosion of US competitiveness' hypothesis must remain a distinct possibility.

Lipsey and Weiss studied this question from the viewpoint of US imports.[60] It was found that imports from American-owned affiliates abroad were more capital- and research-intensive than other US imports. The imports from affiliates indeed were seen to account for much of the high capital intensity that characterises US imports overall (and in this lies a further explanation for the Leontief Paradox). These results are interpreted as meaning that the MNE combines its ownership advantages of low cost physical and human capital and technology with complementary factors of labour or natural resources in the host country. Thereafter the home country imports the resulting research or capital intensive goods from its foreign affiliates. This seems to indicate that trade is taking place according to comparative advantage, but as Fig. 4.1 shows, exports of affiliates to the US represent only a small proportion of US multinational trade. What Lipsey and Weiss are showing is that where US MNEs invest in natural resources or undertake manufacture or assembly of labour intensive operations abroad, then this is trade creating. But as suggested earlier much, indeed most, of US MNE activity may not be of this type.

Together, these two studies add a little to knowledge about MNE trade. The question as to whether or not MNE generated trade causes an erosion of comparative advantage is, however, left substantially unresolved and at least open to varying interpretations. In spite of this it is at least possible to show the magnitude of MNE-generated trade, extending the data which were presented in Fig. 4.1.

The magnitude of MNE-generated trade

Earlier figures revealed the importance of US MNE trade in 1970. Since 1970 there has been a significant slowdown in the rate of growth of this trade but it is still of immense importance.

Table 4.7 Percent of US imports supplied by majority-owned affiliates* of US corporations in 1974

Country of origin	% of total US imports from country indicated, supplied by US affiliates†
World	32.1
Developed Market Economies	24.8
Canada	52.3
Europe	13.4
Japan	1.0
Others	10.9
Developing Countries	37.4
Latin America	34.9
Asia and Africa	39.6

* Foreign companies in which 50% or more of equity is held directly or indirectly by a US company.
† Imports may not take place on an intra-firm basis.

(*Source:* UN Economic and Social Council, 1978, Table III–16.)

The figures in Table 4.7 do not relate only to intra-firm trade, since US affiliates abroad may export to US companies other than their parent corporation. Nevertheless the data are very revealing, showing that US MNE affiliates are responsible for one third of all American imports. The role of US affiliates in Canada as suppliers to the USA market is particularly evident: over half of all imports into the US from Canada are supplied by American subsidiaries.

Referring specifically to intra-firm trade, other data have indicated that about 50 per cent of US exports in 1974 were on an intra-firm basis. These took the form of exports from US parent corporations to their subsidiaries overseas and of exports from foreign affiliates in the US to their parent companies or other affiliates outside America. Similarly it has been shown that 30 per cent of UK exports in 1973, 29 per cent of Swedish exports in 1975 and 59 per cent of Canadian exports in 1975 were intra-firm transactions.

The most comprehensive data on intra-firm trade relates to US multinational firms. Table 4.8 gives details of the intra-company sales of US affiliates, classified by the region in which the subsidiaries are located and by the industry in which they operate.

It is clear that the overall figure of 23 per cent of sales of US affiliates accounted for by intra-company sales is heavily influenced by trade flows in natural resources. Intra-company sales in the mining and petroleum industries represented 24 per cent and 31 per cent respectively of total sales, but only 17 per cent in manufacturing industry. On the other hand intra-company flows were quite important in the non-electrical machinery sector, representing 25 per cent of sales overall and 33 per cent of sales of US affiliates located in the Common Market. Regionally intra-company sales were more significant for US affiliates in developing countries, but this reflects the greater importance of extractive industries in the LDCs.

Table 4.8 Ratio of intra-company sales of majority-owned affiliates of US MNEs to total sales, by industry and region (1975, %)

Region	All industries	Mining	Petroleum	Manufacturing					Transport	Trade
				All manufacturing	Chemicals	Non-elec. machinery	Elec. machinery			
All areas	23	24	31	17	14	25	11	22	10
Developed countries	18	24	21	18	16	27	11	25	10
of which:									
EEC	21	97	24	22	22	33	11	28	10
Developing countries	29	23	35	6	8	10	10	3	6
of which:									
LAFTA*	24	8	53	3	1	10	9	3	3
Africa	59	–	66	–	0	–	0	–	0

– = insignificant.

* Latin American Free Trade Area.

(*Source:* UN Economic and Social Council, 1978, Table 3.)

In general the data are difficult to interpret because of lack of knowledge of the types of transfers involved, as between finished goods, intermediate components, capital items etc. What is certain is that intra-firm trade has important balance-of-payments implications for both home and host countries. This issue has been touched upon earlier in the chapter and arises again in the context of both the impact and control of multinational firms in Chapters 5, 6 and 7. Reliance on MNE-generated trade may be perceived as severely limiting national hegemony, undermining the ability of home and host governments to achieve their own domestic policy objectives. The role of intra-firm flows is also highly relevant to the trend towards protectionism in international trade policy. If protectionist fears materialise, this will have profound implications for the MNEs themselves. The advantages of internationally rationalised production could be greatly reduced and MNEs could be left in certain instances with completely redundant plants.

The impact of customs unions on trade and foreign direct investment

As was pointed out in the theoretical section, the formation of a customs union has been postulated to produce both static and dynamic effects. While the distinction between the two is by no means clear-cut in practice, the former are essentially concerned with trade flows, whereas the latter would include changes in levels and flows of foreign direct investment. Most studies have been undertaken on the static effects resulting from the formation of the European Economic Community and have related to aggregate rather than MNE trade. The research has shown that the positive trade creation effects have outweighed the negative trade diversion influences, although on balance, when expressed in terms of GNP, the net static effects have been shown to be small. The trade diversion effects are crucial in the present context. Thus it would be expected that in US industries which suffered a loss of exports after the EEC's creation, there would be a greater stimulus to foreign direct investment. One study estimated that US manufactures exported to the EEC in 1967 were $250 million lower than they would have been, had the customs union not been formed; but 80 per cent of this decline was accounted for by reductions in imports of chemicals and petroleum products. The general conclusion, therefore, is that the trade diversion effects on US exports have not been great.

Even if the trade diversion effects of the EEC would not explain the very rapid growth of US direct investment in the Common Market from the mid-1950s onward, the rise in the number of US subsidiaries operating within the Community could be related to the dynamic effects of the union. Various points have been put forward in this context. In the first place it has been argued that union formation would have the effect of reducing investment risks and thereby stimulate investment flows. Again, because of the abolition of tariffs between members of the union, the size of the foreign market was much increased. Previous national markets may have been too small to achieve economies of scale, thus inhibiting foreign direct investment. At the empirical level, Scaperlanda approached the problem by examining whether or not the EEC's creation had caused a reallocation in US direct investment between EEC and non-EEC Western Europe.[61] Scaperlanda compared US direct investment in the two areas for a period before the signing of the Treaty of Rome (1951–58) with that for the years 1951 to 1964. The results showed that since 1959 both of the European areas had received an increasing proportion of US investment at the expense of the rest of the world; but there was no significant difference between the shares of investment being allocated to the EEC as compared with non-EEC Western Europe. The conclusion was that factors such as familiarity with the country in which investment was to be located (particularly relevant to the UK), international differences in the application of technology, etc. outweighed the influence of the creation of the Common Market.

In other work, Scaperlanda in association with Mauer analysed the determinants of US direct investment in the EEC.[62] Changes in the value of US direct investment in the Common Market during the period 1952–66 were related to variables representing EEC market size, rate of economic growth in the EEC, and tariff discrimination. The results indicated that only the size of market hypothesis could be supported statistically. The non-significance of the tariff variable supported earlier findings regarding the relatively small trade diversion effects of the EEC. Furthermore the stability of the market size variable between the pre- and post-EEC periods suggested that the EEC's formation had little impact on the sensitivity of US foreign direct investment to changes in market size.

In both of these studies, the results set off a debate in which the findings were challenged, particular attention being drawn to the inadequacy of the tariff variable used in some of the work. Consequently the most that can be said is that research has been inconclusive on the issue of whether or not the formation of the EEC has increased the Community's share of US direct foreign investment. There is evidence that the process of European integration has influenced the choice of US companies between exports and subsidiary production (see Table 4.9). What the empirical research seems to indicate is that market size and growth in the EEC has been more important in causing the shift to direct investment than other factors such as tariff discrimination.

In conclusion, it should be pointed out that even if European integration has caused a shift among US companies in their methods of servicing EEC and EFTA markets, this is not necessarily detrimental

Table 4.9 Sales of US manufacturing affiliates in Europe and exports from US to Europe (selected manufacturers, $ million)

	1957	1962	1968
Affiliate sales	4,505	8,650	19,037
US exports	1,326	2,439	4,345
Ratio of sales/exports	3.40	3.55	4.39

(*Source:* Dunning, 1973b.)

from a world trade point of view. In the first place, significant complementarities have already been shown to exist between exports and overseas production. Secondly, the trade creation effects of the EEC's formation are very pertinent to the operations of all companies (including US firms) located within the customs union. To exploit the EEC market would require companies to develop so as to supply all the previous national markets, thus necessitating increased exports. Thirdly, the EEC may have caused companies to rationalise their production facilities and service the total Community market from a smaller number of plants of minimum efficient scale. The end-result of this process would once again be increased trade.

Concluding remarks on empirical research

It is evident from the empirical research quoted that answers to the many serious questions posed by MNE activities in the field of international trade have barely begun to be considered. Certainly the relationships between trade and investment as different modes of foreign involvement are becoming clearer. Large firm size seems to be an important influence when the choice is made in favour of foreign direct investment rather than exporting; this has been shown to be the case for both US and non-US MNEs. Here size appears to reflect a host of factors such as greater resources of capital and skilled labour, higher R & D expenditures, greater ability to bear risks, oligopolistic market power and so on. When the servicing of *particular* foreign markets is considered, tariff barriers and the size and growth of the host country seem to be important determinants of the choice between foreign direct investment and exporting. Regarding the choice between investment and licensing, research by Parry on the pharmaceutical industry has indicated that non-tariff barriers may virtually force a company to engage in licensing, while a downward trend in tariff barriers may also encourage a greater prevalence of licensing. Work on utilising both ownership- and location-specific variables to explain the general commitment to foreign involvement as well as the mode of the involvement, has, however, only been partially successful as yet.

While considerable progress has been made in these latter directions, studies of the interaction between trade and investment have merely scratched the surface. There is ample evidence to indicate that some complementarities exist between foreign affiliate production and parent company exports. The additional exports take the form of materials and components for further processing, finished products for resale where the affiliate manufactures only part of the product line abroad, etc. Such facts are important, for example, to considerations relating to the home country balance of payments (see Chapter 7), but say nothing about the aggregate effects of MNEs on world trade. When this home country evidence is taken together with results relating to the trade performance of affiliates, the picture becomes only a little clearer. This is because the impact of foreign affiliates on trade seems to depend very much on the type of investment – as between resource- labour- and market-oriented investment etc. – and the nationality of the investment. Moreover, no answer can be given to the question of whether or not MNE-generated trade is consistent with what is deemed to be the comparative advantage of the nation. As the discussions on the studies by Cornell and Lipsey and Weiss indicate, the same results are capable of varying interpretations. Finally, and again relevant to the comparative advantage issue, virtually no data are available on prices in international trade, and particularly on the relationships between the transfer prices used in intra-MNE trade and arm's length prices. In total the picture is far from clear on a number of major issues concerning MNEs and international trade flows. This is a cause for serious concern, given that all multinational firms probably account for about one half of total world trade.

The role of intra-firm trade takes on increasing significance at a time when there is a renewed interest in protectionism. The liberal international economic order prevailing during the thirty years following the Second World War produced undoubted economic gains, but more recently attention has been focused on the costs associated with international interdependence. These costs form an important part of the discussion in Chapter 5, on the impact of MNE trade and investment activities on host countries, and in Chapter 7, on the effects on home countries; similarly issues associated with the regulation of MNEs are dealt with in Chapters 6 and 7, where consideration is given to the efforts of national governments to improve the trade and balance of payments contributions of multinational firms.

Appendix 4.1 The choice between exporting and overseas production

Assume an MNE with some degree of monopoly power in the foreign market, which it can supply either through exports or through overseas production. The marginal costs of exports (production costs in the

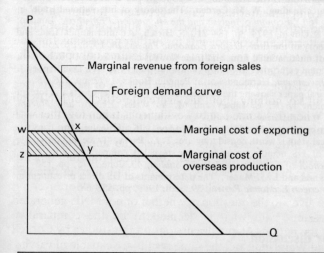

Marginal revenue from foreign sales

Foreign demand curve

Marginal cost of exporting

Marginal cost of overseas production

Fig. (App.) 4.1 The choice between exporting and overseas production. (*Source*: Horst, 1974b.)

home country plus M) are assumed the same for all levels of supply, and similarly the marginal costs of overseas production are deemed constant. The profit maximising strategies are indicated by the intersection of the relevant marginal cost curve with the marginal revenue curve (points x and y). The choice between exporting and overseas production depends on whether savings from overseas production (represented by the shaded area wxyz) are greater or less than the costs of control and coordination C.

Further reading

1. For a review of developments on international trade theory, a standard international economics text is most suitable, for example: **B. Sodersten**, *International Economics*, London: Macmillan, 1971, Ch. 1, 4–7; **M. Kreinen**, *International Economics: A Policy Approach*, New York: Harcourt, Brace & Jovanovich (2nd ed.), 1975, Ch. 11, 12.
2. An excellent summary of empirical tests on trade theories is: **R. M. Stern**, 'Testing trade theories', in P. B. Kenen (ed.), *International Trade and Finance*, London: Cambridge U.P., 1975, particularly pp. 3–35.
3. The classic work on the testing of the neo-factor and neo-technology theories is: **G. C. Hufbauer**, 'The impact of national characteristics and technology on the commodity composition of trade in manufactured goods', in R. Vernon (ed.), *The Technology Factor in International Trade*, New York: Columbia U.P., 1970, pp. 145–231. The summary of the trade theories given in Table 1 on pp. 147–8 is very good.
4. A clear, concise summary of the Leontief Paradox and the suggested explanations for its resolution is contained in: **R. Findlay**, *Trade and Specialization*, Harmondsworth: Penguin Books, 1970, pp. 92–106.

5. The Corden and Hirsch articles relating to the integration of trade and investment theory are worth reading: **W. M. Corden,** 'The theory of international trade' in J. H. Dunning (ed.), *Economic Analysis and the Multinational Enterprise,* London: George Allen & Unwin, 1974, pp. 184–210; **S. Hirsch,** 'An international trade and investment theory of the firm', *Oxford Economic Papers,* **28,** 1976, pp. 258–70.
6. A discussion of multinational firms and trade flows is contained in: **D. Robertson,** 'The multinational enterprise: trade flows and trade policy', in J. H. Dunning (ed.), *International Investment,* Harmondsworth: Penguin Books, 1972, pp. 326–56.
7. A good empirical paper showing the complementarity between exports and foreign direct investment is: **R. E. Lipsey** and **M. Y. Weiss,** *Exports and Foreign Investment in Manufacturing Industries,* New York: National Bureau of Economic Research, Working Paper No. 131 (revised), May 1976, particularly pp. 1–45.
8. Other empirical studies worth considering are: **T. G. Parry,** 'Trade and non-trade performance of US manufacturing industry: revealed comparative advantage', *Manchester School of Economic and Social Studies,* 43, June 1975, pp. 158–72; **A. E. Scaperlanda** and **L. J. Mauer,** 'The determinants of US direct investment in the EEC', *American Economic Review,* 59, Sept. 1969, pp. 558–68.

Questions for discussion

1. Dropping the assumption of international immobility of factors of production, can the Heckscher-Ohlin model explain investment flows between countries? Indicate the other assumptions of the H-O theory, and the implications for trade and investment of progressively relaxing these assumptions.
2. Discuss the relationships between the various theories which are incorporated into the neo-factor and neo-technology models of trade.
3. Discuss the similarities and differences between the neo-factor and neo-technology theories of international trade, and the ownership-specific and location-specific factors identified in theories of foreign direct investment.
4. Under what conditions is foreign direct investment likely to increase international specialisation and enhance comparative advantage?
5. Consider the kinds of proxy variables that might be used to represent the ownership-specific advantages of firms and the location-specific attributes of countries.
6. The world appears to be entering a new era of protectionism, with quotas and non-tariff barriers increasingly being used to limit imports. In what ways might the trade and investment flows of multinational firms be affected by these trends in the world economy?
7. In general, what factors might distinguish MNE-generated from other trade flows?

Multinationals and economic development in host nations

Summary

1. Neo-classical theory predicts that the most important direct gains to host countries from increased foreign direct investment derive from higher tax revenues, from economies of scale and from external economies generally. The effects on the balance of payments could be adverse, and the absence of perfect competition may mean that the cost advantages of MNEs accrue to the parent company abroad rather than to the host country.

2. This neo-classical model is over-simplified and of limited value. The alternative approach is to review the various areas under which gains and losses could arise; and then assess each case on its merits, bearing in mind that foreign investment must be judged against whatever was a feasible alternative.

3. The effects of direct foreign investment on host countries may be considered under four headings (although it must be noted that the impact will also be influenced by the controls imposed over the resources transferred, a topic which will not be considered fully until Chapter 6):

    Resource transfer effects.   The foreign firm may make a positive contribution through the supply of capital, technology and management. But the MNE may raise most of its capital within the host economy, with disadvantageous effects if domestic savings are diverted from other productive uses. The realisation of the gains from the acquisition of technology also depends upon the terms under which the technology is transferred, and upon the suitability of the technology.

    Trade and balance-of-payments effects.   The balance of payments benefits from any initial capital inflow. To be set against this is the continuing outflow of dividends, royalties, and interest and administrative charges to the parent company. Another important issue is that of transfer pricing, which in turn is related to the role of tax havens and exchange rate speculation. The impact of foreign investment on levels of imports and exports is also significant, both in relation to the balance of payments and to economic growth. With development policy in the early 1970s stressing the role of exports of labour-intensive manufactures, foreign investment in labour-intensive industries or processes has assumed considerable importance.

Competitive and anti-competitive effects.   MNEs operate within oligopolistic market structures and possess greater economic power than indigenous competitors. But the effects of MNEs on economic performance in host countries are not easy to predict: some of the influencing factors are the form of the investment (as between an acquisition and a new establishment); the competitive situation in the host state; and the degree of economic development in the recipient country.

Sovereignty and autonomy effects.   Foreign investment inevitably involves some loss of economic independence for host countries, given that ultimate decision-making resides with the parent firm abroad. As a result, the ability of the host government to pursue its desired policies in areas such as taxation, trade etc. is reduced.

4. The empirical evidence on these issues indicates that the postulated adverse effects of MNE operations have perhaps been over-stressed, but equally the gains from foreign investment appear to be less than hypothesised. For example, in many cases MNEs do seem to adapt their technology when investing in labour-rich LDCs; conversely the gains from manufactured exports seem to be small because of the low value added locally, because of the substantial financial concessions offered by host governments and so on.

5. A major study by Lall and Streeten attempted to assess the overall impact of foreign direct investment in six developing nations. It was found that for five of the six countries the net balance of payments impact was negative. When expressed in net income terms it was estimated that almost 40 per cent of the companies in the sample produced negative effects.

6. Such net negative effects are much more likely in the less developed countries – with which this chapter is principally concerned – than in developed countries. There is the added complication that in the LDCs the impact of foreign investment may be considered not only in terms of the effects on income, but may be assessed against a much wider set of development goals. The need to consider each individual case on its own merits is perhaps the strongest conclusion to emerge from the empirical studies undertaken to date.

The key feature of direct foreign investment is that it provides the recipient nation with a 'package' of knowledge, capital and entrepreneurship. It may thereby make a positive contribution to economic growth and development in host countries. But there are costs as well as benefits associated with inward direct investment. For example, the repatriation of profits to the parent company may cause balance of payments difficulties for the host state; MNEs may use their monopoly power to exploit host country consumers; host governments fear a loss of economic independence as decision-making resides with corporate managers abroad, and so on. The aim of this chapter is, therefore, to assess both the gains and the losses associated with MNE activities in recipient states, with particular focus on the impact of multinationals on less developed countries.

Although the present chapter is concerned solely with the effects of MNEs on recipient countries, leaving the analysis and discussion of host nation control until Chapter 6, it is important to note that the two topics are closely interrelated. The impact of multinational firms will inevitably be influenced by the controls imposed over the use of the resources being transferred. This must, therefore, be borne in mind in the following pages. Controls of some sort or another are, moreover, virtually inevitable given the basic conflict of interests between firms and countries. The goals of MNEs and of host countries may coincide on certain issues, but there may also be a wide range of issues – balance of payments improvement, tax avoidance, income distribution, anti-competitive behaviour, transferred technology and so on – where objectives differ and where, consequently, conflicts arise. As will be explained, the outcome of the conflict and thus the effects on the host country will hinge essentially on the relative economic leverage of the two parties.

The benefits and costs of foreign direct investment: a theoretical approach

Neo-classical analysis of the effects of foreign investment derives from an article by MacDougall published in 1960.[1] MacDougall analysed the static effects of a flow of capital into a country (Australia), everything else being held constant. This inward direct investment was considered as increasing the host country stock of capital and reducing the home country capital stock in a simple one-for-one manner. The conventional assumptions apply, namely that the perfectly competitive economic system is in long-run full employment equilibrium. Additionally the balance of payments is assumed to be in equilibrium and to be maintained at that level without cost; terms of trade effects are ignored; returns to scale are assumed constant and there are no external economies; finally, there is no taxation. In Fig. 5.1, GL relates the capital stock to the marginal physical product of capital, given the

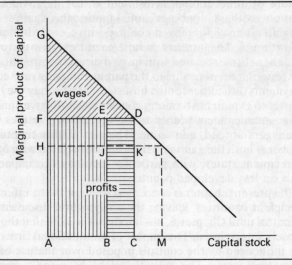

Fig. 5.1   The benefits and costs of foreign direct investment (*Source*: MacDougall, 1960).

amount of labour. The initial stock of capital is AC, of which AB is domestically-owned and BC foreign-owned. Profits on domestic capital are FEBA, and on foreign capital EDCB, while wages amount to GDF. Suppose that direct foreign investment increases from BC to BM, then foreign profits become JLMB. Since the marginal product of capital, and hence the profit rate, has fallen, total profits on domestic capital decline to HJBA. Although the increase in real wages amounts to FDLH, FEJH is merely a redistribution from domestic owners of capital. The host country as a whole gains EDLJ. The interpretation of this simple model was that this host country gain would be small in relation to the profits accruing to the new foreign capital (KLMC).

By dropping certain of the assumptions of the model, more important benefits may be obtained by the host nation. Suppose, for example, that a rate of tax t is imposed by the host country on foreign profits. Then the profits accruing to the owners of the extra foreign capital decline from KLMC to $1 - t$ (KLMC).[2] If the profits tax was of the order of 50 per cent then clearly taxation makes a significant difference to the gains derived by the host country. Conversely, although the terms of double taxation agreements may be fairly complex, some of the tax revenue accruing to the host government will represent a loss of revenue to the home government.

Introducing the possibility of external economies from additional foreign direct investment further increases the likelihood of benefits to the host country. These external economies may arise from the introduction of technology and know-how by foreign firms which is gradually diffused throughout the host economy. Similarly, foreign firms may introduce production methods which facilitate economies of scale, so that the proportionate growth in output is greater than the proportionate increase in labour and capital inputs; this again seems likely to bring a gain to the recipient country.

It would be wrong to suggest that the effects of foreign investment are all beneficial. Once the assumption of perfect competition is dropped, for example, then the range of possible outcomes, including adverse outcomes, is considerably increased. Cost advantages may not be passed on to consumers in lower prices or to workers in higher wages, but rather accrue as profits to the parent company. And oligopolistic competition has been shown to be a notable feature of the MNE. Moreover fluctuations in the net inflow of private capital and the fact that at least part of the foreign profits earned will be remitted back to the parent company, may create balance of payments difficulties. These problems, in turn, may require deflationary measures which will lower the rate of growth and produce unemployment. In total, therefore, the predictions of the model are fairly ambiguous. The approach is also fairly limited: in particular the comparative static approach is not very useful when analysing a dynamic force such as foreign investment. MacDougall's welfare analysis has been extended in several ways, but all the developments have taken place at a fairly high level of abstraction, and the models have been oversimplified representations of reality.[3]

If this framework is abandoned, however, it is necessary to revert to the equally unsatisfactory procedure of reviewing the various areas under which gains and losses could conceivably arise; and then judging each individual case on its merits. This creates difficulties since in most areas, e.g. balance of payments, there is no *a priori* way of knowing whether the MNEs' contribution will be positive or adverse. A further problem arises because the discussion must focus on whether foreign investment leaves the host country better off than it would have been under whatever was a feasible alternative. For example if the investment from abroad did not occur, would this be offset by indigenous investment?[4] Do the foreign firms employ labour which would otherwise have been unemployed? Does the presence of the foreign firm generate more or less entrepreneurship in the country than there would have been in its absence? In the following discussion of the gains and losses for the host country, the possible alternatives must be clearly borne in mind. The effects of foreign direct investment may be reviewed under four broad headings: resource transfer effects; trade and balance of payments effects; competitive and anti-competitive effects; and sovereignty and autonomy effects.

Resource transfer effects

Direct foreign investment can make a positive contribution to the host economy through the supply of capital, technology and management. To the extent that such inputs are scarce locally, then foreign investment may make it possible for output to be increased sharply.

Provision of capital

Multinational enterprises, by virtue of their large average size and other characteristics, have access to enormous financial resources for investment. These funds may be available from internal sources, but in addition MNEs may have easier and perhaps more privileged access to various external capital markets and financial institutions. By providing capital in these various ways, the MNE may make a contribution to filling the resource gap in the host economy between desired investment and domestic savings. Apart from the direct provision of capital, MNEs may have other positive but indirect effects on the supply of funds. In the first place MNE affiliates may mobilise local savings by offering attractive investment opportunities in domestic capital markets; without the MNE these local savings might remain idle or be used in less productive activities. Secondly, foreign direct investment may stimulate the flow of official aid from the MNEs' home country and from international agencies.

These potential benefits provided by the MNE may be reduced by various offsetting influences. For example it has been shown (Chapter 1) that the actual inflow of capital from MNEs is often fairly small, with most finance coming from reinvested profits and local savings. This is not particularly important if the funds could not have been used productively elsewhere in the economy (as in the argument put forward in the previous paragraph). On the other hand if the MNE borrows locally and diverts domestic savings from other productive uses, then local firms may be starved of investment funds. A second point is that private direct investment may be a fairly expensive way for a host country to acquire foreign capital. There certainly seems to be evidence that the rate of profit of MNEs is well above the long-term rate of interest ruling in international capital markets; but this is not a very valid comparison since capital is only one, and perhaps the least important, component in the package brought by the multinational firm.

Technology

The crucial role played by technology in the growth process is now widely accepted. Modern growth theory stresses that it is the technological application of labour and capital and not merely the presence of these factors of production which influences the rate of economic growth in an economy. One model developed states, for example, that the equilibrium growth rate in the long run is a function of the rate of technical advance and of the rate of growth of the labour supply.[5] Since the multinational enterprise is an important agent for both the production and diffusion of technology, then the potential importance of the MNE as a key to progress in host countries becomes clear.

Technology represents knowledge incorporated into new processes etc., which in turn must be capable of converting inputs into consumable outputs at competitive costs. For host countries and especially less developed host countries domestic production of technology would not be feasible. The process of creating new technology through research and development is an enormously costly, hit and miss affair, and the necessary skilled manpower is not available in the LDCs. However, by adopting established technologies, host countries, it may be argued, can by-pass the risky invention and innovation stages and thereby make a significant leap forward. The introduction of new technology could be cost-saving, reducing the cost of inputs necessary to obtain a given amount of output. Or new technology could mean the introduction of new production activities, products or processes. Or again the introduction of technology could enable one or a number of firms to meet competitive pressures successfully. It does not follow from this that the transfer of technology by MNEs to host countries will be unequivocally beneficial. The benefits to be gained by host states depend upon the terms under which the technology is transferred, including the price and the method of supply. In addition, since the know-how was produced by the industrialised countries to meet their own requirements – notably to exploit economies of scale in serving large markets, and to economise on scarce labour – the advantages to be gained by the host country will depend upon the suitability of the technology and associated products transferred. This is particularly pertinent to the LDCs, whose most abundant factor is that of unskilled labour.

Pricing and associated terms of sale.   Many of the potential difficulties in the transfer of technology undoubtedly emanate from the unique characteristics of technology itself and its association with the multinational firm.[6] In particular there is no free market in which a host country could buy knowledge. The marginal cost of using or selling an already developed technology is zero for the owner of that technology. Conversely, from the point of view of the purchaser in say an LDC the marginal cost of developing an alternative technology might be enormous (or infinite if the capability did not exist at all). Within these two limits there is no price which *a priori* could be considered more or less appropriate. An objective pricing formula requires that the amount of technology traded or transferred can be measured accurately, and a price thereby determined. Since this is not possible, price determination requires negotiation and bargaining. In such a bargaining process the host country is inevitably at a disadvantage, because it cannot know all there is to know about what is being bought until the technology has been purchased.

The direct price paid for the technology will in most cases be reflected in the royalties and licence fees which foreign firms charge their overseas affiliates. In some cases, however, a wholly-owned subsidiary may not pay royalties or technical fees separately, as the benefits of the technology accrue in any event as dividends to the parent firm. The direct price may in fact be a less important cost in obtaining technology than the associated terms and conditions of sale. Technology contracts may frequently incorporate tie-in clauses which require the licensee to buy expensive machinery, technical services, intermediate parts and other inputs from the parent corporation or from its other foreign subsidiaries. In addition, restrictions may be imposed on the freedom of the licensee or affiliated company to buy and sell products related to the technology transferred. Conditions may also be incorporated relating to the termination of contracts and arbitration of disputes.

Some of these criticisms of the terms under which technology is transferred represent criticisms of the international patent system. This is so because patenting is a common procedure for transferring manufacturing technology at least in certain sectors, and the sale of patented technology often includes restrictive clauses of the types noted above.[7] Various other specific criticisms of the patent system have also been made. The most common argument is that the majority of patents taken out are not used for production within the country concerned, but have the effect of blocking the domestic market from cheaper imports and preventing local firms from using the patented or other competitive technology. The point may not have too much validity: many patents are never used simply because they cannot support a viable and competitive product, and therefore 'non-use' may not be an abuse of patent protection. Furthermore, alternative imports or technology may simply not be available.

Appropriateness of technology. Much of the effectiveness of know-how and innovations will depend upon the transfer to host countries of *appropriate* technologies. Thus the technology transferred should be appropriate to the relative factor endowments of a country. If, for example, a country is well endowed with unskilled labour, then innovations should be biased in an unskilled-labour-using direction. The problem is shown diagrammatically in Fig. 5.2. Three factors of production are assumed – capital (K), skilled labour (S) and unskilled labour (U). The ray from O to K_1, S_1, U_1 represents the relative availability of the three factors of production during a particular period. Ideally, projects established should utilise all three factors fully. If, however, the projects use technologies which are inappropriate – perhaps relying chiefly on capital and skilled labour – then the likelihood of unemployment among the unskilled labour force exists. In the diagram, if the products use factor inputs in the combination shown by the ray from O to K_1, S_1, U_2, then U_1 U_2 unskilled labour remains unemployed.

This 'factor-proportions problem' is enormously important to the developing countries and a wide range of literature has emerged on the

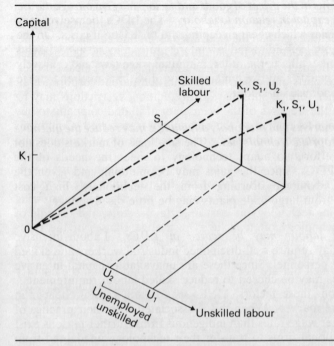

Fig. 5.2 The factor proportions problem.

subject.[8] If capital intensive technologies are being imported into these countries by multinational firms then this places severe limits on the degree of labour absorption possible. And yet underemployment and unemployment on a massive scale is perhaps the principal problem facing the LDCs. The introduction of excessively capital-intensive technologies may have other adverse effects: income inequalities may be worsened; local firms may be encouraged to operate similarly capital-intensive techniques because of the 'demonstration effect'; and production may be biased towards the sophisticated commodities for which the technology has been developed.

The evidence on the extent of the adaptability of foreign firms to the particular labour surplus conditions existing in the LDCs will be presented later in this chapter. At this point it is worth noting that there may be particular factors which work against adaptation:[9]

(i) *Technologies appropriate to conditions in the LDCs may not exist.*   It is suggested that at any point in time there are only a very few techniques for producing a commodity, and such techniques, because they were developed in the advanced countries, have become increasingly capital-intensive. The technologies required by the LDCs may have been scrapped long ago as obsolescent.

(ii) *Distortions in the prices of goods and factors may encourage the use of too much capital in relation to labour.* The LDCs themselves may operate policies which cheapen capital and raise labour costs. On the one hand capital subsidies and low interest rates may act as a stimulus to investment, while on the other, minimum wage laws and relatively high fringe benefits and redundancy pay provisions may encourage firms to economise on labour.

(iii) *Small markets and monopoly advantages may reduce the incentive to find appropriate technologies.* The smallness of markets does not encourage efforts to adapt technology to meet the needs of the individual LDCs, since the gains may be minimal; and given the monopoly advantage accruing from the technology, high cost production from large-scale plants may be little disadvantage.

(iv) *Skilled labour may be scarce in LDCs.* Labour-intensive processes may require well-disciplined industrial workers and skilled supervisory personnel. Since these are unavailable, capital-intensive technologies may be chosen to reduce skilled labour requirements.

Apart from these factors, MNEs may obtain capital cheaper in international markets. When this is associated with their practice of paying higher wage rates than indigenous firms, further reasons exist for multinational firms to transfer their technology unadapted from the home country. Nevertheless, even if there is only limited scope or incentive for changing the technology *in any one industry* in accordance with relative factor endowments, this need not be disastrous. Thus there are considerable differences *as between industries* in relative capital- and labour-intensity. Textiles, footwear and food processing, for example, are relatively labour-intensive industries. Furthermore even within the technologically-advanced, capital-intensive industries, some processes and activities are labour-intensive, e.g. the wiring of boards in the electronic equipment field.

There is a further issue on appropriateness which is important and this relates to the *suitability of products* rather than the *appropriateness of factor use.* The products marketed by MNEs have been seen to be biased towards sophisticated, high technology commodities, and heavily advertised, differentiated consumer goods. Such products, e.g. cosmetics, breakfast cereals, hi-fi equipment, may not be suitable for low income countries either because they are within the reach of only a small élite or because their consumption by a wider population may be at the expense of more essential items. What the argument is saying is that private values represented by market prices do not reflect social values, and therefore the market should be ignored. The difficulty comes in deciding what is and what is not beneficial in different circumstances.

When everything is taken into consideration, 'if the return on the superior technology brought by foreign investment is entirely absorbed by the foreign companies, prices of commodities to consumers and the prices of factors of production in the economy remaining unchanged, there is no direct benefit to the economy'.[10] The conclusion is therefore that once the process of technology transfer is introduced, the close association assumed by neo-classical theory between technology and economic growth becomes much more tenuous.

Management

The provision of foreign management and managerial skills may produce important benefits for the host country. In the first place these may be scarce factors and the inflow of entrepreneurial ability and skilled management thereby improves the balance of the local economy. The spin-off effects may be even more important: local personnel who are trained to occupy managerial, financial and technical posts in the MNE affiliate may later leave the firm and help to stimulate indigenous entrepreneurship. Similarly there may be beneficial demonstration effects on local suppliers and local competitors. On the other hand there could conceivably be few positive results if management and highly skilled jobs in MNEs were mostly reserved for home country nationals; and adverse effects if local producers were choked off by the competition of foreign-owned subsidiaries. Furthermore it has been suggested that the gains from training local personnel in the practices of MNEs may not produce external benefits in developing countries, since these practices may have little relevance to the normal methods of business operation. The practices of large, complex multinational firms may not be appropriate in small indigenous companies manufacturing fairly basic products, and perhaps relying heavily on personal contacts.

In concluding this discussion it is worth considering the relevance of the dynamic element to the assessment of resource transfer effects. When a subsidiary is first established there will normally be an inflow of capital; but thereafter the growth of the firm may be financed either from retained profits or from local savings. It is possible that the main transfer of technology may also take place early in the life of the subsidiary. On the other hand, both the degree of involvement of local personnel in management, and relationships with local suppliers, may increase with the number of years the subsidiary has been operating, as well as with its performance. It has been concluded on the basis of such factors that the net positive impact of foreign direct investment can be expected to be at a peak early in the life of the subsidiary and to decline thereafter. The point of decline could be postponed if the subsidiary enlarges its character and functions, but this depends a great deal on parent company policy regarding the autonomy it is prepared to grant its affiliates. It may also depend upon the location of the affiliate, as between developed and less developed host countries: MNEs are unlikely to decentralise important decision-making functions to the LDCs. These comments, it must be added, assume that host governments do not intervene to try to increase the net positive benefits from inward direct investment.

Trade and balance of payments effects

These are two separate but related issues. The balance of payments is an important policy issue for host governments, as shortages of foreign exchange may act as a constraint on growth in just the same way that a deficiency of savings does. This is essentially the conclusion of the 'double-gap' (savings and foreign exchange) theory[11] Even if savings were adequate domestically, these could not be used to buy investment goods from abroad, until the resources had been converted into foreign exchange. Increased foreign aid, import substitution policies and greater direct foreign investment were all seen as means by which the foreign exchange bottleneck could be relieved in developing host countries.

When a multinational company establishes a foreign affiliate, the capital account of the balance of payments obviously benefits from any initial capital inflow, although this may only be a once-and-for-all effect. To be set against this is the continuing adverse impact on the current account balance of payments, representing the payment of dividends, interest, royalties or administrative charges to the parent company. The gains and losses extend much further than this, however. If the MNE subsidiary was established as an export supply point – whether based on raw material extraction, component assembly or manufacture etc. – there are favourable trade effects. Market access is thus an important benefit for the host country, although market-sharing agreements and so on may limit the actual size of export markets. To obtain the net effect it is also necessary to take account of the raw materials and intermediate inputs which the MNE may import. Alternative import-substituting types of foreign investment may have positive balance of payments effects in releasing valuable foreign exchange, but the net impact depends on the import propensity of the MNE in the host country. These trade issues will be raised again, in a development context, in following paragraphs.

Another important and emotive issue relating to the balance of payments is that of transfer pricing. The transfer price is the price at which a transfer or sale of goods takes place *within* a firm, regardless of whether or not the firm spans different countries. Such prices can be quite different from the prices that would obtain in arm's length transactions, and therefore can be used to shift profits clandestinely between affiliates and the parent company or between affiliates themselves. The chief factors relevant to the pricing of intra-firm transactions will be:[12]

(i) Inter-country differences in tariffs, taxes and subsidies.

(ii) Restrictions imposed by host governments on the remission of profits abroad.

(iii) Existence of local shareholders.

(iv) Exchange rate factors, e.g. instability of rates, or multiple rates, with the rate applicable to profit remittances being unfavourable.

(v) Political and social pressures: these may range from trade union pressures for increased wages consequent on the level of declared profits to government threats of nationalisation because of exploitation.

The relative significance of these various factors as inducements to use transfer pricing is difficult to judge. Corporate tax rates do not differ that much between countries. On the other hand, the expansion of intra-firm trade, the growth of global business strategy, and increasing protectionism are all factors which may increase the importance of transfer pricing. The existence of thriving tax havens in the Bahamas and elsewhere and the operation by MNEs of 'shadow companies' also bear witness to the fact that very large sums of money can be made and lost by financial manipulations.[13] In so far as transfer pricing operates against the interests of any host country, then the result is that the balance of payments gains from foreign investment are less, or losses more, than they would otherwise have been. But the costs are not simply balance of payments costs: local shareholders may lose part of their legitimate profits, workers may lose if wage increases are curbed, and consumers may pay higher prices than necessary.

Before leaving this issue some comment is necessary on the role of MNEs in exchange rate speculation. This has become potentially more important since the Bretton Woods system of fixed exchange rates collapsed. Thus there has developed an increased incentive for MNEs to shift their liquid assets around in times of monetary instability to protect their interests or to seek short-term financial gain. In the process this is likely to accentuate the pressure on the currencies involved and may have destabilising balance of payments effects. At the same time, the growth of the Eurodollar market has substantially increased borrowing facilities; and large MNEs, generally rated as prime credit risks, have the possibility of borrowing large amounts in this market to finance their 'speculative' activities.[14]

Aside from the balance of payments question, economists have always been interested in the more direct relationship between international trade and economic development. It is self-evident that development and trade are related in some manner. Internal markets in many LDCs are small because of low incomes. This could hinder the installation of large scale capacity which would raise productivity and incomes and thereby widen the market. By engaging in international trade the countries concerned might be able to break out of this vicious circle and expand their markets and incomes.

Views on the actual association have, however, changed considerably over time. To the classical economists, trade was seen as an 'engine of growth' as it facilitated the exploitation of international comparative advantage. By the 1950s it was obvious that for the LDCs exports of primary commodities were not having the propulsive effects on development predicted by the classical school. Imperfections in the international trading system, such as oligopolistic competition, discriminatory pricing and product differentiation, discredited the concept of export-led growth for developing countries. The result was that many countries turned to policies which involved the substitution of imports by domestic production, through the control of investment decisions and the protection of the domestic market from international competition. But by the mid-1960s these import substitution policies were also seen to be ineffective and inefficient: domestic markets were too small to support optimal-sized plants, involving excess capacity and the loss of economies of scale; the industries attracted by protectionist policies were frequently capital-intensive and therefore did little to increase the level of employment; as a result of the necessity to purchase capital goods and intermediate inputs abroad, the assumed savings of foreign exchange did not occur; and, rather than creating domestically-owned and controlled industry, protection encouraged foreign direct investment.[15]

As a consequence of such factors, a new orthodoxy emerged in the late 1960s and early 1970s which stressed the role of exports of labour-intensive manufactures as an engine of growth. In essence this represents a return to the static theory of comparative advantage, with trade based upon different factor proportions prevailing in various countries. Four routes have been suggested for the development of manufactured exports:[16] local raw material processing; conversion of import-substituting industry to exporting; new labour-intensive final product exports, e.g. textiles, shoes, toys, sporting equipment; and labour-intensive processes and component specialisation within vertically integrated international industries, e.g. semiconductors and other components for Japanese, US and European electronic firms, automotive parts for motor industries in the developed countries etc. Of these various types of exports, it is in the latter two fields that the major developments have been taking place, and equally, these are the sectors in which multinational companies are particularly involved.

The pendulum has thus turned full circle for development policy in the LDCs – from primary commodity exports through import substitutes to manufactured exports.[17] This creates major difficulties when trying to assess the impact of MNEs in host countries. Multinational firms have been heavily involved at each of these stages, but the fact that a particular policy has not in retrospect proved successful cannot be considered as a condemnation of the companies themselves. For the future too all that can be said is that the MNE is a potentially significant contributor to economic development, if development policy based on exports of labour-intensive manufactures proves to be successful.

Competitive and anti-competitive effects

Industrial organisation theory has shown that both the efficiency of resource allocation and the distribution of economic welfare are strongly influenced by the structure of the markets in which firms operate. This emerges from the links between the structure of markets and the conduct and performance of firms within these markets. Where the market structure reveals high seller concentration, a significant degree of product differentiation and high barriers to entry facing potential competitors, then this confers on existing firms a degree of market power which they may exploit in various ways.[18]

For any given market structure, foreign affiliates operating in the market may be deemed to possess greater economic power than indigenous competitors. This derives from the fact that they are part of larger and international organisations. For example, because the affiliates are part of larger enterprises, their share of local output may inadequately reflect their market power: the affiliate will have access to centralised facilities provided by the parent company and to the MNE's total knowledge and expertise. Similarly, the international nature of the MNE increases the options available, so that, for instance, product, pricing and promotional strategies for any affiliate may be devised to take specific account of the competitive position existing.

Evidence has already been presented to show that US manufacturing MNEs, at least, have certain distinctive structural characteristics. The MNEs tend to be larger than all US firms; they produce under conditions of imperfect oligopoly, are more capital intensive and advertise more. Equally, in the host countries in which the MNEs operate, the structural characteristics of the industries in which affiliates are represented tend to mirror the situation in the United States. But this is not very meaningful, since it does not say whether or not the market structures in host countries would have exhibited these same characteristics, e.g. high concentration, high degree of product differentiation etc. even without an MNE presence.

The situation may be presumed to be different for an acquisition as compared with a new establishment, and for the setting up of an affiliate in a developed as opposed to a developing country. In the LDCs, where MNEs will be likely to face little if any effective indigenous competition, the potential monopoly impact of transnational companies may be a very real fear. In such circumstances the MNE may be able to engage in a wide variety of practices which lead to higher profits, lower efficiency, higher costs, the erection of barriers to entry, and so forth. Moreover, if MNE investment was induced by host country tariffs, this could lead to an influx of foreign firms on the 'follow-the-leader' model, producing excessive product differentiation and a proliferation of inefficient small-scale plants. In a developed host country, on the other hand, the entry of an MNE may have the effect of breaking up a cosy, oligopolistic market structure and thereby stimulate competition and efficiency. But over time, because the affiliate possesses certain advantages over local firms, its market share may tend to increase. If the affiliate ultimately takes over a market leadership role within the industry, it will then be able to use its market power to operate restrictive practices and raise barriers to entry.

Entry by means of a greenfield venture would generally be preferred to that of an acquisition. The establishment of a new enterprise increases the number of firms in an industry and therefore reduces the degree of seller concentration. A merger or take-over, on the other hand, leaves the degree of concentration in the market unchanged. However, the implications that can be drawn from this depend partly on the existing economic strength of the acquired firm and partly on the overall level of competition within the industry. If the acquired company was small and inefficient, and operating in a non-competitive industry, the entry of the MNE might have a beneficial effect on competition. Equally, other circumstances could be postulated in which the acquisition would weaken competition in the industry.

The effect of MNEs on market structure, conduct and performance in host countries is thus not easy to predict. Apart from the influences noted above, the strength of host government anti-trust legislation will have an important effect. Similarly, the encouragement given by governments to industrial restructuring as a means of creating viable competitive indigenous firms will also be relevant. All that can be concluded is that in some industries and in some countries the impact of MNE affiliates will be small. In other cases the impact may be dramatic; but a dramatic effect may be exactly what is required in an industry whose performance had previously been sluggish, non-competitive and inefficient.

Less obviously, MNEs will have an impact on the competitive environment in host countries through their labour relations activities. The foreign firms concerned are bound to be influenced by practices and work methods in their home countries, although these may be alien to the host country. To give only a few examples of differences between the USA and UK: in America, contracts are for the most part legally binding for a fixed term, and single-union representation at the negotiating table is the norm; the degree of unionisation in Britain is about double that in the USA; the UK unions are much more politically aware (and perhaps motivated). But apart from home/host country differences, potential problems may emerge because of firms' multinational status: the freedom of action of the subsidiary is limited by the need to secure approval of the parent; negotiating difficulties may lead to threats to withdraw and to transfer investment projects elsewhere; and from the labour side a multinational firm may be assumed to have a greater capacity to pay. In the LDCs the impact may be even more fundamental. The foreign firms may pay high wages, introduce a shorter working week, and institute generous welfare services. While socially desirable, these innovations may accentuate duality, provide a stimulus to inflation and generally hinder economic development.

Sovereignty and autonomy effects

Although many of the factors noted previously could be either gains or losses to the host country, the sovereignty and autonomy effects of the MNE would always be seen as a cost. Even if foreign firms provide a stimulus to the local economy, this involves some loss of economic independence. Such problems arise essentially from the international nature of MNEs so that policies towards any one affiliate may presumably be constrained by, and be subordinate to, the pursuit of some global objective. Ultimate decision-making does not therefore reside with the subsidiary. Decisions on investment and financial policy, marketing, purchasing, employment and trade policy may all be taken by the parent company with resulting costs to the economy. For example, sovereignty costs could arise in the area of sales and marketing, due to the centralisation of product and market development policies. In the developed countries in fact the most emphasised problem is that of technological dependence, resulting from the centralisation and co-ordination of R & D in the home country.

The feature common to these decision-areas is that all lie within what may be broadly called long-term, strategic and planning areas. Such entrepreneurial-type decision-making functions may be contrasted with the short-run and operational decision-areas which encompass production-scheduling, costing and budgeting, labour relations, maintenance and repair etc. The greater the volume of foreign direct investment in a host country, the more reliant the economy will be on external decision-making in these strategic areas. This means that the economy becomes more reliant on allocated as opposed to self-generated growth.

There are other equally important aspects relating to the reduced ability of the host government to pursue its desired policies. The MNE is less responsive to monetary policy measures because it can draw on funds elsewhere; government fiscal policies may be circumvented by transfer pricing; trade policy may be determined by marketing considerations of the parent firm or by political conditions imposed upon it by the home government, and so on. Host governments in the LDCs may also be in weak bargaining positions *vis-à-vis* multinational companies. This may mean that the companies concerned secure excessive protection or tax concessions, and that the host government undertakes expensive infrastructure investment (e.g. roads, harbours, education). Profits earned by the MNE in these circumstances may be connected with low or negative social returns.

Concluding comments

This discussion began by considering foreign direct investment as a general inflow of capital from abroad; and the effects of overseas investment were analysed using a standard neo-classical model. Rejecting this framework in favour of a less rigorous but more realistic approach, consideration has been given to a wide variety of potential gains and losses associated with the activities of multinational firms in host countries. It must be obvious from this debate that it is not possible to make any net evaluation of the effects of MNEs. Many of the issues are highly controversial and admit to varying interpretations. In addition no attempt has been made to consider what might have happened if the foreign investment had not taken place. But the costs of inward direct investment need to be compared with the costs of the alternatives. Would the project have been undertaken at all or would it have been undertaken much less efficiently in the absence of foreign investment?

Of equal importance is the way the effects of MNEs on economic development are to be judged, which depends very much on the definition of 'economic development'. The latter is a wider concept than that of economic growth. And yet in conventional economics the two have been treated as virtually synonymous, the only measure of development being used for policy and analytical purposes being the growth of *per capita* Gross National Product. However, economic development should relate to a country's performance in terms of all the economic policy objectives set by the host government concerned, and not merely to its growth performance. Policy objectives are normally set in terms of: economic growth; reasonably full employment (or in the LDCs, a reduction in unemployment or underemployment); price stability; and balance of payments equilibrium; to which might be added equitable distribution of income, and economic independence. If such development goals are used, then the assessment of the impact of MNEs becomes very complex. Accepting *per capita* GNP as the sole objective means that the effects of inward direct investment can be calculated by any technique for measuring the costs and benefits of investment generally. With a variety of development goals, on the other hand, all the possible trade-offs have to be considered. For example, in many LDCs great stress has been laid upon economic independence, which, if this means a reduced level of foreign direct investment, may also mean lower economic growth. On the other hand reduced 'material income' may be offset by higher 'psychic income', representing greater nationalistic

satisfaction.[19] Other issues concern the desired degree of industrialisation since the latter may raise productivity and economic growth
without making any impact on the massive unemployment problem
faced by some LDCs. Perhaps the most important problem is that
relating to the distribution of income in host countries. In general in
the recipient area there are likely to be gains for labour and losses for
capital; but among labour groups too the benefits may be confined to a
small caucus of MNE employees while the great mass of the population
remain unemployed or underemployed. The inequalities may further
apply by regions, i.e. urban and industrial v. rural areas; and by sector,
i.e. manufacturing, mining and plantations v. food for domestic
consumption. Furthermore, inequality may be sustained by the
socio-political power of the elite groups in developing countries.
Overall, the firmest conclusion that can be reached is that the MNE
may or may not have a positive effect on the policy objectives relating
to growth, employment, prices and the balance of payments. On the
other hand, it will almost certainly have an adverse effect on income
distribution (at least in the LDCs) and on economic independence.
This means that development based on foreign direct investment is not
neutral as regards social policy, but it does not mean that development
and social progress is incompatible.

No comment has yet been made on the issue of whether or not the
impact of MNEs differs as between developed and less developed host
countries. And yet it is primarily in the LDCs that broader
development goals are formulated, so that the effects of MNEs are
obviously considered differently. Much of the preceding discussion
relating to the costs associated with MNE operations also referred
chiefly to the developing countries. Thus the possibility of net adverse
effects from an MNE presence is much more real in the LDCs. Fears of
loss of sovereignty and autonomy are often less acute in the richer
countries (with the exception of countries such as Canada and
Australia), and the larger industrialised countries at least may be able
to offer more effective countervailing power to the MNE. As both
home and host to the MNEs, such countries have a greater
understanding and acceptance of the ethics of 'big business'. Again,
the developed nations as a group are capital-rich with high-income
consumers, and therefore the problem of obtaining inappropriate
products or inappropriate technologies is hardly likely to apply.
Indigenous firms in the developed countries may also have a greater
potential for assimilating the know-how brought by the multinational
firm, and may provide greater competition for the MNE. In all these
ways the industrialised countries seem likely to obtain a greater share
of any benefits brought by multinational firms. By the same token it
means that if the LDCs are to increase their net benefits or reduce their
net losses from MNE operations, a great deal hinges on devising
effective means of regulating the companies.

The impact of the MNE on economic development: empirical results

In presenting the empirical evidence a distinction is made, as in the previous section, between: resource transfer effects; balance of payments impact; competitive and anti-competitive effects; and sovereignty and autonomy costs. In addition some consideration is given to various studies which attempt to measure the aggregate impact of foreign direct investment. Most of the evidence relates to the LDCs, but where possible developed country examples are also quoted.

Resource transfer effects

Capital

In the early post-war period capital was stressed as the key factor in development. Foreign direct investment was therefore seen as a source of funds which supplemented domestic savings, and which might relieve foreign exchange shortages. In fact the contribution of foreign capital to world-wide capital formation has been small, e.g. during the 1960s foreign direct investment in Latin America represented at most 4-5 per cent of total capital formation. This does not appear to have mattered greatly, however, since the evidence of the last twenty years has been that capital has been less scarce than expected. This was firstly because the level of domestic savings was quite high in some LDCs; secondly because more foreign aid (as well as foreign investment) became available, and thirdly, because the capital/output ratio turned out to be lower than development models had postulated. In the 1960s the share of gross investment in the GNP of LDCs was almost 20 per cent and the share of savings in GNP over 15 per cent.[20] A deficiency of savings has seemed only to be an acute problem at the very early stage of the development process. Once LDCs have achieved a certain measure of growth, they appear to be able to develop their own indigenous means of mobilising savings.

A more significant problem would arise if it could be shown that MNEs have drawn on these local savings and deprived indigenous firms of funds. Certainly foreign affiliates have been shown to generate a large proportion of their capital requirements locally: in the period 1966–72, for example, finance from the parent corporations represented only about one-fifth of total funds employed by US affiliates in all developing countries.[21] The remainder came from depreciation provisions, other foreign funds raised in third countries, retained earnings, and locally-raised loans and equity (although arguably the reinvested profits should be considered as a foreign exchange inflow since the funds could have been repatriated by the affiliate). However, there have been no systematic attempts to test whether foreign firms enjoy preferential treatment from host country financial institutions when borrowing locally or whether in the process local firms are starved of funds. Where foreign firms do use local savings, moreover, a distinction should be made between equity financing and borrowing. The former is obviously preferred from a host country viewpoint since local equity shareholders receive the same return on their investment as do foreign investors. The limited evidence on this issue relating to a number of LDCs suggests that foreign affiliates do not have a significantly different financing pattern (borrowing v. equity finance) than do domestic firms.[22]

Technology
Recent theoretical developments, backed up by empirical evidence, have shown that it is chiefly the technological application of factors and production such as capital and not merely their existence which produces economic growth. That is, quality matters more than quantity. Econometric studies relating to some industrialised countries during the period 1950–62 indicated that between 60 and 85 per cent of measured economic growth resulted from increased output per unit of input (factor productivity): only the remaining 15–40 per cent was attributable to increases in inputs of labour, capital and land.[23]

It is this technology component which MNEs are pre-eminent in providing to host countries. There are admittedly fears in recipient states about technological dependence on the countries and corporations providing the know-how, but technological dependence *per se* is not particularly important. As has been argued, host country research and development should not be encouraged if the economy was likely to grow faster or more efficiently by borrowing technology and using the freed resources in other ways. In other words, comparative advantage in the production of technology should be pursued like any other comparative advantage. What is more relevant is, firstly, the appropriateness of the technology obtained, and, secondly, the costs of the technology received, since it is these factors which will determine whether or not the recognised association between technology and economic growth is actually translated into net benefits at the host country level.

Appropriateness of transferred technology. In this instance, an appropriate technology for the LDCs is taken to be one in which factor substitution takes place to reflect differing factor availabilities (i.e. labour abundance). It is easy to quote individual examples where technologies have or have not been adapted to take account of different circumstances in the LDCs. Thus adaptation of existing technology in India enabled buffalo milk to be used instead of cow's milk as the basis for powdered baby food. Again, a Japanese glass manufacturer set up a subsidiary in India that is half the size of the parent firm but employs three times as many workers. In Kenya, on the other hand, criticism has been directed at the fact that imported corrugated iron sheets are used instead of local materials such as timber and bamboo for roofing. And in Brazil, a tyre plant was said to be a virtual copy of a factory in the home country, while a tractor manufacturer was reported as claiming to ignore labour cost differentials entirely when choosing machinery.[24]

The broader empirical studies which have been undertaken have produced conflicting results. This is partly a reflection of the methodology of the studies themselves, but also indicates that the actual practices employed by foreign-owned firms in the application of technology are quite complex. Mason found that indigenous firms and US-owned MNEs in the Philippines and Mexico did not have significantly different amounts of plant and machinery per factory worker.[25] But such results could be interpreted either as implying adaptation by the MNEs or that local firms copied the unadapted technology of the MNEs through a 'demonstration effect'. In another study, Reuber found that about 30 per cent of a sample of 78 MNEs drawn from a range of industries and countries adapted their technology in some way when moving into the LDCs.[26] While other findings do not necessarily support this result in terms of the degree of adaptability, they do confirm that the situation may differ widely across industries and countries. Courtney and Leipziger, for example, found that in six of eleven industries studied, technology differed between affiliates in developed and less-developed countries, but not systematically in a more labour-using or capital-using way; in the other five industries technology did not differ significantly.[27] A further piece of research, using data relating to Ghana, revealed that MNEs used plant and machinery embodying different factor proportions from those in domestic industries; but whether or nor the multinational firms used more capital-intensive or labour-intensive methods varied from industry to industry.[28]

The explanation for adaptation or lack of adaptation is the critical element for policy, but on this issue evidence is piecemeal. Most of the results quoted above would not support the argument of a lack of choice of technology. Moreover the evidence of Forsyth and Solomon conflicts with the hypothesis and limited evidence that MNEs use more capital-intensive methods because of shortages of skilled labour in the LDCs. It has been found that the degree of adaptation of MNEs to local factor costs and availability was partly a function of competitive pressures. Where product differentiation and the degree of market power was high, adaptation was low. There is other evidence of factor price distortions in many developing countries, wages paid being higher than the marginal social cost of labour and capital being under-priced as a result of credit subsidisation and interest-rate ceilings.[29] The position is thus complex, but in trying to develop policy implications it is worth quoting from the results of a recent study by Morley and Smith relating to Brazil: ' . . . the evidence suggests that the choice of technique is not so limited as it is often portrayed to be and that the failure of firms to adapt may well be the result of their limited search in a permissive environment rather than technical factors'. Therefore ' . . . if LDCs want multinationals to employ more labour-intensive methods, they should be prepared to reduce the permissiveness of the environment. This means allowing greater competition from imports and avoiding "overkill" in granting favors to attract foreign firms'.[30] Furthermore, because of prestige factors LDCs may sometimes insist on developing industries that are capital intensive by their nature, and also resist the importation of 'outdated' or second-hand equipment when, in fact, the latter could permit a more efficient use of local resources.

What is encouraging is that some major MNEs are now consciously attempting to introduce appropriate technologies for the developing countries: Ford's low cost 'modern model T' (Fiera), for example, is designed to be manufactured in small job shops where brake presses and simple welding jigs are to be used instead of the stamping dies and automated equipment operated in the United States. If this production technology is successful in the first plant in the Philippines, Ford plan to introduce it throughout the Asia-Pacific region.[31] Assuming this turns out to be satisfactory, it may well stimulate other MNEs to think rather more seriously than they may have done in the past about the possibilities of adapting technologies in their Third World locations.

Cost of transferred technology.   This issue is closely linked to that of the balance of payments and transfer pricing, and some of the evidence relating to the overpricing of imports where technology transfer is involved will be presented in that context. Basically, the alleged problems associated with the transfer of technology are, firstly, that the royalties and licence fees charged by MNEs are too high; secondly, that tie-in clauses in technology contracts require the licensee to purchase capital equipment and intermediate parts from the parent company, when such items could have been obtained more economically from elsewhere; and thirdly, that technology contracts frequently incorporate export prohibition clauses, limiting the sale of goods using this imported technology to the receiving country. The level of royalties and licence fees cannot really be adjudged empirically because of the lack of any objective method of pricing technology. What can be assumed is that where royalty payments etc. are settled through bargaining, the agreement reached will depend a great deal on the relative negotiating strengths of the parties involved. In the industrialised countries, firms which are potential licensees will often be large and sophisticated, and moreover specialised government agencies may sometimes exist (e.g. MITI and JETRO in Japan), to undertake or assist with the negotiations. Developing countries may be at a disadvantage because of a lack of the necessary bargaining skills at both firm and government levels.

Regarding tie-in and export-restrictive clauses there is a certain amount of evidence mainly relating to some Latin American countries. In an investigation of 250 contracts for technology transfer in Bolivia, Colombia, Ecuador and Peru, it was found that 81 per cent of the contracts prohibited exports totally and a further 5 per cent incorporated some restrictive clauses on exports.[32] These figures refer to all firms making technology contracts, including wholly-owned foreign affiliates, joint ventures and indigenous firms. Where Andean-owned firms alone are considered, 92 per cent of the contracts prohibited the exportation of goods produced with foreign technology. For three of these same countries – Bolivia, Ecuador and Peru – two thirds of the contracts for which information was available (136) included tie-in clauses. The most important tie-in arrangement was the requirement to purchase materials from the technology supplier. Some of the contracts also made such tied purchase conditional on a maximum price being paid for the goods purchased. Other contracts, in addition, prohibited, limited and controlled the use of local materials. It is difficult to interpret the implications of these restrictive arrangements, but certainly they do seem to present fairly formidable obstacles to the entry of LDCs into world trade in manufactures. That such restrictive practices may seriously affect the net benefits available to host countries from technology transfer is also evidenced by action taken in the United Nations. Thus in 1975 a 'Code of Conduct for the Transfer of Technology' was formulated with 40 restrictive business practices in technology transfer being prohibited. To give one example from this code, technology suppliers would not be able to limit exports of licensees' products. These control aspects of technology transfer will be considered further in Chapter 6. It should be noted in conclusion that with the attention being given to these issues in the last few years, host country governments and indigenous firms must now be fully aware of the problems associated with technology contracts. It may thus be assumed that host countries and firms will be commensurately more careful when negotiating terms and conditions.

Employment
The importance of employment creation in the LDCs as an objective of economic development has already been noted. In general, however, the contribution of the industrial sector to employment growth has been disappointing.[33] To take an example from Brazil, while gross value added in manufacturing increased at an annual rate of 6.5 per cent during the 1960s decade, numbers of employees in manufacturing increased annually by only 1.1 per cent; in India the equivalent figures were 5.9 and 3.8 per cent; and in Nigeria 14.1 and 5.7 per cent.

By virtue of their very existence in host nations, MNEs clearly make some contribution to increasing the level of employment. Considering the *direct* impact on employment in developing countries, the United

Nations estimated that MNEs had created 2 million jobs by 1970. This represents roughly 0.2 per cent of the total active population of the LDCs, and compares with an unemployment total of about 50 million.[34]

These comparisons are not very meaningful, and what is required is some assessment of whether the MNEs' contribution to employment is greater or smaller than it might have been. This will depend partly on the *choice of techniques* and partly on the *composition of output*.

The discussion above on the *choice of technology* implied that criticisms of MNEs for using capital-intensive techniques (and thereby minimising employment creation) may not be valid in many instances or at least that the responsibility often rests with the developing countries themselves. In some industries MNEs have a greater absorptive capacity for unskilled labour than indigenous firms. On the other hand, there have been studies looking at the macro-employment implications of adopting particular technology policies, which have indicated considerable potential for increasing jobs. While not merely referring to MNE-created employment, it was calculated that a ten-year 'technology freeze' policy in Puerto Rico could have increased 1963 employment from the actual figure of 600,000 to 1 million jobs, if the level of industrial output had not been affected.[35] But the latter is a heroic proviso, and in general there are serious problems associated with these types of studies.

Equally important in respect of employment creation is the *composition of output*. The most significant issue relates to the relative merits of import-substituting and manufactured export-promotion policies. The evidence is fairly clear, namely that labour abundant countries are likely to create more employment by following an outward-looking than an inward-looking strategy. In a study relating to Korea, Westphal and Kim concluded that the employment-generation effect of export expansion achieved during the 1960s was far greater than would have been attained from an equivalent amount of import substitution.[36] Again, Sheahan in research on Mexico found that the mix of industrial goods exported in the 1960s used 16–20 per cent more labour per unit of output than industrial import substitutes.[37] Multinationals are, of course, strongly represented in both import and export sectors in the LDCs. These results, therefore, primarily reflect the fact that while import substitutes may be produced by MNE affiliates using either capital-intensive or labour-intensive methods, the new phenomenon of manufactured exports from the LDCs is almost exclusively based on the utilisation of cheap labour by multinational firms.

Apart from the direct employment effects of MNEs there is also the *indirect* impact to be taken into consideration. There may be various indirect employment effects, arising from the competition of MNEs with local firms and from the use of the earnings resulting from their operations. In the present context, however, the employment effects of the purchase of intermediate goods are most relevant. One study found that linkages between the activities of MNE affiliates oriented towards local markets were considerably higher than in export-oriented affiliates (Table 5.1). In this work relating to foreign investment in developing countries, it was established that MNE affiliates engaged in import substitution activities obtained about 60 per cent of their inputs from locally-based firms. On the other hand, export-oriented affiliates derived nearly 60 per cent of inputs from their parent companies or suppliers of the parent companies located abroad.

Table 5.1 Sources of inputs for MNE affiliates in developing countries, by type of investment (1972)

	Type of investment	
	(% of total value of inputs)	
Sources of inputs	Local market orientation	Export orientation
Indigenous local firms	52.4	27.8
Locally-based foreign subsidiaries	7.4	9.3
Parent company	28.2	50.8
Parent company suppliers	2.6	8.4
Other	9.4	3.7

(*Source:* Reuber *et al.,* 1973.)

Although it is the kind of result that might be expected *a priori*, the evidence is not completely unanimous on this. What is fairly clear is that in general MNEs have a tendency to import more than local firms, as borne out by studies relating to both developed and developing countries. This conclusion is relevant, of course, not only to the indirect employment effects of MNEs but also to the balance of payments impact.

Balance of payments impact

Trade effects

The evolving views with regard to the impact of trade on economic development were discussed in the theoretical section of this chapter, and some of the evidence relating to the relative merits of import substitution and export promotion policies has been presented from an employment viewpoint. The balance of payments impact follows directly from this and therefore little extra needs to be said. The general view on import substitution policies in the LDCs is that the industries concerned 'have been employing too capital intensive a technology, operating on too small a scale, and earning their countries too little in terms of income, foreign exchange or employment'.[38] Nor have such policies reduced the dependence of the countries concerned on foreign countries and foreign firms. The aim of this section is thus to focus on the role of the MNEs in the export of manufactured goods from the LDCs. With the renewed emphasis on the importance of trade (exports) in development, this is bound to become an increasingly important issue for the developing countries.

Table 5.2 shows the growing importance of manufacturing exports to some LDCs during the 1960s. The data also reveal that a very small

Table 5.2 Manufactured and total exports from selected LDCs

Country	Value of manufacturing exports (1969, $ million)	Rate of growth per annum (%) Manufacturing exports (1962–1969)	Total exports (1960–1970)
Hong Kong	1484	20.1	13.8
Taiwan	570	36.5	24.2
India	547	6.1	3.9
Mexico	380	19.8	6.2
South Korea	365	77.1	38.2
Brazil	244	16.2	8.0
Argentina	208	11.7	5.0
Pakistan	197	23.7	6.3
Philippines	138	10.2	6.6
Iran	133	8.7	10.9
Malaysia	130	18.0	3.6
Nigeria	38	18.1	10.1
UAR	33	4.8	3.0
Colombia	26	19.6	4.8
Chile	23	8.4	9.2
Indonesia	20	21.3	3.9

(*Source:* Helleiner, 1973.)

number of countries account for a very high proportion of total LDC manufactured exports. By 1973, in fact, ten countries – Hong Kong, South Korea, Mexico, Brazil, India, Singapore, Malaysia, Argentina, Pakistan and Colombia – were responsible for 78 per cent of exports of manufactures.[39] Multinational firms have obviously played an important part in determining the rates of growth and the country-concentration of manufactured exports, but figures are not readily available on the subject. One estimate of the MNEs' share of exports of manufactures from various countries is shown in Table 5.3.

Unlike the position for foreign investment overall, non-US MNEs are about as important as US MNEs in this trade. Japanese companies are particularly prominent within the group of non-US multinationals, with a large proportion of investments being directed towards the small Asian economies in order to utilise the supplies of unskilled labour and low wage rates. Regarding European MNEs, it is possible to cite examples of companies which have moved part of their production to the LDCs for the purpose of exporting: Volkswagen in

Table 5.3 Share of MNEs* in the exports of manufactures from selected LDCs (circa 1972)

Hong Kong	Taiwan	South Korea	India	Singa-pore	Brazil	Mexico	Argen-tina	Pakistan	Colom-bia
	At least			Nearly			At least		30% or more
10%	20%	15%	5%	70%	43%	25–30%	30%	5–10%	

* Excludes multinational buying groups, e.g. Montgomery Ward and Sears-Roebuck of the USA and Marks and Spencer of the UK, which are important outlets for manufactured exports from Hong Kong, South Korea and Taiwan.

(*Source:* Nayyar, 1978.)

Brazil and Rollei in Singapore are examples, and companies such as Philips, Olivetti and Dunlop also have export-oriented manufacturing facilities in Third World locations. In general, however, European firms have been much less active in this field and most of their investments in developing countries have been concerned with import substituting activities.

Most of this export expansion is associated with MNE manufacture of simple labour-intensive products, and with the establishment of labour–intensive processes for manufacturing or assembling components. Thus, clothing, leather luggage and baseballs are sewn together in Mexico, the West Indies and S.E. Asia for Japanese and US firms; and a wide range of automobile parts and accessories are produced in numerous LDCs, e.g. radio circuits and antennae, piston rings and cylinder linings in Taiwan, auto lamps in Mexico, diesel engines and braking equipment in India, etc. The electronics industry, nevertheless, is still by far the most important, with the semiconductor sector being particularly significant.

The case of semiconductors[40]
This industry came into being in the early 1950s. It was initially dominated by the USA with three firms, Texas Instruments, Fairchild and Motorola in the forefront, although subsequently European companies such as Philips, and Japanese firms, including Hitachi and Toshiba, have become increasingly competitive. Semiconductors are produced by a three-stage process. The first two stages involve complex, delicate operations and as a rule take place in the advanced countries. The third stage, consisting of assembly and testing, is labour-intensive, tedious and repetitive; this operation has generally been located in the LDCs in the so-called 'offshore locations' (although in some cases testing represents a fourth stage which is undertaken back in the developed countries). With extremely rapid technological change in the industry and product life exceptionally short, cost reduction is crucial; hence the moves to exploit lower labour costs by offshore assembly in the Far East, Mexico, the West Indies, and elsewhere. To take an example of only one company – Fairchild –

affiliates were located in five different countries (see Table 5.4), the primary aim of this diverse locational pattern being to minimise risks. In spite of the vast distances involved, it is profitable for firms such as Fairchild to airfreight components to the Far East or Mexico for assembly, then perhaps to airfreight them back to an advanced country (possibly in Europe) for testing, prior to final sales. As Table 5.4 indicates, Fairchild employed nearly 6,500 people in offshore locations in 1970; but in fact some of the electronics companies now employ as many as 15,000 workers in these Far Eastern and Central American countries.

Table 5.4 The offshore locations of Fairchild

Location	Number of Employees	Year Established
Hong Kong	2,000	1961
Korea	2,000	1964
Singapore	1,500	1968
Okinawa	200	1970
Mexican Border	500	1969
Mexico City	150	1968

(*Source:* Chang, 1971.)

Problems and potential in export-oriented assembly industries in the LDCs

For some countries, thus, exports of manufactures have become very important to the economy. In Mexico, for example, 152 factories employing 21,000 people had been established alongside the border by the early 1970s; and in Taiwan 120 companies had built plants in the Free Trade Zone.[41] But this growth is not without its problems, of which the following should be noted:

(i) A major reason for the growth of offshore assembly is related to the conditions of Sections 806.30 and 807 of the Tariff Schedule of the USA.[42] Under the terms of these, goods can be exported from the USA for assembly abroad and then returned to the USA at highly favourable tariff rates. Essentially, import duties are levied only on the value added abroad. Inevitably, therefore, with the majority of inputs being imported and the majority of output exported, linkages with the host economy are minimal. This is accentuated by the fact that these export industries may be located in specially established export processing zones or free trade zones which are classic enclaves, e.g. in 1965 the Mexican Government began the so-called Border Industrialisation Program establishing a 2000-mile long free trade zone to attract the foreign assembly firms.

(ii) The advantages to host economies are also reduced by the substantial financial concessions offered to foreign investors. A good deal of the value added in the countries concerned may represent tax haven profits for use as a cash revenue for the MNEs' world wide investment programmes. Where such large-scale incentives are used to attract MNEs there are always dangers of 'competitive bidding' by LDCs, as between, say, Taiwan, Hong Kong, South Korea and Singapore.

(iii) Apart from the special incentives, for countries to be suitable locations, political stability, low labour costs and/or limited distance and a docile labour force are important factors. Table 5.5 presents some comparisons of US and foreign labour costs prepared by the US Tariff Commission relating to the year 1970.

Table 5.5   Average hourly earnings including supplementary compensation (consumer electronics products, 1970)

Country	Average hourly earnings* ($)		Ratio of US to foreign hourly earnings
	Foreign	USA	
Taiwan	0.14	2.56	18.2
Hong Kong	0.27	3.13	11.8
Mexico	0.53	2.31	4.4
Japan	0.58	1.60	2.8
Canada	3.50	3.85	1.1

* for equivalent products.

(*Source:* US Tariff Commission, 1973.)

Much lower labour costs are inevitably required in the Far East to offset distance factors in comparison with Mexico. However, such wage differentials may only be transient, which raises considerable doubts as to the long-term position. The requirement of political stability means that the risks of nationalisation are reduced to a minimum, but as already shown, some companies also follow a policy of geographical diversification and multi-sourcing to offset the impact of any political or other disruptions. Finally a docile labour force permits employment to be cut back during recessions and removes the possibility of industrial disputes.

(iv) The range of products is still narrow, and is changing rapidly due to the speed of technological advance in industries such as electronics. The countries concerned must clearly hope that assembly operations will evolve towards integrated production but the prospects for this may not be too hopeful. An associated point is that the simplicity of operations located in the LDCs does nothing to improve standards of skill among the labour force. It should be pointed out that, given these problems, some countries and notably South Korea are trying to make efforts to 'persuade' the companies to establish higher value added processes locally.

(v) In the home countries, particularly the USA, trade unions have begun to campaign against firms setting up 'runaway plants' in offshore locations.

It is therefore important to keep the issue of manufactured exports from the LDCs very firmly in perspective. Although trade is again seeming to act as an 'engine of growth', the rapid expansion of these exports is no measure of the benefits derived by the countries concerned. Nor does it indicate the foreign exchange gains because of the low value added locally. Moreover, while MNE-derived exports of manufactures from the LDCs seem likely to continue to expand fairly rapidly, the trade is still small in relation to exports from multinational firms in the developed countries: in 1970, US MNEs accounted for 11 per cent of total manufactured exports from the LDCs, but 21 per cent of exports of manufactures from OECD countries.[43] Finally, LDC manufactured exports are concentrated in a narrow range of countries and products. The work of Lall and Streeten (relating to a sample of firms in Jamaica, Kenya, India, Colombia and Malaysia, none of which were engaged in processing components) revealed that 'trans-nationality does not appear to have been an important aid to exporting'.[44]

Other balance of payments issues
Of all the potential problems posed by MNEs, *transfer pricing* probably arouses the strongest emotions (see also Chapter 3 pp. 120–3 on this topic). There is, however, a dearth of empirical evidence available on the issue. A major reason for this is that at the micro-level, transfer pricing is difficult to detect, given present disclosure requirements in company accounts, inter-country differences in company laws and so on. A certain amount of information has been made available from individual company studies, and it was such an investigation by the British Monopolies Commission that brought to light the excessive prices charged for drugs in the UK by Hoffmann-La Roche, the Swiss pharmaceutical firm. According to the company itself, transfer prices were determined by 'what is reasonable for tax purposes.'[45] The drugs in question were purchased by the UK affiliate from the group at £370 and £922 per kilo respectively, whereas the same goods were available on the open market at £9 and £20 per kilo. This was in spite of the fact that in the UK as in most other countries, transfer prices are required at least in principle to conform to an arm's length standard. This arm's length price is supposedly determined by reference either to market prices or to some mark-up on prime costs or mark-down on the ultimate selling price.

One of the most well-known pieces of work relates to transfer pricing in Colombia.[46] This study was undertaken by the Colombian government to establish the extent of overpricing of imports and to reduce its incidence by legal action. For the period 1967–70 it was estimated that import prices for pharmaceuticals were 87 per cent greater than the world price; for 1968 the extent of overpricing was

155 per cent. Through government action, annual savings of $3.3 million were achieved, out of an import bill of $15 million. The principal determinant of these practices was probably the quantitative ceiling imposed on profit repatriation by the Colombian government. The extent of overpricing for some other imported products was: rubber 44 per cent, chemicals 25 per cent, and electrical components 54 per cent. Furthermore, studies on other Latin American countries quoted by Vaitsos show generally similar patterns of overpricing; and the same author has linked overpricing with the restrictive clauses which may be contained in contracts for the transfer of technology.[47]

With respect to the impact of taxation on transfer pricing, the US Treasury Department in 1973 published data relating to 871 cases, which they had investigated. The aim was to establish the extent to which US parent MNEs reallocated foreign source income to avoid taxation. It was estimated that reallocations were made in more than one half of the cases examined and that for merchandise trade alone the reallocations deviated from arm's-length prices by $312.5 million.[48] The reallocations were approximations and a significant proportion of the cases could be contested by the firms. On the other hand, the figures could represent an understatement in that only a limited number of firms were investigated.

Various authors have attempted to estimate the extent of discretionary transfer pricing schemes indirectly using statistical methods. Müller and Morgenstern, for example, undertook a study of merchandise exports from companies (chiefly affiliates) in ten Latin American countries.[49] It was estimated that intra-firm exports within Latin America were significantly underpriced for tax reasons, whereas this did not apply to exports to the rest of the world. But, the results are ambiguous at best. The most interesting work is that of Kopits which relates not to the effects of transfer pricing on the prices of tangible goods, but to the use of transfer prices to manipulate intra-firm royalties and licence fees. The latter may be an important means of repatriating profits, thereby influencing the revenues and balance of payments of host countries. Kopits undertook a study on a sample of US MNEs, using 1968 data, to investigate the impact of host country tax rates on intra-firm royalty payments. The results indicated that nearly one quarter of total royalty remittances represented overpricing of intra-firm technology imports by MNEs prompted by tax considerations. In the developed countries overpricing was most prevalent in France, Germany and the UK, amounting to between 30 and 50 per cent of each country's total royalties. In the LDCs the highest incidence of overpricing was found in India and the Philippines. When the overpricing was expressed in terms of tax revenue or foreign exchange losses, it was estimated that host governments lost $38 million in 1968 (a figure which would rise to $60 m. if the total universe and not merely a sample of US firms was taken into consideration). Two thirds of this consisted of British and German losses, derived from the tax-induced substitution of royalties for dividends by the US companies concerned. It was concluded 'that it would be in the interests of certain high-tax industrialised host countries, especially Germany and the United Kingdom, and to a lesser degree Canada and France, if they could adopt and enforce transfer-pricing rules, which led to the use of standard royalties in intra-firm intangible transactions'.[50]

That the potential losses for host countries are very significant has been indicated by some theoretical work based on the value of intra-firm trade by US MNEs and the level of declared earnings.[51] It was estimated that a 12 per cent change in transfer prices on intra-firm trade in 1970 would have equalled the total of interest and dividends earned by US MNE affiliates abroad; an 18 per cent change in prices would have been equivalent to total earnings abroad (interest, dividends, royalties and management fees). The implication is that foreign exchange losses from transfer pricing may be more important than the costs to the host country balance of payments of dividend repatriation, etc.

An associated issue is that of *monetary speculation* by MNEs, since transfer pricing is the major instrument by which large shifts of funds can take place and one that the monetary authorities may be unable to counter. The topic became news with a statement from the Governor of the Bank of England at a conference in 1973 that 'transfers of liquid balances by multinational companies did account for an important part of the transfers which eventually led to the floating of the £, the devaluation of the $, the floating of the yen and the situation of widespread floating in which we now find ourselves'.[52] While this is no doubt a factual statement, no further published details exist. It is possible that MNEs cause monetary crises. If fears of a currency depreciation exist, MNEs acting *individually* may transfer funds into strong currencies to avoid losses. The sum of these individual actions could be enough to produce a 'self-prophesying' impact. The relevance of transfer pricing emerges because national governments are implementing an array of severely constricting controls in an attempt to prevent the overt shifting of funds.

Although transfer pricing effects are potentially more important to host countries, nevertheless *dividend repatriation* and other remittances from overseas affiliates to the parent company are also significant from a balance of payments viewpoint. The classic example which is quoted is that relating to General-Motors Holden's Ltd. in Australia (the subsidiary of General Motors Corporation of Detroit). Although the comparisons are not terribly meaningful, it appeared that in the one year, 1953–54, profits of the Australian subsidiary amounted to 14 per cent of sales, 24 per cent of funds employed, 39 per cent of shareholders' funds (net worth) and 560 per cent of GM's original investment. Dividends paid to the parent company out of these profits amounted to 260 per cent of the original investment and about 8 per cent of Australian export earnings for the year. The implication being drawn was that MNEs required to make only a small initial capital investment in host countries; through re-investment of profits locally, the affiliate could expand rapidly and after a time create balance of payments difficulties by substantial dividend payments to the parent company.

It is obviously true that the balance between capital inflows and the outflows of dividends etc. for any individual subsidiary will change over time. As the rather dated but still interesting results of Table 5.6 show, most recently established affiliates are responsible for the largest capital inflows, and the older affiliates for the bulk of the earnings (earnings are used as a surrogate for remittances).

Table 5.6 Net 1966 earnings and capital inflows of affiliates of US MNEs located in developing countries ($ million)

Year of affiliation	Affiliates in Latin America		Affiliates in other developing countries	
	Net earnings	Net capital inflows	Net earnings	Net capital inflows
1964–66	42	218	5	264
1961–63	26	56	67	50
1958–60	86	70	162	45
1957 and earlier	1,037	−69	1,600	57
Total	1,191	275	1,834	416

(*Source:* Adapted from Vernon, 1972.)

Even so, it is not correct to interpret this as meaning that older established subsidiaries constitute a net drain on the balance of payments position of the LDCs. The crucial question is what would have happened in the absence of the foreign investment. Such an economic drain would exist only if domestic output could have replaced the foreign investment, without any further resource cost to the host country.

Aggregate balance of payments and income effects

The review of the empirical evidence relating to the effects of MNEs on host countries is not yet complete. No consideration has been given to the competitive and sovereignty effects of multinational operations. It is nevertheless a convenient point to stop and try to assess how the costs and benefits of MNE activities net out overall. One major study which has attempted to do this is that by Streeten and Lall relating to 159 companies in 6 developing countries.[53] Some of these results have already been quoted but the research is much wider than perhaps has been indicated hitherto, extending to a comparison of the performance of these 159 companies over 5–7 years in the late 1960s with various alternative possibilities such as: (i) importing the products and (ii) 'most likely' local replacement, where an estimate was made of the likelihood of firms having or being able to obtain the technology to replace the output of the foreign affiliate.[54]

In terms of overall balance of payments effects, it was found that for all countries except Kenya the net impact was negative. The average effects for the various states expressed as a percentage of sales were: Kenya + 2.7%; Jamaica −25.5%; India −11.7%; Iran −55.0%; Colombia −35.3%; and Malaysia −37.6%. The nature of the effects in terms of the ownership of the firms is given in Table 5.7. Very few individual firms recorded positive balance of payments effects – only 11 out of 133 foreign-controlled companies and 3 out of 26 locally-controlled firms – while for 34 firms the negative effect was in excess of 50 per cent of sales.

Table 5.7 Relationship between ownership and balance of payments effects

Classification of firms	Total no.	Total with negative balance of payments effects	Total with negative effects worse than 50% of sales
Foreign Controlled*	133	122	30
Locally Controlled	26	23	4
All Firms	159	145	34

* Wholly and majority foreign owned subsidiaries, plus 24 firms with minority foreign ownership.

(*Source:* Lall and Streeten, 1977.)

In order to identify the causes of these adverse results, it is necessary to look in greater detail at the component balance of payments items. In the first place, the *export performance* of firms in the sample was poor: 35 and 40 per cent of both foreign and locally-controlled firms did not export anything and the median firm exported only 15–19 per cent of its sales. As was suggested earlier, this indicates that the sample mainly contains firms which were engaged in import substitution activities; and indeed exports from the companies in India seemed to be largely a function of government coercion. A second component in the balance of payments is the *net capital inflow.* This comprises the total amount of capital (equity, long-term loans and retained earnings out of foreign profits) brought in from abroad less profits and interest returned abroad. Such figures are not so meaningful in that they do not indicate the total capital contribution of a firm over its life, but the results indicated that the vast majority of firms had a small positive net inflow. Of more interest is the net financial effect which is defined as the capital inflow minus royalties, profits, interest and technical payments. The results here revealed that of the 147 firms with foreign capital only 49 recorded a positive financial effect and as Streeten and Lall comment: 'On the whole the sample foreign firms do seem to be "taking out more than they are putting in" during the period studied'.[55]

A third element in the balance of payments is *import dependence*. This is important because the greater the reliance on imports of components, etc., the smaller is the linkage of the industry to the local economy and the greater is the direct foreign exchange cost. Moreover, the greater the reliance of foreign-controlled firms on imports, the larger is the scope for transfer pricing. The study shows that over half of the total number of firms in the sample imported goods worth over 30 per cent of their sales, and nearly two thirds of firms imported over 20 per cent of the value of their sales. While there is sizeable variation across countries, there is little difference between foreign and locally-controlled firms.

As has been noted at various points, results such as these, while interesting, do not tell the whole story. They do not show, for example, what would have happened had the foreign investment not occurred. In addition, they do not reveal the indirect effects of the investment on the balance of payments via domestic sales and the use of local resources. Such issues pose major methodological problems and, in the event, Lall and Streeten ignore many of the latter effects – usually termed 'externalities'. To give one instance, some of the sample firms were market leaders in their respective industries which may have had effects on price levels, advertising tactics and so forth, but these were not quantified. Bearing this in mind, the procedure followed was to calculate the net effects of the sample firms on national income and then to compare the results with the alternative of local replacement. Of the 159 firms, it was estimated that the net income effect (as a percentage of sales) was positive for 97 companies and negative for 62 companies. There was not much variation between foreign and locally-controlled firms, but sizeable differences between countries; for Kenyan firms, the average net income effect was 12.7 per cent for sales; for Jamaican firms 7.0 per cent; Indian 1.3 per cent; Iranian 5.6 per cent; Colombian −1.5 per cent; and Malaysian firms −4.5 per cent. To quote the authors: 'the most important finding of these exercises, if we accept the premises of the analysis, is that *a very large proportion of manufacturing investments in the sample are undesirable from the point of view of social welfare* ... This finding serves to confirm for foreign investments what has been observed more generally for import-substituting industrialisation policies in a number of developing countries.'[56]

There are clearly enormous difficulties in making meaningful comparisons of actual foreign investments with their 'most likely' local replacements. The procedure followed was to estimate for each sample firm the possibility of replacing foreign technology either with existing local technology or with the purchase abroad of easily available technology. It was assumed that 30 per cent of the total number of firms with foreign equity were totally replaceable by local firms; another one half of firms seemed to be replaceable to the extent of 20–30 per cent of their production, the complexity or non-availability of technology preventing the remainder of their output from being replaced; the final 20 per cent of firms were assumed not to be replaceable at all.[57] The results of these estimates suggested that of the 147 firms with foreign capital, 55 had negative income effects when a comparison was made with the alternative of local replacement. These estimates are extremely tentative, omitting such important factors as transfer pricing, economies of scale, bargaining efficiency and exports when comparing the actual with the alternative situation. Nevertheless, the analysis at least suggests that within the LDCs a significant number of foreign affiliates are yielding negative net social income effects. It was concluded, as a consequence, that projects should be evaluated individually, with host governments being advised to negotiate the best deal possible for themselves in each case.[58]

Competitive and anti-competitive effects

It was noted in the study above that competitive effects were specifically excluded from the analysis. Yet there is evidence that depending upon circumstances the impact of MNEs on competition and efficiency may be very significant. One case often quoted is that of the automobile industry in Latin America: in Chile in 1963–64, 22 firms, most of them MNEs, were assembling less than 8000 vehicles in total, which meant an annual production run of 400 cars per plant.[59] It may be argued that the MNEs were merely reacting to government import substitution policies and tariff barriers, but a more plausible explanation is that of 'oligopolistic reaction'. Thus all the major manufacturers have established affiliates or licensees to prevent other firms gaining a position of advantage in each market. This inefficient industrial structure was not unique to Chile as Table 5.8 shows. The effect of low volume production has been to produce very high cost output. In Brazil unit costs were 35 per cent greater than in the multinationals' home countries, but this rose to a figure of 164 per cent in Chile where even by 1972 output per firm was still as low as 3,290 units.

Other evidence for Latin America indicates that MNEs are most common in highly concentrated industries. In Chile, for example, 1970 data show that 50 per cent of a sample of foreign-owned subsidiaries had a monopoly or duopoly position and a further one third occupied leadership roles in oligopoly markets.[60] What is particularly important is to assess whether or not such market structures are associated with restrictive business practices and excess profits. On this issue, some research has been undertaken on behalf of a US Senate Sub-Committee into the position in Brazil and Mexico.[61] Once again it

Table 5.8   No. of firms, output per firm and production costs in the Latin American motor industry

	No. of firms (1972)	Output per firm* (1972)	Index of production costs† (1970)
Argentina	10	26,859	195
Brazil	10	60,947	135
Chile	8	3,290	264
Colombia	3	8,005	194
Mexico	9	25,530	153
Peru	5	4,759	164
Uruguay	13	491	n.a.
Venezuela	15	5,876	145

* Number of vehicles
† Country of origin = 100
(*Source:* Jenkins, 1976.)

was revealed that market concentration was particularly high in the industries where MNEs were most prominent; and statistical analysis confirmed the expectation that the profitability of affiliates was closely and positively related to this degree of market concentration, as well as to the relative market position of individual firms and barriers to entry.

The powerful market position of MNEs in Brazil and Mexico is very revealing. In Mexico, for instance, one half of the largest 300 manufacturing firms were MNE affiliates in 1972.[62] In markets of very high concentration, where the top four plants controlled over three quarters of production, MNEs produced 71 per cent of sales. Similarly in Brazil, American and other foreign firms accounted for 147 of the 300 largest manufacturing enterprises and 59 of the 100 largest. Again, in those industries where MNEs were dominant, the combined market share held by the top four plants averaged 54 per cent, compared with 39 per cent in industries dominated by Brazilian-owned firms. The two countries are indeed close reflections of each other in terms of the structural sources of MNE power. In both cases the share of total output controlled by foreign firms has been rising rapidly: in Mexico, MNEs increased their share of total market sales from 20 per cent in 1962 to 28 per cent in 1970; in Brazil US subsidiaries alone produced 20 per cent of manufacturing sales in 1970, an increase from 13 per cent in 1966. What is also interesting is that growth by acquisition was an important means of expansion: in the 1971–72 period, three-quarters of the affiliates established in Mexico represented take-overs of going concerns; and in Brazil one quarter of all growth in US firms' assets in the years 1960–1972 was due to acquisitions.

The principal conclusion reached by Newfarmer and Mueller, the authors of this study, was that the progressive industrial denationalisation (the share of host country industry and resources owned by MNEs) witnessed in Brazil and Mexico, has had the effect of diminishing the economic sovereignty of both countries. It was considered that MNEs in these countries possessed enormous economic power which could be misused from the viewpoint of the host nation, but in addition they held considerable potential non-economic power. To quote the authors: 'Since the extensive concentration of foreign holdings in a market results in a few firms making pivotal economic decisions, the structural possibility of joint action for economic and non-economic objectives is always present.'[63]

In the developed countries too there is a certain amount of evidence to show that when MNEs have a dominant position in markets, they may use their oligopolistic power in adverse ways. The behaviour of the oil companies, for example, has been a source of irritation to various host countries at different times. To give a different example, early in 1978 United Brands, the world's largest grower and supplier of bananas, was found guilty and fined by the European Court of Justice on three counts of abusing a dominant market position in the EEC. The corporation was convicted of various restrictive practices including the charging of different prices in different EEC markets and refusing to supply particular distributors.

More generally, some evidence was presented in Chapter 3 (pp. 124–7) on the impact of MNE activities on industry performance in various developed host countries. From a negative viewpoint, there is some evidence that MNEs may compound problems of industry fragmentation, as in the case of the Latin American automobile industry quoted earlier; but equally, a study of the Australian chemical industry revealed that some MNEs, even with tariff protection, installed smaller scale, near optimum-size plant which meant little if any excess capacity.[64] In any event, fragmentation and excess capacity is only likely to be a problem in small, relatively isolated developed countries and not, say, in Western Europe. MNEs may also be able to create additional barriers to entry in host industries through the exploitation of scale economies and their product differentiation, marketing and technological advantages. On the other hand, there are a number of instances quoted where MNE entry has broken down the monopoly position of an established firm in the host country, and even the potential entry of a multinational firm may constrain excess monopoly profits. Furthermore, there may be favourable effects on the competitive position because MNEs are likely to be less collusive than indigenous oligopolists. Overall UK experience has been that US subsidiaries have provided increased competition for established dominant firms and stimulated an increasing awareness of the role of R & D and productive management. One specific study relating to the pharmaceutical industry in the UK indicated that American competition in the market stimulated British companies to undertake high quality research and to perform competitively within a wide range of new drug technologies.[65]

Competition from US multinationals has also encouraged European firms to merge into more viable economic units in some cases. Although the domestic computer industry in the EEC is still in a transient state, the formation of ICL in the UK and of CII-Honeywell Bull in France are examples of different responses to multinational competition.

This is not to say that the conduct of MNEs will always have a positive effect on competitiveness. Various restrictive practices employed by multinational firms have anti-competitive effects (see the discussion in Chapter 3). One of the most frequently quoted of these is the operation of restrictive export franchises, deriving from the common MNE practice of allocating various markets globally. Secondly, the pricing of intra-firm transactions at other than arm's length prices and international price discrimination policies represent further restrictive practices. Thirdly, excessive product differentiation not only raises entry barriers but also entails a waste of resources. It is interesting that such practices do not simply adversely affect the *competitive* position in host countries. In all cases the practices other harmful effects, as, for example, manipulative transfer pricing and export restrictions may create balance of payments difficulties.

A great deal of literature has emerged relating to the impact of the MNE on labour relations, but the area is very short of systematic research. In addition, most discussions relate to developed rather than less developed countries. There are a number of *a priori* reasons for expecting multinational companies to have more unsettled labour relations than domestic firms. In the first place, ultimate decision-making resides abroad, which may produce a range of effects – from increasing employee hostility in the host country, to increasing the possibilities of misunderstanding at a management level; and secondly, different industrial relations procedures and practices may exacerbate conflict. One measure of the impact of MNEs on labour relations will obviously be the *incidence of industrial disputes,* although absenteeism and labour turnover may be more revealing indicators of dissatisfaction. In spite of the *a priori* expectations, evidence for the UK has indicated that foreign-owned firms may have fewer labour disputes than domestic firms, especially after allowing for differences in industry mix.[66] Other research, moreover, based on a sample of foreign-owned companies operating in the USA, found no difference between the strike propensity of these as compared with indigenous firms.[67] Even so, in both cases, there did appear to be some differences in the character of the disputes.

Although in total the dispute record of MNE affiliates may not be any worse than domestic firms, there are numerous examples of issues within the categories noted which have caused difficulties. In respect of the multinational status of such firms, one significant issue concerns the use of withdrawal threats as a bargaining weapon. All of the US automobile companies in the UK have used this threat from time to time, so much so that it has become totally counterproductive. But similar threats have been made in other countries. Ford, for example stated in 1973 that the refusal of unions to relax strict rules on overtime scheduling might force them to shun Belgium for future expansion. Other allegations against MNEs regarding the role of the parent company in negotiations and so on are difficult to substantiate.

Turning to differences in industrial relations traditions and procedures, there is obviously an inclination for an incoming MNE to try to amend the host country system in the light of its own experience. This is particularly so where practices are pursued which the MNE considers to be detrimental to productivity. Union recognition policy is one area of industrial relations that has brought conflict. In Singapore and Malaysia, unions seem to have experienced recognition problems in recent years at the electronic plants of companies such as Texas Instruments, Hewlett-Packard and Motorola. Similar problems have arisen with IBM and Esso in Holland, and with Kodak, Heinz and IBM in the UK. Aside from union recognition policy, factors such as differences in the nature and duration of agreements, plant personnel practices and the level of negotiations may all create difficulties in management/union relations. Given the dearth of hard evidence, there is still great uncertainty over the extent to which MNEs do or do not try to conform to the national conditions as they find them, or whether in fact they should. Chrysler in the UK, for example, which had a notoriously bad labour relations reputation during the early 1970s, nevertheless attempted to make numerous innovations which were in the interests of higher productivity, had they been negotiated and implemented satisfactorily.

With a dispute record no worse than indigenous firms and generally greater productivity, MNE affiliates may appear to have a favourable impact on host economies. More important issues, however, may concern levels of wages and conditions in MNEs, and the impact these have upon remuneration levels and labour availability for domestic firms; research on these topics is still very scanty.

Sovereignty and autonomy effects

It is difficult to establish criteria for judging the impact of the MNE on national sovereignty or autonomy, and the mere assumption that loss of sovereignty entails a cost involves a value judgement. There is the general point that greater foreign investment will increase the difficulties of host governments in pursuing independent policies, and some of the *dependencia* type of issues arising will be discussed in Chapter 8. The problems arise essentially because of differences between the objective of the multinational firm and the objectives of the host government. To make only one point, the MNE may be pursuing some global objective, such as profit maximisation. In the pursuit of this it is likely to set particular, but not necessarily similar, objectives for each of its affiliates, e.g. an affiliate in Brazil may be set a profit objective related to securing a certain share of the Brazilian market, but the latter may conflict with government objectives relating to increasing exports to neighbouring Latin American countries and elsewhere.

It may be argued from this that the greater the degree of autonomy delegated by the parent to the affiliate (and thus the greater the responsibility of the affiliate for setting its own objectives), the lower will be the sovereignty costs to the host government. As a consequence of this view most empirical research in the area has centred round the autonomy/centralisation issue. Autonomy may be assumed to be greater when affiliates have authority which extends beyond short-run operational decisions, that is, are more than mere 'branch plants'. In research on US investment in Scotland, it was established that one third of all firms had no marketing responsibilities for the output they produced.[68] Also – of particular relevance to the technological dependence debate – only one quarter of firms had a significant research and development department in Scotland. Bearing in mind earlier comments on the need to pursue research comparative advantage, nevertheless, this means that a very high proportion of firms are completely tied to the innovative progress of their parent companies. Similar results were obtained in some early research relating to the R & D performance of non-resident owned firms in Canada; although it should be noted that some recent work has thrown doubt on these results, indicating that in a good number of industries there is not much difference between R & D expenditures of foreign-owned as compared with Canadian-owned companies.[69] Another issue which is pertinent to the question of host country sovereignty is that of export restrictions on affiliates. Several empirical studies have shown that parent MNEs impose strict control over the countries to which their affiliates may or may not export.

For the host country, the aim is clearly to try to maximise the net benefits from foreign direct investment. The importance of these and other costs therefore depends upon the extent to which host governments can control the multinational firm. This is the topic of the following chapter, but in the present context it is worth noting that the size, centralised control and possibly global perspective of multinational firms gives them a certain countervailing power vis-à-vis national governments which is not possessed by domestic firms. While it will be shown that host governments, even less developed host governments, are far from helpless in their dealings with MNEs, the power of these firms undoubtedly entails a sovereignty loss for the recipient state.

Final remarks

In the theoretical section of this chapter it was indicated that no clear-cut conclusion could be reached on the issue of whether or not

MNEs bring positive net benefits to host states. The empirical evidence presented essentially bears out this point. The limited empirical work which has been undertaken to estimate the *aggregate* effects of MNE operations suggests that the overall impact is usually positive on national income, jobs and government revenues. Even so, the balance between positive and negative effects seems to be fairly close in numerous instances, with many foreign firms producing a negative income effect when consideration is given to what might have happened in the absence of the foreign investment. Major doubts have been raised about the impact of direct foreign investment on the balance of payments positions of host countries, derived particularly from the payment of royalties, interest charges and dividends and from the uncertain effects of transfer pricing. And there are certain other areas where MNE activity always imposes a cost on the recipient state, principal among these being the cost associated with loss of sovereignty. On the other hand, it has been suggested that in some instances host country policies themselves are to blame for adverse effects, as, for example, when MNEs are 'encouraged' to introduce capital intensive technologies by tax and other incentives. These conclusions thus mean that better host country policies towards foreign direct investment (on issues such as incentives) are a prerequisite for increasing the net benefits attained, quite apart from any controls imposed on the incoming multinationals *per se.*

One issue which has only been touched upon in this chapter concerns the relative impact on host nations of inward direct investment from different source countries and the relative impact of different types of investment (as between import-substitution and export-base types, for example). Regarding the varying forms of investment, it is possible that export-platform type investments may offer greater potential net benefits. But these have not been realised in many instances because of the concessions granted to multinational firms, and the fact that such investments provide few linkages with the rest of the economy. This conclusion is also relevant to the impact of MNEs from different source countries given that, for instance, much of Japanese investment falls into the resource-based and export-platform categories. Apart from this, there is some evidence available that foreign direct investment from less developed home countries may be particularly beneficial to recipient states. LDC multinational firms are insignificant in terms of size and numbers, of course, but they may be expected to increase as the economies of their countries develop. A study of LDC MNEs in Thailand indicated that the sample of firms tended to use labour-intensive technology which was suitable for small-scale production; they were more likely than with other MNEs or domestic Thai firms to buy their machinery locally; they tended to repatriate less of their profits than did other foreign firms; and since they used standard technology, their royalty payments were lower than other MNEs on average.[70] At least in the case of the Thai economy, therefore, LDC multinationals offered significant benefits without many of the costs associated with other inward direct investment.

No comment has yet been made on certain other alleged quasi-economic effects of MNEs such as the impact on income distribution, and on consumption patterns. Derived from the evidence presented on the capital intensity of incoming foreign investment and the use made by foreign firms of domestic savings, it would be expected that MNEs would have an adverse effect on income distribution in host nations. The problem would be exacerbated if chronic unemployment existed in the recipient country, since capital intensive foreign investment could bid up wages for skilled domestic workers who were in short supply, leaving the overall employment situation unchanged. What information there is indicates that other factors in the host country must have a greater influence on the level of income distribution than foreign investment. Thus in research relating to six developing countries with deteriorating income distribution during the 1960s (Panama, Korea, Brazil, India, Mexico and Venezuela), various patterns of foreign investment existed: Panama and Venezuela were among the highest recipients of direct investment from abroad, Korea and India were among the lowest, and Brazil and Mexico were in the middle.[71] Therefore the theoretical conclusion of adverse income distribution effects associated with foreign direct investment has not yet been validated empirically.

Radical economists have emphasised the role of MNEs in transferring the consumption patterns of advanced capitalist countries to underdeveloped countries, thereby extending consumerist capitalism. This topic is associated with that of technology transfer as discussed earlier, with the effect possibly being to increase import propensities in host countries, to adversely influence income distribution and generally to maintain a 'dependency' relationship between home and host nations. Little quantitative information exists on this issue. Although there has been some attempt to relate levels of foreign direct investment in various countries to the degree of consumerism (as measured by the consumption of expensive consumer durables such as cars and television sets), there is to date inadequate evidence to back up the contentions which have been postulated. But as with the income distribution issue, testing is no easy matter given the difficulty of isolating the impact of foreign investment from that of other factors, and it would be wrong to be over-complacent.

Overall, no clear generalisations are possible either in regard to the impact of MNEs on *national income* in developing host countries or in respect of the effects on *other development goals*. In turn, this conclusion indicates serious limitations in existing knowledge concerning the impact of direct foreign investment on economic development. As in the previous section, the empirical results reviewed here have very largely referred to the LDCs. That the impact of MNEs on host developed countries is more favourable is generally accepted. It is not possible to undertake a complete review of the literature to support this view, but in order to counter-balance the LDC emphasis of this chapter, studies relating to one developed country, the United Kingdom, are presented in Appendix 5.1.

Appendix 5.1 The impact of foreign direct investment on the United Kingdom

Several studies have been undertaken into the impact of foreign direct investment – the overwhelming proportion of which is US investment – on the United Kingdom as a whole or on a part of the UK; and the results have been generally favourable in terms of the effects on the host economy. In common with most other country studies, the conclusions are derived from fairly subjective reasoning, and attempts have not been made to fully quantify the benefits and costs of direct foreign investment. M. D. Steuer and various associates undertook an official study for the UK Government which was published in 1973, and the discussion which follows is generally based on the approach of this report.[72]

(a) Balance of payments effects
Following the work of Reddaway and Hufbauer and Adler, the possibility of attempting a quantification of the balance of payments impact of foreign investment has existed. Steuer *et al.* adapted this model and derived various balance of payments estimates based upon the combined effects of foreign investment on exports, imports, import substitution and repatriation. Other work had shown that US affiliates in the UK exported a much higher proportion of their output than the average UK firm, although it seemed that their import propensity was also high. Assuming that the government did not change its macro-economic policy in response to the foreign investment, Steuer estimated that the net balance of payments effect would be favourable, the order of magnitude being about 10 per cent of the output of foreign-owned firms. The model seemed to be fairly robust with regard to changes in assumptions about the proportion of output exported and the greater efficiency of foreign firms, but negative effects were considered to be plausible if the government pursued particular expenditure or taxation policies.

(b) Technology impact
The technology impact essentially hinges on a number of issues. On the negative side: (i) if foreign investment involved the acquisition of British firms, the research achievements of these firms might be lost to the economy; (ii) foreign firms may not undertake R & D in Britain, and the country may therefore become technologically dependent. Against this it can be argued that (i) affiliates may draw on the research

efforts of the parent company at low or zero costs, and the costs and uncertainty of new product development are reduced; (ii) linkage effects diffuse the benefits of parent company R & D throughout the economy.

Statistics on the R & D activities of foreign affiliates in the UK are very scanty. Mansfield quotes an R & D/Sales ratio for US firms in the UK in 1966 of 1.9 per cent; the equivalent figure for domestic US R & D was 2.0 per cent and for all UK industry 1.1 per cent.[73] Comparisons between MNEs and their domestic competitors are not very meaningful, however, because multinational companies are concentrated in the most R & D intensive industries. While unable themselves to make much of a contribution with regard to quantification, Steuer *et al.* suggested that none of the arguments above, whether for or against, were very persuasive. Although this may be so, some of the largest MNEs in the UK, e.g. IBM and ITT, seem to consider themselves vulnerable on this issue and have been at pains to publicise their research contributions to the British economy. On this topic as with a number of others, the Steuer Report was much too complacent.

In common with a number of other Western European countries, the United Kingdom Government has been concerned from time to time about the possibility of technological dependence on the US, the issue coming to the fore most recently in relation to the mushrooming microelectronics industry. It was argued that it was undesirable for British electronic equipment manufacturers to rely on foreign suppliers of integrated circuits (ICs) if their products were to remain competitive in terms of price and performance, for various reasons. Firstly, it was alleged that foreign-owned manufacturers of ICs in Britain, such as Texas Instruments, Motorola and National Semiconductor did not provide the latest and most advanced technology to British equipment manufacturers; this is essentially the 'technological lag' argument. Secondly, American affiliates producing ICs in the UK have concentrated on high volume 'standard' products rather than on the 'special' ICs frequently demanded by the UK equipment producers; the effect has been to raise the cost of integrated circuits to the latter. More fundamentally it has been argued that the UK must have an indigenous manufacturing presence in an industry which is growing so rapidly – providing direct and indirect jobs in 1977 for around 300,000 people throughout the world; and which has fundamental implications for a wide range of end users, in fields as far apart as telecommunications, machine shops, printing and publishing, clocks and watches, car assembly and automated warehousing. This argument would require the UK to enter into large-scale manufacture of both standard and special ICs.

The end result of this debate was that it was decided that public funds should be used to establish an indigenous greenfield company to compete with the dominant US and Japanese MNEs in this field. The aim was to attract British electronics engineers working with US companies to join the new corporation and provide the technical know-how. Apart from this, joint ventures between British and American companies are also being encouraged, although this policy was seen as having possible long-run disadvantages in that there would be little or no UK control over the development of the technology.[74]

(c) Competitive and anti-competitive effects
A significant proportion of the world's largest non-UK firms have subsidiaries in Britain, and these subsidiaries are often large compared to domestic companies. Nevertheless, there is no evidence that the activities of MNEs have led to more industrial concentration in the UK than would otherwise have occurred. It is true that foreign investment is very much an activity of oligopolistic firms, but the evidence is that MNEs tend to enter industries which are more concentrated than average in any event. Typically, moreover, if there is any foreign ownership in an industry, there are several foreign affiliates, not just one. Certainly US manufacturing affiliates in the UK have earned consistently higher rates of return on capital than their UK competitors;but this appears to be due to a more productive use of labour and capital rather than to the exploitation of a monopolistic or oligopolistic position.

On the labour side, results of the investigations into the strike-proneness of foreign firms have already been quoted. As to the argument that foreign firms may reserve top jobs for their own nationals, Dunning found that three-quarters of all US affiliates in the UK had a British Managing Director.[75] Also it was suggested that the US companies employed a larger number of people in the technical and professional grades in Britain than anywhere else in the world. As a final point, in 1970–71, wages and salaries paid by US affiliates were on average more than one fifth higher than in domestic firms.

(d) Regional impact
In the United Kingdom, any assessment of the impact of foreign direct investment will take into account the contribution such investment makes to the problem of consistently high levels of unemployment in areas away from the South and East of England. The topic of US investment in Scotland, one area with particularly serious long-term unemployment problems, was the subject of a major research study by Forsyth.[76] A number of the Steuer and Dunning conclusions for the UK as a whole seemed to be equally applicable in Scotland, but there were differences. For example, Forsyth found that the disputes record of US firms was worse than that of indigenous firms; the spill-over effects (including the diffusion of technological and managerial know-how) of foreign firms on the rest of the economy were small; and

the payment of high wages may have had the effect of attracting workers away from other firms rather than from the pool of unemployed, as well as having some inflationary impact. The fairly optimistic conclusions for the UK as a whole were thus subject to certain reservations in the case of Scotland, although, on balance, Forsyth concluded that American operations conferred a net benefit on the regional economy.

The issue of the effects of multinational activities on regional development has been the subject of various other research studies, the results of which have been somewhat contradictory. Holland and Blackbourn, in work relating to the UK and various other European countries, have argued that the core regions have attracted a large proportion of foreign-owned plants.[77] It was considered that the subsidies payable to firms locating in peripheral regions had not been effective in attracting foreign-owned companies, thus supporting the view that foreign investment may increase regional disequilibria. Other evidence referring to the UK specifically, has indicated that while there was a heavy concentration of overseas controlled manufacturing employment in the South East of the country, there had been some shift towards the peripheral regions since the 1940s. And a study of the movement of manufacturing industry in the UK over the years 1945–65 indicated that foreign-based companies moving plants had a much higher propensity to locate these within the depressed areas than British companies which were setting up new plants or moving existing ones. Overall, it does appear that, at least since the introduction of more active regional policies in the 1960s, overseas investment has tended to favour the assisted areas.[78] This is so in spite of the fact that at a theoretical level, it is not obvious that MNEs should necessarily be more responsive to regional policies than indigenous firms.[79]

In any event, equally important questions concern the impact of overseas investment on these peripheral areas. Young and Hood showed that among many US firms which had established in Scotland as a first location in Europe, the centre of gravity of operations gradually moved towards the core regions within the EEC over time.[80] This implies that the long-term benefits associated with expansion in the size and status of the plants do not materialise in many instances. It is also true that the peripheral regions have tended to attract fairly basic production operations: management in the majority of US plants in Scotland have only routine decision-making responsibilities; conversely, in 1976, of the 124 European regional headquarters of MNEs (from all source countries) located in the UK, 85 were located in London and the majority of the remaining 39 were probably elsewhere in South East England.[81] These types of studies thus indicate that even if short-term effects on the balance of payments and so on are favourable, the long-term impact on peripheral areas such as Scotland is not so clearly beneficial.

(e) Sovereignty and autonomy effects

While these are, perhaps, the crucial issues, the general problems of identification and measurement have already been revealed in the dearth of empirical evidence. It is possible to quote isolated examples where UK sovereignty has been undermined: Chrysler's withdrawal threats to the UK Government in October–December 1975 and the subsequent sale of Chrysler UK to Peugeot-Citroen are obvious examples, but other concrete cases are less easy to find.[82] The Steuer Report, nevertheless, was again over-complacent on this topic. It concluded that because 'the foreign firm is foreign, is here on sufferance, and the possibility of exchange controls, tend . . . to make it more publicly accountable than domestic firms'.[83] On the contrary, the very fact of multinationality places such companies in a unique position to avoid public accountability. The qualitative conclusions of this report on the favourable impact of foreign direct investment on the UK must be heavily qualified as a result of this.

Moreover, even if there is a net favourable effect on the economy this does not imply that there is no need for government policy in respect of foreign direct investment. In the United Kingdom a very *laissez faire* attitude has been adopted to inward investment from abroad. There have probably been no cases of refusal of US or European investment (although the same comment may not apply to Japanese investment). In general, conditions may be attached to permission to invest but not of an extreme kind. The important question is whether such a relaxed attitude has maximised the net benefits to the economy or whether different policy options might be preferred. On this aspect there is no evidence, although on the basis of the empirical results relating to the LDCs, there is a presumption that a negotiated entry is preferable in all cases. Of course, the potential for adverse outcomes is much greater in the LDCs. Since the foreign sector in the UK, for example, only accounts for about 15 per cent of industrial output, any distortions which are being created by the operations of MNEs may arguably be remedied by government action against the domestic sector.

Further reading

1. The classic MacDougall article is an essential starting point: **G.D.A. MacDougall,** 'The benefits and costs of private investment from abroad: a theoretical approach', 1960, reprinted in J. H. Dunning (ed.), *International Investment,* Harmondsworth: Penguin Books, 1972, pp. 129–58. It is useful to refer to this source for the article since a number of other relevant theoretical papers are included, e.g. **A. E. Jasay,** 'The social choice between home and overseas investment', pp. 117–28, and **M. C. Kemp,** 'The benefits and costs of private investment from abroad: comment', pp. 159–62.
2. There are no general references which completely cover the second part of the theoretical section. The distinction between resource transfer effects, trade and balance of payments effects, etc. was made by Streeten and two articles by this author

are worth reading: **P. Streeten,** 'Costs and benefits of multinational enterprises in less-developed countries' in J. H. Dunning (ed.), *The Multinational Enterprise,* London: George Allen and Unwin, 1971; **P. Streeten,** 'The theory of development policy' in J. H. Dunning (ed.), *Economic Analysis and the Multinational Enterprise,* London: George Allen and Unwin, 1974, pp. 252–79.

3. On specific topics the following papers should be consulted:
   MNEs and exports of manufactures from developing countries – **G. K. Helleiner,** 'Manufactured exports from less developed countries and multinational firms', *Economic Journal,* **83,** 1973, pp. 21–47; **D. Nayyar,** 'Transnational corporations and manufactured exports from poor countries', *Economic Journal,* **88,** 1978, pp. 59–84.
   MNEs and transfer pricing – **S. Lall,** 'Transfer pricing by multinational manufacturing firms', *Oxford Bulletin of Economics and Statistics,* **35,** 1973, pp. 173–95; **G. F. Kopits,** 'Intra-firm royalties crossing frontiers and transfer-pricing behaviour', *Economic Journal,* **86,** 1976, pp. 781–805.
   MNEs and technology transfer – **S. A. Morley** and **G. W. Smith,** 'Limited search and the technology choices of multinational firms in Brazil', *Quarterly Journal of Economics,* **XCI,** 1977, pp. 263–87; **C. V. Vaitos,** 'The process of commercialization of technology in the Andean Pact', in H. Radice (ed.), *International Firms and Modern Imperialism,* Harmondsworth: Penguin Books, 1975, pp. 183–214.

4. The excellent study of Lall and Streeten relating to the impact of MNEs on six developing countries is summarised in: **S. Lall and P. Streeten,** *Foreign Investment, Transnationals and Developing Countries,* London: Macmillan, 1977, Part II and particularly Ch. 7, 8 and 9.

Questions for discussion

1. Point out some of the defects of the neo-classical model as a basis for predicting the impact of foreign direct investment on host countries. Indicate the assumption made in respect of what would have happened in the absence of the foreign investment and show the significance of this assumption.
2. Why is the technology contribution of multinational firms potentially so important? What factors will determine whether or not the transferred technology actually produces net benefits for the host country?
3. Discuss the ways in which the balance of payments of host countries may be affected by foreign direct investment.
4. It has been argued (Brooke and Remmers, 1970) that firms consider manipulative transfer pricing as an emergency device only, principally because of the sizeable risks if caught. Do you agree with this?
5. Outline the various ways in which the impact of MNEs may differ as between developed and less developed host countries.
6. Do you believe that it is in the interests of LDCs to establish industrial zones to attract foreign investment in labour intensive industries and processes?
7. Referring to the work of Lall and Streeten, indicate some of the problems in undertaking a cost/benefit study of the impact of direct foreign investment.
8. In the light of the empirical work reviewed, what advice should be given to an LDC government which wishes to maximise the net benefits from inward direct investment?

Economic policy
and the multinational firm

Summary

1. Regulation of MNE activity may be undertaken at an international, national or multinational level. The conclusions of welfare economics would point to an international solution to the control problem: this would entail the dismantling of tariff and non-tariff barriers and exchange controls; the harmonisation of national policy measures in areas such as anti-trust and pollution legislation; and the harmonisation of effective profit tax rates between countries. Additionally, world-wide income redistribution would be required, necessitating global budgets and a supranational political institution.
2. Although economic efficiency would point to an international solution, host governments may be unprepared to give up the necessary sovereignty to permit the implementation of global controls. A wide variety of national controls may therefore be introduced, but all involve some trade-off between efficiency, and sovereignty and equity. Such regulations may relate to the degree of ownership permissible within the host country and/or they may relate to the behaviour of MNEs, with the actual package of regulations depending to some extent on bargaining between the host government and the multinational firm.
3. An intermediate solution is that of multinational controls, where regulations operate across a number of countries making up a free trade area or customs union, e.g. EEC, Andean Pact. At a minimum a multi-regional bloc increases the bargaining power of the host countries *vis-à-vis* MNEs. It might be possible to go further, however, and reproduce an international solution within the boundaries of the union.
4. Numerous proposals have been put forward for generalised international agreements, but these are seen very much as long-term schemes. Greater interest attaches to the more limited voluntary codes of conduct which are being developed and implemented by various organisations, of particular importance in this regard being the OECD code. Work is also being undertaken by the International Chamber of Commerce and by the UN, but conflicts of interests between countries appear to be a major stumbling-block to progress.

5. At the national level a wide range of controls are being operated by host governments. In some countries the regulatory provisions may be fairly permissive; but in other states, particularly in Latin America, very stringent controls exist, including strict screening procedures at time of entry, repatriation ceilings, indigenisation requirements, permitted ownership levels and closed sectors, terms of technology contracts, etc. In the developed countries a generally more liberal attitude prevails, although Japan is an example of a country which has controlled inward direct investment very tightly in post-war years.

6. With respect to multinational controls, the EEC is a good example of a multi-regional bloc which aspires to reproducing a global solution, but the progress which has been made is very limited as yet. The Andean Pact, on the other hand, through Decision 24, has introduced a very comprehensive and restrictive set of rules to regulate MNEs. The bargain offered to foreign investors in this case seems unacceptable, for reported new investment since the Pact was formed has been insignificant.

7. There is little evidence as to the effectiveness of the controls being implemented. The international codes of conduct suffer in being voluntary. Unilateral controls may be effective in some instances in increasing the net benefits for individual host countries but a great deal depends upon the circumstances prevailing. In many cases host governments will be more concerned with attracting a greater volume of foreign investment than with the control question and in Europe, for example, governments actively compete to offer the best package of incentives to MNEs.

In the last few years, demands for control over the activities of multinationals have become increasingly vociferous. In response to these demands a wide range of countries – of varying political persuasions and degrees of development – have acted to impose onerous regulations on MNEs. For the future also, greater regulation of MNEs would seem to be virtually inevitable, unless the companies themselves are prepared to undergo radical change and adaptation.

Controls, whether national or international, are designed to remedy the perceived abuses of such firms and thereby maximise the net benefits of foreign direct investment. From the viewpoint of the host country, it was concluded earlier that the MNE might or might not have a positive effect on government policy objectives relating to growth, employment, prices and the balance of payments; and a substantial MNE presence would certainly affect economic independence adversely, and perhaps also income distribution, particularly in the LDCs. Essentially problems arise from the asymmetry of goals between the investing firm and the host (or home) country. Government intervention designed to alter the terms under which direct investment is obtained from abroad and/or the behaviour of multinational affiliates might thus be expected to remedy such divergences.

The key feature of MNEs is that they engage in activities across national boundaries, and thereby influence resource allocation throughout the world. *National* means of control may either be inadequate or may harm the beneficial global resource allocative effects of the MNE. *International* action might therefore be necessary to improve efficiency and equity on a world scale. The purpose of the first section of this chapter is to provide a theoretical framework within which the necessity (or otherwise) for national or international controls may be determined. This is followed by a review and assessment of some of the types of regulations being planned or currently operated by host governments and international bodies.

Control of the MNE: a theoretical framework

The normative theory of government intervention

In considering the role of government in the economy, it is first necessary to recall briefly the marginal conditions which must be satisfied to achieve an efficient economic system, and to relate efficiency in resource allocation to the welfare or well-being of individuals in society.

An efficient economic system is said to exist when it is impossible to redistribute final goods between consumers so as to make any one consumer better off without making another worse off; when it is impossible to redistribute resources between products so as to produce any more of one good without producing less of another; and when it is impossible to redistribute resources among products so as to produce a more preferred collection of goods.[1] These necessary conditions for efficient resource allocation are satisfied in a *perfectly competitive economy.* Provided that the decisions of consumers are rational, and are based on complete knowledge of the alternatives available, perfect competition also produces a *social welfare optimum* (*Pareto optimum*).[2]

A difficulty arises when it is revealed that a Pareto optimum equilibrium in the economy is not unique. The initial distribution of wealth in a perfectly competitive economy is an important factor in determining the Pareto optimum position obtained. A large number of Pareto optima may thus exist, each corresponding to a different distribution of income and resources. Welfare economics does not permit a ranking of different Pareto optima since interpersonal comparisons of utility are not possible on the basis of any objective criteria. As a consequence of this, the potential exists for government intervention to redistribute final income among consumers or redistribute resource ownership, and still achieve an income distribution which is Pareto optimal. It is also possible that government interventions to redistribute income may cause the economy to diverge from a Pareto optimum efficient position. It is at this point that the government must balance its own *efficiency* and *equity* goals. For example, intervention producing a more desirable distribution of income and a rise in social welfare must be balanced against the fall in social welfare resulting from a decline in efficiency.[3]

A second difficulty exists with the conclusions of welfare economics: the ability of the market economy to maximise efficiency is dependent on the existence of *perfect competition*. The conditions for perfect competition are very stringent. For example, there must be no imperfections in factor, service or product markets; there must be no economies of scale in production; and there must be no divergences between marginal private and social costs or benefits. More generally, free markets must produce a stable general equilibrium where all resources are employed. Where these conditions are not met and market failure occurs, a rationale exists for state intervention in the private market to maximise efficiency.

Summarising, government intervention may be justified in the following circumstances:

(i) *To redistribute income in accordance with some equity goal.* Here, normative judgements by government regarding the optimal distribution of income have provided a powerful motive for increased intervention in the economy during the twentieth century.

(ii) *To remedy imperfections in the market economy and thereby improve economic efficiency.* Imperfections include principally imperfections of competition and knowledge, and externalities. Where imperfectly competitive conditions exist, governments may pursue anti-trust policies to stimulate competition. But problems exist in industries where economies of scale are present, since the plant size necessary to achieve the optimum scale of production in these circumstances may also produce a monopoly situation. The solution in such cases lies in government-regulated monopoly.

As noted previously, perfect competition only produces a welfare optimum if consumer decision-making is rational and is based on knowledge of the alternatives available. The decisions of consumers may not maximise their own welfare if they are not informed of the whole range of choices available or if they are irrational or short-sighted. The regulation of conditions of work (e.g. the limitation of working hours, establishment of minimum wages, etc.), controls over conditions of sale (e.g. advertising standards), the regulation of education, and so on are all examples of government limitations on freedom of choice. Because of imperfections of knowledge, government decision-making is believed to be superior to private decision-making in these instances.

Pareto optimality requires that welfare maximising decisions by individual consumers and firms simultaneously maximise social welfare. This will not hold where the action of one individual affects the welfare of another individual and the external welfare effect is not taken into account. These externalities may be external benefits – where the eradication of pollution in one part of a river improves the fishing for the owner of another part of the river – or external costs – where a rubbish tip constitutes a health hazard to neighbouring residents. The end result of the presence of externalities is non-optimal output levels of different goods and the adoption of inefficient techniques of production. (A diagrammatic presentation of the problem of externalities is given in Appendix 6.1.) A special case of externalities refers to public goods ('collective goods'), important examples of which are defence and, in the present context, technology. The key characteristic of such goods is that the market economy will under-allocate resources to them. This derives from the fact that because an individual can benefit as much from other peoples' purchases of public goods as his own, there is little incentive for anyone to provide himself with the goods. As public goods are consumed collectively, provision must also be made collectively, and since the market mechanism does not operate effectively the state must assume the role of providing the goods.

(iii) *To remedy stabilisation problems.* Since the publication of Keynes' General Theory, it has been accepted that the market economy will not necessarily adjust automatically to a full employment level of output. To avoid periodic bouts of involuntary unemployment, therefore, governments have taken on another key role in the management of the economy. Government fiscal and monetary policies are also important in the attainment of internal and external balance in the economy.[4]

As with any other firm, MNE affiliates operating in the national economy will be subject to action taken by governments to solve these three groups of problems. It remains to be considered whether the types of economic policy measures at the disposal of governments are as effective when applied to MNEs as opposed to indigenous firms; or whether MNEs are able to exploit their multinational status to frustrate the implementation of government economic policies; or whether indeed national means of control are relevant and should be applied to the international firm.

International aspects of government intervention

The economic system is not, of course, closed. Nevertheless, with perfect competition in domestic markets, and assuming no transfer costs, free trade also permits an open economy to operate with optimum technical efficiency in production and to maximise utility, subject to certain assumptions. In a closed economy, economic efficiency occurs where the marginal rate of substitution in consumption (MRS) equals the marginal rate of transformation in production (MRT). The opportunity to trade permits the community to increase its welfare; and the conditions for efficiency then become MRS = MRT, with the latter including transformation through international exchange.

As in the case of the closed economic system, the optimum in terms of efficiency may not be an optimum welfare position given that a large number of Pareto-optimal situations exist. Free trade would permit the attainment of an international social welfare optimum, if those gaining from free trade can compensate the losers.[5] Such compensation does not in practice occur, however, requiring as it does intergovernmental economic transfers. On the other hand, tariffs which might be used to improve the distribution of income internationally, would also reduce economic efficiency. On the one hand, the terms of trade could be improved by tariffs but on the other there would be negative effects associated with the misallocation of resources in production and with the distortion of consumption. On the assumption of no retaliation and assuming a country possesses the monopolistic power to be able to affect the terms at which it trades, an optimum tariff exists which will produce a welfare gain for the country concerned. However, host developing countries, at least, are generally much too small relative to total world trade to be able to do this. And overall, while tariff protection is common, most interventions could not be justified in terms of the optimum tariff.[6] On the whole the presumption lies in favour of free trade, although the possible conflict on a world basis between optimum efficiency and optimum welfare still exists.

The conclusion that free trade is consistent with Pareto optimality once again depends on the absence of market imperfections. But the only first best argument for tariffs as a form of intervention is the optimum tariff. Otherwise imperfections should be dealt with through government intervention in the domestic economy and the operation of tax/subsidy policies.

Although trade theory does not deal fully with international investment and MNEs, there is inevitably a preference for free capital movements. Caves expresses the view as follows: 'In the absence of externalities and market imperfections, the case for free movement of direct investment as a means of maximising world welfare is simply the case for allowing any product or factor to flow towards locations where it has the greatest excess of marginal value over marginal cost.'[7] As in the case of trade in goods, where an optimum tariff exists, so with international factor movements there exists an optimal tax. From a national viewpoint and assuming no retaliation, a capital importing country which possesses monopsony power will be able to improve its terms of borrowing by imposing a tax on capital imports.[8] The object of the optimum tax is to improve national welfare, not to maximise tax revenue. In practice, tariffs are also used by host countries as an instrument of policy with regard to foreign capital in place of taxes (or subsidies). The aim is generally to encourage MNEs to replace exports, which are faced by tariff barriers, by direct investment in the host country (Australia, Canada and the Latin American countries are often given as examples). This is only a second best policy; the more efficient policy would be to tax or subsidise foreign capital directly. It has been shown that foreign capital that is attracted by tariffs may inflict a loss on the economy when it might have yielded a gain if the investment had been undertaken without protection.[9]

In summary, economic theory generally supports policies of freedom in both goods and factor markets internationally, except with regard to optimal tax and tariff intervention by individual governments. The remedy for market failure lies in domestic intervention. These conclusions are reflected in post-war economic policies in the developed countries, although import substitution and increased protectionism characterised many LDCs until fairly recently. In the developed economies, policies have generally tended towards growing state intervention at the national level – although the extent and approach has differed sharply between countries. Internationally there was a trend towards liberalisation in trade and payments, at least until the early 1970s. The formation of the IMF, GATT, and OEEC were all steps in the direction of international liberalisation. It is noteworthy that while the GATT deals with trade and the IMF with short-term money matters, there is no international body dealing with capital flows as such. Mention will be made later of the failure to establish an International Trade Organisation (ITO) in the early post-war years, which was to have concerned itself with such issues.

Government intervention and sovereignty

The theory of government intervention is quite clear in its distinction between interventions which concern efficiency and those which concern equity. This review would not be complete, however, without reference to another rationale for intervention, namely that of sovereignty, or more accurately, loss of sovereignty. This is particularly important since sovereignty loss may be perceived to be produced only by the activities of *foreign* firms. The famous Arusha Declaration, which formed the basis for Tanzania's socialist policies in the late 1960s and 1970s, hit at the heart of the matter when it stated that the country 'cannot depend upon foreign companies and governments without sacrificing freedom'.[10] Host governments might therefore choose to intervene and regulate foreign companies as a means of promoting greater political and economic independence. In just the same way that government intervention on grounds of *equity* may be evaluated in terms of its effects on economic *efficiency,* so intervention to promote *sovereignty* may be judged in terms of its impact on *efficiency* and *equity.* In practice, in fact, it would be very difficult to estimate the economic trade-off between the alternative courses of action. But the significant point is that governments should be aware that increased economic independence may only be obtainable at a cost of lower economic efficiency.

The problem of the multinational enterprise

The issue of control of the MNE depends crucially on how the problem of the multinational is perceived. The problem, in turn, depends on the viewpoint, whether international, from the host country or from the home country (although the latter will not be considered directly at this stage).

The rise of the MNE has been shown to be a consequence of imperfections in both goods and factor markets internationally, but particularly in the market for knowledge. On the whole the view accepted in this book is that MNEs, by overcoming such imperfections (e.g. non-tradability in the market for technology, trade inhibiting government economic policies, etc.), have caused greater international specialisation. In this sense, the MNE, like international trade, permits greater exploitation of international comparative advantage. Extending from this is the presumption that MNEs operate, albeit unconsciously, to improve world welfare. But it is no more than a presumption because of the second-best nature of the solution. In a situation where restrictions on trade and factor movements exist, not every move to overcome such restrictions will result in an improvement in real output and incomes.

When considered as a vehicle for overcoming market imperfections, some of the practices of MNEs which may be welfare inhibiting from the viewpoint of an individual country may in aggregate improve world-wide economic efficiency: for example, the need for price discrimination to ensure an adequate private return from MNE investment in the production of technology has already been noted. On the other hand, there are certain characteristics and practices of MNEs which could not be regarded as efficiency-improving. In particular the oligopolistic market structures within which MNEs operate may give rise to restrictive practices and foster inefficiency. Among the many examples which could be given would be practices restricting competition, e.g. collusive territorial market-sharing agreements among multinationals, coordinated international pricing behaviour, pooling of patents and licences, and takeovers of indigenous firms; or policies leading to excessive competition, e.g. 'follow-the-leader' locational strategies producing sub-optimal production units. Similarly the behaviour of individual MNEs as oligopolists in respect of prices charged, advertising and promotional practices, etc. may enable the firms concerned to earn excess profits which are not derived from superior efficiency.

Apart from the possibly adverse effects attributable to MNEs themselves as national and international oligopolies, differences in national policies as between host governments may produce sub-optimal responses on the part of multinationals. Differences in the fiscal, monetary and balance of payments policies pursued by national governments may lead to counter-strategies by MNEs to minimise their impact. The effects of these counter moves (e.g. transfer pricing to reduce the impact of higher tax rates) will be disadvantageous to certain host countries at least. National policies may also distort the potentially beneficial effects of the MNEs in exploiting international comparative advantage, e.g. where MNEs are accused of using inappropriate capital-intensive technologies, it has been shown that the companies may merely be responding to incentives offered by the host country. Furthermore, differential national policies may produce responses from multinationals which have international as well as national repercussions. The potentially destabilising effects on the world monetary system emanating from MNE responses to the exchange rate and balance of payments policies of various governments may be cited as one example of this.

To sum up, therefore, a number of points should be noted which are relevant to the theory of government intervention and to the control of the MNE:

(i) Foreign direct investment and the MNE can be considered as performing the same function as international trade, but operating through factor flows rather than goods flows.

Therefore, free capital flows would tend to increase international specialisation.

(ii) In reality capital flows are not free, and even if all barriers to the free movement of factors were removed, MNEs would still not maximise world efficiency. Perfect competition does not exist, and, as has been shown, any market imperfections or externalities will prevent the attainment of world-wide Pareto optimality. In the case of MNEs, too, the relevant externalities may be external not only to the firm or the industry but also to the country. (One live example of the latter concerns the adverse effects in the Netherlands of pollution of the Rhine in Germany.)

(iii) Irrespective of their impact on global welfare, the operations of MNEs have not had an equal impact on all host countries. This is partly but not wholly a reflection of national policies being pursued. Even disregarding policy imperfections, the MNE is unlikely to have neutral effects on equity generally, e.g. the greater efficiency of MNE affiliates will not produce benefits for a host country if the real efficiency gains are transferred abroad in the form of monopoly profits or lower export prices. Moreover, again from a host country standpoint, the MNE produces adverse sovereignty effects.

Control of the multinational enterprise

The evidence of the foregoing is that control of the multinational enterprise is both desirable and inevitable. In outlining the types of controls that would be indicated by economic theory a distinction can be made between unilateral and multilateral regulation, the former being formulated and implemented by national governments, the latter being operated internationally or at least at a multi-country level.

(a) *International solutions*

Efficiency criteria *per se* would point to an international solution to the control of the MNE. This would entail the dismantling of some controls but the introduction of others. Essentially the following would be involved:

(i) Freedom of movement of products and factors. This would be necessary to achieve the full benefits of international trade and investment, in line with the conclusions of the theory of international trade and capital movements. In this way many of the impediments which hinder the MNEs from exploiting international comparative advantage and maximising international specialisation would be removed. The conditions necessary to achieve this would be fairly fundamental, of course. The minimum requirement would be the abolition of tariff and non-tariff barriers, and the dismantling of exchange controls. In practice, the requirements would be much more onerous than this, extending to the coordination of international interest rates, etc. (see next paragraph).

(ii) Freedom of movement of products and factors would not produce world-wide Pareto optimality in the presence of externalities and market imperfections. The latter are normally dealt with by domestic government intervention. But if domestic policies were uncoordinated, another set of policy imperfections would emerge. Given the international nature of the MNE, operations and activities would be adapted to take these differential policies into account. Therefore to remove the *micro-economic* imperfections and externalities (i.e. derived from the market structures in which MNEs operate) without creating other *policy-derived* imperfections would necessitate internationally coordinated intervention. What would thus be required would be action to equate international private and social costs or benefits and to stimulate competition nationally and internationally. This would entail coordinated monopoly and restrictive practices legislation, pollution laws, and so forth. In addition, government macro-economic policies would have to be harmonised. For example, to eliminate the incentive to manipulate transfer prices, effective profit tax rates would have to be the same in all countries, as would accounting standards and especially income reporting techniques; any restrictions existing on profit repatriation would need to be eliminated; and a further reason would exist for the removal of tariffs and subsidies.[11]

(iii) Even if the previous conditions for Pareto optimality were met, the problem of the distribution of the gains would still exist. It might be possible to achieve, through world-wide income redistribution, a different Pareto optimal position that produced a rise in international social welfare. An international mechanism for ensuring that the gainers compensate the losers would, therefore, be required.

(iv) Finally (and increasingly unrealistically) some supranational political institution would need to be created to legislate within all of the areas noted. The end result would be global budgets, the incorporation of multinational firms under international law, and an international welfare state.[12]

The second section of this chapter will summarise some of the proposals which have been made, based in broad outline on this scenario, ranging from codes of conduct to a 'GATT for Investment'. There seems to be at least one fundamental reason why such suggestions would not be acceptable at the present time, and this relates to the issue of national sovereignty. It is debatable how much sovereignty and autonomy countries actually possess in practice even at present, but the trade-off between sovereignty and efficiency/equity would not be acceptable. Moreover, the income redistributions involved would not be agreeable either to the rich countries, from whom possibly very significant financial contributions would be required, or to poor nations who would be unwilling to rely on international charity.

(b) *Host country solutions*

Failing a global solution, the principles for which are derived from the neo-classical concept of economic efficiency, the possibility of national policies must be investigated.

Where internationalisation of decision-making is involved, as in the previous solution, issues of national sovereignty are effectively ignored; the opposite extreme to this would be national autarky (self-sufficiency) which would require a disregard of the efficiency goal, placing sovereignty and equity as fundamentals. Excluding this case of complete isolationism, host nation policies towards the MNE will be determined by the weighting the country attaches to various goals. Some of the ways in which the characteristics of MNEs may affect these goals are shown in Table 6.1.

Table 6.1   Influence of MNE characteristics on host country goals

Characteristics of MNEs	Example of problems for host country	Host country goal affected
Large, diversified	Monopolistic practices	Efficiency, equity
Multinational	Circumvention of national policies	Equity, sovereignty
Foreign	Loss of autonomy	Sovereignty
Private, Western	Efficient capitalist form of organisation	Efficiency, equity, sovereignty
Technologically advanced	Technologically reliant	Efficiency, sovereignty
Mobile	Level and stability of employment	Sovereignty, equity, efficiency

In theory, at least, there is considerable scope for unlimited government action to attempt to control the MNE. But the only first best justification for restrictions is the optimum tax. How far beyond this point a country decides to go with controls depends on the importance attached to second-best and non-economic arguments and therefore on the trade-off between goals. These will vary enormously between states and it is only therefore possible here to indicate the potential alternative courses of action which exist. In considering the alternatives, a distinction can be made broadly speaking between two types of controls, firstly, those which relate to the degree of ownership of the 'package' of knowledge, capital and entrepreneurship; and secondly, those which relate to specific aspects of the behaviour of the foreign investment package. Countries may try, in practice, to influence both elements, and the actual arrangements possible are infinite in both detail and variety.

Controls relating to degree of ownership. In ascending order of host country control the following arrangements might be distinguished:[13]

(i) No ownership participation by host country – subsidiaries are wholly-owned and managed by the foreign investor.

(ii) Joint-venture – partially-owned by indigenous private or public interests in association with direct foreign investors.

(iii) Licensing-agreement – a host country firm reaches an agreement with a foreign firm under which (a) machinery and technology is acquired from the foreign firm; (b) the host country firm are committed to producing specified products; and (c) over a number of years the local firm pays the foreigner for the machinery and technology.

(iv) Technical assistance agreement – an agreement between a foreigner and a local firm under which management services, technical information or both are provided.

(v) Industrial cooperation – a wide and complex variety of arrangements are possible including the supply or leasing of plants; contract manufacturing or sub-contracting; joint production or marketing; provision of after-sales service; joint tendering, and so forth.

(vi) For completeness it should be noted that a policy of maximisation of host country control would lead logically to one of the following:
Importation of the finished product *or* the rejection of any association with a foreign country and a refusal to import, *or* the nationalisation or expropriation of foreign assets within the host country.

In the first two cases the foreign direct investment package comes more or less complete. Licensing, technical assistance agreements or industrial cooperation arrangements may be described as 'taking the package apart'. In general these alternatives produce a fairly clear trade-off on the part of host countries. To minimise the association with foreign direct investors, host countries must be prepared to forego some of the potential gains from the package or elements of the package.

Irrespective of the kinds of policies followed there are further dimensions to be incorporated. One relates to possible restrictions on the sectors in which foreigners may operate. In the LDCs and in some more developed states the most sensitive sectors seem to be public utilities, mineral exploration and development, iron and steel, retailing, insurance, banking and other services. In the developed countries generally, sectors such as aircraft, petroleum processing and distribution, pharmaceuticals, chemicals, electronics and vehicles – as high technology industries or large employers – are inevitably targets for political intervention and control. In addition, there may be provisions curtailing acquisition of locally owned companies or take-overs through the purchase of publicly held shares. Such regulations may apply only within certain of the sectors noted, or they may be of quite general applicability.

Controls relating to the behaviour of MNEs. Aside from the possibility of controlling the degree of foreign ownership, host countries may attempt to regulate specific activities of multinational affiliates. Some of the wide range of activities which may be involved are listed below:[14]

1. Purchase of inputs locally.
2. Exports of final products and export market controls.
3. Transfer pricing.
4. Profit and capital repatriation.
5. Royalty payments, management fees, etc.
6. Provision of loan capital from local v. foreign country sources.
7. Local participation in top management.
8. Level of employment.
9. Obligations to train local labour.
10. Unionisation of labour force, guarantees on strikes, etc.
11. Allowances against tax liabilities.
12. Credit policies, e.g. subsidised interest rates.
13. Subsidies on energy, transport, capital spending, etc.
14. Degree of competition and forms of competition.
15. Establishment of R & D.
16. Type of know-how acquired.
17. Use of locally owned transportation.
18. Environmental and social protection.

These items can be related to the discussion on the impact of MNEs in the previous chapter. For example, items 1–6 relate to the balance of payments impact of foreign direct investment; items 1, 7 and 9 represent some attempt to maximise the spill-over benefits from the presence of foreign firms; and item 15 reflects host country fears of becoming technologically dependent. In almost all cases the kinds of controls which would emerge would discriminate against foreign firms vis-à-vis indigenous firms. It would be possible to frame more general legislation in some areas, however. Competition policy is an obvious example, but policies on taxes and allowances and even on the local purchase of inputs could also be operated in respect of all firms. Such policies which are directed at improving the functioning of the market are first best policies; in efficiency terms the second best policy of interfering with the MNE would be justified only when first best policies could not be used or would not work.

Items 17 and 18 in the list above are particularly interesting in representing recently emerging forms of control. It has been realised that the value added in the transportation of LDC products is often high. For instance in iron ore, transport costs represent between 20 and 60 per cent of the c.i.f. unit value of the ore. As a consequence some countries are now introducing regulations which require export products to be transported in ships which are registered in the host state. Again, recent concern over the environment has meant that, in the mining industry particularly, host countries may insist that any land which is despoiled in the course of extractive industries, should be rehabilitated and returned to its original condition.

Bargaining over controls.   It is clear that host governments are not unrestrained in their dealings with MNEs. Even if governments do not seek to control the flow of foreign investment directly through taxes, tariffs and other restrictions, attempts to impose regulations either in respect of ownership or behaviour will also influence the flow. The end result might be that foreign direct investment was choked off completely. On the other hand a completely *laissez-faire* policy might mean that some of the potential benefits for the host country from overseas direct investment would not be realised. It was suggested in Chapter 5 that estimates of the impact of international firms on host economies could only be made within a cost/benefit framework. But even if the net benefits from pursuing a liberal policy towards inward direct investment exceeded some agreed level, a different set of policies towards MNEs might increase these net benefits still further. By bargaining with incoming foreign firms, host governments may be able to reach a mutually beneficial agreement on entry terms, in which the distribution of returns falls within the satisficing range for both parties. In this bargaining process all ownership combinations and behavioural patterns may be considered for negotiation.

The outcome of any bargaining programme will depend on the negotiating strengths of the parties. Negotiating strength in turn will depend on what each has to offer. For example, a country with unique supplies of a particular raw material will be able to extract very favourable terms from the MNE. Conversely, for many manufacturing projects, countries in South East Asia, e.g. Taiwan, Singapore, Hong Kong, with small markets and all possessing the advantage of cheap labour, may appear as equally suitable locations. In such circumstances the bargaining power of the host countries will be small and the MNE may be able to exploit this fact by obtaining substantial financial concessions. The list of activities given above would then represent areas where concessions may be offered to the MNE. As an instance, the host government may give guarantees of no strikes or non-unionisation of the labour force, or interest rates may be subsidised, etc.

Any bargain established between the MNE and the host country need not be sacrosanct. Rather bargaining should be thought of as a continuous process. As foreign investors' experience in particular locations increases, their perception of risk may decline. As a consequence of this and the fact that they have more to lose, they may be prepared to concede advantages to the host country which would not have been countenanced earlier.

Concluding remarks on host country solutions.   From the earlier discussion it is clear that in an ideal world national controls would be a sub-optimal solution to the problems of MNEs. The question arises as to whether or not unilateral policies are the best way of achieving equity and sovereignty as well as efficiency in an imperfect world. It does seem likely that some host countries may be able to influence certain aspects of the ownership pattern and/or behaviour pattern in a way which increases the net benefits of foreign direct investment. But a great deal will depend upon the characteristics of the host countries themselves. Host developed countries may have greater bargaining skills and generally more to offer MNEs, in which case controls will still produce inequities between countries. Furthermore, by operating controls at all, host countries are pursuing beggar-thy-neighbour policies, e.g. when a host state insists that foreign affiliates should export more or import less, they do not think of the employment consequences on countries abroad. Policies such as these are protectionist, and the economic implications are the same as the competitive devaluations and tariff barriers of the 1930s (and on the increase again late in the 1970s). In addition, for any individual country the extent to which controls may be used to influence the behaviour of MNEs can be exaggerated: for example, insistence on the establishment of R & D labs is quite meaningless as the MNE may utilise the R & D output anywhere in the world; similarly the local employees occupying top management positions may be figureheads only.

As a final comment, it would be wrong to give the impression that host countries have as a sole or major concern the extraction of the best possible terms from an MNE. For many the much greater concern is simply to attract the companies. The decision of a multinational firm to invest in a particular country will depend upon the combination of social, economic and political factors which will make up the 'investment climate'. Some of these factors are outside the control of host governments, but others are not and it has been suggested that, at least as regards the LDCs, several policies could encourage the inflow of MNE investment:[15]

(i) The provision of information through agencies established in the major capital exporting countries and the promotion of direct contacts with MNEs.

(ii) The provision of fiscal and other incentives, which have been shown to be successful in attracting some types of investment, particularly of the more footloose nature.

(iii) The operation of policies which create a stable economic environment; and also more specifically the implementation of clear and stable policies with respect to foreign investment. In the latter regard, acceptance of internationally or bilaterally agreed codes of conduct on various issues such as arbitration, taxation, exchange controls, etc. will provide evidence of the host governments' fair intentions towards the investor.

(iv) Offers of protection for the foreign investor through the introduction of tariffs and/or quotas against competing imports.

(v) Other more general policies may also be of some relevance, ranging from the provision of infrastructural facilities and of training facilities for the labour force, to the absence of bureaucratic interference in business affairs.

Arguably the use of some of these methods to attract investment would almost guarantee that the net benefits to the host economy were marginal; but the reality of the situation is that in many circumstances a host government may be prepared to pay the price simply for the employment created by the foreign investor.

(c) *Multinational solutions*

In the development of the European Economic Community, the Andean Pact, and so on, another means of controlling the MNE now exists. Such multi-regional blocs may be considered from two points of view. Firstly, to the extent that freedom of goods and factor movements exist, MNEs are being allowed to operate so as to maximise the benefits from international specialisation (although only within the area covered by the agreement). Supranational policies may be devised to remedy market imperfections, e.g. EEC anti-trust policy, and a budgetary policy used to redistribute income. In theory, therefore, it should be possible to operate the free trade area or common market as a microcosm of a free world economy. It goes without saying, however, that even the EEC is a long way from achieving this, e.g. controls on both portfolio and direct investment still exist between the UK and the other member countries; the EEC budget is so small as to be almost meaningless, etc.

A second way of viewing multi-regional blocs is as larger 'countries'. National – rather than international – type solutions may then be operated. Control of the MNE becomes an issue of bargaining again, the difference being that the negotiating strength of the host countries is much improved. A commodity agreement operated by a group of countries, such as OPEC, could be seen in the same way; and the strains within OPEC are indicative of the types of problems faced by such agreements. Controls may be negotiated with MNEs which are more favourable in terms of the net benefits accruing to the group than any individual country could have obtained. But this may be of little help to countries within the group which do not receive a proportionate share of foreign direct investment; such countries may be able to receive more inward direct investment by breaking out of the group and accepting less favourable terms. This is the familiar problem of the Prisoner's Dilemma in cartel agreements.[16]

Solutions to the problem of technology

In concluding this theoretical section it is desirable to focus on one specific problem associated with MNEs, namely that relating to technology, since the chief impact of the MNE in a world-wide sense, and on individual host countries, emanates from the knowledge advantages possessed by such firms.

It was indicated in Chapter 3 that social optimality would require technology to be made available to all potential users without charge. Assuming that the research and development work was undertaken by a private firm, the ideal policy would therefore be for the state to purchase the technology and then place the knowledge at the free disposal of all firms, local and foreign. But there are difficulties with this solution. In the first place there is the problem of trying to assess the present value of the new information, when the market in knowledge is not efficient. Secondly, private firms may try to obtain the full social value of the knowledge, thereby creating redistributional problems between producers and consumers nationally. There would also be international redistribution difficulties, since it would be inequitable if the burden of compensating firms for the production of knowledge fell wholly on the governments of the countries in which some firms were located.

A second international solution could be formulated. At present the patent system and price discrimination are means by which international firms achieve a satisfactory return from their investment in knowledge creation. Assuming that these firms have a comparative advantage in knowledge creation, it would be desirable for efficiency to permit these practices to continue. Because of the fact, however, that the whole of the surplus from technology creation accrues to the firm responsible for its development, and because the value of the technology transferred is not closely related to the price which individual countries pay for it, a large-scale international income redistribution programme would be required.

Alternative approaches which are less permissive might be to introduce an international code for the transfer of technology and to reform the international patent system. The problem is that banning restrictive export agreements, price discrimination, tied purchases, output-related royalty payments, etc. might produce short-run welfare gains, but at a cost of long-run welfare losses. If MNEs do not obtain an adequate return from the production of technology, this would lead to reduced flows of new technology in future. From an individual host country perspective, nevertheless, it might still be possible within a bargaining framework to improve the terms under which technology is transferred. In this sense control of knowledge is simply one of the behavioural controls which host countries may seek to impose upon incoming foreign firms.

The final point which needs to be noted relates to control over the appropriateness of the technology transferred. It was shown in the previous chapter that inappropriate technology may stem from inappropriate host government policies. Otherwise the problem could arise from the fact that with simple technologies, private returns may be low (although social returns might be high). Government-financed R & D may therefore be the answer, or governments may sub-contract the R & D and purchase the knowledge produced at its social rather than its private value. Given that MNEs' comparative advantage lies in the production of advanced technology, there is no necessary reason why such firms would be most efficient at producing simple labour-intensive technologies.

Appraising the solutions formulated

In appraising the various solutions postulated in this section, the unescapable conclusion is that the best solution must be that which is comprehensive and takes a world-wide perspective. The reason for this is that the domain of the means of control should be as wide as that of the multinational firm itself, namely, global. If a comprehensive global solution cannot be implemented, then international regulation of particular activities which give rise to major concern, e.g. technology transfer, would be a second best form of control. If any approach at the world-wide level is impractical, another second best solution would consist of alliances of a number of countries – either on a regional basis (e.g. the EEC) or on a product basis (e.g. OPEC). Third best solutions involve the introduction of unilateral controls by host governments.

The incidence and effectiveness of controls on MNEs

While the multinational enterprise itself is of fairly recent origin, discussions over the regulation of international firms and the implementation of legislation by host countries are even more recent. Active and sustained interest in MNEs by the United Nations and OECD, for example, is a feature of the 1970s. Action by host countries developed earlier, but to take one specific form of control, it was only with the Suez crisis in 1956 that the potential of nationalisation as a policy instrument became clear. With nationalisation, as with other host country policies, a world-wide demonstration effect is identifiable. This is reflected in the progressive introduction of controls over international firms in the natural resource industries, and in the gradual Latin-americanisation and

Africanisation policies adopted by governments towards foreign manufacturing affiliates; similarly the provisions of the Andean Pact relating to the commercialisation of technology have been introduced into legislation elsewhere. What is lacking to date is knowledge of the effectiveness of the controls which have been implemented in relation to the objectives set, and the likely effectiveness of those currently being proposed. Because of this, most of the information in this section will deal with the incidence of regulations and controls rather than with their impact. As in the previous section a distinction will be made between *international, national* and *multinational* controls.

Controls at the international level

Until the late 1960s and 1970s little international attention was given to the regulation of MNEs and foreign direct investment. A proposal for the protection of foreign investment was considered by the League of Nations in 1929, but made little progress. The Havana Charter of 1948, which was to have established an International Trade Organisation (ITO), included provisions relating to the protection of investment and restrictive trade practices. The ITO would have completed a post-war family of international organisations, in which the GATT was responsible for trade affairs and the IMF for short-term monetary affairs, but the Havana Charter was never ratified. Other early post-war efforts to exercise control over MNEs through international anti-trust programmes and through the development of codes to protect foreign investment were similarly unsuccessful.[17] It was not therefore until well into the 1960s, after a 15-year 'honeymoon' of sustained growth in foreign direct investment, that international regulation of MNEs became an important issue.

At the international level numerous proposals now exist for controlling the MNE. These vary widely, particularly in their coverage and in the degree of compulsion associated with them. Most of the 'proposals' inevitably have not progressed beyond this stage, although some remain worthy of consideration, even if utopian, in so far as they relate to the theoretical framework outlined. Categorisation is difficult but three groups of controls can probably be distinguished, ranging from the most comprehensive to the least comprehensive.

(a) *Generalised international agreements*
One of the initial proposals to emerge was that of Goldberg and Kindleberger who in 1969 advocated the establishment of the General Agreement for the International Corporation, similar to the General Agreement on Tariffs and Trade (GATT).[18] The General Agreement was to be based on a number of universally accepted principles, with an agency being established to operate and administer the agreement. This agency would recommend action on the basis of issues/questions

submitted to it by countries or companies. The recommendations would be voluntary and its success would therefore be dependent upon its own performance. Goldberg and Kindleberger believed that only an international organisation of this sort could handle the five problem areas which existed between MNEs and home and host governments, *viz.* taxation, anti-trust policy, balance of payments controls, export controls and securities regulation (i.e. international transactions in stocks and shares). Each of these problems was considered to have a common denominator: the MNE was either unregulated or its operations were being influenced by the overlapping regulations of different countries.

No details of how the scheme would operate were spelt out, but the ideas were undoubtedly influential. Discussions were held subsequently to assess whether or not there was a need for a GATT for Investment (termed an International Investment Organisation) or for a divestment agency, in which D. Wallace, Jr, played a significant role.[19] What was envisaged was an IIO which would evolve over time towards a regulatory body dealing with issues such as capital flows, taxation and transfer prices, anti-trust, security of investment, accounting standards, and problems relating to entry into and establishment in host countries. The principles behind the scheme were threefold: 1. the principle of an open world economy; 2. the principle of international law (this was included because it allowed for a limited number of rules applied to nation states rather than for a world government); 3. the principle of minimum, moderate or reasonable social controls. Social controls would cover some of the above aspects, e.g. standards for determining transfer prices, accounting standards, etc. More ambitiously, standards might be developed for allocating the total tax revenues derived from an MNE among the various countries in which it operated. Wallace was at pains to point out, however, that the proposals would not produce a global welfare state. The IIO, as envisaged, could not be an important instrument for the redistribution of wealth.

During the same period of time, various United Nations agencies were working on issues associated with the regulation of MNEs. More will be said on this work later, but at this point it is worth noting the report of the 'Group of Eminent Persons' published in 1974.[20] This report proposed that a General Agreement on Multinational Enterprises (GAME) should be concluded. This would establish the general conditions for international production, and would provide for an international control body with executive power for settling investment disputes. It was accepted that this was a long-term proposal, with little chance of immediate implementation. The group therefore argued for the conclusion of selective agreements on specific aspects of international production or for voluntary codes of conduct, until eventually a comprehensive mechanism could be introduced.

All of these ideas represent a form of GATT for investment, but none would fulfil the conditions for an international solution set out earlier in this chapter. Other proposals which are closer to this concept have, nevertheless, been suggested. For example, Ball envisaged the creation of a body of supranational company law under which the global parent would be incorporated.[21] Thus on important corporate issues, the MNE would be subject to international and not national laws, giving the firm greater freedom with regard to trade and investment decisions, mergers, and so on. The proposal by Penrose was on similar lines.[22] Essentially it was suggested that MNEs be incorporated under international law and subject to international income tax. In this way many difficulties and distortions emanating from differential tax provisions would be removed. The requirement thereafter would presumably be to use the tax revenues for redistributive purposes.

Because nation states are unprepared to give up the necessary sovereignty to permit the implementation of such proposals, other writers have proposed the formation of an international consultative mechanism. Rubin has suggested an International Corporation Consultative Center (ICCC), which would provide a forum to deal with particular problems and disputes. The ICCC was seen as going further, however, 'to propose means by which the vast network of the multinational enterprise could be turned to world benefit. The example of development *sans* pollution comes to mind.'[23]

The emergence of numerous proposals to control the MNE has also been linked with more general suggestions relating to global economic reform. The success of OPEC, deteriorating terms of trade for raw materials, debt problems, and world-wide inflation and depression in the 1970s has led to a call by Third World countries for a *new international economic order* (see Chapter 9). It was suggested that an overall deal might be struck between rich and poor nations which would inevitably involve the MNE as the principal supplier of technology to the LDCs and a major exporter of manufactures from the LDCs. Hopes that the 1976/77 Conference on International Cooperation (the so-called North–South dialogue) would make substantial progress in this direction were not fulfilled.[24] On issues which concern the MNE, the developed countries did little to open their markets to manufactured exports from the LDCs; conversely the latter countries would not give guarantees on MNE investments in their territories.

What can be said about these various proposals? The fact that they remain as proposals really speaks for itself. The inherent conflict between the global requirements for efficiency and national interests will always provide a stumbling-block to progress along the lines suggested. The interested parties – host governments, local enterprises, international companies, parent governments, local and international unions, international organisations and so on – have aims and motivations which are widely divergent. And yet it would be wrong to be too cynical. While the supremacy of national decision-making is accepted, the need for international action is also appreciated – precisely because there are possibilities of conflicts in goals and practices. Equally some of the proposals for international action recognise realistically that progress towards a comprehensive global solution must be evolutionary. Before writing off these generalised proposals completely, therefore, the limited experience of operating more narrowly defined international agreements needs to be considered. Successful operation of more limited agreements would, at least, suggest that comprehensive regulations might conceivably emerge at some date in the future.

(b) *International codes of conduct*

Leaving aside these generalised international agreements, several codes of business conduct are in the process of emerging. The aim of a code of conduct, at a minimum, is to provide a set of guidelines with which MNEs are invited to comply. A number of points can be noted. Firstly, a code is seen as a voluntary instrument of control, although the body responsible for the preparation of the code might presumably be prepared to act as an arbitrator in dispute situations. Secondly, the principal difficulty with any such codes is that to be acceptable to all the parties involved they might have to be so general as to be meaningless. Thirdly, as a consequence of these previous factors, codes can only be seen as an initial step towards the harmonisation of the laws of individual countries. Even this is much less than a free international solution, since regulation would remain the responsibility of national governments.

Since the concept of a code of conduct as a method of regulation has come into vogue, a number of codes have appeared from various organisations. These have inevitably reflected the bias within the particular organisation concerned. Thus the *Guidelines for International Investment* published by the International Chamber of Commerce (ICC) in 1972, reflects the views of the business community. On the issue of ownership, for example, the ICC code states: 'The government of the host country . . . should recognise that joint ventures are most likely to be successful if they are entered into voluntarily . . . and that there may be cases where investments which deserve high priority are only possible on the basis of total foreign ownership.' On the question of free movement of factors of production, the Guidelines take a strong free market position: 'The government of the host country should place no restrictions on the remittance of loan interest . . . licence fees, royalties and similar payments.' For its part the company is obliged to 'practice fair pricing policies for goods and services in dealings with associated companies'.[25]

The ICC Code was followed up in 1976 by a *Declaration on International Investment and Multinational Enterprises* from the Organisation for Economic Cooperation and Development (OECD).[26] The 24 member states of the OECD are all industrialised countries, but unanimity of view was by no means easy to obtain since states such as Canada and Australia have the same fears regarding MNEs as the Third World nations. As a consequence, the agreed code was toned down considerably from earlier drafts, it not emasculated.[27] Apart from a set of guidelines for MNEs the OECD Declaration incorporates a number of elements which refer to intergovernmental and government–MNE relationships. First, in general, both national and foreign firms should receive equal treatment from member states, i.e. the principle of non-discrimination. Second, intergovernmental consultation procedures should be strengthened. Third, cooperation on the investment incentives and disincentives operated by member states should be improved, and member countries should make such measures as transparent as possible.

The actual guidelines cover information disclosure, competition, financing, taxation, employment and industrial relations, and science and technology. It is difficult to assess their value. On the one hand, the guidelines on corporate disclosure go well beyond existing legislation in many countries – if companies choose to comply. On the other, regarding transfer pricing, the code states only that 'Enterprises should refrain from making use of . . . transfer pricing which does not confirm to an arm's length standard. . . . ' Also, on technology transfer, the guidelines suggest that firms ' . . . ensure that their activities fit satisfactorily into the scientific and technological policies and plans of the countries in which they operate . . . ' and 'when granting licences for the use of industrial property rights or when otherwise transferring technology do so on reasonable terms and conditions'.[28]

Given that compliance is again voluntary, whether such statements mean anything at all depends crucially on the attitude that MNEs themselves, their employees, and home and host governments adopt towards the code. A number of companies have expressed public support for the guidelines in their annual reports and elsewhere.[29] But equally important perhaps is the attitude adopted by international union bodies. The International Confederation of Free Trade Unions (ICFTU) had in 1975 produced its own radical *Multinational Charter* for the *legislative* control of MNEs.[30] Included in the charter were demands for an international convention for the suppression of restrictive practices and for the establishment of rules regarding taxation; for a drastic revision of the international patent laws; for worker participation, and so on. At a minimum the ICFTU have used the Charter as a means of bringing pressure to bear on organisations such as OECD, and the UN. To give an illustration of this, in the Spring of 1977 the unions presented the OECD with details of 15 cases in which it was claimed that multinationals had infringed the OECD code; one of these cases, that of the Badger company, was in fact brought up directly by the Belgian government. In the event the OECD refused to be drawn into making judgements on any of the individual cases, a decision which augurs badly for the future of the code, but also raises the issue of how far codes can be useful if they carry no sanctions with them.[31]

Stemming from the report of the Group of Eminent Persons, the United Nations began work in 1976 on its own code of conduct.[32] The OECD code relates to the industrial countries only; with the UN code the interests of the LDCs will be the main subject of the exercise. It is clear therefore that many of the issues to be raised will be quite different. For example, the principle of non-discrimination in national laws may not be acceptable; the possibility of nationalisation will have to be permitted, provided adequate compensation is paid; strict controls may be necessary over the extraction of natural resources; and greater attention will be paid to adherence to development objectives, respect of human rights, the cultural environment, etc. More important than this is the fact that although the Group of Eminent Persons proposed a voluntary code, Third World opinion seems to be in favour of a legally binding agreement, something which is completely unacceptable at present to the rich countries. With guidelines and codes of conduct already being viewed sceptically in many quarters, the fear must be that a further LDC-biased UN code may sound the death-knell for the whole concept.[33]

(c) *International agreements and codes of conduct on specific issues*
Apart from international agreements and codes which are designed to comprehend the range of problems posed by multinational firms, a number of attempts are also under way to establish international controls within various problem areas. Specifically the latter include: (i) restrictive practices and anti-trust; (ii) technology transfer; (iii) taxation; (iv) irregular practices; (v) employment and labour relations. All of the international bodies, namely the UN, OECD, ICC, etc. are involved in this work, and in summarising briefly the type of controls/solutions envisaged, attention will be focused on the organisation concerned.

Work in the United Nations. As noted, work in the UN is going on in several different agencies. The Group of Eminent Persons Report emanated from the Department of Economic and Social Affairs; its major achievements were the establishment, during 1974, of an ongoing commission on Transnational Corporations and an Information and Research Centre. But the Group made other specific suggestions:

(i) Technical assistance should be provided to LDCs to help these countries negotiate agreements with MNEs.

(ii) The LDCs, either individually or as a group, should establish their own terms for allowing MNEs to enter their markets (these would include nationalisation standards and compensation, labour laws, registration of capital, etc.).

(iii) Work should begin on codes of conduct, conventions and/or model laws relating to the overall activities of MNEs, but also to specific issues such as transfer pricing, technology transfer, and international anti-trust.

Since its establishment, the Commission for Transnational Corporations has been working on a number of such issues, notably the code of conduct for MNEs (see p. 253), the problem of bribery, and international standards of accounting and reporting for multinationals. The importance of prohibiting corrupt practices will be noted in later paragraphs. The establishment of international accounting and reporting standards is also very necessary, being a prerequisite for both understanding and controlling MNEs. To give a simple example within Europe, reporting requirements currently differ so greatly that it is impossible to obtain even the most basic information relating to the size and growth of affiliates in the various European countries from annual accounts. Standardisation is urgently required.[34] In addition efforts are being made at the Centre to build up a comprehensive information bank to facilitate further understanding of the various activities of MNEs and to strengthen the negotiating capacity of host developing countries.[35]

Another important UN agency in this area is the United Nations Conference on Trade and Development (UNCTAD). The UNCTAD report of a group of experts on Restrictive Business Practices was published in 1974, proposing that an international authority be set up that would function as a court of appeal dealing with restrictive trade practices or other offences committed by MNEs.[36] Work in UNCTAD has also been proceeding on a 'Code of Conduct on the Transfer of Technology', which prohibits 40 restrictive business practices in technology transfer. Examples include: (i) technology suppliers would not be able to limit exports of licensees' products; (ii) in legal disputes jurisdiction would be with the laws and courts of the LDCs. The terms of the code are not legally binding.

In summary, therefore, work in the UN is still at a fairly preliminary stage; and it is by no means clear as yet whether or what type of international action will follow. The problem arises once again from the very wide gulf which exists between the Third World countries, who are the dominant group in the UN, and the developed countries who will have the major task of implementation. The divergence of opinion between the two groups is indicated by the view of the rich countries towards the Code of Conduct for the Transfer of Technology: it was felt that the price and terms of technology should be set by market forces even though inappropriate technology with restrictive terms was sometimes sold to LDCs.

Work in the OECD. The OECD is also working actively on many of these same issues. For example the Council of the OECD has issued a recommendation which calls upon member states to pay particular attention to seven categories of known abuses arising from patent and licensing practices. Where these practices have resulted in a restriction in competition, it is recommended that governments consider some form of compulsory licensing. Again, in 1973, the OECD introduced a voluntary conciliation procedure on disputes between member states involving the enforcement of anti-trust laws. Considerable attention has also been paid to international tax problems and emerging from this work has been a model form of bilateral treaty to be used by developed countries in negotiating tax treaties.[37]

Work in the International Chamber of Commerce. The ICC has for many years operated a Court of Arbitration concerned with the resolution of conflicts between private parties and between governments and MNEs.[38] Much more recently (1977), in the wake of bribery and corruption cases involving MNEs, and admissions concerning 'slush funds', etc. the ICC came out with its draft code of conduct on *Ethical Practices in Commerical Transactions,* the aim of which is to eliminate 'irregular practices and improper conduct'.[39] This is again a good example of how hopes and reality tend to diverge: by the time the code was adopted late in 1977 one of the authors of the original proposals was forced to remark that 'this emasculated animal, with its tongue cut out and its teeth extracted, is not likely to make a major impact'.[40] There is no doubt that corruption is an important issue, being so prevalent in many parts of the world that it is an accepted way of life and not regarded as unethical at all. The failure of the ICC code is now, in fact, less of a problem since the US President signed into law a bill that imposes fines of up to $1 m. on American corporations found to have bribed foreign government officials in an effort to obtain business. Officers and directors of corporations which bribe, or which condone bribery of foreign government officials, face five years in prison and fines of up to $10,000 each. The need for such legislation was revealed by investigations undertaken by the US Securities and Exchange Commission which uncovered more than 300 cases of corporate bribery involving over $400 m. in questionable payments.

The foregoing are merely a few examples of the direction in which work is proceeding. Quite apart from the overlap and potential conflict in the proposals emerging from different organisations, there remain considerable doubts about the value of selective agreements. Thus *ad hoc* attempts to control particular problems may result in distortions in other areas. For example, an international anti-trust agreement is only meaningful if uniform conditions are also created in trade, finance and taxation. Moreover, in framing international agreements (although this applies not only to selective agreements) there are dangers in singling MNEs out for special discriminatory treatment, which would impair their competitiveness and efficiency. In any event, as with generalised international agreements, political realities mean that in present circumstances no international body will be created with the necessary powers to implement selective agreements. The fall-back position is again voluntary guidelines on specific issues, with all the weaknesses these entail. As at the present time therefore the prospects for using selective agreements as a means of developing over the years a comprehensive, regulatory international agreement appear utopian in the extreme.

Controls at the national level

There are potentially an enormous number and variety of national controls possible, but very little empirical evidence exists on their effectiveness. In this context the effectiveness of controls would be measured in terms of their ability to achieve host government efficiency, equity and sovereignty goals. With respect to the efficiency goal, it was indicated earlier that bargaining over controls could increase the host country's net benefits from foreign direct investment, but it is not known very precisely how far the countries implementing such controls actually weigh up the costs and benefits. In any event, host nations may also be influenced by equity or sovereignty considerations or by the importance of particular projects to national economic development plans.

Bearing in mind that 'controls' might be positive, i.e. operating more sensible economic policies so as to remove the windfall profits accruing to MNEs from undervalued interest rates, etc. a distinction will be made between ownership and behavioural controls as before.

(a) *Controls relating to the degree of ownership*

(i) *Nationalisation as a policy instrument.*   Prior to the late 1950s, with the exception of centrally planned economies, few instances of nationalisation could be found. Between 1960 and 1974, on the other hand, about 1,400 take-overs of foreign enterprises were recorded in well over 50 different countries. The pace of nationalisation has moreover quickened from an annual average of 47 cases in the 1960s to an average of 140 per year so far in the 1970s. For the period 1956–72, more detailed data are given in Tables 6.2 and 6.3. Over these years about 19 per cent of assets were nationalised with compensation being paid on two-fifths of the total. In the Socialist developing countries alone, over 90 per cent of assets were nationalised and expropriation of assets (nationalisation without compensation) was much more prevalent.

The sectoral distribution of assets nationalised is perhaps as expected, with basic industries such as mining and smelting, oil and agriculture accounting for over one-half of the total.

Table 6.2 The importance of nationalisation (1956–72)

	Growth in stock of foreign investment $m. (S)	Assets nationalised $ m. (A)	$\dfrac{A}{A+S}$ %	Compensation paid $ m.
All countries	43,251	10,096	18.8	4,170
Socialist countries*	571	5,766	91.0	1,275
Other countries	42,680	4,330	9.2	2,895

* Defined as countries with a nationalisation content of over 80%. Includes Algeria, Bangladesh, Burma, Chile, Cuba, Egypt, Iraq and Syria.

(*Source:* Williams, 1975.)

Table 6.3 The sectoral distribution of nationalisation (1956–72)

	% of total assets nationalised
Mining and smelting	20.8
Oil*	18.2
Agriculture	16.5
Manufacturing	16.4
Public Utilities	12.0
Other	16.1
Total	100.0 ($10,096 m.)

* Production, refining, transport and distribution.

(*Source:* Williams, 1975.)

On a country basis, Table 6.4 reveals that UK and US firms have been particularly affected by nationalisation. During the 1960–69 period alone over half of all reported cases of nationalisation involved UK affiliates, mainly in sectors such as agriculture, banking and insurance. During the 1970s US subsidiaries became increasing targets for nationalisation, firms involved in oil and mineral extraction, retail banking, utilities and transportation being principally affected. Large affiliates have been most exposed to nationalisation pressures: for US subsidiaries with assets over $100 m. the expropriation rate has been 50 times greater than for small affiliates with under $1 m. in assets. Of the 342 American affiliates nationalised between 1960 and 1976, 158 cases (46 per cent) occurred in Latin America; while 419 of the total of 521 UK affiliates nationalised were located in South and East Asia, and Africa south of the Sahara.

In spite of the importance of nationalisation as a policy – in the natural resources sector particularly – it is doubtful how effective it really is in increasing the net benefits to the host country. The skills may not be available in the LDCs to manage the nationalised enterprise, necessitating the conclusion of management, sales and technology contracts with the former parent company or other

Table 6.4   Reported cases of nationalisation by major country of origin and region in which takeover occurred

Country of origin	% share of total no. of cases 1960–69	% share of total no. of cases 1970–76	Total no. of cases 1960–76	Africa south of Sahara	West Asia and North Africa	South and East Asia	Western Hemisphere
				Region in which nationalisation occurred			
UK	53	28	521	192	94	227	8
USA	19	26	342	71	66	47	158
France	12	9	146	37	107	1	1
Others	16	37	438	328	52	25	33
Total	100	100	1,447	628	319	300	200

(*Source*: UN Economic and Social Council, 1978, Tables 7 and III–29.)

overseas firms. Control may effectively therefore remain in foreign hands. Moreover, the finance involved in the payment of compensation and in servicing the management contract may mean little net income gain for the host country. Additionally the act of nationalisation may generate countervailing action from the MNE or its home government. On the positive side nationalisation may assist the learning process in LDCs by accelerating the introduction of local personnel into management positions. The take-over of one foreign firm may also improve the country's negotiating position with remaining MNE affiliates or potential entrants (if they are not frightened off completely – and Table 1.10 on page 28 showed that the annual number of divestments has increased sharply since the mid 1960s). On balance, however, the major benefit must be measured in terms of real or perceived increased sovereignty.

(ii) *Joint ventures and other ownership combinations.*   Given that nationalisation is not a sufficient and probably not even a necessary condition for increasing the gains from foreign direct investment, the question is which ownership combination will maximise the contribution to the host economy. Despite the fact that US MNEs at least are claimed to prefer wholly owned subsidiaries, many have settled for second best: Table 6.5 shows that just over half (52.6 per cent) of US subsidiaries in the sample were wholly owned at the date of entry into the host country, the remaining 47 per cent being joint ventures. Among non-US MNEs, however, wholly owned subsidiaries were fairly rare: only 18.9 per cent of affiliates were in this category at date of entry.

What is particularly interesting is the fact that a number of host countries have instituted changes in ownership patterns since the affiliates were first established. Among the 580 US affiliates which were wholly owned at date of entry, only 472 were still wholly owned

Table 6.5 Ownership patterns* of 2,997 manufacturing affiliates of 391 MNEs in developing countries at date of entry and in the 1970s

Home country and type of ownership	No of affiliates classified by ownership pattern *at entry*						
	Wholly owned	Majority owned	Co-owned	Minority owned	Unknown	Total	% of Total
Affiliates of 180 US-based MNEs, 1975							
Wholly owned	472	26	5	20	–	523	47.5
Majority owned	43	137	9	14	1	204	18.5
Co-owned	14	6	64	11	–	95	8.6
Minority owned	24	21	2	175	–	222	20.1
Unknown	27	13	1	17	–	58	5.3
Total	580	203	81	237	1	1,102	100.0
% of Total	52.6	18.4	7.4	21.5	0.1	100.0	100.0
Affiliates of 211 MNEs based elsewhere than in US, 1970							
Wholly owned	186	81	70	43	12	392	20.7
Majority owned	70	315	34	7	2	428	22.6
Co-owned	32	24	228	14	–	298	15.7
Minority owned	50	18	16	348	9	441	23.3
Unknown	20	1	4	22	289	336	17.7
Total	358	439	352	434	312	1895	100.0
% of Total	18.9	23.2	18.5	22.9	16.5	100.0	100.0

* Affiliates of which the parent firm owns 95 per cent or more are classified as wholly owned; 51–94 per cent as majority owned; 50 per cent as co-owned; 5–49 per cent as minority owned.

(*Source*: UN Economic and Social Council, 1978, Table III–26 derived from data supplied by Harvard Multinational Enterprise Project.)

in 1975, the remaining 108 having to permit equity participation by host country investors. There have been other instances where the MNEs have increased their equity ownership, of course, reflecting dissatisfaction with joint venture arrangements, but overall the number of wholly owned US affiliates in the sample declined from 580 to 523. The position with respect to European and Japanese MNEs is rather different, although this may be partly associated with the fact that the latest data refer to the year 1970. The number of wholly owned subsidiaries rose from 186 at date of entry to 392 in 1970, mainly at the expense of co-owned affiliates. Even so by 1970, in 1,503 of the total number of 1895 affiliates, some local equity participation was involved. This reflects greater flexibility on the part of non-US MNEs as compared with their American counterparts and a desire to pre-empt nationalisation threats; the pattern also reflects the more recent growth of non-US multinationals as well as the type and location of the investments.

This table confirms other evidence that strong government policies of requiring joint ventures from foreign direct investors do result in more local participation, but the evidence relating to whether or not joint ventures provide more net benefits to the host country is mixed.[41] Based on his own work and a survey of other studies, Wells concludes on the positive side that: (i) joint ventures appear nearly always to transfer some control from the foreign parent to the local partner; (ii) transfer prices charged to joint ventures are usually lower than to wholly owned subsidiaries; (iii) joint ventures purchase more of their inputs locally than other types of firms.[42] Nothing was said, however, about other possible spill-over benefits, e.g. the production of local entrepreneurs, development of local capital markets. On the negative side, the conclusions were: (i) joint ventures borrow more locally (although this is a disadvantage only if funds are being diverted from competing uses of higher social value); (ii) they pay more for technical services; (iii) they probably export less; (iv) technology is capitalised at a higher rate; (v) the dividend policy of joint ventures is more stable. The evidence seems therefore to be finely balanced, and the effectiveness of joint ventures must depend a great deal on the attitude taken by the host government and how this develops through time. For example as know-how increases locally, this knowledge may be used to put pressure on the foreign partner to reduce the disbenefits. Against this, on the other hand, Penrose has argued that 'if all the government wants to do is to control those aspects of the operation of MNEs which are likely to adversely affect the economic development of a country . . . 5 or 10 per cent of equity can be an equally satisfactory means of obtaining access to information and an effective voice in . . . management'.[43]

Another possibility is to 'break the package open' by purchasing technology through licensing agreements, by acquiring management through management contracts, etc. The case of Japan (see pp.

269–71) is almost a fairy story of how to develop through licensing, but the number of countries able to reproduce the conditions existing in Japan must be very limited.

The overall conclusion is that it is impossible to provide a simple set of rules to guide host governments who may be considering policies on ownership. The stage of development of a country, its size and its national endowments, plus the varying characteristics of investing firms will all influence the choice to be made. Even the widespread dislike of the acquisition of indigenous firms by foreigners may not be logical in efficiency terms: where the acquired firm is unprofitable or only marginally profitable, a foreign company bringing new technology may improve resource use. Similarly efficiency may be improved where a foreign firm with product design and production capabilities acquires a local company with distribution capability. The impression is, nevertheless, that more and more countries are now insisting on local equity participation: legislation in Malaysia requires that 70 per cent of equity must be locally owned by 1990 (although this may only be a bargaining figure); and even in the UK, the government is taking a stake in North Sea oil operations through the equity participation of the British National Oil Corporation (BNOC). In some cases the MNEs have acquiesced to such demands, but when, for example, the corporation insists on 100 per cent control of its subsidiaries, major conflicts may arise with host governments, as IBM have found in India, Indonesia, Nigeria and Brazil.[44]

(b) *Controls relating to the behaviour of MNEs*
To try to give even a superficial impression of the behavioural controls operated by host countries is not possible in the space available, not only because of their diversity, but also because they are constantly changing and evolving. In this section therefore it is only possible to give examples of controls operated by certain countries. Two case studies of Japan and Canada follow, to provide a little more detail on the evolutionary nature of foreign investment controls.

Investment screening. Non-automatic entry; the assessment of investment proposals on a project-by-project basis according to the requirements of a long-term economic plan; and the establishment of a central screening institution, have been suggested by various authors as an important means of increasing the host country's share of the benefits from foreign investment. Moreover, the screening body, it is suggested, should be responsible for undertaking a continuous review of the performance of foreign affiliates. Controls on MNE behaviour would emerge out of the screening process under this type of framework. In going some way to implement this, Kenya, for example has an elaborate screening system to ensure that only those enterprises which will be of 'benefit to Kenya' are allowed in. On the other hand, once the necessary approval is given, the right to repatriate capital and transfer earnings follows immediately. This, in fact, is likely to be much more acceptable to the MNE than any procedure which links a screening process with variations in the terms of entry for investors.

More generally, according to Table 6.6 below, the South American countries appear to operate the most restrictive and the most integrated approaches to investment screening, and indeed have the least permissive approach overall among the developing nations.

Balance of payments.   Whether entry is automatic or not it will always be backed up by other regulations on MNE behaviour. Given the significance attached to balance of payments considerations, controls are very frequently applied in this area. Taking one example relating to exports, the permitted equity holding of foreigners may be linked to the company's export performance: in Mexico, wholly owned subsidiaries may be permitted only if total output is exported, and in India foreign equity holdings have to be diluted to 40 per cent unless the firm operates in the 'priority sector' (designated from time to time by the government) and/or the firm is manufacturing solely for export. The outcome of this was that in 1978 IBM wound up its operations in India and the Coca-Cola plant also closed.[45] Export requirements may be backed up by restrictions on the import of components: permission from the British Government for Japanese electronics firms to invest in the UK was conditional upon the use of a high proportion of British made components. Other countries restrict the raising of capital locally, Australia being one of the first to introduce such a policy; and, of major importance, attempts may be made to limit any adverse effects of transfer pricing. There are a variety of possible ways of dealing with the problem of pricing goods involved in intra-firm trade:[46]

(i) Transfer prices could be scrutinised and fixed directly. A number of developed countries have adopted this method, although US experience has been that it is cumbersome and complex. In the LDCs, on the other hand, because only a limited number of firms will be involved, the task may be more easily manageable and the experience of Colombia (Chapter 5) showed that substantial savings are possible. A related solution would be to channel all imports through a governmental agency, which would negotiate import prices after making comparisons with alternatives.

(ii) Host governments might tax MNEs on the basis of the estimated proportion of their global profits accounted for by the country concerned. Rather than using reported profits, the estimated figure might be derived from the particular country's share of sales or assets. A special case of this is the OPEC device of charging income tax on the notional ('posted') price.[47]

(iii) Tax and tariff rates might be fixed jointly so that the total revenue realised would be the same whether the MNE repatriated profits

Table 6.6 Patterns of foreign direct investment regulation in selected countries

Parameter	Pattern 1 (mostly Asia – excluding India – Africa, CACM)	Pattern 2 (mostly Middle East, North Africa)	Pattern 3 (mostly South America)
Administration	Case-by-case screening largely restricted to award of *incentives* (non-discriminatory)	Case-by-case screening at establishment (degree of discrimination varies)	Separate administration for foreign investment. Screening at establishment
Investment screening criteria	Emphasis on functional contributions of investment. Little indication of extensive cost/benefit analysis. Screening largely for award of incentives	Emphasis on functional contributions and conditions of investment. Little indication of extensive cost/benefit analysis	Criteria formulated for cost/benefit analysis, often extensive. Includes social cost criteria in some cases
Ownership	Few requirements. Few sectors closed to foreign investment	Joint ventures prevalent	Strict regulations on ownership and investment (except Brazil). Large number of closed sectors
Finance	Few repatriation limitations	Few repatriation limitations	Repatriation ceilings in most areas (except Mexico). Screening of foreign loans. Special control of payments to parent company
Employment and training	Announced indigenisation policies but little headway in practice	Local quotas for work force. Few local quotas for management	Specific across-the-board indigenisation requirements
Technology transfer	No controls	No controls	Screening and registration of all technology imported
Investment incentives	Long-term tax incentives for establishment	Establishment incentives limited to five years – in most cases non-renewable	Incentives tied to specific contributions, but incentives may be curtailed for foreign-owned firms
International dispute settlement	Adherence to international dispute regulations. Regional investment regulation: EAC, etc.	Same as Pattern 1. Regional investment regulation: Arab Economic Union	Local adjudication and regional harmonisation of investment regulation: ANCOM, CACM

Note: CACM = Central American Common Market; EAC = East African Community; ANCOM = Andean Common Market.

(*Source:* UN Economic and Social Council, 1976.)

directly (by declaring them) or indirectly (by over-pricing imports). Account would also have to be taken of over-charging royalties or under-pricing exports, and these factors plus other complexities would make this scheme very difficult to operate.

(iv) Host countries which operate a policy of requiring local equity participation clearly hope to be able to undertake internal checks on transfer pricing. But perhaps a more useful procedure would be for countries simply to insist on the right to inspect the books of foreign affiliates, always assuming that the expertise existed locally and/or that manipulative transfer pricing could be established by this procedure.

By its very nature transfer pricing is difficult to detect but as concern has grown in host countries so greater efforts are being made to detect such policies using one or a combination of the measures outlined above.

Employment and training.   Another important set of controls relates to quantitative and qualitative job requirements. LDCs with high rates of aggregate unemployment may simply impose overall job requirements. Thus Indonesia requires that 75 per cent of employees of foreign firms be Indonesian within 5–8 years. The Malaysian government goes further and specifies the proportions in which various ethnic groups are to be employed in an organisation. In other countries job requirements are often part of regional policies: Canada, France, Netherlands, UK, etc. offer major incentives for jobs to be brought to 'depressed areas'. Additionally, lay-offs may be forbidden (Italy) or made very costly (Germany, Belgium).

With respect to qualitative requirements, Argentina requires at least 85 per cent of managerial, scientific, technical and administrative personnel to be local citizens. Regulations may also refer to the training of local workers. Over-rigid requirements can have unfortunate side effects, of course. The premature introduction of nationals into key jobs may keep the affiliate from achieving internationally competitive standards and may adversely affect training (and thus technology transfer).

Technology transfer.   Control of technology transfer is closely linked to the transfer pricing issue discussed above, at least as regards the payments for technology. With respect to the restrictive business practices commonly associated with technology contracts, these may be the subject for bargaining between the host government and the MNE. A number of countries such as Mexico, members of the Andean Pact, certain other Latin American states and India operate very comprehensive regulatory systems. But excluding these countries, many LDCs seem to apply few controls at the national level. This point is borne out by Appendix 6.2, prepared by the UNCTAD Secretariat, which summarises the controls imposed by a wide variety of countries of different social and economic systems and degrees of development. The table in fact indicates that policies which have either a general effect on the transfer process or are specifically related to technology transfer seem to be more widespread in many developed countries.

Other issues. It should be noted that there may be important international political dimensions involved in national regulation of the MNE. To quote one example, early in 1978 the Nigerian government asked all major foreign firms in the country to declare the extent of their business interests in South Africa; and announced that no new government contracts would be given to firms which would not reduce their involvement in South Africa. As an initial action, the government ordered all state and para-statal bodies to withdraw their deposits from Barclays International. While this action is by no means unique, it does indicate that the issue of national control is much wider than one of national and purely economic interests.

As a final comment, it would be wrong to overemphasise the negative aspects of controls (from the MNEs' viewpoint). In the 1960s the smaller Asian countries introduced legislation, which might typically specify: 5 years' exemption from profit taxes; duty-free import of capital equipment; and no restrictions on profit repatriation. In addition MNEs may be offered trouble-free labour: Singapore offers a strike holiday to MNEs for a number of years, and in South Korea a special labour law rules out industrial disputes with foreign firms. More countries are beginning to set up 'industrial free zones', a recent example being the Egyptian industrial park at Alexandria. In Europe, too, competition to attract foreign investment has led to an escalation of incentives, the Irish leading the way with the offer of a remission of tax on export profits until 1990.

(c) *Controls imposed by developed and less developed host countries*
The data presented in Table 6.6 indicated that various patterns of foreign direct investment regulation could be identified among the developing countries. One of these patterns, which prevailed in most African and certain Asian countries, was characterised by relatively few regulations and restrictions, with, conversely, numerous incentives being offered to foreign investors. In these countries indigenisation policies as regards management and the labour force existed, but they were often not mandatory; few sectors were closed to foreign investors; and most countries accepted international dispute settlement procedures. The second pattern, which was mainly found in the Arab countries, was rather less liberal with more regulatory provisions existing. For example, local participation quotas were often mandatory; and employment and training requirements were specified, as were capital and profit repatriation limits. The most restrictive approach was pursued by South American countries. Here,

initial screening procedures were much stricter and screening of technology imports was also widespread. In addition specific indigenisation requirements existed; repatriation ceilings were imposed in most countries; and strict regulations existed on ownership and on the sectors in which foreign investment was permissible.[48]

The situation is evolving very quickly and many of the so-called 'liberal' LDCs seem to have become markedly less so of late. A number of the African countries have tightened up their regulations and in the Middle East the international petroleum industry, at least, has been faced with greater controls. Given these moves, it is fair to say that multinationals generally face a significantly more restrictive regulatory environment in less developed than in developed countries.

The position varies quite widely, however, as will be shown in the discussion relating to two notable industrialised countries – Canada and Japan – in following paragraphs. Within Western Europe, too, the situation differs between, on the one hand, West Germany and the Netherlands and, on the other, France, Sweden and Norway.[49] The former countries are important as capital exporters and therefore have a vested interest in relative ease of access for foreign investment; but in addition the West German economy tends to be run upon liberal economic principles. The UK is also itself a major capital exporter and again a fairly liberal and relaxed policy has been adopted towards inward direct investment (although a more interventionist policy is being operated in respect of oil investment). Nevertheless discussions may be held between the UK authorities and the prospective investors about a variety of factors in important cases and powers exist to prevent take-overs.[50] In the UK also both take-overs and new foreign controlled ventures are expected to be basically self-financing. Contrasting these countries with France and the two Scandinavian states, one difference is that the latter tend to exclude or restrict investment across wide and important sectors of their economies. French policy has varied but is generally very nationalistic and therefore bargaining takes place about the terms and conditions of entry, and local equity participation is very common. In addition take-overs must be entirely financed from abroad, while for new enterprises at least half of the finance must be obtained from non-French sources. In the Scandinavian countries there is a requirement for a majority of nationals on boards of directors and in Sweden firms have the right to restrict, through their articles of association, foreign nationals acquiring shares in their companies. It must be clear from these points that the differences between the countries are really ones of degree, and the regulatory policies operated cannot be compared with those existing in many LDCs. In common with other developed countries, Western European states have been reluctant to adopt any specific laws or regulations to deal with direct foreign investment.[51] Given that the various European countries are in fact competitors for investment, the most important question is not what controls to impose but rather what incentives to offer.

(d) Case studies of Canada and Japan

Canada[52]

In terms of the degree of foreign ownership and control of major industrial sectors, Canada is unique among developed countries; and a key feature of the foreign sector is the overwhelming dominance of US direct investment. It is fair to say that Canada has adopted a schizophrenic attitude towards foreign investors: on the one hand the country has been very receptive to US and other foreign firms, and indeed has adopted policies of high tariffs to encourage such firms to produce in Canada for a large protected domestic market. On the other hand, a succession of reports have urged greater control over foreign investment, principally, it must be said, for nationalistic reasons. The dilemma is the classic one of any host country. In simplistic terms, do people in Canada wish to be 'rich Americans' or 'poor Canadians'?

Serious Canadian investigation into questions of foreign ownership and control dates from the publication in 1957 of the Report of the Royal Commission on Canada's Economic Prospects. More recently three official investigations have been important in paving the way for what could be seen as a fairly significant shift in Canadian policy, firstly, the Watkins Report (1967–68), next the Wahn Report (1970) and finally, the Gray Report (1970–72). What emerged from these and other studies was an expression of the required aims of Canadian policy towards foreign ownership. Three elements were stressed:

(i) The necessity to improve the overall efficiency of the economy to the benefit of all firms.

(ii) The necessity to retain and increase indigenous ownership and control of firms in Canada (where feasible and desirable).

(iii) With regard to the foreign sector, economic benefits should be maximised and costs minimised;[53] the ways in which US firms transmit American law and policy objectives to Canada should be ended; and, the non-economic impacts of foreign firms should be minimised.

During the 1960s certain regulations were introduced in respect of foreign firms. Some Canadianisation policies were brought in; disclosure requirements of foreign firms were increased; and foreign affiliates received from the government 'Some Guiding Principles of Good Corporate Citizenship'. But the various official reports brought home the need for more definitive policies, and the government responded with the 1974 Foreign Investment Review Act. This legislation established a Foreign Investment Review Agency (FIRA) to screen proposals for foreign activity, for the purpose of advising whether or not the activity would provide 'significant benefit' to Canada. For the first 18 months after the Act was passed, the legislation applied only to take-overs of existing Canadian companies by foreign-owned firms; but from October 1975 the establishment of new foreign businesses in Canada and some expansions of existing foreign-controlled firms were also subject to review. The factors to be taken into account in determining whether or not significant benefits would be provided are: (i) the effects on the level and nature of economic activity in Canada, including employment; (ii) the degree of involvement of Canadians; (iii) the effects on productivity, industrial efficiency, technological development, product innovation and product variety in Canada; (iv) the effects on competition; (v) the compatibility of the investment with industrial and economic policies.

These criteria are extremely broad, and the role of FIRA seems to be to negotiate greater national benefits in one or more of the five areas. FIRA is therefore a bargaining agent, not merely a screening agency.

Various other policies have also evolved. One broad set of regulations aims to influence the degree of foreign ownership overall, and in particular sectors. For example, in 'key sectors' such as broadcasting and banking, foreign owners have been required to divest their interests to a minority position. Also taxes on dividends paid abroad discriminate in favour of companies with a Canadian ownership component. A second set of regulations is designed to increase the net benefits of foreign affiliates to the economy through raising exports, the domestic sourcing of supplies and research capacity. Moreover, the Canadian government has attempted to lessen the impact of extraterritorial measures with respect of US anti-trust and trade legislation, e.g. US subsidiaries in Canada were forbidden under the terms of US legislation to trade with Cuba, but the act involved is no longer applied strictly.

And yet the foreign investment dilemma remains. In the first two-and-a-half years of FIRA's existence 209 out of 293 take-over applications were approved with a further 41 cases being withdrawn and only 43 being disallowed. FIRA also approved almost every new business investment.[54] This has led on the one hand to accusations that the Foreign Investment Review Act was being used as a means of facilitating foreign investment rather than reviewing it – thereby undermining Canadian sovereignty. On the other hand, it has been argued that FIRA's favourable attitude to foreign investment permits Canada to continue to enjoy the benefits of international capital flows: the operation of FIRA 'to sustain political goals of national independence (would) inevitably lead to economic costs in terms of foregone aggregate social welfare'.[55] Inward direct investment is thus bound to remain an important economic and political issue. For the MNEs themselves, uncertainties relating to the future course of legislation in Canada can only be exacerbated by the potential secession of Quebec from the rest of the country.

Japan[56]

The Japanese case is almost diametrically opposite to that of Canada. Beginning with prohibitive controls over foreign direct investment, the country is only now beginning to ease the terms under which foreigners are allowed into the country.

Japanese policy towards direct investment from overseas was laid down in the Foreign Investment Law in 1950 which was designed to permit the reconstruction and development of the Japanese economy with the assistance of foreign capital and technology. According to the terms of this law, direct foreign investment would be permitted in Japan only when it contributed to the attainment of self-sufficiency and to the improvement of the balance of payments. These terms were interpreted so strictly by the review body, the Foreign Investment Council, that inward investment was tightly restrained. Thus the main instrument used to obtain foreign know-how was that of licensing. US (and European) firms were happy to supply technology under licensing agreements in these early post-war years, because their foreign investment interests lay elsewhere, principally in Europe, because of cultural barriers, and because returns were reasonable (even if the per unit royalty rate was low).[57] The Japanese government carefully screened licensing proposals, channelling technology into key industrial sectors, and using its bargaining strength in negotiating terms with the licensees.

The position had altered dramatically by the early 1960s: the Japanese economy had been expanding extremely rapidly and a large home market offered good prospects for foreign investors. Moreover, direct investment seemed to be the only way for foreign companies to break into the Japanese market given that tariff and non-tariff barriers were effective in excluding exports. Finally, Japanese firms, becoming increasingly competitive themselves in some sectors as they expanded behind this protectionist wall, were aiming to license increasingly sophisticated technologies. All of these factors made Western firms reluctant to continue with licensing agreements. There was thus some easing in government policy with respect to foreign investment, and the early years of the 1960s saw a growth in joint venture deals. Wholly owned subsidiaries were, on the other hand, still almost totally restricted, except for the so-called 'yen companies'.[58] Still each investment application had to go through individual screening and there were major complaints over administrative delays produced by the complex bureaucratic machinery.

No major moves occurred until the Japanese Capital Liberalization Program which operated from June 1967 to August 1971. Once again the introduction of this was related to pressure from the international business community, but also to pressure from Japanese industrialists who began to fear that hostility from the outside might lead to the imposition of tariff barriers against their exports. Under the terms of this programme a distinction was made between three groups of industries: (i) for category A industries such as motor cycles, watches and radios, where the Japanese were sufficiently competitive, 100 per cent foreign ownership was allowed on an automatic approval basis; (ii) category B industries were those still considered vulnerable. Here foreign ownership of up to 50 per cent was permitted, with greater foreign holdings being subject to case by case screening. (iii) Finally another seven groups of industries were designated as 'restricted', for which automatic approval was granted only if foreign ownership did not exceed 15 per cent.

Table 6.7 Foreign investment and technology imports in Japan

	No. of technology contracts approved*	Foreign investment in subsidiaries and joint ventures ($000)
1951–55	491	26,275
1956–60	832	62,494
1961–65	3,017	180,732
1966–70	4,784	323,922

* Category A (*Source:* Ozawa, 1973.)

The liberalisation programme led to an increase in foreign investment as Table 6.7 indicates, but the total was still very small because of the large number of exceptions and hidden barriers to capital inflows. Also joint ventures remained much more common than wholly owned subsidiaries. All this time the Japanese industry and economy was becoming stronger internationally, and foreign direct investment from Japan into the USA and South East Asia was rising. Increased pressure was again put on Japan to liberalise further, and in 1973 and 1975 new steps were taken to extend the industries in which 100 per cent foreign ownership was allowed. Even so, enormous difficulties still remain in the way of the foreign investor:

(i) Official regulations are purposely left vague to give greater discretionary powers to the authorities.
(ii) The Japanese anti-trust body, the Fair Trade Commission, seems to have as its prime aim the supervision of foreign companies.
(iii) Many foreign firms have experienced severe problems in joint venture agreements because of shared management, low returns, a tradition of debt-financing among Japanese companies, etc. Most of the new foreign investment is consequently taking the form of wholly owned subsidiaries, e.g. in 1976 out of a total foreign investment of $4.6 billion, only $184 million was in joint ventures.[59]

The case of Japan is thus a classic example of the way in which a host country can 'break the package apart' to obtain only those elements which are considered necessary or desirable. But this does not provide much of a general lesson for host countries, since it is doubtful if there are any states outside the developed world which are in a position to take the technology component alone. Typically, for example, the managerial expertise would not exist locally to apply the licensed technology (although a number of the South East Asian countries may soon possess the necessary skills). The Japanese example is, however, of great interest in showing the way in which a ruthlessly single-minded host government, operating a well-planned policy, can gain major benefits from foreign companies.[60]

Controls at the multinational level

In considering controls at the multinational level, only the EEC at present has the potential to develop an international solution to the problem of MNEs of the type outlined in the theoretical section. This is so because the Treaty of Rome envisages a regional grouping extending beyond the customs union and common market to economic and monetary union. The other regional groups such as the Andean Pact and the Association of South East Asian Nations (ASEAN) have lower aspirations, although the Andean group aims to become a common market by the late 1980s. Here the most that can be hoped for is greater bargaining power in dealing with multinational firms. Even so the Andean Pact provides a valuable illustration of the potential existing for regulating MNEs, and an interesting contrast to the other case to be considered in this section, namely that of the EEC.

The European Economic Community solution

In considering the EEC solution it is crucial to understand the aims of the Treaty of Rome. This seeks not only to create a customs union but also to permit free movement of factors of production and ultimately to achieve economic and monetary union. At this point the former national markets would be replaced by a unified EEC market, in which laws and taxes would be harmonised and national currencies either abolished or at least fixed in value in relation to each other; while an EEC budget would replace or supplement national budgets. As a consequence national sovereignty would be surrendered to the EEC Commission and the European Parliament. It is obvious that the EEC is nowhere near achieving this dream, but were it to be in this position, then many of the problems associated with MNEs would disappear. Within the free market (for both goods and factors) MNEs could make rational locational decisions to exploit comparative advantage and increase specialisation; common policies as regards tax rates, investment incentives, etc. would remove any policy imperfections that might distort MNE decision-making; and common policies in respect of anti-trust laws etc. would be devised. The only remaining problem would concern relationships between the Community and the rest of the world.

This is hypothetical but provides an understanding of how MNEs are viewed within the EEC. In its 1973 document *Multinational Undertakings and the Community*, the Commission states that 'measures to be undertaken should not impede the development of a phenomenon with recognised economic and social advantages but . . . merely aim at guarding the Community against its harmful effects with the help of a suitable legal framework . . .' containing '. . . no discriminatory aspect'.[61] The three principles of treatment are thus: (i) legal framework, and opposition to codes of conduct;[62] (ii) non-discriminatory treatment between indigenous and foreign firms; (iii) comprehensive framework, implying a rejection of specific isolated measures.

In outlining problem areas and measures envisaged, therefore, it is clear that many of the EEC's proposals, while attending to the control of MNEs, are also integral components of economic and monetary union. The main areas in which developments are taking place are as follows:

(i) *Harmonisation of company law,* and the creation of a company under Community law called the 'European company'. Progress is very slow and the European company has so far failed to materialise. The advantages of such a company would be very considerable, particularly because it would stimulate the creation, and help the expansion, of European-based MNEs. One important aspect of the draft statute for the European company concerns the proposal for worker participation. If adopted, representatives of labour groups would sit on the boards of many European companies and thus share in the decision-making process. The ability of MNEs to take action which adversely affected the interests of workers might be much reduced.[63]

(ii) *Harmonisation of corporate tax systems.* These proposals aim to provide neutrality between tax locations and provide an equitable basis for relieving international double taxation within the Community. Work on tax avoidance is also in progress. In association with the harmonisation of company law, tax harmonisation would reduce the financial benefits to be gained by manipulative transfer pricing between Community countries.

(iii) *Competition policy.*[64] Articles 85 and 86 of the Rome Treaty deal with competition policy, and thus in this area the Commission already has operational powers to act on a Community-wide basis. As at the beginning of 1975 the Commission had dealt with 17 cases including MNEs and the pace of activity has quickened perceptibly since then. Problems sometimes exist with MNEs over the coverage of anti-trust laws as between countries, but this does not appear to be a difficulty with EEC legislation because: (i) under the Rome Treaty jurisdiction covers the 'enterprise' which comprises both parent, even if outside the EEC, and subsidiary within it; (ii) following the precedent established in one notable case (US Alcoa), the Commission has jurisdiction in all situations where the impact of anti-competitive activity is felt within the EEC, even though the anti-competitive acts take place outside the Community. Under proposals being considered, prior notice would be required for mergers above a certain size, allowing the Commission to consider whether the merger would be liable to hinder effective competition. Joint venture proposals would also be scrutinised and a code of obligations is to be drawn up with respect to take-over bids.

(iv) *Harmonisation of national and regional aids.* Although international investment plays an important part in the implementation of regional policies in the EEC, problems exist because of outbidding by member states. Efforts are therefore being made to harmonise national and regional aids.

(v) *Protection of workers.* In addition to protection that might be afforded by worker directors, other legislation is proposed to increase security of employment, and to harmonise labour law. The Commission also take the view that the growth of European collective agreements can help to solve other problems associated with MNEs.

(vi) *Rules concerning the establishment of European MNEs in LDCs.* Under this heading, measures are proposed to provide guarantees for investment; to establish Community rules regarding transfer prices and license fees; and to institute a development cooperation policy to encourage investments best suited to host country priorities.[65]

(vii) *Increased provision of information on the activities of MNEs.*

The implementation of many of these proposals is still clearly a long way off. One major omission remains even then. There is no provision to compensate member states which may be adversely affected by the proposed legislation. This forms an important part of an international solution and the EEC budget should be seen in this role. But in the medium term between two-thirds and three-quarters of the funds will continue to be used for agricultural support, and the regional and social funds are minute. Failure to solve this issue may place the package of measures envisaged for regulating MNEs, and the whole concept of economic and monetary union, in jeopardy.

The Andean Pact solution[66]
The Andean Common Market (ANCOM) was formed in May 1969 by Colombia, Ecuador, Peru, Bolivia and Chile, with Venezuela joining the Pact in 1973. The agreement provided for the progressive reduction in tariffs and trade barriers between members and the establishment of a common external tariff. An equally important element of the Pact concerned the regulation of multinational

companies (the body of rules and regulations commonly being called Decision 24). The three key elements of control relate firstly, to the ownership of MNEs, secondly, to the transfer of technology, and thirdly, to the regulation of transfer prices.

(i) *Ownership*.   Foreign companies within the ANCOM region that wish to export to other countries in the community and thus operate community-wide must transfer between 51 per cent and 81 per cent of their equity to national investors. These are the so-called 'fade-out provisions'. Additionally, not only must the foreign investor relinquish direct ownership rights, but also a corresponding amount of effective control. Existing companies were given 15 to 20 years to bring about the necessary changes in ownership while new investors were subject to the terms immediately. All new investment projects had, in addition, to be approved by the competent national authority, thereby introducing a selective admission pattern. These are general provisions, and other regulations place restrictions on the sectors in which foreign firms may operate. As a result, foreign companies in banking, insurance and the media were required to convert to indigenous ownership, and no new foreign direct investment was permitted.

(ii) *Technology transfer*.   In contracts for the transfer of technology to local firms numerous practices were forbidden, including: (a) price fixing of the licensed product; (b) terms requiring the purchase of intermediate and capital goods from a specific source; (c) restrictions on the output of licensed products; (d) restrictions on the use of competitive technology; (e) restrictions on exports (in most cases); (f) package deals in which the recipient pays for technology which will not be used, in order to obtain certain services.

(iii) *Transfer pricing*.   The ANCOM Foreign Investment Code also provides for a control system for transfer pricing, involving screening the price of technology, product prices, credit terms, etc. Related to this the Pact limits profit remittances to 14 per cent of registered capital per year, and any reinvestment in excess of 5 per cent of registered capital has to be approved by the national agency. Royalty payments to the parent company are not permitted.

The actual operation of Decision 24 was left as the responsibility of individual countries, so that all member states had to draw up their own legislation on the subject. This was one weakness of the scheme, for although the countries produced legislation which was formally very similar, important differences seem to have existed in implementation from country to country. If such differences are very marked then naturally the objective of regional planning and coordination could be defeated.

Even so, what is certainly true is that the era when foreign companies could establish affiliates in the Andean countries relatively freely ended in 1969. In its place has emerged a fairly restrictive control system in which foreign investors are offered the bargain of a larger community market in return for reduced equity ownership and close control over behaviour. There is no doubt that a larger market makes relatively small LDC countries more attractive for investment, and coordinated action would normally enable the countries to obtain improved terms. The evidence in the case of the Andean Pact seems to be, however, that the package offered to foreign investors offers an unacceptable trade-off. The reported new investment since 1969 has been insignificant, with the exception of investments relating to natural resources. This again provides important lessons not only for other present or potential regional groups but also for individual host governments seeking to regulate multinational enterprises.

Concluding comments

The empirical evidence presented has indicated strongly that irrespective of the efficiency gains to be obtained from international regulation of the MNE, political realities mean that such a framework of control will not be acceptable in the foreseeable future. Even the very modest attempts to formulate voluntary codes of conduct have run into severe difficulties, with implementation certain to pose greater problems. Indeed the fact that a fairly cohesive unit such as the European Economic Community is moving so slowly in the direction of comprehensive controls, is hardly a good omen for prospects at a global level.

In the area of unilateral controls, on the other hand, the evidence shows that virtually all countries, formally or informally, regulate foreign direct investment and the MNE. The aim is to increase the net benefits to themselves, irrespective of the impact on other host countries or the multinational's home country. But, there is little evidence to indicate how far individual countries have succeeded in these efforts to improve their share of the benefits. A great deal must depend on individual circumstances, particularly as regards the importance of the investment to the MNE. As the experience of the Andean Pact seems to indicate, for normal discretionary investments it is possible for host governments to go too far in trying to extract concessions. A distinction must also be made between new and established investments: when an affiliate is established in a particular country, withdrawal is not an easy step to take; although, as the example of IBM indicated, some companies may be prepared to go to this length to retain proprietary know-how. In any event, even if governments manage to implement restrictive controls without effecting a mass exodus, the future flow of new investment may simply dry up. Particularly in a time of high unemployment, numerous other countries may be prepared to step in to compete for the investment by offering fewer restrictions and/or more incentives. This is a game in which the only winner is the MNE itself, and illustrates clearly the possible futility on economic grounds of trying to implement unilateral controls.

Appendix 6.1   The distinction between marginal private and social costs

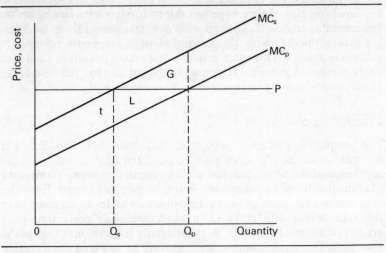

Fig. (App.) 6.1   The distinction between marginal private and social costs.

In the diagram above, MC_p represents the marginal private cost to producer A of pursuing a particular activity. This activity is assumed to impose certain external costs on another party (B), so that the marginal social cost is given by MC_s. P represents the monetary value of the activity to society. In the absence of interference, output will be Q_P, where $P = MC_p$ and profit is maximised. The socially optimal level of output is, however, Q_s. In operating at this point, producer A loses in money terms the area L; this represents profit foregone on output Q_sQ_p. On the other hand, the other party (B) gains the whole area G + L. The net money gain to society is therefore given by the area G.

A number of solutions to the problem of externalities are available to governments. The government could regulate the output level that must not be exceeded (in this case Q_s). Alternatively a unit tax on output (t in the diagram) could be imposed, e.g. the imposition of petrol tax and road tax ensure that the motoring public bear some of the cost of pollution, congestion and road maintenance for which they are responsible. Or again a solution might be sought through court action or through some kind of bargaining procedure. (The latter has particular relevance to negotiations between host country governments and MNEs over the terms of entry.)

Appendix 6.2 Principal issues in regulatory practices of selected countries concerning imports and use of technology

Principal issues	Countries
Policies on controlling costs	
1. Ceiling on remittance arising from foreign direct investments	Algeria, Argentina, Brazil, India, Paraguay, ANCOM
2. Ceiling on remittance of royalties	Argentina, Brazil, India
3. Limitations regarding payment of royalties between subsidiary and parent company	Brazil, India, ANCOM
4. Technological contributions entitled only to royalties and cannot be registered as capital contributions	ANCOM
5. Control on payment for unused patents	ANCOM
6. Control on package licensing	Japan, West Germany, Spain, USA
7. Control on the payment of royalties during the entire duration of manufacture of a product, or the application of the process involved without any specification of time, or excessively long terms of enforcement	Mexico, Spain
8. Control on price fixing practices	Japan, Spain, USA, Argentina, Mexico, ANCOM
9. Control on excessive prices of technology	Spain, Argentina, Mexico
10. Control on improper or discriminatory royalties	USA

Abusive practices either deemed to be illegal or otherwise controlled

(a) *Territorial restrictions*

11. Territorial restrictions on exports

Japan, Spain, Argentina, Brazil, Mexico, ANCOM

(b) *Restrictions on purchases, output or sales*

12. On sources of supply of raw materials, spare parts, intermediate products, capital goods and/or competing technologies

Australia, Ireland, Japan, New Zealand, Spain, UK, USA, EEC, Argentina, Brazil, Mexico, India, Malawi, Zambia, ANCOM

13. On pattern of production

Japan, Spain, Mexico, ANCOM

14. On sales and/or distribution

Japan, Spain, USA, Brazil, Mexico, ANCOM

(c) *Post-expiration effects*

15. Limitations on or payment for the use of a patented invention even after the patent has expired

New Zealand, Spain, UK, USA, India, Malawi, Zambia

16. Limitations on or payment for the use of related know-how even after the agreement has expired.

Spain

(d) *Limitations affecting the dynamic effects of the transfer*

17. Control on the purchase of technology already available in the country

Spain, Argentina, India, Mexico

18. Limitations on field of use

USA

19. To use staff designated by the supplier

Mexico, ANCOM

20. Grant-back provisions

Japan, Spain, USA, Argentina, Brazil, Mexico, ANCOM

21. Limitations imposed on the management of the recipient enterprise

Spain, Mexico

22. Limitations on the research or technological development of the recipient enterprise — Spain, Mexico

(e) *Other practices*

23. Not to contest validity of patents — USA

24. Authentic text of contract in foreign language — Spain, Argentina

Patent policies

25. Patents protected provided they are in the social interest — Peru

26. Patents granted, as a general policy, to ensure that new inventions are worked in the country — Canada, India

27. Compulsory licenses, revocation or expropriation of patents are recognised for reasons other than non-working — Austria, Canada, Denmark, France, Finland, West Germany, Ireland, Norway, Sweden, USA, Czechoslovakia, Hungary, Poland, Romania, USSR, Algeria, Brazil, Colombia, India, Iraq, Israel, Nigeria, Peru

28. Regulations on employees' inventions — Denmark, Finland, West Germany, Norway, Sweden

29. Recognition of inventors' certificates notwithstanding the grant of patents — Bulgaria, Czechoslovakia, GDR, Poland, Romania, USSR, Algeria

Promotion of national technological capabilities

30. Incentives to export-oriented activities — Algeria, Argentina, Brazil, India, Mexico, Philippines, Republic of Vietnam, Sri Lanka, Yugoslavia, Romania

31. Provision regarding training of national personnel in foreign collaboration agreements — Algeria, Argentina, Central African Republic, Egypt, Gabon, Ghana, India, Indonesia, Kenya, Liberia, Libyan Arab Republic, Malagasy, Nigeria, Philippines, Somalia, Uganda

32. Preferential schemes for national supply of goods and/or services from national sources — Argentina, Gabon, India, ANCOM

33. Measures to facilitate absorption and diffusion of foreign technology and development of indigenous technology — Brazil, India, Peru, Republic of Korea

(*Source:* UNCTAD, 1974.)

Further reading

1. For a good statement and critique of welfare economics see **C. K. Rowley** and **A. T. Peacock**, *Welfare Economics: A Liberal Restatement*, London: Martin Robertson, 1975. On the specifically international aspects refer to **B. Sodersten,** *International Economics,* London: Macmillan, 1971, Chs. 19–21.

2. On the control of MNEs, Dunning and Gilman have provided a clear summary of the alternatives: **J. H. Dunning** and **M. Gilman,** 'Alternative policy prescriptions and the multinational enterprise', in G. Curzon and V. Curzon (eds), *The Multinational Enterprise in a Hostile World,* London: Macmillan, 1977, Ch. 1, pp. 31–55.

3. A book which considers international control of the MNE is **D. Wallace, Jr,** *International Regulation of Multinational Corporations,* New York: Praeger, 1976. Proposals for international agreements are contained in: **P. M. Goldberg** and **C. P. Kindleberger,** 'Toward a GATT for investment: a proposal for supervision of the international corporation', *Law and Policy in International Business,* **2,** No. 2, 1970, pp. 295–323; and **G. Ball,** 'Cosmocorp: the importance of being stateless', *Columbia Journal of World Business,* **25,** Nov./Dec. 1967.

4. On policies pursued by different countries see:
   Canada: **A. M. Rugman,** 'The regulation of foreign investment in Canada', *Journal of World Trade Law,* **11,** No. 4, July/Aug. 1977, pp. 322–33.

Japan: **T. Ozawa**, 'Technology imports and direct foreign investment in Japan', *Journal of World Trade Law,* **7**, No. 6, Nov./Dec. 1973.
5. The most comprehensive review of unilateral and multilateral controls being implemented is contained in: **K. P. Sauvant,** 'Controlling transnational enterprises: a review and some further thoughts', in K. P. Sauvant and H. Hasenpflug (eds), *The New International Economic Order,* London: Wilton House, 1977, Ch. 22, pp. 356–433.

Questions for discussion

1. What guidance does welfare economics provide on the issue of control of the multinational enterprise?
2. Under what circumstances would free international production produce both an efficiency optimum and a maximisation of world welfare?
3. Why might host countries choose to implement unilateral controls over the MNE in spite of the predictions of economic theory?
4. Referring to the evidence presented in Chapter 5 on the impact of the MNE, which types of unilateral controls would seem likely to maximise the net benefits from foreign direct investment?
5. Discuss some of the ways in which the international trade union movement might assist in the regulation of the MNE.
6. Review the various counter-strategies which the MNE may employ to protect its interests in the face of an increasingly restrictive operating environment.

Chapter 7

Multinational enterprises and home country interests

Summary

1. Neo-classical theory points to the possibility of over-investment abroad taking place from the standpoint of the home country interest. This possibility arises because of a divergence between private and social rates of return. In making foreign investment decisions, private firms will not take account of the fact that new investment abroad will have the effect of lowering the return on all existing investments in the country concerned. Also to the home country, taxes paid abroad represent foreign income lost. A further important conclusion of the theory is that foreign investment will lead to a redistribution of domestic income towards capital and away from labour. Once some of the assumptions of this model are relaxed, however, particularly that of invariant terms of trade, the theoretical case becomes less obvious.

2. If over-investment does take place, the optimum tax represents a first best policy measure for reallocating investment and raising domestic income and welfare, assuming no retaliation.

3. From a short-run perspective, concern over foreign investment has been chiefly related to the possibility of adverse effects on the balance of payments and on the level and skill mix of employment. But whether or not there are significant adjustment costs to the community in these areas depends crucially on what MNEs would or could have done if they had not established overseas affiliates. More recently, disquiet over the transfer of technology, tax avoidance and the anti-competitive effects of MNEs has been increasing in home countries, as has concern over the economic and non-economic power controlled by MNEs.

4. A variety of macro-economic policy tools may be used to remedy any short-term balance of payments and employment problems caused by foreign investment. Capital controls are, on balance, not desirable because of their negative effects on resource allocation and on the level of world output and national income. Strengthened anti-trust policies and so forth may also be needed; and overall, the effective monitoring and control of both the short- and long-run impact of MNEs requires the formulation by home countries of comprehensive policies towards direct foreign investment.

5. During the 1960s, the United States introduced a number of legislative measures to restrict the outflow of capital. The Burke-Hartke proposals of 1972 would have produced, amongst other things, major changes in the taxation of American multinationals, but the proposals were rejected. The possibility of abolishing the deferral provisions of US tax law is still under discussion and research has shown that this would lead to a substantial increase in tax receipts in the US.
6. The United Kingdom has stringent exchange control provisions to limit outward capital flows, with companies being forced to pay a significant 'dollar premium' when acquiring foreign currency (except under special circumstances). Neither the UK nor the US restrictions on capital movements have had much effect on the level of foreign direct investment, because of the possibility of reinvesting foreign profits and borrowing abroad.
7. Empirical studies of the impact of foreign investment have shown that positive balance of payments effects are associated with the 'reverse classical hypothesis'. The hypothesis states that direct investment abroad substitutes for investment in the host country, but does not reduce capital formation in the investing country. That is, foreign investment was 'defensive' and required to maintain markets. On a similar assumption the net employment effects are also likely to be positive. But this does not exclude the fact that there will be major job losses and gains associated with foreign investment, which is important when considering the adjustment costs to be borne by the community. Furthermore, jobs lost are likely to be of a lower skill mix than jobs gained. A study by Musgrave indicated that, overall, foreign investment has led to a small loss of output in the US; the research also confirmed the theoretical prediction of a significant redistribution of domestic income in favour of capital.

There are still wide areas of ignorance regarding the impact of the overseas operations of MNEs on the structure of domestic industry and the concentration of market power; on trade policy; on technological capacity; and on the supply and allocation of skilled manpower in the home country.

Chapter 5 assessed the impact of multinational firms on host countries, particularly less developed host countries. In Chapter 6 the focus was on control of the MNE, and while international or multi-country solutions to the regulation issue could involve both home and host nations, the national control measures discussed only took the viewpoint of the host country. In the present chapter, therefore, the impact and control of the MNE is considered from the home country standpoint, bearing in mind that the countries which are important capital exporters are also major recipients of inward direct investment.

The topic is an extremely important one, particularly in the United States, but increasingly also in Britain and elsewhere. During the 1960s in the United States, for example, the level of capital outflows was seen as a major contributor to the persistent balance of payments deficit; while in the recession-hit 1970s outward direct investment was viewed as exporting production and jobs and thus exacerbating unemployment problems. Other concerns relate to the impact of MNEs on concentration levels and on stabilisation policy through tax fiddling and the like. It is clear from this that the perspective of discussion is different in capital-exporting as opposed to capital-receiving countries. The emphasis in host countries is on issues such as economic growth, productivity and national sovereignty. In home nations, by contrast, the transitional problems of the balance of payments and employment are of prime concern, with relatively little thought being given until recently to the effect of capital outflows on the level and distribution of the national income and on the structure of the economy.

Economic theory and home country interests

Neo-classical theory and outward direct investment[1]

From the theoretical work of MacDougall and others discussed in Chapter 5, it was suggested that there were significant potential gains for the host country from foreign direct investment. Although with the relaxation of certain assumptions adverse outcomes were also shown to be possible, the general presumption was still that direct investment from abroad provided net benefits for the receiving country.

The main theoretical studies on the effects of outward direct investment on the home nation are in the same neo-classical tradition, although the body of literature goes back at least as far as J. M. Keynes. Keynes's attack on British overseas investment mainly referred to the then more prevalent portfolio form of investment, but his remarks on the distinction between the social and private risks of home and foreign investment are worth repeating: 'Consider two investments, the one at home and the other abroad, with equal risks of repudiation or confiscation or legislation restricting profit. It is a matter of indifference to the individual investor which he selects. But the nation as a whole retains in the one case the object of the investment and the fruits of it; whilst in the other case, both are lost . . . . If the Grand Trunk Railway of Canada fails its shareholders by reason of legal restriction of the rates chargeable or for any other cause, we have nothing. If the Underground System of London fails its shareholders, Londoners still have their Underground system.'[2]

Theoretical work on the problem of the allocation of direct investment between home and overseas is, nevertheless, chiefly a product of the post-Second World War period. MacDougall confined his remarks mainly to the impact of foreign direct investment on the host country, but other authors such as Jasay analysed the investment impact from the viewpoint of the investing country.[3] The starting-point is similar, with foreign investment being considered as a replacement for domestic investment. The problem is then viewed as being one of resource allocation in a perfectly competitive world which is in long-run full employment equilibrium. Under these circumstances it can be shown that, from the standpoint of the home country interest, overinvestment abroad may take place.

The essence of the argument stems from two propositions. The first is that the marginal productivity of capital declines as the capital stock increases with a given labour supply and state of technology. The second is that with perfectly competitive markets the rate of return paid to capital and the wage rate paid to labour are equal to the value of their respective marginal products. As a consequence, as capital is transferred from country X to country Y, the rate of return to capital in Y is reduced while the return to the remaining capital in X increases; opposite changes take place with respect of wage rates in each country. A corporation will invest abroad to gain a higher return than at home, but this additional investment overseas will have the effect of lowering the return to all units of country X's investment already in country Y. This means that the social rate of return on overseas investment will be less than the private rate; whereas with domestic investment, social and private rates of return will be equal. Assuming no risk differential, companies in country X will continue investing in Y until their private returns on both home and foreign investments are equal. With the social rate of return abroad being lower than the private rate, the social return on foreign investment at this point will also be lower than the domestic return; and therefore the level of investment abroad will be excessive from the national viewpoint. There may thus be a conflict between the private and social optimum level of investment; and as Jasay has pointed out, even if the foreign investment was undertaken by a monopolist, there would still remain a tendency to overinvestment on the part of the capital-exporting country.

The essential point can be seen by referring again to the diagram in Chapter 5, which is reproduced as Fig. 7.1. Foreign investment in the host country (all of which is taken to be from one source) is assumed to increase from BC to BM. This additional investment produces an income of CMLK for the investors concerned, a return which is greater than that obtainable at home (thereby providing the motivation for the investment). On the other hand, because the marginal product of capital declines from CD to ML in response to this increase in investment, profits on existing foreign investments decline from BCDE to BCKJ. This loss may not be perceived by the foreign investors making the marginal investments abroad, and therefore the social return to the home country from the new foreign investment is lower than the private return by the amount of the loss (JKDE). This loss of profits JKDE accrues to the host country in terms of wages. In the case of domestic investment, conversely, only a distributional issue is concerned: the loss of profits would accrue to domestic labour in the first instance, but government has the power to alter this income distribution created, if it so wishes.

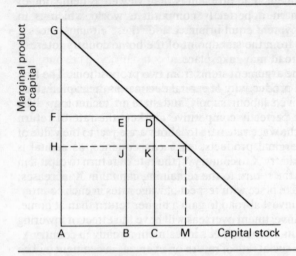

Fig. 7.1 The benefits and costs of foreign direct investment (*Source*: MacDougall, 1960).

The basic weakness of this model is that it assumes invariant terms of trade. And yet in the perfectly competitive world of the type hypothesised, foreign investment is likely to alter the terms of trade. In turn any change in the terms of trade will have a significant impact on the marginal social return from foreign investment and thus on the relationship between social rates of return at home and abroad. For a simple two-country, three-goods (exportable, importable and non-traded) general equilibrium model, it has been shown, however, that it is not possible to predict the direction of any change in the terms of trade without making further assumptions about the price elasticities of demand and supply involved.[4] Therefore it has been argued that the presumption that 'under competitive conditions capital-rich countries tie up too great a proportion of their resources in foreign ventures' must be dismissed.[5] Foreign investment may either be too much or too little, but because the terms of trade effects are indeterminate, it is not possible to know whether one situation or the other applies.

It has been argued by Frankel, additionally, that the effect of new foreign investment on the return to units of capital previously in existence – the intra-marginal effect – would usually be small or negligible for the domestic economy, since the home country would normally own only a small fraction of the foreign country's total assets. As a consequence, the difference between social and private rates of return would also be negligible. The conclusion reached, therefore, was that: 'Except where the intra-marginal effect may be significant, the domestic economy . . . should favour foreign over domestic investment as long as the marginal product of the former exceeds the latter's. Enterprise investment decisions will tend automatically to be consistent with this criterion, since enterprises tend to place capital where the return expected from it is greatest.'[6]

In spite of this, other arguments may be put forward to support the thesis that the volume of foreign investment could proceed beyond the point warranted by the national interest. The first point relates to the question of risk and derives from the argument postulated by Keynes. The risk involved in investment abroad is likely to be greater than that of a similar type of domestic investment. This should be taken into account in the expected returns. But there are various types of risk that the firm may not consider, such as expropriation and the emergence of unfavourable regulations. Although the individual firm would be affected by such factors, whether its investments were at home or abroad, the national economy suffers only if the investment has been made abroad.

Of even greater importance than this is the fact that taxes on profits arising out of domestic investment accrue to the home government, whereas taxes on the profits of foreign investment accrue to the foreign government. Again there is a divergence between private and social interests. To the foreign investor whether the tax authority is in the home or in a foreign country matters little. To the home country, on the other hand, taxes paid abroad represent foreign income lost. Thus, whereas the private investor may compare net of tax returns at home and net of tax returns abroad, the relevant comparison for the national interest is between pre-tax returns on domestic investment and returns on foreign investment after paying foreign taxes.[7] The national interest requires that the latter must at least equal the former. If foreign investment is pushed by private firms to the point where after-tax returns are the same both at home and abroad, the home country is earning a lower social return on capital employed abroad than on capital invested at home. Referring to Fig. 7.1, if the host country captures part of the rectangle CMLK, that amount is lost to the home country. As will be shown, Grubel applied these theoretical considerations to an analysis of private and social rates of return on US manufacturing investment in Canada, Australia, South Africa and Western Europe; the conclusion reached was that private rates of return were generally positive, but that social rates of return from investing abroad rather than in the US were strongly negative.[8]

A third factor which is relevant to the debate concerns external economies. Balogh and Streeten consider that this provides 'the essence of the case for curbing foreign and encouraging domestic investment'.[9] Considering an investment which raises world product, if the entire increase resulting from this investment can be appropriated by the investor, then social and private returns are equal. Normally speaking, however, some part of the increase in output would not accrue to the foreign investor: a new cost-reducing investment would raise wages or lower prices, so that in the host country, workers, other entrepreneurs and other consumers might benefit. Suppliers of competitive products and some other income groups would suffer losses, but overall there would be likely to be a net addition to host country incomes. The argument has been expressed slightly differently by Frankel, who stressed the 'development benefit' of foreign investment, and the productivity gains resulting from technology transferred from the home country.[10] These are lost to the home country, it is argued, except for any increase in the after-tax profits of investing firms or any reduction in import prices. Therefore, to be of benefit to the national interest, it has been concluded that the foreign investment return (after tax) should be sufficiently in excess of the pre-tax return on domestic investment to compensate for the development gains foregone.

When all points are taken into consideration, the theoretical case for restricting outward direct investment is by no means strong, particularly once some of the other restrictive assumptions of the models, e.g. perfect competition, diminishing marginal productivity of capital, etc., are abandoned. Moreover, while stress has been laid on the divergence between private and social interests, not all such divergences provide arguments for limiting outward direct investment. For example, the operation of a firm abroad in the extractive industry may provide not only the company itself but all domestic industry in the home country with a secure supply of primary materials at stable prices. Additionally, the productivity gains from foreign investment may not only benefit the host country. Productivity in the home country may also benefit where direct investment overseas results in economies of scale for the investing firm.

Before leaving this issue, it is worth re-emphasising the theoretical conclusion concerning, not the level of domestic income, but rather the distribution of that income. Given the assumptions made, the export of capital will improve the return to the remaining capital in the home country, but lead to a decline in the domestic wage rate. There is thus a redistribution of domestic income towards capital and away from labour, although the gains to the former fall short of the losses to labour.[11] This conclusion may be relevant in determining the negative attitude adopted by trade unions towards outward direct investment.

Home country policies towards international direct investment – long run

The previous chapter indicated that efficiency criteria would point to a comprehensive international solution to the control of the MNE. For the present and for the forseeable future such a solution will not be forthcoming. Certain international policies are being devised through codes of conduct, etc., but the main controls over MNE activity are those operated by host governments. These may be designed to increase the net benefits from foreign investment, but many such controls also relate to the sovereignty goals of host nations rather than to any efficiency or equity criteria. Although sovereignty issues may not be seen as important to *home* countries, there is still no necessary symmetry between the goals of the MNE and the goals of its home nation (i.e. what is good for General Motors is not necessarily good for America). It is important to emphasise, even so, that home country policies emanating from the asymmetry of goals will normally reduce world-wide economic efficiency and will inevitably have adverse repercussions on host countries.

As indicated in the discussion on host country regulations, the range of possible controls on foreign investment and the MNE is restricted only by the ingenuity of the legislators, and this also applies to home country controls. Nevertheless, theoretical discussion has concentrated on the operation of an optimum tax on overseas investment earnings. As noted earlier, the concept is analogous to that of the optimum tariff, whereby a country can turn the terms of trade in its favour by the imposition of an import tariff, if it possesses monopolistic power in international trade.

The purpose of the optimum tax on foreign investment earnings is to maximise national income in the capital exporting country. Any such tax will have a number of effects on the domestic economy. In the first place, it will affect the allocation of investment between home and overseas, with increases in taxation tending to discourage capital outflows and stimulate domestic investment. Furthermore, if the movement of capital abroad depresses the foreign rate of return, the home country possesses an implicit monopoly power, which perfectly competitive investors may not fully exploit. In these circumstances, the imposition of a tax by the home country, which reduces the outflow and supports the foreign rate of return above its competitive level, may increase the net revenues accruing to the home government. Secondly, changes in tax rates will influence not only the allocation of investment between home and overseas but also the actual level of capital formation. This in turn will have implications for current incomes and savings and for the growth rate of national income. Policies which therefore maximise current income and consumption may not be optimal in the longer run if capital formation is greatly reduced. Such dynamic considerations need to be taken into account when changes in tax rates are being contemplated. Third, as noted previously, foreign taxes paid on overseas earnings represent a loss to the domestic economy; and although the firm itself may be indifferent as to which country receives its tax payments, the home government will not be. A high domestic tax may recoup some of those lost revenues. Policy regarding the taxation of overseas investment earnings may in these ways have a significant impact on aggregate income and consumption. If the theoretical possibility of over-investment abroad by the lending country is correct, then the optimum tax represents a first best policy measure for reallocating investment and raising domestic income and welfare.

A note of caution is necessary. The literature concerning the home country impact of foreign direct investment has generally looked at investment as a one-way process only. But the USA and the major European countries are not only important sources of foreign investment but are also the major recipients of such investment. Thus the potential for retaliation needs to be taken into account when contemplating policies (such as the optimum tax) against foreign direct investment.[12] If, for instance, outward investment is restricted by country X, foreign firms located in country X might be tempted or persuaded to return to their home country Y, thus offsetting the initial welfare gains made by country X. Even without two-way investment flows, the threat of retaliation is present. As an example, action by one country A to raise its tax on foreign investment income earned in country B, could lead to action by the host country B to change its tax rates to offset the impact. The overall effect would be to restrict capital flows below the world optimum and below the level which would be of mutual advantage to both countries. This situation is analogous to that resulting from the spread of protectionism in the field of international trade.

The short-run impact of outward direct investment on home countries

The discussion to this point has been concerned with the effects of foreign investment on the level and distribution of real income in the home country, and therefore has focused primarily on long-run issues. In this long-run analysis, full employment is assumed, as is balance of payments equilibrium. In the case of the balance of payments, any temporary disequilibrium is assumed to put pressure on foreign exchange markets, eventually producing adjustment through an exchange rate change; or if exchange rates were fixed, the net monetary inflow or outflow implied by the disequilibrium would cause price and income changes which would effect an adjustment indirectly. With respect to any unemployment arising from jobs displaced through foreign production, this would be assumed to be strictly temporary and full employment would be restored as real wages adjusted. The important point is that the adjustment process and the costs of adjustment are ignored.

While the theoretical focus of analysis has been on long-run issues, much more attention has been paid at the practical policy level to the possible short-run, transitional problems associated with outward direct investment. This is once again an area where private and social costs diverge: private investors acting individually are unlikely to allow for the adjustment costs to the community that may arise because of their direct investments abroad. A case in point could arise if foreign direct investment gave rise to a large volume of imports that created unemployment; in this case some transitional costs would have to be borne by the investing country.

The central problems are therefore to identify whether or not MNE operations create adjustment problems for the home country, and if difficulties do exist, how burdensome they actually are. Considering *balance of payments issues* first of all, a number of possible effects may result:

(i) The initial capital transfer may be assumed to affect the balance of payments adversely. However, this implies that the transfer takes the form of a movement of funds, whereas capital exports may be represented by capital equipment and materials for plant operations overseas. In any event, even if capital exports are not 'tied', an export demand will inevitably be generated as the affiliate begins to manufacture. And in subsequent years the export of equipment, materials and spare parts is likely to continue from the parent company to its affiliate.

(ii) Sales by affiliates abroad may displace exports from the parent company or stimulate imports into the home country, but once again the exact movements are by no means certain, as earlier chapters have indicated. For instance, the marketing and service activities of the overseas affiliate may create a demand for complementary commodities manufactured only by the parent company.

(iii) As the affiliate becomes established, the home country balance of payments will benefit from the repatriation of profits earned overseas, from royalty payments to the parent company, and so on.

(iv) While strictly a long-run issue, the home country balance of payments will also be affected to the extent that foreign direct investment raises the national income of the recipient country and hence stimulates import demand.

Turning next to the short-run *employment effects,* again various possibilities exist:[13]

(i) Production displacement effect: employment losses will occur to the extent that MNEs service foreign markets by production from overseas affiliates rather than by exports from the parent company.

(ii) Export stimulus effect: this represents the positive effects on domestic employment arising from foreign affiliates' demands for home country exports of capital equipment, intermediate goods, complementary products, etc.

(iii) Home office and supporting firm effects: further stimuli may be given to non-production employment in the home country by the centralisation of management functions at the parent company. Moreover, the operation of foreign affiliates may lead to increased demands in the home country for legal and public relations services, management and engineering consultants, etc. The number of jobs affected would be small in both of these categories, but highly skilled personnel would be involved. The employment effects on home countries must consequently be viewed not only in terms of the impact on the level of employment but also on the mix in employment.

From the points noted, it is clear that even at the theoretical level there is no obvious presumption that foreign direct investment *per se* creates significant adjustment problems for a home economy. Countries face transitional problems for a wide variety of reasons, some of which may be much more important than those created by overseas direct investment. For example, a certain degree of job turnover is inherent in the normal operation of any labour market. Even under equilibrium conditions there would exist simultaneously a certain number of unfilled vacancies and a group of unemployed job seekers. The process of economic growth particularly produces major dislocations in labour markets, as there is a constant shift of workers from marginally productive jobs to higher technology activities where productivity is higher.

The short-run impact of foreign direct investment depends crucially on a number of issues.[14] The first relates to what MNEs would or could have done if they had not established affiliates overseas. In other words, does the direct investment abroad substitute for domestic investment, does it substitute for domestic consumption, or does it supplement both? Secondly, the overseas direct investment impact depends upon whether or not full employment or under-full employment exists in the home country. And thirdly, the impact is dependent upon whether or not the outward financial flow associated with the foreign investment is offset by a transfer of real resources through higher exports and/or lower imports.

The various possible effects on investment, consumption, employment and prices are given in Table 7.1. Only extreme cases are shown, *viz.* zero or total resource transfer, *or* zero or total domestic displacement. In the former instance, it is therefore assumed that the foreign investment is either completely offset by increased exports and/or lower imports (full transfer), or the outward financial flow does not affect levels of exports and imports at all (zero transfer). In practice, the situation would fall somewhere between these extremes. Similarly, it is unlikely that foreign investment will either completely displace domestic investment (I_f substitutes for I_d) or fully supplement it (I_f is supplementary).

As indicated, adverse employment effects occur if foreign investment substitutes for domestic investment or domestic consumption *and* the financial outflow is not matched by higher exports and/or lower imports. Even if adverse employment effects do

Table 7.1 Effects of outward direct investment on the home country

	If substitutes for I_d*		If substitutes for C_d*		It is supplementary	
Initial full employment†	1. Full transfer	2. Zero transfer	3. Full transfer	4. Zero transfer	5. Full transfer	6. Zero transfer
Employment	No change	Decrease§	No change	Decrease§	No change	No change
Prices	No change	No change§	No change	No change§	Increase	No change
Investment‡	Decrease	Decrease	No change	No change	No change	No change
Consumption	No change	Decrease	Decrease	Decrease	No change	No change

* I_f = foreign investment, I_d = domestic investment, and C_d = domestic consumption
† With under-full employment initially the effects would be similar, except as regards column 5 where the results would be:
    Employment: increase
    Prices and investment: no change
    Consumption: increase
‡ Accelerator effects of investment are ignored
§ Assuming inflationary conditions exist, the effect might be to check inflation without reducing employment.

(*Source:* Musgrave, 1975.)

not occur immediately when foreign investment substitutes for investment or consumption at home, through multiplier/accelerator effects, the number of jobs would eventually be reduced. Adverse balance of payments effects occur whenever there is 'zero transfer' (or less than 'full transfer'). Since at this stage no policy measures are being considered to deal with the adverse impacts, the balance of payments is simply taken as being in short-run disequilibrium. The price effects are more difficult to predict. It might be, for example, that where I_f substitutes for I_d or C_d and there is zero transfer, some dampening of the rate of inflation may occur. On the other hand, with full employment, full transfer and I_f supplementing I_d or C_d, inflationary pressures would be exacerbated.

On the basis of reasonable assumptions about the degree of substitutability of investment and degree of transfer, it is probably fair to conclude that some adjustment costs to the community can be expected from outward direct investment; but the importance of these is essentially an empirical question, which is discussed later in the chapter.

Before leaving this assessment of the short-run, partial equilibrium problems which may face the home country as a consequence of outward direct investment, there are a number of other, related issues upon which attention has begun to be focused in the United States and elsewhere. These are now considered.[15]

(a) Export of technological advantage
One issue which has given rise to considerable disquiet, particularly in the United States, concerns the transfer abroad of technology. Chapter 5 indicated that host country fears over the transfer of

information related to the appropriateness and the price of the technology. In the USA, concern has arisen over the fact that most of the flow of new technology in the post-war years has been from America to the rest of the world; and from the fact that despite cutbacks in government support, R & D expenditures in the US are still greater than those in all other OECD countries combined. It is argued that multinational firms, as the main vehicle for transferring information, combine US capital and technology with cheap labour abroad and in the process erode US comparative advantage and damage the interests of US labour. More specifically, there seem to be a number of strands to the argument: firstly, the capital and technological advantage of the USA is eroded (it will be recalled that a similar view to this was presented when comparisons were being made between Japanese and US direct investment abroad in Chapter 4 pp. 150–1); and the international competitiveness of its manufacturing industry is impaired. Secondly, the manufacturing sector shrinks, with adverse effects on jobs and wages in the industries affected. Thirdly, the share of national income derived from the repatriated earnings of US affiliates abroad increases. This has an adverse effect on income distribution in the United States, but additionally increases the dependence of the country on the economic performance of foreign nations.[16]

It is clear that these issues are closely related to the potential balance of payments and employment problems discussed previously. The weakness of the case is that it is considered only within a partial equilibrium framework. It is probably true that the export abroad of a particular industry's technology will reduce the returns to the immobile factor, labour, in the short run. These short-run losses produce adjustment problems for the economy, and are a legitimate cause for concern. But it may be more important to consider the longer run impact of technology transfer: although output in the affected industries may decline, production in other sectors of the economy will be stimulated as a result of changed production patterns and higher incomes overseas. It has been shown, within a general equilibrium framework, that labour will derive long-run benefits from technology transfer, if the new product is relatively capital-intensive and factors are immobile internationally.[17] These gains take the form of increased real wages for a fully employed economy and additional jobs in an under-full employment situation. On the other hand, where capital is mobile internationally, the conclusion is that there will be no long-run gains or losses as a result of the transfer of technology.

There is a further aspect to this, which relates to technology transfer within a dynamic product cycle framework. In the early stages of the cycle, an increase in domestic employment will be experienced, as the new product is accepted in home and foreign markets. Later, job displacement could be presumed to arise in the innovating industry at home as the MNE transfers technology and production facilities abroad to exploit lower labour costs. However, by this time the domestic industry concerned may be entering into a new cycle with higher technology products (see the examples in Chapter 2, pp. 82–4, including that of radios, transistors and printed circuits); this may have the effect of retaining domestic employment. Foreign production utilising the original technology provides the profits to finance R & D and thereby enable the source country to continually up-grade its technology.

(b) Tax avoidance and inequitable taxation

The possibility of establishing an optimum tax on foreign investment earnings, as a means of raising domestic income and welfare, has already been discussed in the context of long-run policies towards overseas investment. This question has short-run dimensions also. Suppose the level of taxes on MNEs' overseas earnings are lower than those applied to their domestic earnings; this will provide an incentive for multinational firms to invest abroad. Since this will stimulate the growth of MNEs' foreign operations, it will also exacerbate the problem of domestic job displacement. As will be indicated, much of the debate in the United States over the tax treatment of multinationals is related to this short-run jobs question.

Aside from this, there is another dimension to the tax treatment of MNEs, which concerns the possibilities of tax fiddling. Through manipulative transfer pricing, the operation of 'paper companies', and the sophisticated use of tax havens, it is argued that MNEs may be able to avoid home country taxation. The fact that host countries frequently offer tax holidays and other fiscal incentives is seen as a further means of escaping domestic taxes.

(c) The power of multinational firms

One of the criticisms applied to MNEs in recipient nations is that their multinationality enables them to circumvent and frustrate economic policies pursued by host governements. And a similar criticism has been applied in home countries, once again particularly in the United States. The same points regarding the ability of MNEs to escape the impact of government macro-economic policy measures apply; while at the micro-level also, home governments may find it more difficult to implement their policy objectives.

But this is really part of a much wider issue which relates to the power of MNEs and the sovereignty of their home governments. The country-ownership concentration of MNEs; their concentration in particular industries in certain countries; and the concentration of foreign holdings within a small number of firms, are all potential sources of political and economic power. These structural features of MNEs may facilitate conduct, either by individual firms or by groups of firms, which adversely affects the economic performance of the home country, as well as that of host nations. Thus aspects of business conduct such as monopolistic pricing, predatory and restrictive practices, manipulative transfer-pricing and so on may have harmful effects upon long-run structure and performance.

Home country policies towards international direct investment – short run

In the previous chapter, among a number of justifications for government involvement in the workings of the economy, the possibility of intervention to remedy general equilibrium problems was noted. Within this general area of stabilisation policy, governments possess a wide range of fiscal and monetary tools to deal with short-run problems in the economy. The possibilities of altering the rate of exchange or adopting other measures to influence international goods and factor flows are also present. These alternative courses of action have been grouped into two broad sets of policies, *viz. expenditure changing* and *expenditure switching* policies.[18]

The effects of expenditure switching and expenditure changing policies on the level of employment and the balance of payments can be represented diagrammatically as in Fig. 7.2.[19] The horizontal axis shows the level of real expenditure, and the vertical axis measures the competitiveness of the home economy *vis-à-vis* foreign countries, which can be represented by the exchange rate. A movement to the right along the horizontal axis means that an expenditure increasing policy has been instituted through tax cuts, higher government expenditure, interest rate changes, etc. A movement up the vertical axis implies that an expenditure switching policy aimed at increasing exports and reducing imports has been introduced. This could result from devaluation or a downward float in the exchange rate. The two curves in the diagram show all combinations of expenditures and exchange rates producing internal balance (full employment and stable prices) and external balance (where exports = imports, at a given level of capital movements). X is the equilibrium position for the economy where both internal and external balance exist.

Suppose that the effects of outward direct investment are such as to cause the home economy to depart from both internal and external balance to a point such as Y. With floating exchange rates being operated by most countries over the last few years, any short-run departure from internal and external balance occasioned by outward direct investment would not seem to be too much of a problem. A downward movement in the exchange rate should stimulate exports and reduce imports, while also producing a favourable effect on the level of employment. The only adverse impact is on the terms of trade and the rate of domestic inflation. Short-run difficulties might still exist, of course, as the adjustment process worked itself through. With a fixed exchange rate system on the other hand, as operated in the international economy between 1945 and the early 1970s, specific

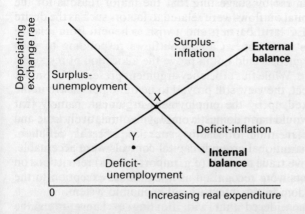

Fig. 7.2 Policies to achieve internal and external balance in the economy (*Source*: Swan, 1963).

government policies would be required to affect both the level of employment and the balance of payments. However, policies to raise internal demand and increase domestic employment would cause the balance of payments deficit to widen, and some countries might be either unable or unprepared to devalue.

This was the kind of situation in which the United States found itself during the 1960s. The abandonment of fixed exchange rates or a once-for-all devaluation were rejected because of the effects this would have on the international monetary system and the gold- and dollar-exchange standard. Thus other short-run solutions had to be sought. The causes of the US deficit were numerous, including overvaluation of the dollar, the level of foreign aid and the high level of foreign military expenditures, but most discussion focused on the level of private capital outflows. There was a considerable measure of agreement that capital controls should not be imposed, even as a short-run solution to the US balance of payments deficit, for several reasons: (a) controls would interfere with the optimum allocation of resources and lower world output and national income; (b) controls could decrease the exports from the US that were fostered by capital outflows; (c) the effectiveness of controls would decrease over time because of the long-term diminution of earnings from foreign investments; and (d) even in the short run, controls might encourage firms to decrease the repatriation of earnings so as to build up precautionary balances at subsidiary level. Nevertheless, a strong case for the imposition of capital controls to relieve the US balance of payments was made by D. A. Snider.[20] It was argued that capital controls met the four criteria of acceptability – effectiveness, employment, institutional and efficiency – better than any other measured proposed. Snider rejected the misallocation of resources (efficiency) argument by suggesting that the major reasons for the growth of US capital outflows were related to factors such as the desire to circumvent EEC tariff barriers and a wish to benefit from relative boom conditions in Europe. Capital outflows responding to such criteria, it was argued, would not improve the allocation of resources and world welfare. While this efficiency argument presented by Snider may not be correct, the view still proved to be quite persuasive in the US. It was backed up by the employment argument, namely that capital controls would harm domestic employment relatively little and certainly less than other measures such as internal deflation. Moreover, on institutional grounds capital controls were acceptable. Unlike quantitative trade controls (e.g. import quotas) restrictions on capital movements were recognised as a legitimate exception to the principle of freedom in the international economic system.

It might be considered that with floating exchange rates the arguments in favour of capital controls would be considerably weakened. That this has not proved to be the case is a reflection of the changed economic conditions of the 1970s. The various combinations of economic circumstances illustrated in Fig. 7.2 do not include unemployment, inflation *and* balance of payments deficits, but this is the situation in which many countries find themselves. Calls for capital controls may thus re-emerge, since a depreciating exchange rate will be less effective in a situation of world recession, and the stimulation of internal demand is being considered only cautiously for fears of renewing price inflation.

Irrespective of the effectiveness of the macro-economic policy tools available to home governments, there may be other short-run adjustment problems of foreign investment which require further measures. These derive from the fact that the possible employment effects of foreign investment relate both to the level and the skill mix of employment. With perhaps a tendency for MNEs to increase the demand for higher skilled at the expense of lower skilled employees in the home country, a number of measures would seem to be necessary. These might include, for example, policies to increase retraining programmes, policies to minimise the upheaval costs for displaced workers, and earlier notification by firms of impending closures. The aim of such measures would be to assist advance planning and to reduce the dislocations involved as workers find new employment. Such redundancies might result, say, from an MNE decision to shift labour-intensive operations to the Far East.[21]

It should be pointed out finally that the range of policy measures necessary to encompass other issues such as tax avoidance, anti-competitive effects, and the like extends much more widely than this to include anti-trust legislation, tax policies, laws controlling the transfer of technology, etc. Indeed, a large number of the policies which were reviewed in Chapter 6 in relation to host country regulation, have a counterpart at the home country level.

Emerging from this, it seems clear that what is fundamentally required is a comprehensive policy towards MNEs. The foregoing discussion has tended to consider the policy instruments available to regulate MNEs on an *ad hoc* basis. But because of the comprehensive nature of the effects of MNE operations, there is a strong likelihood that piecemeal policies may create further imperfections. For example, the use of exchange control legislation may indeed influence the balance of payments account, but in the process there may also be effects on industrial structure and competition. This arises from the fact that the firms hardest hit by such legislation are small firms, whereas large companies may find it relatively easy to borrow abroad.

Apart from the direct and indirect impact on the domestic economy, a comprehensive policy would also have to take account of the effects on host countries. The rich, industrialised countries have responsibilities to aid the socio-economic development of Third World nations and therefore cannot turn a blind eye to the foreign operations of MNEs. More than this, since multinational firms cannot operate separately from the political life of host countries, home governments may inevitably become involved. Similarly, home governments may be drawn into issues as a consequence of legislation introduced by host countries to regulate MNEs.

A policy towards outward investment will also need to take account of the interrelationships with inward direct investment. There is obviously the question of possible retaliation to consider. In addition, it is not inconceivable that foreign affiliates within a particular country may themselves become parents to overseas investments, (e.g. where US affiliates in Canada used their Canadian operations to obtain preferential access to Commonwealth countries by means of direct investment).[22] Furthermore, revenues lost by home governments from outward direct investment are partly recovered by taxes on inward direct investment. And, even if there is some loss of jobs, etc. as a result of home country firms transferring production facilities abroad, this matters little if the gap is filled by incoming foreign firms – particularly if the latter are more productive than the firms they replace.

The construction of such a comprehensive policy is inevitably difficult because of the conflict of views between industry and government. As the problem was expressed, in a UK context, the divergence of view between the two parties was seen to derive from:[23]

(i) Different perceptions of the contribution of foreign production to the home country balance of payments.

(ii) Different assessments of the competitive advantages to be gained by foreign production.

(iii) Different assessments of the relative attractiveness of the home country as a manufacturing base.

(iv) The problem of establishing any principles which would apply to the majority of firms and which could therefore provide a framework for policy.

(v) The lack of comprehensive information relating to the main issues.

In many respects these differences of perception between MNEs and home governments mirror the divergent views of MNEs and host governments and may give rise to the same conflicts. And equally the case for a considered and comprehensive policy is just as strong.

Home country legislation and foreign direct investment

US legislation and the multinational enterprise

In spite of the above comments, the United States has not developed a coherent set of policies to deal with the real or perceived problems associated with outward direct investment. And the same comment might equally be applied to inward investment. In both instances the origins of many of the policies seem rather accidental, while other legislation is related to fairly short-term economic or political considerations.

In respect of controls on direct investment abroad, these are of fairly recent origin and parallel the rapid expansion of international production by US firms during the 1960s. Until that time, there was broad agreement in the United States that a liberal trade and investment policy was in the best economic (and political) interests of the country. The involvement of the US in the establishment of the IMF, the GATT, and the ill-fated ITO are all reflections of this attitude. Concern first began to be voiced about the balance of payments deficit in the late 1950s, although at first foreign investment was not cited as the villain of the piece. The remedial measures applied included policies to tie economic aid and overseas military procurement to the purchase of US goods, to curb duty-free tourist imports, and to restrict bank lending to foreigners. In July 1963, the Interest Equalisation Tax (IET) was introduced. This related only to portfolio investment, but in essence it was the first response to the disquiet beginning to be felt about the level of capital outflows. The aim of the IET was to reduce the net outflow of capital by taxing US purchases from foreigners of foreign equities or debt obligations of three or more years maturity.[24]

The Voluntary Credit Restraint Program (1965) and the Mandatory Control Program (1968)
Controls designed to improve the US balance of payments deficit were eventually applied to direct investment abroad in 1965. As part of the

Voluntary Credit Restraint Program, US corporations were asked to cooperate in limiting the outflow of capital to their affiliates in industrial countries and to increase dividend remittances. Although the Program did lead to some reduction in private capital outflows, persistent deficits continued, and international confidence in the dollar fell following the devaluation of sterling in 1967. Thus, on 1 January 1968, the voluntary programme was replaced by a Mandatory Control Program. Individual corporation investment quotas were set for each of three geographical areas, based on the experience of the firms in the 1965–66 period. The most stringent quotas applied to Schedule C countries (continental Western Europe) and the least onerous to Schedule A countries (LDCs).[25] In the case of the voluntary programme, Canada and the LDCs were exempt, but only Canada was excluded from the 1968 measures after the assurance that funds would not be routed through Canada to affiliates elsewhere.

The controls implemented had a significant influence on capital transfers from the US in the late 1960s, as Table 7.2, showing data from the US Department of Commerce, reveals:

Table 7.2 Direct investment transactions,* excluding Canada (1965–69 in $ billion)

Selected transactions	1965	1966	1967	1968	Projected 1969
Capital transfers (excl. use of foreign borrowings)	2.99	2.79	2.79	0.25	1.12
Reinvested earnings	1.02	1.08	0.92	1.21	1.67
Use by direct investor of long-term foreign borrowings	0.11	0.65	0.56	2.22	2.30
Direct investment (inc. use of foreign borrowings)	4.12	4.52	4.27	3.68	5.09

* Data relate to 3,300 OFDI reporters (i.e. corporations reporting to the Office of Foreign Direct Investment of the Department of Commerce).

(*Source:* Willey, 1970.)

On the other hand, the impact on foreign direct investment was probably not very great because medium and large corporations, at least, were able to raise money abroad. The sharp rise indicated in the table in the use by direct investors of foreign borrowings is indicative of this. Some investment projects may have been delayed, of course. Additionally, the investment plans of smaller firms may have been adversely affected; and at least there were extra costs associated with overseas borrowing in terms of higher interest rates to be paid and the managerial time spent in fund raising.

As a means of restricting capital outflows the mandatory controls may have been successful, but this is not a measure of their effect on the US balance of payments. As was discussed in the previous section, the linkages between trade flows, remitted income and direct investment are all important. This point was emphasised by the appearance, soon after controls were introduced, of the influential Hufbauer and Adler study. The report did not give unequivocal support to the notion that foreign direct investment was advantageous to the balance of payments but, on reasonable assumptions, such an outcome seemed possible. As a consequence of this and the fact that most authoritative opinion was opposed to the mandatory controls, pressure increased to remove them. However, while some liberalisation was introduced into the programme in 1969, the US Government was committed to maintaining controls until fundamental improvement was achieved in the balance of payments. It was not finally until early 1974 that controls over the outflow of dollars for direct investment abroad were removed; the interest equalisation tax was also abolished at this time.

As the 1960s moved into the 1970s, the focus of concern in the US shifted from the balance of payments *per se* to more general macro-economic problems. During the 1960s the rate of exchange of the dollar had been viewed as sacrosanct, and therefore the obvious solution to the balance of payments deficit – devaluation of the dollar – could not be applied. But with the revaluation of a number of major currencies against the dollar in 1971 and the subsequent abandonment of the fixed exchange rate system, this became less of a problem. Unemployment and inflation began to be seen as greater difficulties. Moreover, new concerns associated with the belief that MNEs were exporting the technological heritage of the US, that American tax policy was subsidising foreign investment and so forth, began to loom large.

The proposed Foreign Trade and Investment Act (Burke-Hartke Bill)
Trade unions in the US – represented by the American Federation of Labour (AFL) and Congress of Industrial Organisations (CIO) – had generally supported the liberal trade and investment policies followed in America during the post-war years. But the trade unions began to take an increasingly protectionist stance during the 1960s. Multinational firms were seen as exporting jobs, and as reinforcing structural change in the US economy which was shifting workers from highly unionised production industries into non-unionised higher technology and service industries. The Director of the AFL-CIO Department of Research summarised the union position as: 'One of the underlying causes of the deterioration of the US position in world trade is the operation of US-based multinational companies with far-flung foreign subsidiaries . . . (They) have exported American technology, with the loss of US production and employment, for the private advantages of the firm. They are a major factor in the rapid and substantial loss of US production in such relatively sophisticated goods as radios, televisions and other electrical products, as well as in shoes

and apparel. . . .'[26] This American trade deterioration, the unions claimed, had resulted in a net loss of about 900,000 job opportunities from 1966–71.[27]

The AFL-CIO proposals for the control of outward direct investment and the MNE were contained in the 1972 Foreign Trade and Investment Act. This was first introduced to Congress in September 1972 by US Representative James Burke and US Senator Vance Hartke, with the twin objectives of limiting the flow of imports and discouraging foreign direct investment. The bill contained a number of features affecting taxation, imports and capital and technology exports.

(i) Taxation. In assessing the Burke-Hartke proposals, it is first necessary to review US tax legislation as applied to MNEs. US tax treatment of international business rests primarily on the foreign tax credit and the principle of tax deferral. The *foreign tax credit,* which dates back to 1913, means that US corporations are entitled to a credit for tax paid to a foreign country on income earned in that country. For example, if the pre-tax profits of a foreign affiliate amount to $1000 and profits in that country are taxed at a rate of 35 per cent, then the host government would receive $350 in taxes. If the US tax rate was 50 per cent, then the corporation's tax liability to the US government would be $500, from which would be deducted the amount of foreign tax paid. Thus the actual tax payable to the US government would be $500 − 350 = $150. This foreign tax credit system ensures equal tax treatment for companies whether they operate in the US only or both in the US and abroad, since the same total rate of taxation would be paid. (The system is based on the concept of 'capital export neutrality'). Alternative schemes exist: foreign investment would be favoured if there was no taxation of income earned overseas; while domestic investment would be favoured if foreign tax payments were only permitted to be deducted from foreign income rather than credited against US tax liabilities on that income (the latter system is termed 'national neutrality'). The three schemes are shown in Table 7.3.[28]

Scheme 3 was essentially the Burke-Hartke proposal. It can be seen that this would place a heavy burden on the foreign operations of US firms. US MNEs would be taxed more heavily than domestic competitors in America. Moreover, since tax rates in many of the overseas countries in which US MNEs operate are about the same as American tax rates, the Burke-Hartke proposals would also adversely affect the competitive position of US multinationals *vis-à-vis* foreign competition.

The second major element of US tax legislation is the *tax deferral provision.* This permits the deferral of US tax on profits earned by US subsidiaries abroad, until the profit is remitted to the parent corporation. Thus the investing firm is provided with an interest free

Table 7.3 Alternative means of taxing foreign investment

	Foreign tax credit scheme (Scheme 1)	Exemption (Scheme 2)	Deduction (Scheme 3)
Profits of foreign affiliate	$ 1,000	$ 1,000	$ 1,000
Foreign tax rate	35%	35%	35%
Foreign tax payable	$ 350	$ 350	$ 350
Dividend paid to parent (all profits repatriated)	$ 650	$ 650	$ 650
US tax rate	50%	50%	50%
Pre-credit US tax	$ 500	–	$ 325
Tax credit	$ 350	–	–
US tax paid	$ 150	–	$ 325
Total tax paid	$ 500	$ 350	$ 675
Effective tax rate	50%	35%	67.5%

(*Source:* Bergsten, 1976.)

loan for the period of deferral, thereby encouraging the retention and reinvestment of foreign earnings. Tax deferral therefore discourages dividend repatriation and is an inducement to foreign investment.[29] The Burke-Hartke Bill proposed the elimination of this deferral provision. This proposal could not be criticised on grounds of equity because the deferral provision discriminated against domestic investment. Nevertheless the companies themselves would be adversely affected. Work by Stobaugh *et al.* has suggested that initially both the US balance of payments and US tax revenues would benefit.[30] However, reduced availability of funds to foreign affiliates would eventually lower investment and ultimately profit, to the benefit of foreign rivals. Using results derived from a computer simulation model, it was estimated that in a period of between five and eight years, deferral would result in lower US tax revenues and a worsened balance of payments (this issue is considered more fully in Appendix 7.1).

(ii) Imports. The Burke-Hartke proposals contained two major provisions in regard to imports. Firstly, import quotas were to be imposed on a country basis for virtually all imports, except where bilateral agreements existed between the US and other governments or where the failure to import would disrupt the domestic US market. Secondly, sections 807 and 806.30 of the Tariff Act would be repealed; these offshore assembly provisions (OAP) permit US firms with assembly operations abroad to enjoy re-entry of US-made components into America, with duty being paid only on the value added in the foreign location.

The proposed abolition of the OAP is interesting because US imports under sections 806.3 and 807 increased dramatically from

$593 million in 1966 to $5.2 billion in 1975. And countries such as Mexico, Korea and Taiwan which have been major recipients of this investment have achieved high rates of growth (see Chapter 5). Ending of the provisions could therefore be seen as a blow to LDC development efforts. Research by Finger has indicated that elimination of sections 806.3 and 807 would have reduced the foreign value added embodied in US imports (from both developed and developing countries) by an estimated $2.7 billion in 1972. Even so, the positive trade balance effects on the US of abolition of the OAP were estimated to be small.[31] Moreover, it was believed that economic welfare would decline in the US, as the output of components would fall to such an extent as to more than offset the increase of domestic assembly, the basic reason for this being lack of competitiveness. The Burke-Hartke proposals could thus have produced negative effects both in the US and abroad.

(iii) Capital and technology exports.   The AFL-CIO sponsored bill also proposed that capital exports be prohibited whenever such outward investment flows would reduce employment in the US. Similarly, the licensing and transfer of patents could be regulated where necessary to protect domestic employment.

In total, the 1972 Foreign Trade and Investment Act was an attempt to put a sharp brake on the expansion of outward direct investment, with a view to improving the balance of payments and, particularly, to improving employment prospects in the United States. The proposals naturally were subjected to detailed study, some of the results of which will be given in the next section. These studies at least suggested that the impact on the US might be the reverse of that anticipated by the Bill's sponsors, and as a result, the legislation was not passed by the US Congress.

This Bill was, nevertheless, evidence of a change in attitudes within the United States. In 1972 the Domestic International Sales Corporation (DISC) Statute came into force. A company which qualifies as a DISC is not subject to income taxation on its current or retained export earnings (although one half of these earnings are taxable as dividends). The DISC legislation, therefore, provides a subsidy to US exports by effectively reducing the taxation of export earnings of firms located in the USA by approximately 25 per cent. This inevitably has some adverse effect on the foreign investment of American firms; but, arguably, merely offsets the positive incentive to overseas investment provided by the tax deferral scheme. Following on from this Statute, it was only with some difficulty that the US government obtained legislative authority to enter into the Tokyo Round of trade negotiations in the GATT. By the terms of the Trade Reform Act (1974), it was obvious too that the concern expressed by the previous Burke-Hartke Bill had made some impact: MNEs which shifted production facilities abroad were compelled to offer employment opportunities to US workers losing their jobs as a result of any such move, and were required to assist in relocating them. In addition, any affected employees were to be given at least 60 days notice before the move. As part of the 1974 Act, a further attempt was made to abolish the offshore assembly provisions in the tariff code, but again this was defeated. Attempts to take America down the slippery path of import and investment restrictions were thus staved off for the time being. In doing this and in introducing adjustment assistance, the US government was accepting that economic benefits accrued from multinational operations abroad and from free trade. The pressures for change are still building up, nevertheless. The US Treasury have implemented new guidelines which will create a tax incentive for US MNEs to charge their foreign subsidiaries more for research and development undertaken by the parent corporation. And in 1978 the US President put forward proposals to remove the deferral scheme, and tax foreign source income before it was received in America. On the other hand, the elimination of favourable tax treatment for DISCs was also envisaged, since it conflicted with the rules of the GATT.

Other US legislation
Inevitably, political factors have been important in some US legislation which directly or indirectly affects MNEs. Since the 1917 Trading with the Enemy Act, the US has imposed restrictions on the commercial and financial relations between its nationals and certain, particularly Communist, countries. Such restrictions may range from the banning of any contact, to the regulation of sales of 'strategic goods'.[32] Since such legislation applies to both parent and subsidiary companies, it has been a bone of contention between the US and various host countries from time to time, where the latter do not operate the same restrictions on trade with Communist countries.

On a different aspect, although attempts are being made to introduce an international code of conduct relating to business corruption, the United States has acted to bring the issue into the open. Companies whose shares are quoted on the New York Stock Exchange are obliged by the Securities and Exchange Commission to disclose any illegal or improper payments made to government officials, politicians, etc. abroad, by parent or subsidiary companies. Because the shares of many non-US MNEs, e.g. ICI and BP, are quoted in New York, such companies are also affected by the legislation.

Both of these examples – East/West trade and corruption – are evidence of a phenomenon whereby US law imposes itself as world law because of the predominance of US multinationals. The extra-territoriality provisions of US anti-trust law are particularly well known in this regard: a case in point was the United States criminal investigation of an alleged international uranium cartel during 1977. Evidence seems to suggest that this worked against consumers' interests everywhere. However, to quote *The Economist,* 'does this justify the attempt to regulate ... foreign companies in foreign countries dealing with foreign markets for a foreign raw material?'[33] US anti-trust law is even more far-reaching than this. It was shown in the case of the 1975 merger of two Canadian paper companies, that if two such foreign companies, which export in substantial volume to the US and have significant assets there, undertake to merge, US courts may be deemed to have jurisdiction over the merger.

In concluding this section on US legislation, it is worth pointing out that the American government has operated a variety of schemes to protect and encourage overseas investment. Insurance is provided for US investors against losses due to wars and civil disorders, expropriation and currency inconvertibility. While such schemes have operated since the end of the Second World War, the programme has been the responsibility of OPIC – the Overseas Private Investment Corporation – since 1969. The system involves written approval by the host government of OPIC's insurance role with any particular project, and of OPIC's international arbitration rights in the event of expropriation. Whether or not this has any deterrent value, to a country considering confiscation of assets, is debatable. The work of the agency focuses on private investment in developing countries, although in the 1970s OPIC has come under increasing pressure not to insure projects which have detrimental effects on US jobs or the US balance of payments. Equally, OPIC is required to follow standard risk management practices with the eventual aim of financial self-sufficiency, meaning, therefore, a kind of portfolio approach to its project coverage and the insurance of many less risky projects. In criticising the present operations of OPIC, Bergsten considers that the agency's role should be essentially developmental.[34] As such, the organisation should only insure investments in the poorest countries in South Asia and Africa where risks are high and home country support is still required to attract foreign investment. Bergsten's view is that OPIC should have minimal concern with standard risk insurance practices and should be allocated public funds to support its activities.

As an adjunct to this, the long-surviving Hickenlooper and Gonzalez Amendments might be noted. These commit the US government to stop bilateral aid and oppose multilateral aid respectively in cases of uncompensated expropriation. Both are ineffective since they may merely exacerbate any dispute situation, and since 1973 the US President has been given the authority to waive the Amendments.

UK legislation and the multinational enterprise[35]

Regulation over outward direct investment from the UK is related to the likely effects of the investment on the balance of payments. Therefore close controls are placed on the *method of financing* direct investment. This is to ensure that the cost will not fall on the foreign exchange reserves until after equivalent benefits have accrued to the balance of payments through the repatriation of earnings. In understanding the way these controls operate it is first necessary to explain the difference between the official rate of exchange for sterling and the rate of exchange in the investment currency market.

Investment currency and the dollar premium

From the end of the Second World War no official foreign exchange has been provided for portfolio investment outside the sterling area. British residents wishing to obtain funds to purchase foreign securities have had to obtain the foreign exchange from another UK resident disposing of existing portfolio investments. This purchase and sale of foreign currency relating to portfolio investment takes place in a separate market for investment currency (often termed 'investment dollars'). The aim of the arrangement is to stem the outflow of portfolio funds which it is feared would take place in a free market situation. Generally the demand for investment dollars has been greater than the restricted supply meaning that the investment currency rate stands at a premium (the so-called dollar premium) above the official rate of exchange, as Table 7.4 indicates. The

Table 7.4 Price of investment currency in the UK (selected years)

Year (last working day)	Price of investment currency (No. of US dollars to the pound sterling)	Effective dollar premium (%)*
1963	2.5112	11.4
1966	2.2904	21.8
1969	1.7391	38.0
1972	1.9099	22.9
1975	1.2396	63.2
1976	1.1672	45.8
1977	1.4208	35.0

* Calculated in relation to the official parity until 1972 and to the concurrent spot rate thereafter.

(*Source:* Bank of England, 1978, and earlier editions.)

premium has varied widely over time: in 1962 it was as low as 3 per cent, whereas in 1975, at a time of major weakness in the British economy, it was over 60 per cent. In 1962 direct investment through the investment currency market was permitted for the first time, the premium in this instance representing an effective tax on multinational investment. From 1963 to 1977 portfolio investment was subject to an additional penalty, namely that when foreign securities were sold, investors were only allowed to recoup the premium on 75 per cent of the proceeds; the remaining 25 per cent of the proceeds had to be sold at the official rate of exchange (this was called 'the surrender rate'). But this requirement was lifted from 1 January 1978.

The development of controls over direct investment
Until 1961 foreign exchange was provided at the official rate for all overseas direct investments that met official requirements. Only direct investment within the sterling area was freely permitted, however, with investment elsewhere being subject to the criteria laid down by the authorities. In 1961 non-sterling area direct investment was permitted only if 'clear and commensurate benefits' would accrue to UK export earnings and the balance of payments within two to three years. From the following year direct investment which did not meet these criteria was permitted provided foreign exchange was obtained through the investment currency market.

Controls were tightened in 1965–66 for both sterling area and non-sterling area investments, as part of a general economic package designed to assist the balance of payments, and restore confidence in the sterling exchange rate. For investments in Australia, New Zealand, South Africa and the Irish Republic (the main developed sterling area countries) companies were asked to postpone or cancel projects that were to be financed from the UK. Non-sterling area direct investments which were beneficial to the balance of payments could no longer receive foreign exchange at the official rate and had to make use of the investment currency market. Any other direct investments had to be financed abroad.

Other changes were made subsequently in response to varying economic circumstances. For example, in 1972, in anticipation of membership of the EEC, exchange controls were eased so as to allow companies to spend £1 m. per project per year in direct investment in the Community, using foreign exchange obtained at the official rate. Previously the only direct investments permissible with official exchange were those which met the very tight 'super-criterion' rules (defined below). But in 1974 with a Labour government returning to power and the pound in difficulties this concession was removed. On accession to the EEC, the UK in fact agreed to a progressive removal of restrictions on capital movements within the Community over a period of five years up to 1977; but national governments are permitted to retain controls when balance of payments difficulties exist. The 1974 restrictions noted above were made in response to such difficulties and since then there have been only minor attempts to ease exchange controls.

As at 1978, therefore, the situation was as follows:
(i) A category of 'super-criterion projects' is defined. These are projects which are expected to pay for themselves in a period of 18 months, either through repatriated profits or other benefits to the UK balance of payments. In these cases £250,000 (or 50 per cent of the total cost of the investment, which ever is the greater)

is permitted to be financed at the official rate of exchange. From 1 January 1978 there was some change in these rules in relation to direct investment in the EEC. Here the amount of foreign currency which can be bought under the supercriterion is £500,000 or half the total cost of the project. In addition the length of time over which the cost of the investment has to be recouped is three years. For EEC and non-EEC investment the remainder of the foreign currency must be provided through the investment currency market or by other means. Apart from the supercriterion projects, therefore, direct investments cannot be financed by capital outflows at the official exchange rate, but must use investment currency, overseas borrowings or retained earnings from foreign subsidiaries.

 (ii) Any overseas investment has still to be approved by the Bank of England. The Bank requires that two thirds of all foreign earnings must be repatriated each year. Therefore expansion abroad, which might be financed by retained overseas earnings, is restricted to the one third of profits not subject to repatriation rules.

(iii) Since 1972 there has been virtually no distinction between sterling and non-sterling area countries from the viewpoint of portfolio investment. However, outward direct investment in the sterling area continues to be permitted freely with foreign exchange bought at market rates.

What has been the effect of these controls? As in the case of the United States, controls seem to have done fairly little to limit outward direct investment and for a similar reason. That is, most foreign investment is made by larger companies who are able to borrow abroad. Apart from the negative factor of the controls, a number of positive factors actually encouraged foreign borrowing during this period. Firstly, the growth of the Eurocurrency and Eurobond markets during the 1960s made it much easier to obtain capital abroad for foreign operations. Secondly, since interest rates abroad rose less sharply than those in the UK during the 1960s, this partly offset the higher risks of overseas borrowing. For smaller companies which do not possess the same ability to borrow abroad, on the other hand, exchange controls may act as a severe deterrent to direct investment. For example, any such companies which must resort to the investment currency market for finance, would find the very high dollar premium payable in recent years a big disincentive.

During the 1960s and into the mid-70s, in a period of continuing weakness in the balance of payments, it can be argued that a case could be made for exchange controls, at least as a second and third best solution. From 1977 through the 1980s, the situation is completely different, in that North Sea oil has assured fewer balance of payments difficulties for the UK than in past years. On these grounds, therefore, a relaxation of controls should be expected. But, as in the case of the

United States, it is likely that new criteria may be used to justify the retention of direct investment controls. The Trades Union Congress (TUC) is opposed to relaxation on the grounds that a major flow of funds into continental Europe would take place, leading to the export of factories and jobs and domestic unemployment. Here the UK government will have to balance union resistance against the advantages of relaxing exchange controls. Such a relaxation would ease any upward pressure on the exchange rate brought about by the balance of payments surplus, and prevent a revaluation of sterling which would have detrimental effects on exports. Relaxation would also fulfill EEC Treaty obligations, and facilitate direct investment.[36] Moreover it would overcome a problem which seems to exist in the UK, namely that of a surplus of investment capital and a shortage of attractive investment opportunities. These arguments for retaining or easing controls over direct investment abroad are essentially selfish motivations derived from the UK domestic interest only. From an international point of view, the economic case remains one of permitting freedom of trade and factor movements to maximise world welfare.

Empirical studies of the effects of foreign direct investment on home countries

The aim of this concluding section is to review the results of some of the empirical studies which have attempted to assess the effects of outward direct investment on home countries. This section has been included following that on legislation, because in reality legislation or legislative proposals have generally emerged before the studies. The latter have thus tended to provide ex-post rationalisations for, or critiques of, the regulations. Emphasis is placed on studies relating to the United States, as the home of the largest proportion of foreign direct investment, and the focus is primarily on short-run issues.

Foreign direct investment and the balance of payments

US concern over the impact of foreign investment initially focused on the balance of payments, and the 1965 voluntary restraints on dollar outflows abroad stimulated various attempts to assess the actual trade and payments impact of direct investment overseas. The major initial study was that undertaken by Hufbauer & Adler for the US Treasury published in 1968.[37] Immediately preceding this, somewhat similar research had been undertaken for the UK by Reddaway and others (1967 and 1968), and although the studies differ in terms of their assumptions, time periods covered, data sources, etc., it is useful to consider the two reports together.[38]

A crucial assumption in any such empirical investigation concerns what might have happened if the foreign direct investment had not taken place. Three extreme possibilities exist:

(a) Classical assumption
This postulates that foreign investment produces a net addition to capital formation in the host country but a similar decline in capital formation in the home country.

(b) Reverse classical assumption
In this case direct investment abroad substitutes for investment in the host country, but does not diminish capital formation in the investing country. This is essentially the 'defensive investment' argument, which states that foreign investment was required to maintain markets, as exports were likely to be excluded by host country policies designed to promote self-sufficiency.

(c) Anti-classical assumption
Again a given investment abroad does not reduce capital investment in the home country. But in the host country, capital formation is increased as a result of the foreign investment. This situation could occur when MNEs establish projects in the host country that local firms were incapable of undertaking. The assumption implies that foreign direct investment increases world capital formation. With the reverse classical and classical assumptions, international capital flows do not change total world capital formation.

The Hufbauer-Adler study investigated all three hypotheses, whereas Reddaway limited his analysis to the reverse classical hypothesis. The belief was that if, for example, a 'British company had not established a factory to produce pharmaceuticals in New Zealand, then a factory with roughly the same capacity would have been established by a non-UK company to make the same type of products.'[39] In essence, therefore, it was assumed that there was no alternative to the investment decision, since the New Zealand market for pharmaceuticals could not have been served by exports. The export displacement resulting from the investment is taken to be low or zero. This is a major weakness of the Reddaway study. It is easy to see that for some foreign investments there is no alternative, particularly if a number of firms of comparable size and efficiency in an industry are in world-wide competition, and if host country tariff barriers act as a constraint on exports. But it is debatable how much of total foreign investment would fall into this category. Hufbauer and Adler, by pursuing alternative hypotheses, allowed for the possibility, for instance, that the foreign market could still be served by productive capacity in the home country (i.e. the classical assumption, implying high export displacement as a consequence of direct investment abroad.)

Comparisons of the Reddaway and Hufbauer-Adler results under the reverse classical hypothesis are shown in Table 7.5. For the period 1955–64, using data for 60 British firms, Reddaway concluded that on average an addition of £100 to UK foreign direct investment would benefit the balance of payments on current account in the long run by £8.1 per annum (item 7 in Table 7.5) or £4 more than the return from a fixed interest loan at the rates then current. At the time the investment was made, by contrast, there would be an adverse effect on the balance of payments amounting to £89 per £100 of direct investment (less whatever amount the company raised through long-term finance overseas); the difference between £89 and £100 arises from the fact that some of the foreign direct investment takes the form of capital equipment exports (item 1(a) in the table).

For the United States, Hufbauer and Adler found that a much higher proportion of direct investment would take the form of capital equipment exports, so that the immediate adverse balance of payments effect of investment amounted to just $73 for every $100 invested. In the long run the US balance of payments benefited by $11.7 per annum. As a consequence of these higher return figures on US investment, the recoupment or payback periods were shorter for US than UK overseas investment. The other major differences between the two sets of results were in the exports of capital equipment, parts and components from US and UK parent companies to their subsidiaries and other local firms abroad. These exports were very small in the case of UK companies but highly significant for US firms, which may reflect the policies of the respective parent companies, or the relative efficiencies of home country suppliers.

When the Hufbauer-Adler classical and anti-classical results are included, the range of balance of payments outcomes relating to foreign investment widens considerably. The long-run balance of payments impact is estimated to vary from +$6.6 to −$15 per $100 of direct investment, with a payback period ranging from $6\frac{1}{2}$ years to never. As can be seen by referring to Table 7.5, the export displacement effect is very important to the result obtained. With the reverse classical assumption, export displacement (item 3) is negligible; on the other hand once the possibility of significant export displacement is allowed, as in the classical model, negative net balance of payments outcomes are possible.

These studies were very valuable in drawing attention away from the immediate balance of payments impact of direct investment overseas to the more significant, indirect trade effects. The focus by Hufbauer and Adler on the question of what would have happened in the absence of the investment was also a major contribution. Even so, the research approaches were by no means universally accepted and a lengthy debate and numerous new studies emerged over the following years.[40] Most of this research was undertaken in the United States, either following Hufbauer and Adler by applying econometric

Table 7.5 Reddaway and Hufbauer-Adler estimates of balance of payments effects – derived from reverse classical assumption

		Reddaway values for UK (1955–64)	Hufbauer-Adler values for USA (1961–62 to 1964–65)
1. (a) Capital equipment exports to subsidiaries	} % of value of overseas direct investment	10.5	27.0
(b) Capital equipment exports to local firms		3.1	23.8
2. (a) Parts and components exports to subsidiaries	} % of subsidiary sales	3.2	4.2
(b) Parts and components exports to local firms	} sales	0.7	3.5
3. Differential between export displacement and assoc. exports produced by subsidiaries and local firms (% of sales)		−1.7	2.3
4. (a) Imports (% of subsidiary sales)		−1.5	−4.3
(b) Imports (% of local firms' sales)		n.a.	−3.7
5. (a) Royalties and fees (% of subsidiary sales)		0.6	1.2
(b) Royalties and fees (% of local firm sales)		0.3	–
6. Remitted earnings as a % of post-tax earnings		50.5	50.5
7. Post-tax rate of return on investment (%)		8.1	11.7
8. Reverse classical recoupment period		14 years approx.	9 years approx.

Notes:

1. (a) This represents the proportion of the total value of direct investment abroad which takes the form of exports rather than capital outflows. For the USA, for example, the immediate adverse impact on the balance of payments of $100 of direct investment is only $73 (less whatever amount the company raises on long-term overseas financing) since $27 of investment is in the form of exports. (b) Apart from exports to subsidiaries, foreign direct investment also has an indirect benefit for the home country by encouraging local firms to buy equipment from the investing country (particularly in the case of the USA). This may be necessary if local firms are to remain competitive with foreign subsidiaries.

2. (a) This represents the continuing trade effects of foreign direct investment, as subsidiaries purchase parts and components from the parent company. (b) Similarly local firms continue to buy from abroad through a demonstration effect.

3. This represents the difference between the export of finished products from the parent company which may be stimulated by improvements in sales and servicing associated with the foreign subsidiary, and any export displacement caused by the production of foreign subsidiaries or local firms. Export displacement will be small under the reverse classical assumption.

4. Export of finished goods and components back to the investing country from the foreign subsidiary or local firms.

5. Payments for patents, licences, management services, etc.

6. Total remittances including dividends paid.

7. Post-tax earnings as a percentage of total investment.

8. The number of years before post-tax earnings abroad offset the initial investment, e.g. the Reddaway post-tax rate of return of 8.1 per cent is the equivalent of about 6 per cent per annum on a replacement cost basis after adjusting for stock appreciation. This means an average payback or recoupment period of approximately 14 years.

(Source: Adapted from Hufbauer a...)

methods to published statistics, or relying on the results of company surveys. The econometric studies have tended to show that foreign direct investments made because the firms must do so to hold and increase their markets were beneficial to the balance of payments; if therefore most investments were to fall into this category, US foreign direct investment would have a positive effect on the balance of payments in the long run. There are a number of general weaknesses with such investigations: the models may not give sufficient weight to 'anticipatory exports' (i.e. goods exported from the USA in anticipation of building the plant abroad) nor to 'associated exports' (i.e. complementary products which may be exported by the parent after the establishment of a foreign subsidiary). Furthermore the studies do not take account of 'balancing exports' that result after the first plant built abroad is operating at capacity. These exports may be required since consumption may expand smoothly whereas additional plant capacity can only be added in large steps. Finally, econometric models do not reveal the dynamic effects of overseas direct investment in terms of maintaining the competitive position of home country firms. A leading researcher in the field concluded: '. . . at the present time econometric models . . . should not be used for national policy making'.[41]

Foreign direct investment and employment

Following the Hufbauer-Adler report, there was growing concern in the USA not only with the balance of payments effects but also with the employment impact and other general domestic ramifications of overseas direct investment. Some of the more qualitative, policy-oriented studies which emerged focused on these types of issues, and particularly on the employment question. Certain of these investigations were patently biased, designed merely to provide public relations material for various interest groups, and consequently the results and conclusions varied widely. The results of the more useful studies are summarised in Table 7.6.

The debate probably began with the AFL-CIO claim that 500,000 jobs had been lost in the USA between 1966 and 1969 due to imbalances in the development of external trade (study No. 1 in Table 7.6). A high proportion of these job losses were claimed to be due to the impact of 'runaway' firms in setting up labour-intensive operations in offshore locations. Because of major weaknesses in the methodology – in particular no allowance was made for possible offsetting employment gains arising from associated parent company exports etc. – the results obtained were fairly predictable, and widely criticised.

Any study claiming respectability must attempt to include all possible direct and indirect employment effects associated with foreign investment, in the same way that Reddaway and Hufbauer-Adler had tried to do for the balance of payments impacts. As Table 7.6 shows, most studies indicated large positive employment effects resulting from the creation of non-production jobs in the US. These arose from the centralisation of management functions at parent company headquarters and from the expansion of associated service industries (i.e. home office and supporting firm employment effects). Moreover, capital equipment and parts and components exports from parents to subsidiary companies and local firms also boosted employment in the United States (i.e. export stimulus effect). Together these two factors had produced about 5–600,000 jobs in the US by the end of the 1960s. Given the difference in data and methodology and in the period to which the studies referred, the various investigations produced reasonably similar results. As was noted earlier with respect to the balance of payments studies, however, the major area of dispute concerns the production displacement effect. This is very sensitive to the assumption made regarding the percentage of foreign markets retained by US firms in the absence of foreign investment. The point is brought out particularly clearly in Hawkins' work, where three alternative hypotheses are tested. Firstly, only 5 per cent of the production of US affiliates abroad would have been retained in the US if the foreign investment had not been made. This is similar to the reverse classical assumption made by Reddaway. Secondly, 10 per cent of production would have been retained in the US, and thirdly, 25 per cent. The employment loss associated with these assumptions ranged from 190,000 to 791,000 jobs.

In just the same way that the reverse classical assumption was associated with a net positive balance of payments effect in the long run, so this assumption was also associated with a net employment gain for the US economy from foreign direct investment. As yet, nevertheless, no comprehensive evidence is available on the proportion of foreign investment which falls into this category, and is therefore necessary to maintain firms' market positions abroad. Such evidence may indeed never be forthcoming given that world markets are dynamic and continually changing. The most that can probably be said is that on likely assumptions, jobs displaced and jobs produced by foreign direct investment seem to approximately offset each other.[42]

The employment adjustment problem
The precise relationship between job gains and losses may in any event be less important than another issue, namely that of the adjustment problem created for the home economy by the job movement arising from overseas direct investment. Some measure of this will be given by the overall number of jobs created or destroyed through foreign investment – on the basis of the studies quoted up to 1.5 million jobs. But this is a minimum figure and the actual movement may be much higher because of differences in the employment mix as between jobs produced and jobs lost. The work of de la Torre, Stobaugh and Telesio

Table 7.6 The effects of MNEs on US employment: summary of selected studies

Study	Source of data	Estimate of % of foreign markets retained by US firms in the absence of foreign investment	Employment effect (No. of jobs)*			
			US production displacement effect	Export stimulus effect	Home office and supporting firm employment effect	Net employment
1. Ruttenberg, AFL-CIO study (1971)	Aggregate official data	Inferred to be high	-500,000 jobs between 1966-69 due to adverse trade movements, of which MNEs account for an 'important part'†	n.a.	n.a.	'Important part' of -500,000
2. Stobaugh and associates (1971)	9 case studies and aggregate data	Low or zero in the long run	-†	+250,000	+350,000	+600,000
3. Emergency Committee for American Trade (1972)	Sample survey of 74 companies	Inferred to be low	n.a.	+300,000	+250,000	Substantially positive
4. US Chamber of Commerce (1972)	Sample survey of 158 companies	Inferred to be low or zero	n.a.	+311,345‡	n.a.	Positive
5. R.G. Hawkins§ (1972)	Aggregate data	Assumption 1 (5% of production of US affiliates retained in the US)	-190,000			+279,000
		Assumption 2 (10% of production retained)	-381,000	+260,000	+209,000	+89,000
		Assumption 3 (25% of production retained)	-791,000			-322,000
6. US Tariff Commission (1973)	Unpublished statistics on operations of US firms with foreign operations	Assumption 1 (average share of foreign markets actually held by US exports during period 1960-61)¶	-603,100	+286,000	+321,000	+488,000‡‡

* For an explanation of these effects see pp. 291-2.   † Negligible.   ‡ Based on net trade.

§ Apart from the assumptions on US production displacement, Hawkins made a number of other assumptions, namely: a) 47% of exports to affiliates would not have occurred in the absence of the affiliates; b) 63.7 workers were required per million dollars of manufacturing output in US exports.

‡‡ The net result includes 629,000 jobs created in the US by foreign-based MNEs. It is doubtful whether, in fact, this should be brought into the calculation.

¶ Calculations were also undertaken on the basis of two other assumptions, namely: a) that 100% of the markets held by US exports were displaced by MNEs; and b) that 50% of the markets held by US exports were displaced. The net domestic employment impact in the two cases was -1,297,000 jobs and -417,800 jobs respectively.

(*Source:* US Tariff Commission, 1973; Hawkins, 1972.)

has confirmed that the jobs added in the US as a result of foreign direct investment are of a higher skill level than the jobs lost.[43] The employees dismissed from low-skilled jobs cannot readily fill these higher-skilled positions; rather they must look for unskilled job vacancies elsewhere in the economic system. Similarly skilled and professional workers in existing jobs may be encouraged to move to new positions becoming available in MNEs. The total adjustment may therefore be well in excess of 1½ million jobs. Moreover, the position may be complicated by particular geographical or industry concentrations of employment creation and destruction.

These figures are derived from all foreign investment decisions taken up to about 1970, and do not reveal the annual displacement of jobs. The latter relate to the investment decisions made during any particular year. As part of the work quoted in Table 7.6, Hawkins made some estimates of the job effects for 1968. On the basis of assumption 2 (i.e. 10 per cent of the production of US affiliates retained in the USA in the absence of foreign investment), the number of jobs lost in 1968 alone might have been about 40,000 and the jobs gained perhaps 50,000.[44] These 90,000 jobs represent between 4.5 and 6 per cent of the annual expansion of the US labour force of 1.5–2 million people. While small, this still represents an adjustment burden with which significant costs will be associated. The closures of large plants may have a devastating effect on local communities and present major transitional problems. What must finally be assessed is whether such short-run costs will be more than balanced by long-run gains. Before coming to this, however, consideration needs to be given to the relationship between domestic and foreign investment since this is critical to the impact of MNE operations on home countries.

Does foreign direct investment supplement or substitute for domestic investment?

The empirical results quoted have indicated that the impact of foreign investment on the home country is crucially linked to the question of what MNEs would have done if they had not established affiliates overseas. It has been shown that the reverse classical assumption, namely that direct investment abroad does not diminish capital formation in the source country, tends to be associated with positive balance of payments and employment effects in the home nation. But comprehensive evidence as to the proportion of foreign investment which falls into this 'defensive' category is not available. What is perhaps surprising is that little attention has been paid to type of investment when considering this problem, just as at the theoretical level inadequate regard has been given to the distinction between investment type. Resource-based investment is *prima facie* of the reverse classical (or anti-classical) type: firms invest abroad to exploit resources which are unavailable at home. Thus to counteract its high dependence on resource imports, Japan, for example, is investing heavily abroad to secure supplies of resources. For the firms concerned, extractive ventures will frequently be part of the parent company's vertically integrated operations. With regard to investments which are designed to exploit cheap labour abroad the situation is rather more complex. It is clear that the investments would not have been made in the home country unless much higher wages were offset by higher productivity; and therefore the investment abroad would not substitute fully for domestic investment. But if it is assumed that capital resources within a corporation are limited, then overseas investment must have an adverse effect in the short term on capital investment domestically. In the longer term, on the other hand, this international division of labour type investment will again comply with the reverse classical assumption. Both of these types of investment are essentially defensive in aim, and a defensive motive could also be attributed to horizontal investments where exports were impossible because of tariff barriers, etc. In the latter type of activity, nevertheless, it is much less obvious that MNE outward investment leaves home country capital formation unaffected. Because of this, and because of the differing patterns of outward investment by source countries, it would seem that the foreign investments of countries such as Japan and Sweden are more clearly biased towards reverse classical conditions than, say, American investment. In turn there is a greater likelihood of home country gains in these former instances. On the other hand, some studies have indicated that direct investment by US MNEs in other industrialised countries is associated with size of market and financial variables, but that external factors do not seem to have much impact on domestic US investment. This would seem to suggest that foreign investment does not totally substitute for home country capital formation. But the evidence is very limited and from the viewpoint of countries such as the United States and the United Kingdom, the answer to the question of whether or not foreign direct investment supplements or substitutes for domestic investment is still indeterminate.[45]

The overall long-run effects of foreign direct investment on home countries

Reflecting the focus of public concern, most empirical studies have aimed at assessing the impact of foreign direct investment on particular problem issues in home countries such as the balance of payments or the level of employment. The overall long-run effects refer to the impact of overseas investment on national income and the distribution of that income. From a theoretical viewpoint it was suggested earlier that over-investment abroad might occur because of a divergence between private and social interests, because of the loss of profits' taxes to host country governments and because of development benefits foregone through the transfer of technology. Of equal importance, it was suggested that foreign direct investment could be associated with a redistribution of domestic income away from labour and towards capital.

An important study on the long-run effects was that undertaken by Musgrave. As has been stressed by all the research quoted in this empirical section, Musgrave's results depended heavily on whether or not US investment abroad did or did not mean less investment in the US. To quote the author: 'if foreign investment is additional, US productivity will not be reduced and there will be a clear income gain. But if some displacement occurs, the outcome is in question and has to be established by careful analysis. The reasoning presented in this report leads us to believe that investment abroad is in substantial degree in displacement of domestic investment, but it also suggests that the gains from increased foreign earnings largely offset the loss of domestic output, so that only a small net loss results.'[46] The loss of domestic output arises from the fact that the displacement of home investment makes domestic labour less productive. Conversely foreign earnings rise because of the investment of US capital abroad at higher yields than at home.

An important element in such calculations is the rate of profits' taxation. Thus Musgrave suggested that the loss of income to foreign treasuries was one of the major reasons why the estimates showed a net loss to the US economy. The foreign tax credit scheme operated by the US means that about 90 per cent of taxes paid on foreign subsidiaries' earnings go to foreign treasuries. This could be seen as additional support for the argument that higher US taxes on overseas earnings were required (*à la* Burke-Hartke); but the position is not straightforward since higher taxes would generate further external effects which would need to be taken into account. (Because of the importance of this issue, a review of some of the studies undertaken into the likely effects of tax changes is provided in Appendix 7.1.)

In any event the much more significant long-run effects of foreign investment appear to relate to the distribution of domestic income. If the US capital stock abroad as at 1968 had been invested in the home country, it was calculated that labour income after tax would have been 4 per cent greater and post-tax capital income would have been 17 per cent smaller. This represents an important shift.. The evidence available therefore indicates that union concern in the United States, and more recently in the UK, over outward direct investment is not misplaced. The *net* effects of investment seem to be small *on reasonable assumptions*. But in the short run, adjustment problems may be created for labour, and in the long run, labour seems to be at the wrong end of a distributional shift in national income as a result of outward capital flows.

Nevertheless, there are still wide areas of ignorance. Indeed the fact that it is necessary to make assumptions about the interrelationships between the foreign and domestic investments of MNEs when undertaking empirical studies speaks for itself. This in turn is partly a reflection of inadequate attention being paid to the distinction between various types of outward direct investment. Most of the empirical results quoted, moreover, have referred to foreign direct investment from the USA, which reveals that there is a greater dearth of information regarding the impact of outward investment from, for example, the United Kingdom. In the latter case, data on the home and foreign operations of UK firms remain inadequate for analytical purposes. Indeed a major study of UK industry abroad, published in 1976, ended only with a series of questions: 'What . . . is the effect of UK industry abroad on the structure of domestic industry and the concentration of market power? on employment and the distribution of income? on tax revenue? on trade policy? on the UK's access to raw materials and energy supplies? on its technological capacity? and the supply and allocation of its skilled manpower?'[47] The implication was that the answers to most of the questions were unavailable. And in the UK, as in the US and most other source countries, there have been no attempts as yet to construct a comprehensive national overseas business policy.

Appendix 7.1   Home country taxation of MNEs

Virtually all the empirical work undertaken on home country tax systems relates to American multinationals. The empirical studies have tended to focus on the impact of changing or removing one or more of the elements of the US tax system, the two principal components of which are the foreign tax credit scheme and the deferral provision. An equally important issue, of course, relates to the question raised by economic theory as to whether the tax system operated leads to a divergence between social and private rates of return. Grubel undertook a study of this issue in relation to US direct investment in various European countries, Australia, South Africa and Canada during the period 1960–69.[48] The results showed that the pre- and post-tax rates of return earned by US manufacturing firms were higher on investment abroad than on investment in the US; that is, the private rate of return was positive overall and for investment in all countries except Spain, France and Canada. However, the social rate of return requires a comparison between the before-tax return at home and the after-local-tax return abroad. On this basis of comparison the all-country average shows a negative return of 5.9 per cent per year. Positive social returns were achieved only from investments in Belgium/Luxembourg, Germany, Denmark, Switzerland and South Africa. Grubel was careful to point out the various weaknesses of the analysis, but still considered that: ' . . . the evidence is sufficiently reliable to conclude that the export of capital from the United States for direct investment in manufacturing and the internationalist policies guiding the taxation of income from this capital do not clearly raise US welfare and probably lower it'.[49]

In considering the impact of altering American tax policy, Horst analysed three proposed changes, using data relating to US MNEs in 1974: i. repealing deferral; ii. increasing R & D charges to foreign subsidiaries; and iii. eliminating the foreign tax credit.[50]

(i) The removal of the deferral provisions would mean that US taxable income would include the value of the foreign subsidiaries' retained earnings; and it was estimated that US taxes to be paid as a consequence would rise by about $500 million (with the MNEs' after-tax income falling by a roughly similar amount). The parent companies' investment was calculated to rise by about 4 per cent, with the subsidiaries' investment declining by 9 per cent, although a great deal depended on the assumption made about the elasticity of investment with respect to the cost of capital. The elimination of deferral would have little effect on foreign taxes paid.

(ii) Regarding the possibility of US MNEs being required by American law to increase R & D charges to their foreign subsidiaries, the impact is very dependent on the assumption made: in all cases US taxes would rise substantially, but the foreign taxes paid would only fall sharply if the host government would allow the multinationals to deduct these R & D charges from the subsidiaries' taxable income. The foreign government could protect its tax base by disallowing higher deductions for R & D expenses, although the double taxation implications of this would inhibit new investment by US MNEs.

(iii) The impact of repealing the foreign tax credit and allowing only a deduction for foreign taxes (essentially the Burke-Hartke proposal based on the concept of 'national neutrality') would inevitably have the most dramatic effects: US taxes paid would rise by approximately 50 per cent with a consequent decrease in total corporate earnings and in new investment. Foreign taxes paid would not fall by more than 3–10 per cent, but the volume of overseas investment would drop sharply.

Other work has looked at the problem from the viewpoint of estimating an *optimum tax* on foreign investment earnings: this has indicated that the system of national neutrality would produce a result close to that obtained from an optimum tax.[51] It would appear therefore that significant welfare gains could be obtained if the United States changed to a system based on tax deductions rather than tax credits as at present, and if deferrals were eliminated. But important provisos need to be made to this conclusion. In particular host countries would almost certainly be provoked into implementing retaliatory policies. Moreover, the profound adverse impact on MNE

profitability would have far-reaching direct and indirect consequences
on both home and host countries.

Further reading

1. The basic theoretical articles are: 1. **A. E. Jasay**, 'The social choice between home
   and overseas investment', 1960, reprinted in J. H. Dunning (ed.), *International
   Investment*, Harmondsworth: Penguin Books, 1972, pp. 117–28; 2. **M. Frankel**,
   'Home versus foreign investment: a case against capital export', *Kyklos*, **18**, 1965,
   pp. 411–32; 3. **T. Balogh** and **P. Streeten**, 'Domestic versus foreign investment',
   Bulletin of Oxford University Institute of Statistics, **22**, 1960, pp. 213–24. Interested
   readers should also consult: **M. Beenstock**, 'Policies towards international direct
   investment: a neoclassical reappraisal', *Economic Journal*, **87**, Sept. 1977,
   pp. 533–42.
2. For the theory of the optimum tax see **M. C. Kemp**, 'The benefits and costs of private
   investment from abroad: comment', 1962, reprinted in J. H. Dunning (ed.),
   International Investment, op. cit., pp. 159–62. See also **R. E. Jones**, 'International
   capital movements and the theory of tariffs and trade', *Quarterly Journal of
   Economics*, **81**, 1967, pp. 1–38.
3. The argument for introducing controls over capital movements to assist the balance
   of payments is given in **D. A. Snider**, 'The case for capital controls to relieve the US
   balance of payments', 1964, reprinted in J. H. Dunning (ed.), *International
   Investment, op. cit.*, pp. 357–74. And the history of US and UK controls during the
   1960s and early 1970s is in **Sir A. Cairncross**, *Control of Long-Term International
   Capital Movements*, Washington D.C.: Brookings Institution, 1973, Ch. 3 and 4.
4. The following studies are important:

   Taxation: **T. Horst**, 'American taxation of multinational firms', *American
   Economic Review*, **67**, 1977, pp. 376–89.

   H. G. Grubel, 'Taxation and the rates of return from some US asset
   holdings abroad, 1960–69', *Journal of Political Economy*, **82**,
   1974, pp. 469–87.

   Aggregate effects: **P. Musgrave**, *Direct Investment Abroad and the Multinationals:
   Effects on the United States Economy*, report prepared for the
   Subcommittee on Multinational Corporations of the Senate
   Foreign Relations Committee, Washington DC: US Government
   Printing Office, August 1975.

   C. F. Bergsten, T. Horst and T. H. Moran, *American Multinationals
   and American Interests*, Washington DC: Brookings Institution,
   1978.

   T. Houston and **J. H. Dunning**, *UK Industry Abroad*, EAG
   Business Research Study, London: Financial Times, 1976.

   Employment effects: For various articles relating to the employment impact, refer to **D.
   Kujawa** (ed.), *American Labor and the Multinational Corporation*,
   New York: Praeger, 1973.

   Balance of payments effects: Apart from referring to the Hufbauer-Adler and Reddaway
   reports in the original, a series of review articles by Dunning are
   very revealing: **J.H. Dunning**, 'The foreign investment controversy', *Bankers Magazine*, May 1969, pp. 307–12; June 1969,
   pp. 354–60; and July 1969, pp. 21–5.

Questions for discussion

1. Differentiate between private and social rates of return in the context of outward direct investment. Review the various areas in which private and social interests may diverge.

2. 'Once the assumptions of perfect competition, divisibility of factors and products, diminishing marginal productivity of capital, constant terms of trade and adjustments to equilibrium positions, are abandoned, it is impossible to say with certainty whether, from a national point of view, investing abroad is preferable to investing at home . . . Much depends on the industries and the conditions in which the investment takes place.' How far do you agree with this view of Balogh and Streeten?

3. Consider the meaning and implications of the *classical, reverse classical* and *anti-classical* assumptions when undertaking empirical studies of foreign direct investment.

4. What is meant by the following:
   (a) Dollar premium?
   (b) The concept of 'capital export neutrality'?
   (c) Domestic International Sales Corporation?
   (d) 'Supercriterion' projects?

5. Discuss the case for and against the abolition of exchange controls by the United Kingdom.

6. 'The protectionist approach to (outward direct) investment is based on a willingness to forego the potential economic gains in order to obviate, at least temporarily, the necessity to make costly internal economic adjustments' (Kujawa, 1973). Discuss.

7. Discuss the view that with the operation of a floating exchange rate system there are no longer the same pressures in home countries to implement controls on outward capital flows.

Alternative perspectives on the MNE

Summary

1. While the viewpoint adopted in previous chapters essentially accords with what may be termed a 'contemporary orthodox approach', alternative models exist, *viz.* 'global neo-classical', 'radical' and 'mercantilist'. All of these models provide different conclusions on the impact of multinational corporations on the world economy and similarly have very different implications for the future of the MNE.

2. The global neo-classical model sees the unhindered operation of MNEs as the way to maximise world efficiency and domestic economic welfare; in this scenario, the nation state's control over economic affairs will gradually be replaced by the operation of international firms and the establishment of other international economic institutions. The mercantilist model provides a view of the future which sees the demise of the interdependent world economy; the economic conditions which provided a favourable environment for MNEs are seen as coming to an end, and with the world economy fragmenting into regional economic blocs, the reign of the American MNE is believed to be ending.

3. Numerous radical theories have been postulated, in which the MNE is regarded implicitly or explicitly as the new agent of imperialism. The possible motives for imperialist behaviour by the rich countries are numerous, including declining rate of profit in the home economy; the need to find markets to absorb domestic surplus; the interests of the State in maintaining macro-economic prosperity at home, in pursuing its 'urge to dominate' and in extending its national institutions and value systems abroad; and motives derived from class issues, such as the need to draw attention away from internal conflicts between dominant and subordinate classes.

4. 'Dependence' and 'the development of underdevelopment' in the poor countries are believed by the radical school to be principal outcomes of imperialism. In the first case, technological dependence, high import dependence, restricted export markets, and limited foreign aid sources are all components of the dependence model. In the second case, the transmission of the tastes and preferences of the rich to the poor countries and the

misuse or misallocation of resources in the Third World countries, restricts their development potential.

5. The MNE is considered to be an integral part of the process by which imperialist relationships develop between rich and poor countries; and it is seen as being particularly important in the post-World War Two neo-colonialist period.

6. Many of the theories of imperialism cannot be readily tested empirically. It has been shown that the US economy is heavily dependent on imports of basic raw materials; that a relationship may exist between US direct investment in a host country and the political persuasion of the host government; that US military assistance to host governments and US direct investment are positively correlated; that some notable US international firms are heavily reliant on American government military contracts; that by various measures, LDCs are highly dependent on the industrialised countries, and so forth. But these empirical studies do not prove that imperialist relationships exist or that multinationals are agents of imperialism.

7. Nevertheless, the major conclusion of the chapter is that multinational activity must be assessed in political and social as well as in economic terms. Although it may not be possible to identify cause and effect at an empirical level, the interrelationships between politics and economics are apparent both from the research work quoted and from the case studies presented – ITT in Chile, Lonhro, the oil companies and OPEC, Chrysler and Lockheed.

Conflicting perspectives

On the basis of the characteristics of multinational companies already examined, it is not surprising to find that present activities and motivations and future development paths are the subject of heated debate. Contention surrounds many issues including the presence of MNEs in more concentrated or oligopolistic industries, the influence such firms exert in the development of Third World nations, the actual or potential conflict of interests with host nations, the massive MNE involvement in world trade, and so on. And yet the same, generally agreed facts about MNEs are open to many different interpretations depending on the viewpoint taken, with the result that long-run predictions vary widely. To take one example, the varying perspectives lead to differing evaluations of the effects which MNEs will have on the world economic order. The aim of this chapter is to identify these differing viewpoints on multinational enterprises, with particular focus being placed on the radical models. The scene is then set for the final chapter of the book which considers the future of the MNE. In broad terms it is possible to classify analyses of MNE activity as follows:

(a) Global neo-classical analysis

This is based on the central belief that the market mechanism must be allowed to operate unhindered in order to produce a 'fully rational international division of labour that will optimise the productive resources of the world'.[1] Further, this view suggests that increasing economic interdependence, and technological advances in both transport and communications, will effectively make the nation state outdated. Both world efficiency and domestic economic welfare are regarded as being advanced by a diminution in the nation state's control of the economy and the continued growth of multinational corporations. The MNE is regarded as the most effective medium for integrating and organising resource utilisation on a global scale. As a corollary it is seen as the institution most likely to survive changing international political relationships. Throughout this process the impact of the MNE is considered to be essentially benign – aiding, for example, the transfer of resources from the developed nation core to the less developed periphery.

(b) Radical critiques

Within this group are an extensive collection of critical theories. They have in common a rejection of the applicability of neo-classical optimisation and the optimism with which it is surrounded. More Marxist-oriented writers offer long-run analyses in terms of the inherent contradictions of the capitalist world economy (falling rates of profit, cyclical crises, etc.); while others see MNEs as both the product of, and agent for, a global hierarchy of economic dependence. In all of these approaches the MNE is, to a greater or lesser degree, regarded as the new agent of imperialism. As has been observed: 'for Marxists the large firm and not the nation state or the market is the institution through which the dynamic of capitalist accumulation is expressed'.[2]

Particular attention has been given in recent years to the *dependencia* model. The mechanisms by which wealth and benefits are transmitted are regarded as being similar to those in the global neo-classical view, but in this case the forces are considered as malevolent and exploitive of the periphery. Increasing firm size and uneven development are dominant principles. Their operation results in the concentration of decisions and power in the large, urban, financial and industrial centres with the growth of the developing world being retarded by this system. Although this analysis embraces trading and political relationships, foreign direct investment is also considered to be of major significance in establishing the *dependencia* relationship.

(c) The 'mercantilist' model

Both of the previous perspectives regard the nation state as playing a diminishing role in the world economy as a result of MNE expansion. In contrast, the mercantilist view considers that the nation state and the interaction of national interests are the major determinants of the future direction of the world economy.[3] This view is based on the belief that the world economy will become less interdependent as the conditions which originally facilitated the emergence of the MNE have now changed. This is related, it is alleged, to the relative decline of US power and growing conflicts among developed nations, as each pursues economic policies which reflect domestic economic priorities. This model forsees the future development of regional economic blocs, so that international trade, monetary institutions and investment patterns will increasingly become interregional rather than truly international.

Although the emphasis in this model is on future developments, it does establish a framework within which recent policies on control can be viewed and is introduced at this stage with this in mind.

(d) Contemporary orthodox

Most academic writing by economists on MNEs falls into none of these categories, but broadly supports the view that MNEs produce net benefits to the world economy. The theoretical basis for this approach remains neo-classical, both in trade and welfare theory. Increasingly, however, there is a recognition of the necessity to take the long and wide view of MNE operations by applying a cost-benefit perspective to the activities of parent corporations, affiliates and even to individual projects. Arising from this is an acknowledgement of the need for the state to intervene selectively and flexibly in order to minimise the externalities associated with MNE activity. In many instances it is also recognised that control can only be undertaken on a supranational basis. Similarly it is accepted that over-restrictive legislation will be self defeating. The approach taken in previous chapters is broadly that of the contemporary orthodox.

All of the perspectives outlined are open to question and have very different implications for the future of the MNE, as shall be seen in the next chapter. But, before turning to the future of the multinational enterprise some attention will be focused on assessing radical critiques of foreign direct investment. This is necessary both to balance the approach taken earlier and to reflect the volume of radical literature emerging in recent years (particularly from Third World nations). Two important points should be noted immediately. Firstly, within the radical literature there are a bewildering number of viewpoints stemming from internal disputes within particular schools of thought. Only the main issues are considered here. Secondly, foreign direct investment and MNEs are more often considered implicitly than explicitly within broader discussions of imperialism. It is nevertheless clear that MNEs are a vital component in radical models of the world economy.

Imperialism: definitions and motivations

Definitions

Imperialism was originally associated with the direct extension of political sovereignty and highly centralised government as practised by the major European powers in the second half of the nineteenth century. Historically it has been associated with three analytically distinct phenomena – colonialism, industrialisation and foreign direct investment – although these can rarely be considered separately. In all of these contexts it has combined both political and economic overtones. These latter have been expressed variously as 'the network of means of control exercised by one economy (enterprises and government) over another' and 'the internationalisation of capitalism'.[4] In effect, imperialism describes an international *relationship* which involves both economic and political dimensions, private and public interests. It is a relationship of a special type 'characterised by a particular asymmetry – the asymmetry of dominance and dependence'.[5]

The definitions embrace a wide variety of forms of political and economic behaviour by both governments and private sector institutions. These could include trading relationships, aid programmes, militarism and so on. While imperialism can in theory exist without foreign direct investment, most radical writers would accept the stated view that 'no study of imperialism can begin without an understanding of the nature of the multinational corporation: its goals, its interests and its methods of operation'.[6] This view pertains particularly in radical analyses of the post-Second World War period of alleged 'neo-imperialism' (i.e. imperialism without colonies) during which US economic and political influence expanded rapidly.

Motivations

The explanations provided by the radical models for the growth of imperialism and the associated expansion of the MNE are quite different to those formulated in Chapter 2. They are of course wider and much less specifically related to MNEs as such and hence are presented here only in summary form.

(i) Declining rate of profit.   One of the earliest explanations in the radical tradition was the Leninist view that declining rates of profit in the home economy encouraged the export of capital abroad, which in turn produced an imperialist relationship between home and host countries. It is doubtful whether this offers a comprehensive explanation of MNE expansion over the last 20 years. While the concept of a general profit rate may be relevant to the competitive

industrial sector of the advanced capitalist economies, in the oligopolistic sector where MNEs typically operate, profit margins are themselves determined by corporate price, output and investment policies. Although this is so, it has been argued with some justification that differential rates of profit between home and host economies may still constitute a justification for foreign investment.[7] In this case the relevant comparison is between marginal and not average rates of profit between home and abroad. Even if average profit rates in, say, the LDCs are lower, the return from any particular investment project may be higher than that attainable in the home economy.

(ii) Underconsumption and surplus absorption. Based on the classical theory of underconsumption associated with the work of Hobson and Luxemburg, this approach may be summarised as follows:[8]

1. The identification of a chronic tendency in a capitalist economy for aggregate demand to be insufficient to absorb all of the output produced.
2. A consequent and continual need to find new outlets for surplus production in order to avoid economic crises.
3. Foreign countries and territories are viewed as representing important potential markets for domestic surplus (initially taking the form of exports, but later involving foreign direct investment).
4. An imperialist foreign policy provides access to these markets for the imperialist country.

In terms of this model, a level of output exists in each economy which represents socially essential production. This is the minimum volume of production required to maintain its (growing) population at a standard of living necessary for survival. The difference between this level of output and total productive potential is 'surplus', in the sense that there is some potential flexibility with regard to its allocation. Since the rate of growth of output potential is assumed to expand more rapidly than that which is socially necessary, outlets are required: hence trade, government activity (including military expansion) and foreign direct investment. Baran and Sweezy have made one of the major modern contributions to this theory.[9] While they regarded direct investment abroad as an outlet for investment-seeking surplus generated in the corporate sector of the monopoly capitalist system, foreign investment was not considered as being a major absorber of 'surplus'. It was regarded as a method of removing output (and profit) from LDCs rather than of channelling surplus into them.

Baran and Sweezy have been criticised for concluding that modern capitalism cannot find ways to avert its stagnationist tendency. Thus they reject price cutting or government fiscal policies as possible ways of raising domestic consumption. Both of these they regard as possible, but unlikely, in a monopoly capital situation, given the economic and political power of capitalism. Higher government expenditure, for example, might require higher corporate taxation which could be resisted by the companies. Having assessed all other alternatives, military spending emerges as the only effective way of absorbing surplus. It has the claimed additional attraction of preserving the interests of the capitalist oligarchy and its foreign direct investments, as part of a necessary programme of exerting global influence. The link with MNEs arises from the fact that the 'principal requirement of the foreign corporations is for a stable and highly favourable environment for their investment and trading activities'.[10] Such an environment may be created by military expenditures overseas.

(iii) The role of the state. It is important to stress that in the two main groups of theories considered in the preceding paragraphs, the imperialist relationship is one which emerges from implicit links between states and large corporations aimed at maintaining macro-economic prosperity. Such links are at the root of radical analysis. There are however a wide range of more explicit ways in which state and corporate activity are claimed to be related, some of which are considered under this heading. While it is not possible to argue that all international activities of the state have an economic explanation, there is at least some coincidence in the international *objectives* of companies and of their domestic governments. Hence the hypothesis, for example, that imperialism is designed to increase aggregate economic gains for the home country through trade and investment. Although such concepts are plausible they are often very difficult to verify, especially when any one hypothesis is taken in isolation. For instance, in the case of US exports, the fact that net exports since the Second World War have rarely exceeded 1 per cent of GNP makes it difficult to conclude that aggregate gains through exports are significant. On the other hand the radical case is much better served when imports of raw materials are considered (see Table 8.1) although it is not necessarily *proven* by the import pattern.

Table 8.1 Relative dependence of the US on selected imported raw materials (1967)

Product area	Imports as % of total domestic use
1. Carpet wool; copra; crude rubber; fibres, gums and barks; raw silk; abrasives, beryllium; chromium; cobalt; manganese ores; mica; nickel; titanium	90–100
2. Asbestos; bauxite; fluorspar; tin	60–89

(*Source:* The Bureau of Census, see Cohen, 1973, p. 139.)

This issue will be examined further in the empirical section, where the evidence as to whether or not the US economy is structurally dependent upon imperialism will be reviewed. It is sufficient at this point to accept the hypothesis that a country *could* use its power to improve the terms of trade (by lowering the effective price of strategic imports), to extend its export markets in order to increase export earnings, or to create a more favourable climate for private sector foreign investment and thus raise receipts from repatriated profits. Governments may also have an important role in creating markets for their military equipment industries; and several writers have developed theories of convergence between military industry and government in the US.[11]

It has been suggested that the role of the state in support of its interests (including foreign direct investment) frequently emerges in more ephemeral ways. Thus actions of a state could arise from a 'generalised missionary spirit' reflecting such a belief in a nation's institutions and value systems that it feels justified in aiding their extension abroad.[12] A closely related motivation is that stemming from an 'urge to dominate' which is claimed to be inherent, at both individual and national level. In these cases gains, in terms of 'psychic satisfaction', may not be readily measured in economic terms. Schumpeter, however, certainly regarded the 'urge to dominate' as having important economic consequences and it has appeared implicitly in more recent work.[13]

One recently emerging, and potentially important, strand of analysis should be noted in this section. The exact nature of the role of the state in mixed economies and the economic functions it should undertake relates to the growing interest in 'corporatism'. This can be defined as an economic system in which the state directs and controls predominantly privately-owned business according to four basic principles: unity, order, nationalism and success. This framework for analysing the mechanics of the mixed economy sees the role of the state in the economy changing, so as to take a directive as opposed to a merely supportive role. This necessitates growing involvement in the internal decisions of private firms to apply the guiding principles. So, for example, cooperative effort may be considered as preferable to competition in certain industries (e.g. computers) for reasons of *nationalism* or to ensure *success;* while market regulation by the state may be employed to bring *order* to specific markets (e.g. shipbuilding). The existence and growth of such a relationship is consistent with the claims of the radical school that political and economic power converge. One study of the genesis of corporatism in the UK examines its emergence in response to changes in the UK economy – namely, industrial concentration; declining profitability; technological developments; international competition; and economic crisis.[14] Thus while corporatism has developed, *inter alia,* to counteract corporate power, it can itself prove to be a powerful vehicle for support of both domestic and international corporate activity emerging from that state.

(iv) Class-based motivations. From the radical perspective imperialism is a class phenomenon, and numerous class-based hypotheses have emerged in the literature. A number of illustrations may be noted.[15] In any unequal society the dominant class are regarded as having interests in promoting their own *social legitimacy* by, for instance, generating international antagonisms of particular types in order to support business interests. Imperialism of this type draws attention away from internal conflicts between dominant and subordinate classes. A second class based motivation for imperialism may result from the interests of military and civilian government bureaucracies in *organizational expansion*. Imperialist expansion will increase the power and prestige of the agencies involved.[16] Since the civilian and military agencies represent arms of government, this point is closely related to those noted in section (iii).

The MNE and imperialism

The economic explanations of imperialism which have been discussed in previous sections concern many more activities than foreign direct investment. Even so, the MNE is involved both directly and indirectly in foreign aid programmes, military installations, general issues of foreign policy and so on. It is regarded as both a cause and an effect of imperialism.

From the radical viewpoint, MNE expansion is a characteristic phenomenon of mature capitalism within which various monopolistic pressures lead to the search for new investment outlets. These views are expressed in the under-consumption and declining profit rate hypotheses. Modern radical thought on the other hand considers that the MNE invests in host countries so as to accumulate more capital there; the surplus generated abroad is then transferred back to the investing country. This 'suction-pump' explanation does not distinguish between capital stocks overseas and flows of current income. In particular it does not take into account the role of reinvested earnings in MNE expansion, but rather concentrates on comparing remitted earnings and new capital outflows from the home economy. This latter emphasis is clearly too narrow.

One particularly important issue surrounds the link between modern imperialism and national sovereignty. Radical writers are quick to point out that even where a national government is not dominated by business interests, the strength of MNEs globally means that the host country concerned has almost no choice in particular situations as regards type and capital intensity of technology, sources and prices of intermediate products and capital equipment, volume of production and exports and so on. While this is often superficially true, there is plenty of evidence from countries like Mexico and Venezuela to show that states, with substantial restrictions covering the terms under which foreign investors operate, can continue to attract foreign capital. Moreover, it is illuminating to observe the growing attempts by centrally planned economies (particularly the USSR) to establish close cooperation with multinational firms. Although both these examples often involve breaking up the MNE package to the advantage of the host economy, they do present a challenge to the Marxist view of the inevitable net cost of MNE activity to recipient nations. In radical eyes the state will be corrupted by foreign firms and will become both reluctant and, ultimately, unable to introduce appropriate legislation or administrative measures to govern their behaviour. While there is ample evidence of pressures existing between MNEs and host governments, it is not easy to conclude that MNEs have dominated economic events to a degree where *all* the effects of capital imports have been evil and where economic nationalism has been subjugated to their power. Orthodox analysis highlights actions possible to counteract abuse by MNEs through policies on taxation, trade, competition and so on. In sharp contrast is the radical view that government policy is not independent of the underlying economic structure.

One modern and representative radical view of the MNE could be summarised as follows:[17] First, no country should ever under any circumstances permit foreign corporations to own and operate enterprises within its borders, since they can never be instruments of economic development; second, where MNEs do exist, they should be immediately nationalised; third, foreign capital should be accepted only in the form of loans; and finally, the acid test as to whether any group in a country is genuinely devoted to the cause of national independence and economic development is its attitude towards foreign investment.

An essential part of the radical critique of the MNE is the identity of ownership of these corporations with particular countries. It is acknowledged that while the trend is towards an internationalisation of both stockholding and management, this is offset by the separation of ownership and control and in effect means little. While European investors do buy stock in US MNEs, the corporations in turn may reinvest in Europe on terms and in directions determined by US nationals; the contention is thus that the scope for exploiting the US national interest remains. Such issues come into even sharper focus when, for example, the post-Second World War growth of US foreign direct investment in Europe and Latin America is considered. In both these cases there was considerable coincidence of foreign and corporate policy. The reconstitution of the system of international payments under US leadership permitted the US to run a continuing deficit in its balance of payments and facilitated the financing of foreign manufacturing and military activity. Moreover, in the European case, the prosperity and type of economic development sponsored by the Marshall Plan, which had as its political aim the prevention of the spread of communism, provided an ideal environment for the establishment of foreign affiliates.

Perhaps the most fundamental dimension of the perceived association between the MNE and imperialism stems from the radical view of *capital*. Capital is seen not in abstract or quantitative terms only, but rather in terms of its exploitive, hierarchical relationship with labour. Its accumulation has been achieved over long periods of history and a substantial part of its ownership currently resides within MNEs. The multinationals in turn are committed to an ethic of growth, further accumulation and diversification both geographically and industrially. It is through this mechanism that the historical record of exploitation is seen to be linked to the MNE, particularly since international investment has been growing much faster than world output.

The consequences of imperialism: neo-colonialism and dependence

The radical theoretical studies which have emerged over recent years have concentrated on analysing the consequences of the essentially post-war phenomenon of neo-colonialism (or neo-imperialism). Neo-colonialism may be defined as 'the survival of the colonial system in spite of formal recognition of political independence in emerging countries'.[18] With variations, radical writers view the process of neo-colonialism as operating on developing countries in two basic ways, firstly through its effects on their resource development and allocation, and secondly through a transmission of the tastes and preferences of the rich countries in such a way as to distort and damage their economic development. The end result is reflected in the structure of global prices, an outcome which is alleged to have been reinforced by the large-scale expansion of multinational firms.

On the *resources* issue, the neo-colonialist relationship is regarded as both causing distortions in the utilisation of available resources, and as inhibiting the growth of factor endowments, e.g. human capital. The use by MNEs of high technology plant may be inappropriate (see the discussion on the factor proportions problem, Chapter 5), and the importation of skilled and professional manpower may limit the possibilities of developing local skills. The net effect will be to restrict development potential. Some radical writers would go further and claim that the production system of poor countries has been actively subordinated to that of the developed world. This has been characterised as 'the development of underdevelopment'.[19] Although this view is not always supported by other radicals, most would accept that neo-imperialism results in a new form of dualism between a high profit/high wage international oligopolistic capitalist (MNE) sector and a low profit/low wage competitive local capitalist sector. At a minimum this dualism is considered as representing non-optimal use of resources. Moreover, this occurs alongside a process of alleged 'decapitalisation'. That is, most new investment is funded by the generated profits of past investment and there is therefore a limited or non-existent inflow of new capital.[20]

As regards *tastes and preferences,* it is hypothesised that these are influenced by the 'demonstration effect', creating demands for products which can only be supplied by the MNE affiliates rather than by indigenous firms. An imperialist relationship is thus reinforced.

These issues have given rise to much work, especially by radical economists in the Third World on the nature of 'dependence'. There are many overlapping dimensions of this concept in an economy, including: specialisation of production and exports, especially on primary products, which have unstable markets; high import dependence for industrial products and food, often purchased under unfavourable terms of trade; specific dependence on foreign-owned corporations in vital sectors where the effects on employment, income distribution and so on spread throughout the economy. Technological dependence and reliance on only a few sources of foreign aid are other aspects of the phenomenon. In each of these areas, dependence is a matter of degree and in some instances exploitation may not be involved. Further, dependence in some of these areas may operate to the disadvantage of the capital exporting nations themselves, as the post-1973 oil situation has indicated.

Viewed more formally, dependence may be regarded as placing structural limits on development in Third World countries.[21] It may be hypothesised that industrial development is strongly conditioned by balance of payments fluctuations. Dependence may be instrumental in producing balance of payments deficits (and thus in retarding development) for various reasons including poor terms of trade for producers, and profit repatriation. The necessity thereafter for foreign finance creates a vicious circle: 'Foreign capital and foreign aid thus fill up the holes that they themselves created.'[22] The MNE is widely regarded as an integral part of the process and as being capable of contributing to almost all aspects of dependence. Multinational companies may be important to an LDC in securing external markets for the commodities, but thereafter the level of export earnings is highly dependent on the efficiency and goodwill of these firms. Foreign investment may be seen as a way of solving problems created by earlier imperialist behaviour, but this very process accentuates dependence. There are also links between foreign aid and foreign investment since aid to an LDC creates a market for the products of the multinational. This self perpetuating process is characterised by Hymer as the 'New Imperial System'.[23]

These dependency issues are equally important to the orthodox analysis of the impact of foreign direct investment on host countries. The essential difference between the radical and orthodox views is that the former school regards *conflict* as the principal (if not sole) element in interactions between home country governments and firms, and host countries, while the orthodox school considers that there are also some elements of harmony and benefit. In an attempt to clarify this debate Cohen introduces a model comprising four analytical concepts:[24]

(i) Exploitation loss (EL). On an opportunity cost basis, if the absolute benefit gained by the *exploited* from present relationships is x and the benefit from the best alternative opportunity is y, then x–y represents exploitation loss.

(ii) Exploitation gain (EG). On a similar basis if the *exploiting* participant's gains from the present organisation of relationships is w and the best alternative is v, then w–v represents exploitation gain.

(iii) Cost of escape (CE). To avoid EL, the *exploited* must incur transition costs to a new set of relationships. If the present value of CE > EL, then it will not pay the participant to try to escape from the status quo. This, it is argued, explains why exploitation often persists for long periods in real-life situations. Conversely if CE < EL the exploited participant will not accept the status quo, and will try to change his strategy in order to escape.

(iv) Costs of maintenance (CM). To preserve EG the *exploiting* participant must prevent this escape and transition to a new organisation of relationships; but this will only be worth while if the expected value of CM < EG. If CM > EG, it will not pay the exploiting party to try to maintain the status quo, despite the gain from exploitation.

Cohen's model assumes a non zero-sum game in which all four of these variables are critical in determining the outcome. Clearly all the factors are likely to vary frequently as relationships alter, and the model is therefore pertinent to understanding relationships between MNEs and nations in both the developed and developing parts of the world. There are many situations which illustrate these principles. For example, in commissioning work on a major docks and harbour project, an LDC may resolve to move from its traditional contractor source. In attempting to do so it may discover that the cost of escape involves significant increases in total project cost because the existing contractor has the plant, labour force and additional services already on site in the country. Conversely a new contractor would have to establish these from scratch. In these circumstances, a reduction in the tender price and good credit terms from the original contractor may be sufficient to maintain the status quo. The MNE response in such cases may be to form consortia to further raise the cost of escape by competitive tendering. For the MNE thus CM < EG; for the LDC, CE > EL at least in the short term. Another illustration of these principles is to be found where LDCs attempt to take over the export distribution of their agricultural products from a major MNE. Here CE might involve incurring expenditure in establishing distribution, warehousing and marketing facilities in a number of countries at very high cost. In addition the prices obtainable may be lower or less stable. Consequently a modest expenditure (CM) by the MNE represented by political contributions, employment creation or higher producer returns may readily offset the proposed change.

Empirical evidence on economic imperialism and foreign direct investment

Methodological issues

That there is no general theory of economic imperialism which commands wide acceptance must now be clear. There are rather a number of related propositions regarding relationships between states and corporations (including MNEs), the nature of exploitation, the motivation for foreign direct investment and so on. All of these have stimulated a number of verification attempts, but such studies face severe methodological problems, both because of difficulties in formulating testable hypotheses, and because of data availabilities. In effect, therefore, while writers have been claiming to 'test' theories of economic imperialism for over a century, much of the output is impressionistic and unsystematic. Moreover, relatively few have formally incorporated the MNE as such since they have been more concerned with macro relationships between states.

At this macro level, concepts of imperialism such as inequality, dependence and exploitation can be quantified in a number of ways, using techniques derived from other areas of economic analysis. If inequality is defined as the uneven distribution of particular values (such as GNP or investment) across countries, then Lorenz curves etc. can be used to derive a measure of the relative position. Similarly, various tests of economic concentration can be applied to show, for example, trade dependence between economies. Such approaches can measure the extent of inter-state and inter-area relationships. But the reader is only able to impute imperialist forces as being the underlying cause, depending on personal theoretical preference. What is much more difficult is to prove specific propositions linking, say, MNE activities to imperialism.

Within these limitations, this section concentrates on exploring some of the empirical evidence on economic imperialism under headings which have a particular bearing on the operations of MNEs. As in the theory section the emphasis is on examining radical studies.

A consideration of selected hypotheses

(a) The 'institutional necessity' for foreign investment

While not denying the importance of the profit motive in explaining MNE development, several authors have suggested that other factors even more fundamental to corporate capitalism created the necessity for overseas investment in countries like the US.[25] These emerged, it was claimed, from the fact that the technological advantage possessed by large domestic corporations had only been achieved at high cost; moreover, these firms operated in unstable imperfectly competitive markets and required economies of scale to maximise returns. As a result, the corporations were believed to put pressure on the state through persistent lobbying, in order to preserve an international system which would facilitate their expansion and enable them to recover their costs. Initially, free trading arrangements would meet these requirements, but ultimately foreign direct investment was seen as the only method of achieving corporate objectives. Apart from the role imputed to the state in this process, the view expressed is very similar to orthodox theories of MNE growth.

The latter hypotheses are not testable and a more conventional form of the 'institutional necessity' model derives from the assumption that US capitalism depends on investment in LDCs for raw materials, especially those of strategic importance. Table 8.2 illustrates the growth of US imports of basic raw materials over the period of major MNE expansion, indicating greatly increased reliance on external supplies of the minerals concerned. Without foreign sources, the minimum requirement for the US economy would be a period of significant readjustment. Such readjustment, it is argued, would affect the whole economy and, in particular, could erode the domestic market position of MNEs by plunging the country into economic decline. Although the presentation of the facts as in Table 8.2 is fairly typical, such evidence does not prove that foreign direct investment aimed at securing raw material supplies is both indispensable and imperialist. It is true to say that US raw material imports, at around 5 per cent of GNP, have a significance far beyond their nominal value, and that a reduction in the level of imports of some of the items would have serious employment effects in the US. But this does not allow for the possibilities of substitution, if required, nor does it demonstrate conclusively that imperialism is necessary since the US market would be attractive for exporters of raw materials in any event. Furthermore, over two-thirds of total US investment assets are located in developed countries and two-thirds of US imports and one-half of the profits of US affiliates emanate from these countries (such as Europe) where true 'imperialist' relationships do not exist.

Before concluding this section, it is worth while briefly considering the position of Japan, since the country is particularly dependent on external sources for supplies of basic raw materials and foodstuffs. In

Table 8.2 Selected minerals: net imports* as a percentage of domestic mine or well production† in the USA

	Average 1937–39	1966
Iron ore	3	43
Copper	−13	18
Lead	0	131
Zinc	7	140
Bauxite	113	638
Petroleum	−4	31

* Net imports = imports − exports

† These data do not deal with total consumption. The latter includes refining from scrap and use of inventories. This table only represents the change in the dependency on imports as compared with use of domestic natural resources.

(*Source:* Magdoff, 1966.)

order to reduce the proportion of resources imported from third parties, Japan is pressing ahead with direct investment abroad under a 'develop and import' strategy, a policy which gained particular momentum following the Arab oil cutback and price increases. Prior to and during the Second World War, Japan pursued imperialist policies in South East Asia in order to secure vital resources, and for the future too a question-mark must hang over Japanese intentions. Resentment has been building up among the Association of South East Asian nations, the view being expressed that Japan has been treating the countries as little more than colonies. But even developed countries such as Canada have expressed concern. Thus a Canadian government official has been quoted as saying that 'It is not much of an exaggeration to say that Japanese governments have looked upon Canada in recent years as a large open-pit mine; as an endless and reliable source of raw materials to satisfy the Japanese industrial appetite . . . it will be necessary for Japan to recognise the quality and the competence of Canada in a variety of economic and non-economic fields; to do more than, as is now the case, regard Canada primarily as an object of its "Resources Diplomacy". '[26] As the pace of Japanese direct investment abroad quickens, such issues seem likely to come increasingly to the fore.

(b) The state and the MNE

One important implication of the above concerns the extent to which the interests of the state and the MNE coincide over issues concerning exports, imports and investment income from abroad, or in the general requirement to ensure a favourable environment in foreign countries. A number of empirical studies which explore the relationship are examined in this section.

(i) Open door policies. The radical perspective on much of US foreign policy is expressed in Magdoff's claim that 'the underlying purpose (of imperialism) is nothing less than keeping as much as possible of the world *open* for trade and investment by the giant multinational corporations'.[27] The implications of this view are that political developments between the US and some regimes have a measurable impact on US trade and investment policies. Thus a move to the left in a regime results in policy changes by the US Government which reduces opportunities for trade and investment by US firms. A move to the right reverses the process and US Government and MNE interest revives.

In an attempt to test these general propositions, Rosen examined five Western-oriented LDCs which underwent significant internal political shifts between 1960 and 1972.[28] In establishing his hypotheses, Rosen stressed the explicit connections between official US foreign aid and private investment and trade, in that the former was designed to support and reinforce the latter. These links are reflected, for instance, in guarantees provided by the state to private firms against the risks involved in foreign investment. Some official statements go further in confirming the relationship between private and politically-sourced finance: 'The position to which the US and other developed countries adhere is that private foreign investment should be considered as development aid' (quoted from a US Senate Committee Report).[29] Again, the US Secretary to the Treasury, George Schultz, is quoted as saying: 'When (private investment) capital is rejected (by an LDC), we find it difficult to understand that official donors should be asked to fill the gap.'[30]

Figure 8.1 presents Rosen's evidence for Brazil. By the end of period 1 (1960) conditions most favourable to inward investment prevailed. These included unrestricted movement of foreign investment funds; unlimited repatriation of profits; and guaranteed free admission for equipment. Though brief, period 2 (under the left-wing Presidency of Quadros and Goulart), saw some important policy changes, resulting in the expropriation of an ITT subsidiary and the nationalisation of both Standard Oil and Shell. Following a military *coup d'état,* period 3 saw a further policy switch to encourage foreign investment, with a commitment being made to the US government to pay compensation for expropriations. The resultant surge of investment from abroad led to foreign firms controlling 62 per cent of foreign trade and 40 per cent of the capital market by 1968. In summary the Brazilian figures, especially on investment and trade, are fairly consistent with expected relationships: US exports and direct investment increased significantly during the years when favourable policies were being pursued by Brazil and declined when a left-wing regime was in power; the pattern of US economic and military aid to Brazil is not so clear, for during the 'half closed' period the level of aid from America was at least as high as during the open periods, whereas the Rosen hypothesis would indicate a positive correlation between aid, investment and trade. With regard to the total study, Rosen concluded that for the five countries (including Indonesia, Chile, Greece and Peru) actual movements of investment, trade and aid tended to behave as predicted by radical theory, although there were some unexplained changes. It was stressed, even so, that the causal and motivational aspects of the theory could not be confirmed or denied by such simple tests.

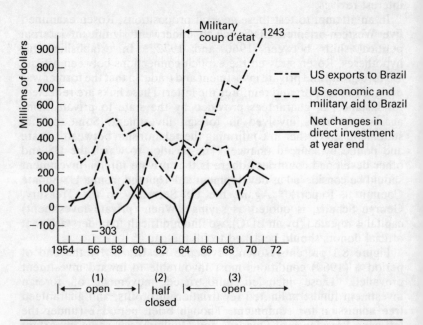

Fig. 8.1 US direct investment in Brazil, and exports and military aid to Brazil (*Source*: Rosen in Rosen and Kurth, 1974. p. 122).

(ii) The military and the MNE. Numerous propositions have been advanced to trace this relationship. One of the most basic, if informal, hypotheses is that US Governments have a vested interest in imperialist policies because of the correlation between periods of fairly high military expenditure and periods of relatively high levels of aggregate demand in the US economy. The MNE is linked into this process either by having close interests in arms-related expenditure, or through a general involvement in the politics of aid and investment as discussed above. In the empirical attempts to explore this general hypothesis, it has again been easier to show coincidence of certain variables rather than offer conclusive evidence that imperialism has been designed for high military spending.

Table 8.3 Relation between US military assistance given to and US private direct investment in nations*

US military assistance	US private direct investment $0–25 m.	$25–300 m.	$300+ m.	n‡
$0–8 m.	79	43	19	71
$8–656 m.	14	38	63	33
$656+ m.	8	19	19	15
Total†	100	100	100	119
n‡	66	37	16	119

* Entries show percentage of the 119 nations in the study (all of which were independent as of 1965). Total US military assistance (1950–65) and US private direct investment (1957) are both given in million dollars.
† Column totals may not sum to 100%, because of rounding.
‡ n shows number of countries.

(*Source:* Odell in Rosen and Kurth, 1974, p. 149.)

The work of Odell gives some important insights into the relationship between US military aid and private investment.[31] His hypothesis is, in fact, broader, *viz.* that the amount of US military assistance given to a country is positively related to the level of 'American economic interest', in which is included the importance of the country as a source of raw material imports, the level of foreign investment in the country, and the proportion of US trade conducted with the country. For the purpose of this study the investment findings in Table 8.3 are of particular note, in that they suggest some relationship in the expected direction at least during the Cold War years: of the 66 countries with a low level of inward investment, 52 (79 per cent) also received little military assistance from the US; these countries with low investment and low military aid (the upper left cell in Table 8.3) include Nigeria, Czechoslovakia and Burma. Conversely, 13 (83 per cent) of the 16 countries with substantial investments obtained high or intermediate levels of military assistance; included in this group are Peru, Brazil, UK, France and West Germany. To complete the picture, countries such as India and Spain fall into the cell showing medium levels of both aid and investment. Although these relationships, showing a correlation of military aid with economic interests, were confirmed when country size was included in the test, Odell invited cautious interpretation of the results, both because of data approximations and because he did not feel that they provided an unambiguous validation of the theory.

Other radical commentators have been less concerned to apply standard tests to data than they have been to show the identity of interests between major US enterprises and the military expenditure of the state. Thereafter inferences are drawn on a variety of imperialist propositions.[32] Thus Melman presents data on prime US Government military contracts and the principal contractors, an extract of which is shown in Table 8.4. While these are formally public companies, several largely operate on behalf of one customer (the US Government), and have very large parts of their production equipment actually owned by the US State. In 1967, for example, equipment in this category was valued at $114 million in General Electric and $79 million in General Dynamics. It is reasonable to assume that the form of 'state-management' prevailing in the US does mean that foreign policy, military aid and overseas investment are inextricably linked with the affairs of these companies. While the documented activities of Lockheed in particular have added fuel to radical allegations, it is not valid to conclude that in their overseas investment such companies are driven by imperialist motives. Indeed a number of them, particularly the aircraft firms, are not even multinationals in the sense of having manufacturing facilities in various countries; but they are all international companies operating on a world-wide scale. That the activities of such firms have been advanced by US foreign policy in the last 20 years is undeniable. As a corollary, the future shape of foreign policy will inevitably bear some relationship to the best interests of these particular corporations.

Table 8.4 US prime military contracts awards, 1961–67 (largest ten contractors)

	7 year total ($ m.)	% of total sales in period
Lockheed Aircraft	10,619	88
General Dynamics	8,824	67
McDonnell-Douglas	7,681	75
Boeing Co.	7,183	54
General Electric	7,099	19
North American-Rockwell	6,265	57
United Aircraft	5,311	57
American Telephone & Telegraph Co.	4,167	9
Martin-Marietta	3,682	62
Sperry-Rand	2,923	35

(*Source*: US Department of Defense, Directorate for Statistical Services, quoted by Melman, 1970, p. 77.)

(c) Dependence

There is fairly wide agreement that empirical evidence (see Chapter 5) does point to various conditions of 'dependence', especially between rich and poor countries. This is expressed, for example, in the LDCs' concentration on a narrow range of products, whether raw materials or manufactures; in their dependence upon a narrow range of buyers for their exports; in the high proportion of foreign trade in GNP; in the requirement for capital and manpower from developed economies; in the high level of service charges on loans when compared with receipts from exports and so on. Although some countries are less dependent on exports of primary commodities than in the past, others are still frighteningly reliant on one or a few basic commodities. The resultant inability of many LDCs to be able to plan within a reasonably extended time horizon is one of the most serious constraints on their development efforts. Table 8.5 illustrates this problem by relating the level of reserves in different countries to the annual value of their imports.

Table 8.5 Reserve holdings of primary producers

| | Primary producers of: | | | | | | | | |
	Tin	Coffee	Cocoa	Sugar	Rubber	Tea	Petroleum	Iron ore	Copper
Number of countries	5	12	6	5	4	2	10	6	4
Ratio of reserves to annual imports	48	.32	.29	.20	.44	.38	1.33	.16	.39

Note: The ratio of reserves to imports for groups of commodity-producing countries was derived from figures in International Monetary Fund, *International Financial Statistics,* 1972 Supplement.

(*Source:* Krasner in Rosen and Kurth, 1974, p. 187.)

Of the primary producing countries in this period, only those who were petroleum producers were left with flexibility in longer term planning, in that they were relatively unconstrained by the level of current export earnings. In other cases reserves were so low in relation to annual imports that any fall in current export earnings would pose very severe problems. Taking the example of the five sugar producers, the volume of reserves represented only 20 per cent of the annual value of imports, or expressed differently, reserves were adequate to finance 10 weeks' imports. The example of the copper producers is particularly interesting given the problems faced by Zambia (by far the largest copper producing country) during the late 1970s because of the slump in world copper prices. Precisely because of the low level of reserves, imports had to be severely restricted and the economy virtually ground to a halt. It is vital to note, of course, that the main production facilities in most of the countries concerned are owned by MNEs and that MNEs are also major purchasers at the next stage of distribution. It is not difficult to see therefore that there is scope for influencing the dependence of producing countries through pricing policies, decisions on production and extraction rates and so forth.

More generally, there are various possible ways in which foreign direct investment by MNEs may create or increase dependence. The centralisation of decision-making by MNEs can create a geographical hierarchy, within which some countries are unlikely ever to be able to make key decisions in MNE-controlled sectors. The MNE must thus be relied upon for technology, marketing and finance. Emerging from such relationships the MNE may indirectly maintain dependence since it may be in the interests of certain privileged groups in the LDCs to maintain their presence. Further, individual MNEs may pursue particular policies, for example, charging low export prices, paying a high level of dividends to the parent company and discouraging local competition, all of which in their various ways perpetuate dependence. These types of issues were reviewed in some detail in Chapter 5.

On a related point, Rosenstein-Rodan examined the hypothesis that the changed composition of the foreign capital inflow to Latin America (from loans and portfolio investment in the nineteenth century to private direct investment in the twentieth) brought with it a requirement to transfer a higher proportion of profits to the source of funds.[33] The evidence seemed to support the hypothesis; and although it was not possible to draw final conclusions, the author suggested that as the scarcity of technological know-how in LDCs was reducing, a large volume of equity investment may be a relatively costly way of achieving development. Moreover, because it required higher returns it may actually maintain dependence by making less capital available for local activity.

The introduction of standard MNE 'packages' of finance, technology, management and so on, irrespective of the stage of development of the economy, may also increase dependence in absolute terms. This is on the assumption that the recipient country could have been more autonomous by separate purchase of the component parts of the package. This is not only an LDC problem. Canada is one of the most extreme cases of a developed nation with dependency problems. Over 80 per cent of output in sectors such as electrical machinery, chemicals, rubber and transport equipment is accounted for by the largest MNEs. In many such cases the costs of reducing dependence may be very high, although this is not always the position. Taking the computer industry in Europe as an example, it is clear that while market penetration by MNEs is high, local capacity could readily be expanded under appropriate conditions to recapture the market.

One of the most difficult dependency propositions to test is the relationship between foreign direct investment and cultural dependence (i.e. the demonstration effect – the 'Coca-Cola culture' effect). While there is ample general evidence that cultural transference is associated with trade, communications and industrialisation, the link with foreign direct investment is more difficult to verify. One recent study of 48 developing countries which each had at least $1 m. of US manufacturing direct investment did attempt this.[34] It was tentatively concluded that there was a relationship between the levels of consumption of expensive consumer durables (in this case cars and TVs) and the advertising intensity of the foreign direct investment in the countries concerned. It is debatable however whether this actually represents a test of the cultural dependence hypothesis and there are problems in distinguishing cause and effect.

It is at least possible to hypothesise that the growing strength of some governments in LDCs might result in economic and political action which could counter the power of the MNE and so reduce dependence. Reference to two representative studies suggests that such host government action may be countered by the multinationals. One of these examined the way in which wealth deprivation policies (including war, taxation, expropriation etc.) of host governments had influenced Standard Oil and Shell over the period 1918–69.[35] The conclusion was that in spite of some important actions against them, the companies had been very resilient when faced with hostile government policies and had invariably adapted their operations and returned to plan fairly quickly. In another examination of MNEs in the natural resources industries, some interesting examples were provided of the ways in which international companies have developed strategies designed to protect themselves against nationalisation.[36] These include the practice (especially by international copper companies) of raising capital from the host government, from customers and from international financial institutions, with repayments to be made from output. Policies of this type in effect cement any relationships of dependence which might exist. It is, however, clearly difficult to generalise from case-by-case studies. As Chapter 6 has indicated there are plenty of individual countries which have used their powers of regulation to the full in order to tackle dependence problems, some of them with notable success.

(d) Exploitation

In trying to devise measures of exploitation, problems arise in establishing what is 'fair', or 'reasonable' in MNE behaviour. This will vary according to perspective. For example, a radical viewpoint such as that taken by Emmanuel would contend that exploitation is inherent in trade relations.[37] His 'unequal exchange' thesis is based on the view that poor countries, simply because they have relatively low wage levels, export at prices which reflect these levels. On the basis of comparative input costs, the poorer countries' prices must be lower than those for products from developed countries and hence trade is inevitably imperialist. Even Emmanuel would concede that both parties might nevertheless gain from trade, although in unequal proportions.

Taking a more orthodox point of departure, exploitation in this context could be regarded as meaning that most of the value (or benefit) from an investment or trading relationship accrues to the MNE. Accepting the limitations of such a definition, exploitation could show itself in a range of ways, including inefficient use of resources in a host country; too rapid development of primary resources; underpayment for local factors (labour and land and possibly capital); and a wide variety of individual corporation malpractices involving the misuse of economic power, 'political' activity and so on.

In reviewing a number of African cases, Schatz illustrates various exploitive practices pursued by foreign companies.[38] These cover instances of gross overpricing for equipment and construction projects in Ghana, Nigeria and Sierra Leone; the provision of credit from foreign suppliers at excessive interest rates and short pay-off periods; and overcharging for managerial services provided by MNEs on government-sponsored projects. A large volume of such work has been undertaken, especially by radical LDC economists which, although often qualitative, does point to issues of substance.

On a more formal basis, Moran developed a model for the study of exploitation in natural resource investments and applied it to the activities of the Anaconda and Kennecott Corporations in the Chilean copper industry.[39] In the early years of copper development, the corporations clearly undertook considerable risks. But because the Chilean government was inexperienced in handling MNEs, between 1913 and 1924, Braden (Kennecott's subsidiary) paid under 1 per cent of the value of gross sales in taxes. As the host country's bargaining skills and experience in operating concessions increased, the 'exploitation' potential decreased. By the end of the Second World War, the corporations faced an effective tax rate of 80 per cent. As Moran points out in his general model, exploitation may require an element of complicity on the part of elite groups in the host country, who (as in the Chilean case) exert pressures in different directions according to their interests. Aside from the Chilean example, other countries in the Third World have also shown that taxation policies can be used to reduce the economic rents which accrue to MNEs in natural resource extraction. One of the most comprehensive studies, relating to the petroleum and mineral industries, is that by Mikesell.[40] His work highlights the movements in the balance of power between MNEs and host countries, the end results of which may have been reduced potential for some of the more overt forms of exploitation of former periods. The problem for LDCs pursuing these tactics is that the multinationals concerned may react by withdrawing completely, to the detriment of the host country.

MNE imperialist behaviour: some cases

In recent years the activities of particular MNEs have demonstrated how economic power can be employed in a way which has imperialist overtones. Several of these cases are well documented and while not necessarily typical, are worthy of brief examination.

(a) ITT and Latin America

In several instances ITT has exerted specific political pressures in order to solve major business problems in certain Latin American countries. In 1965 the intention of the government of Peru to reorganise its telephone industry apparently led ITT to approach Dean

Rusk (Secretary of State) to request that the US Department of State might intervene at the highest level on behalf of the corporation.[41] Doubtless such communications are fairly typical, and would not attract undue attention were it not for the subsequent problems between the same corporation and the Chilean government in 1970–71. Official US Government enquiries on this latter case made the incident of international significance. From making suggestions to the US Government that the latter should intervene in the political affairs of Chile in order to prevent the Marxist Allende regime from coming to power, the corporation apparently became actively involved with the Central Intelligence Agency to implement its objective.[42] Thus the underlying economic motive, namely ITT's desire to preserve its interests in the Chilean telephone system, was to be achieved by bringing down the Government through economic sanctions, social disorder and a new regime. At the same time as ITT was working out its plan to overthrow Allende, corporation executives were going through the motions of negotiating a formula to permit the Chilean State to take over the ITT share in the Chilean telephone company. It is more than possible that the fundamental principles involved in this case and the publicity which it was given resulted in a re-examination of the *modus operandi* in a number of MNEs. Indeed this case was among those which were instrumental in initiating international moves towards codes of conduct and specific action against bribery activities.

(b) Lonrho

The activities of this British-based MNE which has widespread interests in industry, and particularly mining, in Africa, came into the public eye in April 1974. A series of board-room disagreements led to a large number of revelations concerning the affairs of the company. These included avoidance of UK taxation by directors through 'offshore' payments, the withholding of information from shareholders and board members, duplicity in dealing with black and white African countries, the breaking of economic sanctions taken by the United Nations against the illegal regime in Rhodesia and 'special payments' of £836,000 passing through the chief executive's personal account. Subsequent political concern in the UK led to an official enquiry into the company's affairs.[43] The inspectors' report, published in mid 1976, was highly critical of many aspects of the company's operations including transactions involving Rhodesian and South African copper mines. It also emphasised the active involvement of Roland ('Tiny') Rowland, the chief executive of Lonrho, in the politics of Africa. And the affair was given added publicity by the criticism of Mr Angus Ogilvy who was a director of the company but more important a member by marriage of the Royal Family: he was held to have been 'negligent in fulfilling his duties . . . to an extent that merits severe criticism'.[44] The whole affair raised many questions about the behaviour pattern of an MNE both as regards its shareholdings and its attitudes to the host nations within which it operated. As the UK Prime Minister of the day described it, Lonrho revealed 'the unacceptable face of capitalism'.

As a postscript to the Lonrho case, the Tanzanian Government decided in 1978 to expel Lonrho from Tanzania because of the nature of the company's activities in Southern Africa. The action was taken because the company had contravened the United Nations mandatory sanctions against Rhodesia and South Africa in spite of repeated assurances to the contrary given to black African states. Lonrho was forced to sell its assets in motor distribution and textiles to the state-run National Development Corporation in Tanzania at a 'fair price acceptable to the Government'.[45]

(c) Activities of the multinational oil corporations

Although the operations of the world's seven major oil corporations ('The Seven Sisters') had frequently been studied, the events immediately surrounding October 1973 raised new questions about their real and potential power. At this time and over the following months the Organisation of Petroleum Exporting Countries announced huge increases in the price of oil, cut output levels and introduced embargoes against America and Holland as a package of political and economic measures. While these dramatic OPEC initiatives appeared to show where the power truly lay, namely with a cartel of states, the ensuing events over the following four or five months gave enormous allocative discretion to the oil corporations. This happened by default since the consumer governments could not agree on a basis for rationing supplies, and left the allocation to the oil multinationals who then became the centre of debates on whether loyalties were to host or home nations. In the US, in particular, these events and the subsequent price rises coincided with announcements of record profits from the oil companies. The net result was a period of almost unprecedented public criticism about their activities. This culminated in a series of hearings by a Sub Committee of the Foreign Relations Committee which examined the strategies and tactics of the companies for the previous 20–30 years.[46] From a mass of evidence it became clear that the US Government had effectively delegated its responsibility for all supplies to the companies over a long period, on the assumption that private and public benefit coincided. Although a number of other issues concerning intercompany agreements, policies and methods of operation were examined, the major lesson was summarised by the committee as: 'In a democracy, important questions of policy with respect to a vital commodity like oil, the life-blood of an industrial society, cannot be left to private companies acting in accord with private interests and a closed circle of government officials.'[47] This example is important in that it emphasises that excessive MNE power is not simply a concern of poor nations. Clearly, supranationality goes far beyond that.

Because oil is so crucial a commodity, it is not surprising that the names of the multinational oil companies arise frequently in international affairs. The revelations which emerged over the involvement of Shell and BP in assisting the illegal regime in Rhodesia are an example of this. It appears that from the first days of Rhodesia's unilateral declaration of independence (UDI) in 1965 and the resultant imposition of sanctions, oil continued to flow through South Africa. The reason for this was that Shell and BP considered themselves bound by South African law which prohibited any attempt to control the destination of oil products sold by their subsidiaries in South Africa; the oil corporations argued that this South African law prevented them from complying with the UK sanctions order. The disturbing features of the case are firstly, that no information became available about the Shell and BP operation until 13 years after the initial imposition of sanctions, and secondly that the UK Government was apparently fully aware of 'sanctions busting' by the oil companies.

(d) Chrysler UK

This case is interesting because it again reveals the strength of the bargaining power that MNEs possess in their dealings with developed as well as underdeveloped countries. Chrysler UK, a subsidiary of the American Chrysler Corporation, had been consistently unprofitable. Between 1964 (when Chrysler took a minority holding in Rootes Motors) and 1975, the UK company made net losses of £69 m. In 1975 alone losses amounted to £35 m. The end result of this was that early in November 1975 Chrysler presented the UK Government with three options for the British subsidiary: liquidation by end January 1976; Chrysler to give the UK company to the Government; or Chrysler to transfer a majority interest (>80 per cent) to the Government. The UK Prime Minister said of the meeting: 'The Government were presented with a pistol to their head.'[48]

The UK Government was in an impossible situation: unemployment was already high and Chrysler's closure would have entailed direct and indirect job losses of 55,000 people; and the balance of payments was heavily in deficit, exacerbated by a very rapid rise in motor vehicle imports. The Government therefore had to persuade Chrysler to remain in Britain. Agreement was ultimately reached, with the Government committed to supporting Chrysler UK to the tune of £162.5 m. between 1976 and 1979 with no equity participation in the company, and with no assured long-term future for the firm. Chrysler, moreover, was being supported to compete with a state-owned motor company British Leyland, which itself was receiving a massive infusion of public money. By force of bargaining and skilful timing the corporation was able to extract support from the Government without reducing either its ownership stake in the subsidiary or operational control. Taken together, the whole case points to the ability of an MNE to find and exploit political pressure points.

That the Chrysler Corporation viewed the British Government with contempt was shown again in 1978, when the corporation sold off its entire European interests (including Chrysler UK) to the French group Peugeot-Citroen. The UK Government was given no prior warning of the proposed deal. This was in spite of the fact that loans had been made available by the Government to Chrysler to ensure the continued presence of the American corporation in Britain, and in spite of the corporation's commitment to a 'planning agreement' in the UK which should have involved the unions and the UK Government in any discussions which took place about the future of the UK affiliate.

(e) Lockheed Aircraft Corporation
The general issue of US and other multinational companies making improper payments overseas has been in the headlines frequently over the last few years. One of the first major cases was associated with the suicide of the chairman of United Brands in 1975, the corporation having paid $1.25 m. in bribes to a Honduran Government official in an attempt to bring down the export tax on bananas. Since then a number of US federal agencies and Congressional Committees have brought to light several similar bribery cases. These involved such names as Exxon which made payments in excess of $45 m. in recent years; Northrop, one of America's leading arms exporters, which paid out $130 m.; Gulf Oil, which paid $10 m., including $4 m. to help finance the re-election of President Park in South Korea; and Lockheed which disbursed over $24 m. Under US law such payments have now to be disclosed.

While it was technically legal for these companies to use funds to obtain business, the Lockheed case deserves special mention because of the position of individuals involved in foreign countries. Lockheed had admitted to such payments for a long period but struggled to avoid disclosure of the recipients' names because of the inevitable impact on future business. Information did become available, however, and this revealed extensive payments to senior individuals in Holland, Germany, Italy, Sweden and Japan. The revelations, early in 1976, resulted both in the resignations of the chairman and vice-chairman of Lockheed and in considerable political turmoil in some of the overseas countries concerned. These included the Dutch constitutional crisis over the alleged payment of $1.1 m. to Prince Bernhard (husband of Queen Juliana) in 1961–62 when the Lockheed F104 Starfighter was being sold to Holland. Similarly, it appeared that payments over a period of years had been made in Japan to a number of key officials, including the former prime minister.

As in the other payments' cases, fundamental issues of the use of economic power and the ethics of large business emerge. These do not only pertain to MNEs, but are emphasised in that context because they have important implications for the type of business–government relations which support oligopoly power.

Concluding remarks

The issues considered in the preceding pages, when taken in the context of earlier chapters, serve to highlight the fact that there is no possibility of a 'value-free' assessment of foreign direct investment. The more extreme views are never likely to converge. The reader is left with the problem of identifying the values underlying any analysis of the MNE, given that these are rarely defined and stated explicitly. More commonly the reader is likely to be presented with an implicit argument without any real knowledge of the positions of the protagonists. This criticism applies particularly, though by no means exclusively, to some of the weaker radical contributions. On the other hand, on occasion, the orthodox studies are equally open to criticism for the narrowness of their empirical focus.

Having said this, the present chapter is extremely important in drawing attention to the fact that multinational activity must be assessed in political and social as well as in economic terms. As has been pointed out: 'Politics and economics are interwoven strands in the fabric of the world order . . . An international economic system is affected by the international political system existing at the time, and vice versa. The behaviour of governments on economic issues will be affected by their political calculations, which will in turn be determined in part by the structure of world politics. At the same time, political steps by governments must often rest on economic capabilities.'[49] These interrelationships, of course, make it extremely difficult to separate cause and effect at an empirical level, a point which has been noted at various times in the chapter. However, it is not necessary to accept the close relationships postulated by the radicals between, say, military activities and foreign direct investment, to admit that some association whether planned or unplanned is entirely feasible and, indeed, likely. Similarly no matter which way causation runs, the issues are still important. The case studies quoted above perhaps make this point particularly clear: the spectacular example of ITT's involvement in Chile reveals that economic power can readily be used for political ends. For these reasons the present chapter is a vital input to the study of the economics of multinational enterprise. It is also a necessary prelude to the final chapter of this book which looks to the future, with economic power and the ownership of MNEs becoming more diffuse but with possibly fewer signs of changes in political and military strength.

Further reading

1. For one of the most convincing statements of the global neo-classical position see **H. G. Johnson,** *International Economic Questions Facing Britain, the United States and Canada in the 1970s,* London: British-North American Research Association, June 1970. For a lucid exposition of the *dependencia* model see **O. Sunkel,** 'Big business and dependencia: a Latin American view', *Foreign Affairs,* **50,** April 1972,

pp. 517–31. A comprehensive examination of the alternative global neo-classical, *dependencia* and mercantilist models for the future is provided in a paper by **R. Gilpin,** 'Three models of the future', in C. F. Bergsten and L. B. Krause (eds), *World Politics and International Economics,* Washington: Brookings Institution, 1975, Section 1, Ch. 2. See also Section 3 of this book for three useful papers on broad economic trading relationships affecting the MNE.

2. For a good contemporary survey of imperialism, see: **A. Lauterbach,** 'Changing Concepts of Imperialism', *Weltwirtschaftliches Archiv,* **113** (2), 1977, pp. 322–347; and **B. J. Cohen,** *The Question of Imperialism,* London: Macmillan, 1973. The book of readings edited by Radice is also very useful: see **H. Radice** (ed.), *International Firms and Modern Imperialism,* Harmondsworth: Penguin Books, 1975. The paper by **Stephen Hymer,** 'The multinational corporation and the law of uneven development', is reprinted in this volume (pp. 37–62); and the two following articles by **C. Palloix** and **G. Ádám** also refer specifically to the MNE. The involvement of ITT and the Kennecott Copper Corporation in Chile is highlighted in Salvador Allende, 'Speech to the United Nations', pp. 233–47, a speech made less than a year before Allende's death and the overthrow of his government by a military *coup d'état.*

3. The section on the empirical evidence relating to foreign direct investment and imperialism draws extensively on **S. J. Rosen** and **J. R. Kurth** (eds), *Testing Theories of Economic Imperialism,* Lexington, Mass.: D. C. Heath, 1974, which should be consulted on this topic.

4. For a good review of the material available on MNEs in LDCs, and the varying interpretations put on the data, see **S. Lall,** 'Less developed countries and private foreign direct investment: a review article', *World Development,* **2,** No. 4 and 5, April–May 1974, pp. 43–8.

5. In order to balance the coverage in this chapter and consider a full statement of the position in favour of private direct investment in LDCs, see **G. L. Reuber** *et al., Private Foreign Investment in Development,* Oxford: Clarendon Press, 1973.

Questions for discussion

1. Examine the basic premises which underly the different economic perspectives on the MNE. To what degree is there any common ground among them?
2. Assess the extent to which the theories of foreign direct investment discussed in Chapter 2 embrace the motivations for expansion postulated by radical commentators.
3. Comment on the validity of the following quotation (Lauterbach, 1977): 'Essentially all the specific charges (relating to foreign direct investment and imperialism), no matter how justified they may be objectively in a given case, merely reflect the deeper reasons for the prevailing resentment: (economic) nationalism.'
4. Critically evaluate the usefulness of Cohen's model of dependency in understanding the political economy of Canada or Mexico.
5. 'In LDCs the principal product of foreign direct investment is poverty.' Discuss.
6. Establish a series of tests which could provide widely acceptable measures of exploitation by MNEs. (Assume total access to both corporate and government data.)

The future of the MNE:
a critical appraisal

Summary

1. The global neo-classical, radical and mercantilist models offer extreme predictions for the future – ranging from a world economy organised and controlled by MNEs to a world in which multinational firms become fragmented on a regional basis.
2. Although the predictions are unrealistic, the models are valuable in highlighting the emergence of certain new international economic issues. These, and other important issues which will influence the future operations of MNEs, include:

Proposals for a New International Economic Order. The far-reaching NIEO proposals for international economic reform will not be implemented. Even so, they are indicative of a new mood within Third World countries, which, at the least, may be reflected in greater unilateral regulation of MNEs.

Improvements in East–West economic relations. Growing opportunities exist for Western companies with the growth of East–West trade. The characteristics of MNEs – in terms of size, access to capital and world-wide distribution networks, flexibility and experience in operating with foreign partners – place them in a particularly favourable position to benefit.

International trade and monetary issues. Protectionist forces, reflected in a growth of non-tariff barriers, are evident throughout the world economy, which may have a significant impact on multinational operations. 'Defensive' foreign investment may be encouraged, but intra-MNE trade will be hampered.

Changing distribution of power. The United States' economic position within the world economy has declined, although it has remained militarily the most powerful state. This is relevant both to the future of US MNEs; and to the expansion of non-US multinationals which do not have the support of substantial foreign aid and military expenditures from their home governments.

Regional economic cooperation. The proposed enlargement of the EEC and possible developments in economic cooperation elsewhere in the world offer both improved market prospects for MNEs and improved bargaining power for the participating host countries.

Resource shortages.   Although the widely forecast growth of producer cartels has not materialised, the prospect of long-term resource shortages will inevitably strengthen the bargaining power of host economies *vis-à-vis* MNEs.
3. Overall, a restrictive world economic environment seems likely to exist in the immediate future. In spite of the global efficiency gains to be achieved by international action to introduce controls or to remove imperfections, national regulation of the MNE seems certain to be the most prevalent form of control. Changes in the economic environment may mean even fewer areas of open access for MNEs, as home and host countries seek to maximise their net gains from foreign direct investment. MNEs will require increased flexibility to meet the varying demands of nation states and the end result is likely to be a slower growth of direct foreign investment. The net effect will be that global economic efficiency will be retarded to the detriment of all countries.

In this, the final chapter of the book, the aim is to try to outline some alternative views of the future of the multinational enterprise. The various perspectives on the MNE which were noted in Chapter 8 offer not only different interpretations of the present, but also divergent views of the future. The present chapter begins with a discussion and critique of these predictions. Thereafter, in order to maintain the perspective taken throughout the rest of the book, the future of the MNE is evaluated from what has been termed the contemporary orthodox standpoint. To do this, the various conclusions reached regarding the efficiency of the MNE, the impact of multinationals on home and host nations, the need for and effects of national and international forms of control, etc. are drawn together. These conclusions are then set alongside the changing international economic and political environment under which MNEs seem likely to operate into the 1980s and beyond, to suggest an alternative scenario for the future.

Some alternative models of the future of the MNE[1]

The global neo-classical model

The explicit ineffectiveness of the nation state as a unit for control of resources which lies at the root of this model, leads to international economic problems being best solved by a world federal government. This is a world in which there is an irreversibility in the intermeshing of economic interests between countries and a recognition of the benefits accruing from MNEs' coordinating resources. The nation states are assumed to recognise that MNEs can relieve them of many of their economic responsibilities, and to find that MNEs will in general act in the interests of both the nation state and world order. By an unspecified process these two sets of interests, national and international, are assumed to coincide in the long run.

Some very dramatic changes are required in international relations in order to give credence to this model. More immediately, however, there are signs that its basic assumptions are open to question. It is hypothesised that bargaining advantages will always be on the side of the MNE rather than the nation state, and because of this nations would have to pay a high economic price to reassert their sovereignty. It is believed therefore that governments would shrink from driving out multinationals and regaining their sovereignty simply because this would mean lower standards of living, higher unemployment and the like. In reality, economic nationalism in developed countries and, especially, in LDCs has often outweighed any disadvantages associated with reduced MNE activity, and many nation states have shown a determination to choose their own route in development. Moreover, the 1973 oil crisis showed the power of host nations when faced with MNEs, and reminded both parties that the growth of MNEs has been dependent on favourable political environments. It is certainly true that some host countries actively compete with each other by offering attractive incentives to attract multinational investment; but equally, most countries try to regulate the ownership and behaviour of MNE affiliates in their own interests by means of a wide variety of controls.

Perhaps the strongest challenge to this view of the future lies in the changing composition of foreign direct investment. When so predominantly sourced from the US, direct investment overseas was undoubtedly related to that country's widespread political and military influence. However, much of the major new MNE activity from Japan and Western Europe has little political back-up and the home nations concerned have not as yet been prepared to take on wider world roles. The ensuing growth of competition among MNEs for markets in host nations, taken together with policies of national self interest, point to a quite different future and one far removed from harmony of interests.

Radical models

Since much radical writing is couched in terms of historical determinism, the theoretical contributions examined previously all have a predictive element which implicitly or explicitly involve the MNE. These range widely, from the belief that cyclical crises and social disorder will lead to a transition to a socialist scheme of organising production, to the contention that a new world order of dominance and dependence is emerging with the MNE as its focal point.

One of the most lucid statements of this position is to be found in Hymer who saw the operation of two Marxist-based principles as crucial in determining the future impact of the MNE.[2] One is the law of increasing firm size, that is, the tendency for firms to grow from the workshop to the factory to the national, and subsequently to the multidivisional and multinational scale of operations. The other is the law of uneven development, namely the tendency for the international economy to produce wealth and poverty, development and underdevelopment. Operating together, these two laws are seen to result in a hierarchical division of labour within the firm and in the centralisation of decision making in a few key cities in developed nations. To Hymer, income, status, authority and consumption patterns would all radiate out from these centres along a declining curve, thus perpetuating inequality. MNEs thus would continue to generate dependence and there would be a strong tendency towards coordinated action in their exploitation of the periphery.

Writers in the radical tradition face the familiar basic dilemma of trying to predict where power will lie between the MNE and the state, and between MNEs of different origins. As Rowthorn summarises the debates, the particular differences of opinion concern the relative strength of US capital and hence its ability to dominate Europe and Japan; and the nature and severity of the antagonisms between capital of different national origins.[3] For example, if US capital does dominate in a super-imperialism, the existing MNE pattern will be reinforced. The alternative view is that US hegemony will be effectively challenged by Europe and Japan, resulting in an imperialism wracked by internal contradictions.[4]

Perhaps the major weakness of all these models is their assumption of the passivity of the so-called periphery of host nations. There is now ample evidence that many are less pliable when faced with corporate pressures than they once were. Moreover, it would appear that natural resource shortages may continue to have the effect of adjusting the global balance of economic power in favour of some parts of the periphery.[5] Effectively used, there is scope for using this power to redefine the terms on which MNEs have access to nation states. Clearly the days of open, unrestricted host economies are past.

Models which view the future as being strongly influenced by collective action by the industrial powers have to make particular assumptions about common interests which may be invalid. Western Europe, US and Japan are already involved in active competition for their respective domestic markets. Protectionism, concerns over economic growth, the balance of payments and currency stability, together with political chauvinism, are all real or potential causes for disharmony among the principal source nations.

It would nevertheless be naive to suggest that dependence will not continue to be a by-product (albeit unplanned) of MNE activity or that distortions will no longer occur in host economies. Whether or not foreign direct investment is beneficial or exploitive will continue to depend on the type and volume of investment, its terms and the policies of the host government. The opportunities for change rest simply in the potential alteration of the balance of power. On the other hand, the radicals would argue that this could do no more than bring the flow of capital *out* of the host countries closer into line with that put *into* such economies by MNEs, rather than redress the balance completely. And it would probably be added that any change in the balance of power could only be short term. The periphery might become less peripheral (in Marxist terms) but could never become central.

The mercantilist model

The mercantilist world of the future would require basic changes in the operations of the MNE. A malevolent form of mercantilism would result in each grouping of nations being in serious conflict with the other over issues relating to international trade and investment, exchange rates and the balance of payments. The beggar-thy-neighbour practices of the 1930s would be widespread. Protectionist policies could in turn require the fragmentation of MNEs and a redirection of investment policies in order to gain access to markets. A more benign form of mercantilism would present the MNE with a world in which regional blocs would act to attempt to stabilise the world economic system. The ensuing increase in economic and political interdependence would bring both advantage and disadvantage. The advantage might lie in established affiliates having access to larger markets, while disadvantages could lie in exclusion from other regional groups offering markets, materials and perhaps more optimal manufacturing locations.

This model assumes a significant and permanent decline in the central role of the US in the world economy. While it is probably indeed true that the US can no longer afford to run very large balance of payments deficits to support political commitments abroad, purchase foreign assets and simultaneously pursue policies for domestic full employment, it does not immediately follow that there is an obvious alternative to the US. Europe and Japan for example have grown in economic strength, but Europe is still politically divided; and both areas depend on the US for security. US MNEs may thus continue to have powerful advantages over their rivals in many national states. Moreover, the growth of European and Japanese MNEs also provides the home governments of these multinationals with a valid interest in maintaining an economic order favourable to foreign direct investment.

Where this model is particularly useful is in emphasising the need to consider the future of the MNE within the broader framework of changes in world political movements. MNEs are sensitive to political climates, especially in their long-run planning. But they are also capable of flexibility and ingenuity, which could enable them to benefit from changes which might occur within a world moving in a mercantilist direction.

Comments on the alternative models

There is no doubt that the models considered in the preceding paragraphs focus attention on some important trends within the international economy. The moves towards protectionism can be seen throughout the world and present a major challenge to the liberal international economic system which held sway for twenty-five years following the Second World War. Similarly the European and Japanese expansion and the emergence of the oil-producing states has created a more heterogeneous group of major economic powers. Furthermore the continuing and perhaps increasing income inequality between rich and poor countries, and the dependence of the latter states, is brought out clearly in the radical models; while the refusal of the Third World nations to accept this state of affairs means that international economic reform, through the forum of the United Nations, etc. will be blocked unless the interests of these countries are explicitly taken into account. The future of the MNE will be influenced by all these and other factors.

The individual models formulated, however, concentrate on an over-narrow range of issues. The global neo-classical model may be accepted insofar as it highlights the role of the MNE in producing a more efficient world-wide allocation of resources. But the step which follows from this, namely, that optimality will be produced in a world which is regulated by the multinational enterprise, is not plausible. The pursuit of private benefit will still lead to unacceptable social costs being incurred without national or international controls. Moreover, the model fails to take account of political realities. The radical view may be embraced insofar as it identifies power, abuse and dependence. It is considered suspect in its underlying determinism and in the way it discounts the emerging political and economic strength of the periphery. The mercantilist perspective is credible in so much as it identifies a resurgence of economic nationalism and protectionism, but less so in its predictions on the extent to which this has changed or will change the world economic order in the short term.

In formulating a more comprehensive view of the future of the MNE, the remainder of the chapter attempts to summarise the economic benefits and costs which have been shown in this book to accrue from multinational activity – taking the perspective of world economic welfare and home and host country interests. It is the balance of benefits and costs to the different parties which will determine whether their approach to MNEs will be in harmony or in conflict. The changes in the international economy are then superimposed upon this framework to provide a considered alternative perspective on the MNE.

A further assessment of the future of the MNE[6]

The impact of multinational firms

(a) *Global effects*[7]

In various chapters of the book the question has been raised as to whether or not MNEs operate so as to enhance world economic efficiency and welfare. The conclusion that has been reached from both theoretical and empirical standpoints is that the MNE may have negative as well as positive effects on world welfare, and that on balance the position remains uncertain. On the positive side, it seems likely that the operations of MNEs have resulted in an increase in the volume of world investment, implying a higher rate of real savings with MNEs than without. In particular there is evidence that 'export platform' type investment mainly supplements domestic investment. But because there are redistributional effects to be taken into consideration, an increased global level of investment does not necessarily mean higher world welfare. With respect to economic efficiency, the fundamental case in favour of foreign direct investment is that when the MNE package is transferred to a host country, where it is combined with lower cost indigenous inputs, then there is an improvement in the international allocation of resources. In this way direct investment abroad may be considered as performing the same function as international trade, but operating through factor flows rather than goods flows. In addition it is argued that by internalising market imperfections MNEs produce a more efficient distribution of resources, and their ability to take a global perspective and engage in world-wide scanning may also improve resource allocation internationally. Further ways in which MNEs may improve international economic efficiency include: the favourable effects of training programmes for employees in host nations; technology-transfer linkages with local suppliers and customers; the stimulus to competition in host country markets; and the realisation of economies of scale in managerial functions and R & D. And because MNEs may be able to ensure full appropriability of the returns to investment in new information, a greater incentive will exist to undertake R & D programmes; in this way world-wide R & D expenditures may be increased.

On the negative side, there is the alternative view that MNEs themselves create market imperfections and thereby distort resource allocation. Since they generally operate in oligopolistic markets, MNEs may exploit patent protection, raise entry barriers and operate a variety of restrictive practices. Moreover, 'follow-the-leader' type investment strategies by MNEs may create excess capacity and thereby waste resources; while other investments made to protect an oligopolistic position or in response to trade barriers may not complement the comparative advantage of home and host countries and may therefore be equally detrimental to international resource allocation. Similarly manipulative transfer pricing may distort the allocative mechanism. Finally, multinational firms may be able to by-pass government regulations designed to stimulate competition and efficiency and circumvent market mechanisms.[8] In spite of this it seems likely that MNEs have improved world-wide economic efficiency.

(b) *Host country effects.*[9]

Irrespective of the global economic effects of foreign direct investment, the operations of MNEs have not had an equal impact on all countries. The net outcome of the activities of multinational firms on recipient countries will be determined by four sets of factors: resource transfer effects, trade and balance of payments effects, competitive/anti-competitive effects and sovereignty/autonomy effects. With respect to resource transfer effects, the foreign firm may make a positive contribution through the supply of capital, technology and management. There may also be net balance of payments gains if the capital inflow and the export performance of the MNE affiliate offsets remittances back to the parent company and imports of finished and unfinished goods, capital equipment, etc. Again, in the same way that MNEs may increase global efficiency by stimulating competition and inducing greater efficiency among rival firms, so there may be positive efficiency gains for the host country.

The one area where losses are inevitably involved is that of sovereignty: inward foreign investment necessarily entails some loss of independence for the receiving countries, given that ultimate decision-making rests with the parent corporation. Nevertheless, in each of the other broad categories of effects too, a negative impact may be nearly as likely as a positive impact, depending on the particular circumstances. Some of the empirical evidence quoted in Chapter 5, for example, indicated negative balance of payments effects for 5 out of 6 host developing countries studied. In general, it seems likely that foreign direct investment has had, on aggregate, a net beneficial effect in terms of national income, jobs and government revenues particularly in developed host countries; in the LDCs the balance between positive and negative effects may be much finer in many instances. The crucial factor in assessing the contribution of MNEs is the assumption of what would have happened if the investment had not been made: if local entrepreneurs could not have undertaken the investment then a gain in capital formation has occurred, which in turn leads to positive conclusions about the impact of foreign direct investment on income and employment in the host countries. Similarly on the balance of payments side, the outcome is dependent again on issues such as whether or not the goods would have had to be imported, if the investment had not been made.

There is one other issue which needs to be considered and this relates to host country objectives. Even if direct investment leads to gains in, say, the rate of economic growth and the level of income in a recipient country, this may be unacceptable to the state concerned if the country is pursuing a different or wider set of development goals. If economic independence and an equitable distribution of income rate highly as national objectives, then clearly there is a much greater likelihood of the host country viewing the effects of foreign direct investment as adverse. Arising from this, there is then a higher probability of controls being imposed over inward investment and the activities of MNE affiliates.

(c) *Home country effects*[10]

The literature relating to the impact of outward direct investment on home countries has tended to distinguish between short- and long-run effects. The latter relate to the effects on home country national income and output. Income and output gains will be derived from higher returns on capital or technology, expressed in terms of repatriated profits and royalties from affiliates, lower-priced imports or higher-priced exports. Home government revenues may also rise due to taxes on foreign source income. Finally, the labour force allocation may be improved as employment demands change in favour of highly skilled professional and managerial jobs. The theoretical conclusion on outward investment is, however, that over-investment abroad may take place from the standpoint of the home country interest; and the limited evidence from the United States is that, overall, foreign investment has led to a small loss of output and, more importantly, to a redistributional shift in domestic income away from labour and towards capital.

In any event, more concern has been expressed in home countries about the short-run impact of outward investment. It has been argued that adverse effects may arise in the following areas: balance of payments (although this is less of a concern under the present floating exchange rate system); level of employment, through the displacement of production jobs; erosion of capital and technological advantages, meaning that the international competitiveness of the country's manufacturing base is reduced; tax fiddling through the use of tax havens, transfer pricing and tax holidays offered by host countries; circumvention of domestic economic policies, meaning difficulties in the attainment of national objectives; and abuse of economic and non-economic power. Some of these concerns are particularly marked in the United States. On the tax issue, for example, it is argued that the tax deferral provisions encourage MNEs to engage in a variety of shady practices and indeed provide a specific incentive to make investment abroad rather than in the US. The types of concern expressed have changed over time and differ as between home countries – in the United Kingdom the job displacement argument is crucial and balance of payments issues are more important than elsewhere – but the end result is again the regulation of foreign direct investment.

Conflict, bargaining and regulation[11]

Considering only the global impact of multinational corporations, if the ultimate goal was that of world-wide economic efficiency then international regulation of MNEs would be required. As previous comments have indicated, MNEs have certain adverse effects on international resource allocation, and these could only be solved through international action designed to introduce controls or to remove imperfections. Thus coordinated action would be required in respect of monopoly and restrictive practices, pollution, etc. Moreover, tariff and non-tariff barriers, subsidies, exchange controls and so forth would have to be abolished. Profits' tax rates would have to be the same in all countries, as would accounting standards and income reporting techniques. Even then, to achieve world-wide optimum welfare, an international budgetary mechanism would be required to ensure that the countries gaining from foreign direct investment compensated the losers. It is fairly evident that these requirements are utopian in the extreme. Nevertheless the sub-optimality of the alternative, namely that of national regulation, is well recognised – witness the attempts by the OECD, the United Nations and other bodies to introduce international codes of conduct. Equally there is an awareness in both home and host countries that uncoordinated national controls are a fertile breeding ground for the financial and other manipulations which MNEs are uniquely in a position to operate. And there is a realisation that over-restrictive legislation – analogous to the impact of tariff and non-tariff barriers in international trade – is a form of protectionism which will lower the overall world volume of foreign direct investment to the detriment of all countries.

World-wide efficiency considerations are thus one constraint on the actions of national governments. But maximum global gains are not the only factor, and alongside this numerous other criteria may be used by governments in assessing the desirability or otherwise of foreign direct investment. Included in a government's objective function might be growth, full employment, income distribution, price stability, the quality of life, economic independence, and economic security. Given this situation, there are many potential areas of conflict between governments and multinational corporations, as the latter pursue possibly quite different objective functions. Taking only the balance of payments issue, a host government will be interested in as high a financial capital inflow as possible to establish the particular MNE project concerned, and thereafter is concerned to minimise the import bill (by local sourcing of components, material inputs, etc.), to minimise remittances, and to maximise export receipts. For its part, the MNE may be interested in financing as much as possible of the project locally; it may also prefer its parent company or other MNEs as suppliers for reasons relating to price, quality or delivery dates; while in addition, on the export side, host government pressures may conflict with the MNE's plans for the world-wide division of markets between subsidiaries. Conflict does not only occur between MNEs and host governments. Home governments also have balance of payments objectives which may or may not coincide with the plans of the multinational. And, of course, regulations imposed by home and host governments to control their respective balance of payments may then produce inter-country conflict. To give one illustration, the United Kingdom as home to MNEs requires the repatriation of two-thirds of foreign earnings each year and, except under special circumstances, effectively forces companies to rely on overseas borrowings for financing their direct investment abroad. It is not difficult to see that conflicts may arise when host countries introduce other legislation to limit remittances and the raising of capital locally. In addition, differences in regulations between host countries themselves may produce conflict as the countries compete for the favours of the multinational.[12]

In inter-country conflicts, however, MNEs may merely be pawns in what is a much wider game than that relating to foreign investment alone. And MNEs may have many areas of common interest with their home government. The main direct area of tension is, therefore, that which exists between MNEs and host governments. The outcome of the conflicts will be reflected in extreme cases in expropriation (by the host country) or divestment (by the MNE), but more usually economic conflict will end in economic compromise. The outcome of the bargaining process by which an agreeable compromise is reached will depend upon the negotiating strengths of the respective parties which in turn will reflect their economic leverage. As has been suggested, the host country's leverage will be substantial when (a) its domestic market is large and rapidly growing; (b) its local resources are valuable and the local policy climate is favourable; and (c) a large number of viable options are open to the country, but few options are available to the MNE.[13] Conversely, the MNEs' leverage will be high when (a) the economic value of the package offered is substantial, and (b) the options open to the company are numerous but the host country has few viable options. The bargaining process by which a compromise is achieved may either be explicit or implicit. Thus some host countries may operate an investment screening agency which actually involves itself in bargaining over terms of entry, forms of ownership, and behavioural controls. Alternatively, states may simply introduce legislation and apply it across the board to all prospective investors. But because the acceptability of the regulations to MNEs will be reflected in the volume of investment attracted, host states will be able to judge whether or not the controls need to be loosened or tightened and thus an implicit bargaining process may take place.

Virtually all countries now operate some kind of control mechanism in the attempt to maximise the net benefits (both short- and long-term) from foreign direct investment. 'Benefit', of course, may mean different things to different countries depending upon the weighting that is attached to various national objectives. The end result may be that host governments make quite different judgements on the role which MNEs can play in their economy. As a result, some – such as Tanzania at present – will effectively reject direct investment; others – such as Taiwan and Singapore – will base much of their development on it. Similarly the types of controls operated may vary widely: many countries insist on local equity participation, the most noteworthy being the 'fade-out provisions' which apply within the Andean Common Market; a country such as the Philippines relies primarily on entry controls; other nations bar foreign investors from a range of sectors. In general multinationals face a substantially more restrictive regulatory environment in less developed than in developed countries, and in a few of the latter states, such as West Germany and the UK, there is still a widespread belief that a liberal and relaxed policy will maximise the benefits from inward direct investment.

An interim view of the future

Most of these controls represent moves away from the requirements for international economic efficiency, and thus will adversely affect global resource allocation. But because MNEs are a vehicle for overcoming market imperfections – including imperfections derived from uncoordinated policies towards foreign direct investment – then the allocational losses will be less than might be anticipated. In any event, as indicated, global economic efficiency will be only one criterion by which host (and home) countries determine their policies towards foreign direct investment. National controls are, and will continue to be, a fact of economic life. Some progress may be made in the way of developing international policies on certain issues – the international patent system (relevant to the transfer of technology) and restrictive practices being two possible areas for action. However, codes of conduct seem likely to have a bleak future, the conflicts of interest between countries being too great to permit acceptable compromise.

The future therefore seems likely to be one of conflict and compromise between MNEs and governments. Even fewer areas of 'open access' will exist for multinationals. The corporations will be required to be increasingly responsive to the objective function of both home and host countries and therefore to accept that ownership and operating conditions may vary widely among affiliates. The elements of the package provided by MNEs are therefore changing, with money capital becoming less important in relation to management and know-how, as home and host states try to 'de-package' and 're-package' according to their own requirements. MNEs which do not possess this flexibility may retreat to their domestic base or try (probably unsuccessfully in the long run) to switch to more amenable production locations. The need for *US* MNEs to be more 'foreign market oriented' will also derive from the fact that many will lose their unique managerial and technological advantage through the diffusion process, and, faced with greater indigenous competition, will be increasingly required to plan products for markets. Increased competition among MNEs of different national origins is a further dimension.

In some areas of the world, MNEs will retain a very strong bargaining position. In such cases where, for instance, they are able to play off one country against another (as in Europe and the Far East at present), the multinationals will continue to be able to extract substantial financial concessions from governments. But the parts of the world where such tactics are possible also seem likely to shrink: EEC policy will almost certainly change to prevent competitive bidding; and the fact that other host countries are viewing MNE projects on a cost/benefit basis means that the cost to the country of offering tax holidays, subsidised interest rates and the like will be questioned more closely.

How are these trends likely to affect the volume of foreign direct investment? Within the evolutionary framework postulated, there seems no reason why MNEs should not continue to expand and prosper, assuming flexibility of approach. The key issue for many multinationals is whether or not they will still be able to appropriate the returns from their investment in new information. The ability of MNEs to internalise and overcome market imperfections suggests that this will be possible. Even if the equity ownership of affiliates is significantly diluted, MNEs may still have close control over management and know-how. On the other hand, close regulation over behaviour will be a constraint (and if the end result is lower levels of world-wide R & D expenditures, this will adversely influence the rate of economic growth). Given trends already emerging in the world economy, the future pattern of foreign direct investment seems likely to be weighted more heavily towards vertical integration, and export-platform type investments. In these cases, once the MNE is aware of the terms under which it operates in host countries and assuming stable policies, there are relatively few uncertainties on the production and assembly side, which should encourage multinational operations.

Before making a final judgement on such issues, account needs to be taken of new factors which may change the shape of the economic environment within which MNEs operate and it is these which are now considered.

The MNE and the future : some open questions

(a) *Proposals for changes in the international economic order*[14]
There has been a growing contention over recent years as to whether the economic dependence of the LDCs on the developed world and on private sector enterprises like MNEs can ever be reduced without some structural changes in the economic order. Much of the debate on this has centred around the UNCTAD proposals for a New International Economic Order (NIEO).[15] Part of the package of proposals included a scheme to regulate MNEs by a code of conduct which would attempt to ensure that their operations supported the development objectives of the Third World. Within the framework created by the code, it was proposed that LDCs would embark on a series of measures to take more initiative in their own development. These would, for example, include the development of collaborative production, research and marketing systems using their own joint resources in order to offer a viable alternative to the package offered by MNEs. The keynote to this order would not only be greater self-reliance but also a new pattern of international trade which would involve a much increased volume of imports and exports between the LDCs themselves.

It will be obvious that these proposals presume the possibility of making radical changes in the world order in order to direct more resources towards the development of the Third World. Even at the first level of providing greater economic security for the LDCs, an integrated and internationally planned programme would be needed for primary commodities. The implementation of this would require compensatory financing arrangements to offset fluctuations in export earnings. But more than this, stabilisation and intervention schemes would be necessary in many commodity markets to give consistently better returns to the producer. Furthermore, debt relief schemes would be required to reduce the debt servicing difficulties of the LDCs. In order to effect more permanent changes it is recognised that the process of change would have to go much further. Thus a new order would require, for instance, stringent measures to reduce dependence, adjustments in international laws and trade patterns, together with international monetary reform.

Any implementation of these proposals, even on a limited scale, would have profound effects on MNEs. Implementation would, however, need extensive cooperation from many groups who have been highly critical of the proposals. The critics' objections vary, but include the claim that it is an overtly political rather than an economic plan; that it almost involves an abolition of the market system of international exchange; and that it implies a burden of guilt to be expiated by the actions of developed nations. There are many other criticisms founded on practical problems, which question the realism underlying the scheme.

In general, the NIEO proposals seem to be founded more on hope than reality. In some senses that matters less than the fact that such a scheme should have emerged in recent years. From the MNE viewpoint, the very appearance of the plan is enough to signal the direction which future policy towards them might take. If only one of the elements of the proposals, such as commodity market planning, was attempted, many existing MNE operations would have to be adjusted. The more long-term proposals would necessitate the global re-examination of affiliate patterns in some corporations, and would call into question the very existence of others. Furthermore, even if the NIEO proposals make no progress whatsoever, the plan is indicative of a more aggressive, less acquiescent attitude on the part of the Third World countries. This may be assumed to be reflected in greater unilateral regulation of MNEs even if multilateral regulation, as implied by the NIEO, fails.

(b) *East–West economic relations*

Multinational corporations are finding new opportunities with the growth of East–West trade, consequent on improved political relations between the Eastern bloc and the West. From the viewpoint of the socialist countries concerned, numerous benefits are likely to emerge from increased contact with the West: domestic industry may be stimulated by foreign competition, and gains would be attainable from higher quality products and from the import of capital and technology. The actions of the Eastern bloc to date would appear to suggest that they see the gain largely in terms of buying technology on a selective basis.

Multinational firms are in a particularly strong position to benefit from the links developing between East and West.[16] In the first place, large size is a characteristic of many MNEs and size probably improves the bargaining position of the companies when negotiating with state monopolies or large industrial combines in the socialist countries. Secondly, large MNEs have access to varied sources of capital and large financial resources. This is important given the massive size of some of the projects concerned and the requirement for enormous credit facilities. Thirdly, the concentration of American MNEs in industries manufacturing machinery and transport equipment gives these companies a particular advantage since many Eastern bloc projects require these types of products. Fourthly, MNEs may be seen as particularly suitable partners since the totality of the project may be contracted with a single company; where an order has to be spread over a number of firms, there is inevitably less flexibility. On the marketing side, a further advantage possessed by the MNE is access to a world-wide distribution network; this is important given the problem some of the Eastern bloc states seem to be having in marketing their products successfully in the West. Finally, the experience of many MNEs in operating joint ventures, managerial supervision schemes, turn-key projects and so forth is a major asset, when these are precisely the kinds of industrial cooperation arrangements sought by the Eastern countries.

With the slowing of growth rates in the West, and greater competition in many Western markets, the Eastern socialist countries may offer increasingly attractive opportunities for multinationals in the future. Moreover, although tough negotiations may be involved in setting up contracts, relatively few risks are likely to be entailed thereafter, and certainly far fewer risks than exist in Third World operations.

(c) *International trade and monetary issues*

The rapid post-war growth of the multinational enterprise was undoubtedly aided by the prevailing liberal international economic system, represented at the institutional level by the IMF, the GATT, the World Bank, etc. With the ending of the Bretton Woods system of fixed exchange rates, and with world-wide high unemployment levels and inflation rates, protectionism has re-emerged as an important issue in international economic affairs. Side-by-side with the continuing negotiations in the GATT to further reduce tariff levels between countries, non-tariff barriers have been introduced in numerous industrial sectors as nations seek to insulate their economies against imported unemployment and inflation. Protectionism forms the basis for the mercantilist model outlined earlier; but the realisation within the developed countries of their close interdependence probably precludes the predictions of this model being fulfilled.

At this stage it is difficult to see the way in which the international economy will develop in the future. What is clear is that the liberal international economic order is probably dead and this, in itself, has certain implications for multinational firms. On the one hand, trade barriers would seem to be likely to encourage 'defensive' foreign direct investment; similarly an increase in 'buy-national' policies (which have always existed in government and public authority purchasing) could also stimulate defensive investment, given that there is less likelihood of discrimination against locally registered companies.[17] On the other hand, proposed foreign investments are likely to be more closely scrutinised by host countries to assess their effects on competitive indigenous firms and thus to establish the net job gain or loss. And equally, home countries will look more carefully at the effects on jobs within the parent company, while exchange controls may create problems for the financing of investment. The net effect will obviously depend upon the type of investment and the location and is obviously highly complex. For existing multinationals, difficulties will be created for world-wide sourcing and intra-corporation trade and in some locations MNEs may find themselves with redundant plants. On the other hand, the effects of protectionism on MNEs may not be so severe as on firms which export from a national base; the former may be able to offset some of the impact by, for example, a little more ingenuity in respect of transfer prices.

Multinational corporations will also be affected significantly by exchange rate movements, which seem likely to be long term in nature, and which principally affect the dollar *vis-à-vis* currencies such as the yen and the German mark. The decline in the dollar means that Europe's location specific advantage of relatively low labour costs may no longer exist. If the exchange rate movements were taken in isolation, some US corporations might choose to divest their European operations and export from the USA. But if protectionist pressures were to build up, such corporations could find themselves excluded from the European market. The overall impact in respect of US MNEs is therefore not easy to predict. What is certain is that European and Japanese companies will be increasingly likely to invest in the USA as the location specific advantages of America become more evident.

(d) *The changing distribution of power*

The United States position in the world economy and its dominance in policy making has declined. On the other hand the US has remained militarily the most powerful state, so that while America has shown less inclination to intervene militarily in recent years, its deterrent potential has remained. Moreover, Europe and Japan as the major new economic power blocs depend heavily on the United States for their security, which gives America a lever over the economic policies pursued by the former countries.

Reflecting the growing economic strength of the non-US industrialised world, MNEs from these countries – when expressed in terms of the number of affiliates established – have been growing faster than US MNEs over the past few years; and this trend would be expected to continue. Indeed the number of source nations will tend to expand further as firms in the higher income LDCs and corporations in socialist countries see opportunities abroad. Excluding the US, countries such as Japan, West Germany and the UK will continue nevertheless to be of principal significance. The issue which needs to be considered is how the changing balance of power will affect the multinationals. The fact that neither European or Japanese MNEs have the support of substantial foreign aid and military expenditures from their home governments could be seen as limiting their access to a number of economies and perhaps increasing the vulnerability of their overseas operations to expropriation. On the other hand, the fact that many of the host countries concerned will have strong trade ties with

Europe or Japan and may, in fact, be trade-dependent upon them, means that the home governments can use this *economic* power in support of their multinationals if the need arises. There is some evidence too that non-US MNEs are more flexible in coming to terms with host governments. Additionally, the lack of a colonial past may be an advantage in some instances. Thus part of the resentment which is often focused upon American MNEs by African and Latin American nations reflects the US neo-colonialist reputation; the involvement of the Soviet Union and China in many Third World countries is another factor which will operate to the detriment of US but perhaps not European MNEs. The Japanese case is rather different. The aggressive economic power of Japan may make certain host governments in Europe and North America fairly reluctant to accept Japanese direct investment except under closely defined terms. Moreover, Japanese imperialist behaviour in South-East Asian countries before and during the Second World War has not been forgotten.

Once again, therefore, there is no simple answer to the question of the impact of the changing distribution of power on MNE activities. In some markets the wider US role may outweigh other factors and maintain the dominance of American MNEs. In other cases non-American MNEs may be much more acceptable politically. To some extent these kinds of issues are already reflected in the host country concentration of investments from different sources (see Chapter 1).

(e) *Regional economic cooperation*
Prospects for economic cooperation between countries, whether taking the form of free trade areas, customs unions or more tenuous links, will undoubtedly have an impact on MNE activity. The EEC, already a huge economic bloc, is to be expanded further. While the end result of this may be the dilution of some of the principles of the Treaty of Rome, the continuance of the customs union seems assured. To US MNEs, many of whom do half of their overseas business in the EEC, expansion means larger markets and greater flexibility in producing and sourcing. The enlargement of the Common Market will also attract new non-European MNEs, while also encouraging the growth of European multinationals. Once the Community is able to reach agreement on a common policy towards MNEs (the current outline of which incorporates many of the components required for a true 'international solution') then substantial efficiency gains will be forthcoming.

Elsewhere in the world the prospects for increased cooperation are mixed, but to the participating countries increased bargaining power is gained and to the MNE larger markets may mean fewer risks even if operating conditions are more stringently controlled.[18]

(f) *Resource shortages*
Following the oil crisis in 1973–74 and world shortages of certain key

commodities which sent prices soaring, there was considerable discussion about the possibility of long-term advantage in bargaining switching to primary producing countries. To quote the title of a collection of articles published around this time: 'One, two, many OPECs . . .?'[19] In reality oil proved to be an exception – at that time at least. The scarcity of primary products was seen to be short term only and the different circumstances pertaining in non-oil markets has not permitted the successful formation of more commodity exporting alliances. The formation of other producer cartels is not ruled out for the future, however. For some commodities relatively few countries would need to collude and lack of technological and marketing expertise is not an insurmountable problem. Should other producer organisations emerge then naturally the bargaining power of the host economies will be strengthened enormously, thereby influencing the outcome of discussions with MNEs on prices, concessions, technology and ownership shares.

A final view of the future

The discussion has focused on some of the major issues which will influence the development of the multinational firm over the next twenty years or so. The picture emerging is that of a much more restrictive global economic environment than that previously experienced. Several of the issues examined point to host governments looking closely and often sceptically at what is offered within the multinational package. It is now widely recognised that MNEs are not development agencies and that they should not be allowed discretion in key areas of the economy unless following nationally determined policies of host governments.

Furthermore, it has been realised by host countries (especially LDCs) in the last decade or so that they do have a choice on the form of the package, and that joint ventures, licensing and technical assistance agreements, and other non-equity arrangements are alternative propositions to wholly-owned subsidiaries. The circumstances likely to prevail in the future will almost certainly reinforce these trends. Self-reliance will be the response to dependence. For home governments, too, obsessed by short-term economic problems, the commitment to free capital movements will seem a much less attractive policy than formerly.

The interim view of the future presented earlier suggested that assuming flexibility on the part of the MNEs, conflict could result in compromise, and multinationals would survive and prosper. The changes in the international economy postulated, however, probably tip the balance in a more pessimistic direction. Many prospective MNEs will balk at the complexities of multinationality. For existing MNEs the increasing difficulties of trying to integrate affiliate operations on a world-wide basis will suggest extreme caution. Given the different forms of involvement under which MNEs may operate in different countries, the corporations may be forced to treat their overseas investments on a fairly *ad hoc,* short-term and localised basis. And yet it would be unwise to be too pessimistic. There are signs that some host countries are beginning to take a more realistic view of the opportunities offered by multinational firms. This may prove to be the beginning of a new period of improved relationships between MNEs and host countries. If so, in the long term, foreign investment and MNEs may enter a new conciliatory and expansionist phase.

For the immediate future, nevertheless, the end result of present trends is likely to be a slower growth of foreign direct investment. Of course, international economic trends foresee both a continuation of the slower rates of economic growth experienced over the last few years and a slackening in the expansion of international trade. The relationship between direct investment growth and output growth may not, therefore, change too much, and indeed intra-MNE trade may continue to increase in relation to world trade as a whole. The net result will be that global economic efficiency will be retarded to the detriment of all countries. For home and host countries this cost has to be carefully weighed against whatever economic, but primarily non-economic, gains are to be derived from unilateral regulation.

Further reading

1. Many of the concluding comments in this chapter derive from earlier discussions in the book, but to consider a view of the future derived directly from the theory of the multinational enterprise, see **P. J. Buckley** and **M. Casson,** *The Future of the Multinational Enterprise,* London: Macmillan, 1976, Ch. 5.
2. In order to review the broader aspects of multinational operations and the prospects for the future, the following books are recommended:
   R. J. Barnet and **R. E. Müller,** *Global Reach: The Power of the Multinational Corporations,* New York: Simon & Schuster, 1974.
   R. Vernon, *Storm Over the Multinationals: The Real Issues,* London: Macmillan, 1977.
   T. N. Gladwin and **I. Walter,** *Multinationals in the Firing Line: Management of Conflict in a Hostile World,* New York: John Wiley, 1978.
   An earlier but still interesting book is: **J. N. Behrman,** *National Interests and the Multinational Enterprise,* New York: Prentice Hall, 1971.
3. On the subject of the NIEO, see **J. N. Behrman,** *Towards a New International Economic Order,* Paris: Atlantic Institute, 1974.
4. There are various articles of interest, including:
   H. V. Perlmutter, 'Super-giant firms in the future', *Wharton Quarterly,* Winter 1968.
   H. V. Perlmutter, 'The multinational firms and the future', *Annals of the American Academy of Political and Social Science,* Sept. 1972.
   J. H. Dunning, 'The future of the multinational enterprise', *Lloyds Bank Review,* July 1974.

Questions for discussion

1. Write a critique of the predictions for the future of the MNE provided by the theory of foreign direct investment (see Buckley and Casson, Ch. 5).

2. How realistic are the predictions provided by the global neo-classical, radical and mercantilist models?
3. Consider the ways in which the NIEO proposals would affect MNEs. Sketch out a more gradualist approach to reform which might achieve the same objectives.
4. Do you believe that it would be in the interests of Third World countries to support a scheme for international regulation of the MNE, designed to maximise world-wide economic efficiency?
5. How far would you agree with the view that the hostility and suspicion of multinationals is part of a learning process wherein both nation states and multinational firms learn to make decisions with a greater sense of their mutual interdependence and reciprocity?
6. J. K. Galbraith has argued that the main 'danger zones' associated with the multinational enterprise are: bribery and corruption; currency speculation; insensitivity to the environment; and involvement in the arms trade (Galbraith, 1978). How far would you agree with this assessment from an economic viewpoint?

Notes and references

Chapter 1

1. US Tariff Commission, 1973.
2. Barnet and Müller, 1974, p. 14, quoting Peter Drucker.
3. Weisskopf, 1974, p. 41.
4. Lall and Streeten, 1977, p. 4.
5. Statement of Paul Jennings, President, International Union of Electrical, Radio and Machine Workers in US Congress, Subcommittee on Foreign Economic Policy, 1970, part 4, p. 814.
6. For a comprehensive examination of the definitional problems see, for example, US Tariff Commission, 1973; UN Economic and Social Council, 1978, Annex I, pp. 158ff.
7. This issue is discussed fully in Dunning, 1978b. The point is highly relevant to the discussion later in the chapter on changing forms of MNE involvement. As Dunning (p. 3) states in this regard: ' . . . the traditional role of MNEs as providers of entrepreneurial capital may have passed its zenith. Instead, their future is likely to rest in the provision of technical and managerial services bundled together in a variety of ways. . . .'
8. In the context of US foreign direct investment, foreign affiliates which are organised as foreign corporations and registered abroad are commonly called *subsidiaries*. However, foreign affiliates may also be organised as *branches* through which the parent corporation operates abroad in its own name and always has total ownership. For example Timex Corporation operates in the UK as a branch, whereas the Singer Company (UK) Ltd is a subsidiary of the Singer Corporation. The distinction is nevertheless ignored.
9. It is worth quoting the definition of *foreign direct investment* used by the US Department of Commerce. It includes 'all foreign business organisations in which a US person, organisation or affiliated group owns an interest of 10 per cent or more', together with 'a foreign business organisation in which 50 per cent or more of voting stock is owned by US residents even though no single US group owns as much as 10 per cent'. See US Department of Commerce, 1970.
10. See Dunning, 1974b, pp. 577–81.
11. Buckley and Casson, 1976, Table 1.4.
12. Figures quoted from Sauvant and Lavipour, 1976.
13. UN Economic and Social Council, 1978, Tables III-40 and III-41.
14. Ibid., p. 53.
15. Ibid., p. 36.
16. Witness the furore surrounding Hitachi's attempts to establish a TV manufacturing operation in the UK during 1977. Although the UK government did not forbid the investment, opposition from indigenous TV manufacturers and the trade unions (who claimed that the creation of 500 jobs could put at risk 5,000 jobs) caused Hitachi to withdraw its plans to produce in the UK. See the *Financial Times*, 'Financial Times Survey on Japanese International Companies', 21 Dec. 1977.
17. Torneden. 1975, Table 2.2, p. 22.

18. Possible non-equity arrangements go much wider than this, to range from licensing, franchising or management agreements to highly complex forms of industrial cooperation agreements. The latter include supply or leasing of plants; contract manufacturing or sub-contracting; joint R & D; coproduction; comarketing and provision of after-sales-service; and joint tendering and joint products.
19. UN Economic and Social Council, 1978, pp. 46–7.
20. Litvak and Maule, 1973, p. 267, quote from the *Japan Economic Review* that: 'Due to the aggravating problem of industrial pollution . . . logs should be processed into pulp in the South-East Asian countries for importation into Japan.'

Chapter 2

1. It is interesting to consider whether the prospective MNE in fact needs to have some advantage. In some cases, particularly as regards investment in the LDCs, there will be no effective competition. This is relevant to the discussion by Kojima (1973) of trade-oriented and anti-trade-oriented foreign direct investment. In his discussion of trade-oriented Japanese investment in South East Asia, there is no mention of the requirement of Japanese firms to possess some advantage. This point is considered further at the end of the theory section of the chapter.
2. A summary of the various theories is presented in Buckley and Casson, 1976, Chapter 3. The most recent contribution, synthesising and extending earlier work, is by Dunning, 1977b.
3. Kindleberger, 1969, p. 13.
4. The seminal work is that of Stephen Hymer, 1960, in his PhD thesis; also Kindleberger, 1969.
5. Caves, 1971, p. 5.
6. A public good is a commodity which is available to everyone without charge. In this case the good concerned is only public within the firm itself. Johnson in Dunning, 1972.
7. Penrose, 1968; Kindleberger, 1969; Caves, 1971; Vernon, 1971; Dunning, 1973a.
8. Knickerbocker, 1973.
9. For an early expression of these ideas see Robinson, 1934. More recently McManus, 1972, and B. M. Wolf, 1977, have reformulated the thesis.
10. Aliber, 1970.
11. This was certainly the case at the time the theory was formulated.
12. For example, Grubel, 1968; Levy and Sarnat, 1970.
13. One of the most recent exponents of this view is Rugman, 1976, 1977a.
14. The ideas are derived from Lall and Streeten, 1977, p. 26.
15. Kindleberger, 1969, pp. 19–23.
16. Ibid., pp. 67–8.
17. Coase, 1937.
18. The examples are drawn from Brown, 1976.
19. Buckley and Casson, 1976, Chapter 2.
20. Ibid., p. 69. Present authors' italics.
21. Magee, 1977.
22. The role of labour costs is stressed in Johnson's, 1968a, version of the product cycle model of international trade and investment.
23. Transport costs represent 'natural' trade barriers, whereas tariffs etc. are 'artificial' barriers.
24. Hirsch, 1967; Vernon, 1966.
25. Derived from Kindleberger, 1973, p. 64.
26. Vernon, 1974.
27. Hymer and Rowthorn, 1970; Hymer, 1975.
28. See some recent work of Dunning, 1978a, for a discussion of the relationships between firm- and country-specific factors.

29. The industry types are those suggested by Buckley and Casson, 1976, and Dunning 1977b.
30. See the excellent discussion in Dunning, 1977b, on this issue.
31. An interesting paper which queries the relevance of 'Western' theories to Japanese direct investment abroad is Ozawa's, 1975.
32. Apart from Japanese investment, there is a further type of investment which is difficult to relate to the theory. This is the investment – admittedly very small in volume terms – by MNEs from less developed countries in neighbouring developing states. The firms concerned produce unsophisticated, low technology, undifferentiated goods and invest abroad again to take advantage of plentiful, cheap local labour. For information on the activities of such firms in Thailand, see Lecraw 1977.
33. Ozawa 1975, p. 25.
34. Vaupel, 1971.
35. Vernon, 1971.
36. Parker, 1974.
37. Dunning, 1973a.
38. Hymer, 1960; Caves, 1971.
39. Caves, 1974a.
40. Orr, 1973.
41. Buckley and Casson, 1976, Chapter 4.
42. Horst, 1972a.
43. Interesting comments on the role of size are contained in Lall and Streeten, 1977, p. 28; and in Hufbauer, 1975, pp. 272–3.
44. B. M. Wolf, 1977.
45. Knickerbocker, 1973.
46. Vernon, 1971.
47. Horst, 1975; Buckley and Dunning, 1976. A comprehensive review of these and other recent empirical studies is given in Dunning, 1977a.
48. This section draws heavily on Hufbauer, 1975, pp. 259–61.
49. Grubel, 1968.
50. Stevens, 1969.
51. Paxson, 1973.
52. Cohen, 1972; Rugman, 1976, 1977a.
53. This point is made by Hufbauer, 1975, pp. 265–6.
54. Caves, 1974a; Orr, 1973.
55. B. M. Wolf, 1977.
56. Dunning, 1973a, p. 311.
57. In order to expand, a firm had to receive Government permission in the form of an Industrial Development Certificate (IDC). By refusing IDCs for all regions, except those designated Development Areas, the Government had a potent weapon in 'persuading' industry to establish in regions such as Scotland.
58. Stobaugh, 1971a.
59. Ibid. p. 55.
60. Klein, 1973.
61. Research which supports these conclusions includes Tsurumi, 1969; de la Torre, 1971; Mousouris, 1967; Lary, 1968.
62. Parry, 1975–76.

Chapter 3

1. Baumol, 1967, p. 45.
2. Williamson, 1964.
3. Penrose, 1959.
4. Marris, 1964.
5. Ansoff, 1965.

6. Simon, 1962.
7. Cyert and March, 1963.
8. Aharoni, 1966.
9. Day, 1967.
10. Williamson, 1970.
11. Williamson in Marris and Wood, 1971, p. 367.
12. For further discussion of organisational issues in multinationals, see Brooke and Remmers, 1970, Part 1; and Brooke and Remmers, 1977, Part 2.
13. Leibenstein, 1966.
14. Johnson in Dunning, 1972, p. 455.
15. This section draws on Johnson in Dunning, 1972, particularly pp. 455–8.
16. Arrow in Nelson, 1962.
17. A proof of this is given in Sherman, 1974, pp. 186–7.
18. See Demsetz, 1969, for a criticism of the effects traced by Arrow.
19. Schumpeter, 1947; and Nelson, 1959.
20. Magee, 1977.
21. Johnson, op. cit., p. 460.
22. These issues are dealt with competently in Reekie, 1975, Chapter 7.
23. The distinction is usually made between sporadic, predatory and persistent dumping. Sporadic dumping takes place when a firm wishes to clear stocks without harming its normal markets. Persistent dumping occurs when a producer consistently sells at a lower price in one market than another.
24. Hirschleifer, 1956.
25. Behrman, 1970; and Stubenitsky, 1970.
26. Aharoni, op. cit.; Miller and Weigel, 1971.
27. These include Scaperlanda and Mauer, 1969; Severn in Machlup, Salant and Tarshis, 1972; Kopits, 1972.
28. Knickerbocker, 1973.
29. A conclusion shared by Stevens in Dunning, 1974, after his exhaustive review of studies of the investment and financing decisions of the MNE.
30. Mansfield et al., 1971, p. 13.
31. Baran and Sweezy, 1968.
32. OECD, 1968.
33. Mansfield in Dunning, 1974, p. 169.
34. Parker, 1974.
35. Mansfield in Dunning, 1974, p. 166.
36. Baker and Ryans, 1973.
37. Arpan, 1972–73.
38. Greene and Duerr, 1970.
39. Stobaugh, 1971b.
40. Reddaway, 1967, p. 75. 'Reported' represents authors' italics.
41. Brooke and Remmers, 1970, p. 176.
42. The study of US MNEs was undertaken by Robbins and Stobaugh, 1973, and the quotation from Penrose, 1968, is on p. 272.
43. Groo, 1972.
44. Blackbourn in Hamilton, 1974.
45. Schöllhammer cited in Dunning and Yannopoulous, 1973.
46. Donaldson, 1966, and McAleese, 1971–72, for Ireland; and Forsyth, 1972, for Scotland.
47. Aharoni, 1966, p. 241.
48. Thunell, 1977.
49. Young and Hood, 1976.
50. Pratten, 1976.
51. Caves, 1974b.
52. Solomon and Ingham, 1977.
53. Parry, 1977.
54. Ibid., p. 30.

Chapter 4

1. The multi-fibre agreement was negotiated in the GATT in 1973 to limit imports of textiles into the developed countries from the LDCs. Textiles is one of the basic industries in which protectionist pressures have been increasing, the others being shipbuilding, steel and motor vehicles. A good review of the state of play as at end-1977 is in *The Economist* (London), 31 Dec. 1977, in an article entitled 'From Free Trade to Adjustment', pp. 75–96.
2. The terms of trade are defined as the ratio of export prices to import prices. There has been considerable debate over the movements in the terms of trade for primary products. The results depend crucially on the base year chosen, how countries are grouped etc. A comprehensive study is contained in Hayes, 1975.
3. From 1947, six rounds of tariff reductions have been negotiated in the GATT. The Tokyo Round of negotiations was due to end in 1978.
4. In terms of manufactured goods only US MNE-related exports totalled $28.8 billion, 19 per cent of overall world exports in 1970. The data for this section are from US Tariff Commission, 1973.
5. The commodity composition of US MNE exports is interesting. Exports are concentrated in the following product groups: computing equipment, grain mill products, transportation equipment, soaps and cosmetics, farm machinery and equipment, other food products, instruments and drugs.
6. Holthus and Scharrer, 1974.
7. The concern of this section is with the pure theory of international trade. Pure theory deals with both positive and normative (or welfare) economic issues. The distinction should be borne clearly in mind. Positive (what is) problems include questions such as: what factors determine the patterns of trade between countries? Normative (what ought to be) theory considers questions such as: is free trade the optimal policy or is free trade better than no trade?
8. The Ricardian example is shown in the table:

Man years of labour per unit product, without trade

Produce	England	Portugal
Wine	120	80
Cloth	100	90

Before the establishment of trade, the production of a unit of cloth in England is assumed to require the work of 100 men for a year, while a unit of wine takes 120 men the same period. Although Portugal has an absolute advantage in the production of both commodities, the country would benefit more comparatively speaking by concentrating on wine and importing cloth from England: for costs of 80 man years it would obtain cloth requiring 90 man years to produce domestically. It would be in England's interests to specialise in cloth; it would obtain wine requiring 120 man years at home, in return for 100 man years. For trade to be advantageous, the cost ratios in Portugal (80/90) and England (120/100) must be different.
9. The Ricardian theory in fact assumes that only labour productivity varies between countries.
10. Heckscher, 1950; Ohlin, 1967.
11. See, for example, Stolper and Samuelson, 1969; Jones, 1969; Johnson, 1968b. For a review of the literature on factor price equalisation, see Bhagwati, 1964.
12. Leontief, 1969.
13. Leontief's results were as follows:
The technique used was that of input-output analysis, which was devised by Leontief himself. Input-output analysis shows the relationship between inputs of raw materials, labour etc. and the resulting outputs in various sectors and industries.

Domestic capital and labour requirements per $ million of US exports and
of competitive import replacements (of average 1947 composition)

Factor of production	Exports	Import replacements
Capital ($ in 1947 prices)	2,550,780	3,091,339
Labour (man-years)	182,313	170,004

14. Among numerous contributions, see Kenen, 1965.
15. Vanek, 1959, supplemented Leontief's data to estimate the natural products incorporated in export and import replacements and found the following:

Natural Resource Products	Exports	Import Replacements
($ in 1947 prices)	340,000	630,000

Vanek concluded that capital can be considered a relatively abundant factor in the USA, and Leontief's results were distorted by the omission of natural resources. Resources were viewed as the scarce factor in the USA, but these could enter the production process only in conjunction with large amounts of capital.
16. Posner, 1961; also Hufbauer, 1965.
17. Linder, 1961. The approach is similar to that adopted in 'export base' theories of growth.
18. Drèze, 1960.
19. Johnson, 1968a.
20. Following the suggestions of Dunning, 1973a, Hirsch, 1976, formalises the concepts into a model and Parry, 1975–76, 1976, followed a similar approach in his study of the pharmaceutical industry.
21. This section is derived from Corden, 1974, particularly pp. 195–9.
22. Corden states that this is a 'Mundell-type solution'. Mundell, 1957, developed a theory of international investment within an H-O framework, dropping the factor immobility assumption and introducing restrictions on the freedom of international trade. Because of these trade restrictions, factors of production will tend to be transferred between countries in response to the international differences in factor returns.
23. Hirsch, 1976. On p. 258 of his article, Hirsch gives a comprehensive list of other contributions to the trade/investment decision.
24. It is, however, worth while to refer back to the discussion in Chapter 2, pp. 66–8, when it was suggested in relation to Japanese overseas direct investment that since there may be few or no potential competitors abroad, this crucial assumption of the necessity for some 'advantage' may no longer be valid.
25. Hirsch, 1976, p. 265.
26. Dunning, 1977b. The contribution is subtitled 'A Search for an Eclectic Approach'.
27. Kojima, 1973. The argument is much extended in Kojima, 1978.
28. Hirsch, 1976, p. 266.
29. Corden, 1967, 1974.
30. Viner, 1950; Balassa, 1971.
31. These tests were conducted by MacDougall, Stern and Balassa. A review is contained in Bhagwati's survey of trade theory, 1964.
32. Leontief, 1969.
33. For example, Ellsworth, 1954; Kenen, 1965; Valvanis-Vail, 1954.
34. Baldwin, 1971.
35. Ibid.
36. Keesing, 1965.
37. Gruber, Mehta and Vernon, 1967. See also Keesing, 1967.
38. Hufbauer, 1965; Katrak, 1973; Leamer, 1974.
39. Hufbauer, 1970.

40. Ibid., p. 194.
41. Leamer, 1974.
42. Baldwin, 1971.
43. The suggestion was made by Johnson in Vernon, 1970a.
44. Katrak, 1973.
45. Dunning and Buckley, 1974.
46. B. M. Wolf, 1977.
47. Buckley and Pearce, 1977.
48. Horst, 1972b.
49. Jud, 1973.
50. A brief but highly informative review is given in Hufbauer, 1975, pp. 278–80.
51. Parry, 1976.
52. Hirsch, 1976.
53. Dunning, 1977a.
54. Horst, 1974a.
55. Lipsey and Weiss, 1976.
56. Hufbauer and Adler, 1968; Reddaway *et al.*, 1968.
57. This is the so-called 'reverse-classical assumption'. The issues involved are considered further in Chapter 7.
58. Lall and Streeten, 1977, p. 135.
59. Cornell, 1973.
60. Lipsey and Weiss, 1973.
61. Scaperlanda, 1967.
62. Scaperlanda and Mauer, 1969.

Chapter 5

1. MacDougall, 1960.
2. On the other hand the host country now receives $(1-t)$ (EDKJ) instead of EDKJ, but this is fairly small.
3. Among the developments which might be noted are the formulation of (a) dynamic growth models with foreign investment and trade by Pitchford, 1970, and Brems, 1970; and (b) comparative-static general equilibrium models by Pearce and Rowan, 1966.
4. To take the point further, if investment from abroad could not have been replaced by indigenous investment, then a gain in capital formation has occurred. This, in turn, then suggests positive effects on host-country employment and income. More generally, to the extent that foreign investment supplements investment by indigenous firms in host countries, world capital formation will be increased as a result of MNE activities.
5. The influence of Solow, 1956, and others has been particularly important in stressing the role of technical progress. One model developed takes the form: $G_y = G_t + aG_k + (1 - a)G_n$, where G_y, G_t, G_k and G_n are the percentage rates of growth of output, technical change, capital stock and the supply of labour respectively. For a long-run equilibrium rate of growth this reduces to:
$$G_y = \frac{G_t + G_n}{1 - a}$$
For more details see a macro-economics textbook such as Dernberg and McDougall, 1972.
6. For a discussion see Vaitsos, 1970.
7. Among various articles on the subject see Lall, 1976.
8. The classic work was that of Eckaus, 1955.
9. Mason, 1971.
10. Johnson in Dunning, 1972.
11. Chenery, 1961.

12. Lall, 1973.
13. The activities of the multinational American banks are interesting in this regard. The banks started building up their branches in the Bahamas and the Cayman Islands from about 1970. The growth has been mainly at the expense of the banks' London operations; and by 1977 only one third of the American banks' international business was being conducted in London as against two thirds a few years earlier. See *The Economist*, 24/2/78.

    In general, tax havens may provide a variety of advantages. A small number of countries such as the Bahamas and Bermuda, exempt either all income from taxation or foreign source income channelled through them. Other states, like Panama and Liberia, do not tax income from activities undertaken outside the country, such as sales or shipping, irrespective of where the company is incorporated. Still other countries, like Luxembourg, give full exemption to foreign source income flowing through holding companies. Apart from tax advantages, a major benefit often associated with tax havens is the ability to sustain secrecy about the nature of the firms' operations.

14. A Eurodollar deposit is a dollar-nominated deposit in a non-US (usually European) bank. The market grew up, almost by accident, from the late 1950s as a result of US banking regulations. Its growth since then has been associated with the US balance of payments deficit, the expansion of US firms in Europe and most recently with the oil crisis of the early 1970s. For a description of the Eurodollar (or strictly Eurocurrency) market, see any standard International Economics textbook.

    It is interesting that, during 1978, New York City was proposing to try to attract some of these Eurodollar funds away from London, by permitting banks operating branches in New York to handle offshore deposits free of the reserve requirements and deposit interest rate restrictions imposed by the Federal Reserve; the banks would also be exempt from New York state and city income tax.

15. A good summary of changing attitudes on development is in de Vries, 1966. See also Sachs, 1973.
16. Helleiner, 1973.
17. In actual fact, most recently there has been a revival of anti-trade sentiment. The argument goes that if all or most LDCs try to gain access to the world market for exports of labour-intensive manufactures, the benefits for each single country will be reduced, as a consequence either of falling prices or of market barriers erected by the importing countries.
18. This section draws heavily on Dunning, 1974b.
19. H. G. Johnson, 1965.
20. Streeten, 1974.
21. Bergsten, 1976.
22. Lall and Streeten, 1977.
23. Denison, 1967.
24. Morley and Smith, 1977.
25. Mason, 1971.
26. Reuber, 1973.
27. Courtney and Leipziger, 1974.
28. Forsyth and Solomon, 1977.
29. Morawetz, 1974.
30. Morley and Smith, 1977, p. 287.
31. Quoted in Bergsten, 1976, p. 32.
32. Vaitsos, 1975.
33. Morawetz, 1974.
34. Sabolo, 1975.
35. Weisskoff, 1973.
36. Westphal and Kim, 1973.
37. Sheahan, 1971
38. Helleiner, 1973.
39. Nayyar, 1978.

40. Chang, 1971.
41. Murray, 1972. The points noted in the section following broadly follow Murray.
42. Almost every industrial country has now such a provision in its tariff, whereby domestic components may be sent out of the country for processing and/or assembly and then returned, with the tariff being assessed only on value added abroad. See Finger, 1975, 1976.
43. Nayyar, 1978.
44. Lall and Streeten, 1977, p. 135. See also reference 58 in Chapter 4.
45. Monopolies Commission, 1973.
46. Quoted in Lall, 1973.
47. Vaitsos, 1975.
48. For other transactions, the estimated deviations from arm's-length prices were as follows: sale of intangibles, $52.4 m; loans, $75.9 m; sale of services, $127.0 m; and other transactions, $94.1 m. See Kopits, 1976b.
49. Müller and Morgenstern, 1974.
50. Kopits, 1976a, p. 802.
51. Lall, 1973.
52. Opening address by the Governor of the Bank of England, Lord O'Brien, at a Colloquium at the University of Nottingham in April, 1973.
53. The results are summarised in Lall and Streeten, 1977.
54. A third alternative considered was that of 'financial replacement'. Here the estimates were based on the assumption that the foreign capital was obtained in portfolio form, but that the technology and thus the input requirements of the local firm would remain the same as those of the foreign firm.
55. Lall and Streeten, 1977, p. 142.
56. Ibid., p. 173.
57. The question as to what would have happened in the absence of the foreign direct investment is crucial. It is arguable that if local entrepreneurs could have undertaken the investment because technology was available, they would have done so. If they did not undertake the investment, then it is questionable if it is valid to assume that the MNE investment is replaceable.
58. While not reported here, another important study was that undertaken by Bos, Sanders and Secchi (1974) into the overall impact of foreign direct investment in India, the Philippines, Ghana, Guatemala and Argentina. The effects of foreign direct investment on national income and on government revenues were found to be positive in all cases, but the impact on the balance of payments was always negative. The actual size of the positive and negative effects varied widely as in the Lall and Streeten study, the inference again being that host-country policies can have a marked effect on the outcome. Unlike Lall and Streeten, the Bos *et al.* study did not seek to compare the results of foreign direct investment with the likely results of alternatives available to the host nation.
59. L. L. Johnson, 1967.
60. Vaitsos, 1975, p. 209.
61. Connor and Mueller, 1977.
62. Newfarmer and Mueller, 1975.
63. Ibid., p. 152.
64. This section draws extensively on Parry, 1977.
65. Lake, 1976.
66. Gennard and Steuer, 1971.
67. Jedel and Kujawa, 1976.
68. Hood and Young, 1976.
69. Hewitt, 1977.
70. Lecraw, 1977.
71. Bergsten, 1976, pp. 40–42.
72. Steuer *et al.*, 1973.
73. Mansfield, 1974.

74. For some insights into the debate over microelectronics which was taking place during 1978, see *The Sunday Times (Business News)*, 18 June 1978: 'The Chip that could make Britain into a World Beater'.

75. Dunning, 1976.

76. Forsyth, 1972.

77. Holland, 1976; Blackbourn, 1974, 1978.

78. The study showing a move towards the peripheral regions since the 1940s was that of Dicken and Lloyd, 1976, and the research covering the period 1945–65 was prepared by Howard, 1968. The US Tariff Commission, 1973, considering American investment in Europe as a whole, estimated that one half of all post-war investments were in assisted areas; they explained this in terms of the fact that US companies had been much more alert than European firms in taking advantage of regional incentives.

79. Yannopoulos and Dunning, 1976, have suggested that multinationality would make MNEs both more and less responsive to regional incentives than local firms. For example, since MNEs have no particular commitments to specific regions and fewer preconceived ideas about development areas, they might be more responsive to regional incentives. Similarly, since the MNE has more freedom in shifting its tax burden, this reduces uncertainties which may surround possible changes in regional incentives. Conversely, other factors may make MNEs less responsive to regional assistance.

80. Young and Hood, 1976.

81. Hood and Young, 1976, found few R & D and Marketing functions among US plants in Scotland; the work on the location of European headquarters is by Dunning, 1978c.

82. On the Chrysler issue, see Young and Hood, 1977.

83. Steuer *et al.*, 1973, p. 12.

Chapter 6

1. The marginal conditions which must be simultaneously satisfied to attain economic efficiency are: (a) *The marginal rate of substitution (MRS) in consumption between any two goods or between any good and leisure should be the same for all consumers.* If this condition was violated then consumers would be able to benefit by the exchange of commodities. (b) *The marginal rates of transformation (MRT) between any two products should be the same for any pair of producers.* If this condition was violated, reallocation of output between the producers would increase the total output of one product without decreasing the total output of the other. (c) *The marginal physical products of a given factor for a given product should be the same for any pair of producers.* (d) *The marginal rates of technical substitution between any two factors should be the same for any pair of producers.* (e) *The marginal rate of transformation (MRT) between any pair of goods (or between any good and leisure) should be equal to the marginal rate of substitution (MRS) between the same pair in consumption.* Otherwise, consumers could be made better off without utilising any more factors of production if the output of two products is reallocated. See, for example, Rowley and Peacock, 1975, Ch. 1.

2. Social welfare relates to the welfare of all individuals in society. A fundamental premise in welfare economics is that each person allocates his income among various consumption goods so as to maximise his own individual utility (satisfaction). Utility is a subjective experience meaning that interpersonal comparisons of utility are not meaningful and thus that individuals' utilities cannot be summed together. Social welfare cannot therefore be measured quantitatively. The conditions for an increase in social welfare can be easily formulated, namely, that the utility of at least one individual rises, while the utility of all others is

unchanged. But nothing can be said about the value of the social welfare function if one individual's utility rises, while some other individual's utility falls.

At the point of optimum social welfare, no increase in the utility of one member of society can be made without a loss in someone else's occurring. This optimum is called 'Pareto optimum'.

3. To give an example, government may raise income tax to increase income equality, but this may result in a fall in the quantity of labour supplied, thereby reducing the growth rate.

4. External balance requires balance of payments equilibrium. Internal balance is normally expressed in terms of full employment.

5. This *compensation principle* states that situation x is better in terms of welfare than situation y if the gainers in welfare in moving from y to x gain enough to be in a position to compensate the losers and still have something over. It has been argued that this approach is not very useful from a policy viewpoint since compensation will not necessarily occur and income distribution will be affected. Consequently attempts have been made to make interpersonal comparisons by assigning *marginal welfare weights*. For example if policymakers assume that country A's income is worth $\frac{1}{2}$ for every £1 of income and country B's 1, then it would be possible to calculate whether free trade produced more welfare than a position of protection by calculating the weighted change in welfare. See Shone, 1972, Ch. 5.

6. *The optimum tariff.* The importing country imposing a tariff is subjected to two conflicting forces: a loss of real income due to a reduction in the volume of trade, and a gain in income resulting from improvements in the terms of trade. If the country is big enough to influence the terms of trade, the latter effect may be greater than the former, resulting in a net rise in real income. The tariff rate that maximises this net gain is the 'optimum tariff'. See Sodersten, 1971, Ch. 19.

7. Caves, 1971, p. 22.

8. For a summary of theoretical developments see Corden, 1974.

9. Corden, 1967.

10. Nyerere, 1968. The Arusha Declaration was adopted in February 1967.

11. It should be noted that taken to its logical extreme such policies would lead to the dissolution of the MNE into perfectly competitive units. Even without this there are dangers in reducing the market power of MNEs since the generation of new technology may require concentrated industrial structures and large firm size.

12. The concept of an international welfare state is usually associated with Jan Tinbergen (Tinbergen, 1954).

13. It will be noted that this statement assumes that ownership produces control which may not be correct (see the discussion in Chapter 1). Given that MNEs provide management and know-how in addition to equity, a mere reduction in the supply of equity capital may not *per se* reduce control.

14. Adapted from Streeten, 1974.

15. The following points are derived from Lall and Streeten, 1977, pp. 193–4.

16. The more successful a cartel, the stronger the incentive for any member to break away, and underbid the group. On the other hand if others were to break away, the losses to those who remain might be greater than if they had never joined an agreement.

17. For details see Wallace, 1976, p. 26.

18. Goldberg and Kindleberger, 1970.

19. The proposal for a divestment agency had been made earlier, in 1969, by Hirschman. The proceedings of the 1973 conference referred to were published in Wallace, 1974.

20. UN Economic and Social Council, Report of the Group of Eminent Persons, 1974.

21. Ball, 1967.

22. Penrose, 1968.

23. Rubin, 1971.

24. See *The Sunday Times*, London, 5 June 1977.

25. International Chamber of Commerce, 1972a.

26. OECD , 1976.
27. See *The Economist,* London, 8 Oct. 1977.
28. OECD, 1976, pp. 16–17.
29. The 1976 Report and Accounts of Unilever Ltd stated, for example: 'we have publicly expressed our support for, and our determination to comply with, these (OECD) guidelines . . . '.
30. International Confederation of Free Trade Unions, 1975.
31. *The Economist* referred to the OECD report on these cases as 'three pages of fluff'. In the same article there are some interesting comments on the way in which the US government view the Code. *The Economist,* London, 17 Dec. 1977. On the Badger case specifically, see Blanpain, 1978.
32. The work is being undertaken by the Centre on Transnational Corporations.
33. But this is essentially speculation. In its 1976 document which set out the issues involved in the formulation of a code of conduct, all that was established was that there were three important principles which the code should incorporate. These were: 1. that MNEs should be required to observe the laws of the country in which they operate; 2. that they should adhere to host country social and economic goals and objectives; and 3. that MNEs should abstain from corrupt practices. See UN Economic and Social Council, 1976.
34. The report on international standards of accounting and reporting is being bitterly opposed by the MNEs. With respect to the reporting requirements proposed, Massey Ferguson are reported as saying: 'We regard the report as horrendous. It calls for information that we don't bother preparing even for internal use.' And Ciba-Geigy stated: 'Laying down obligatory standards is likely to be counter-productive, calling for a lot of time and work and yielding few usable results, unprofitable in its concept and wholly unrealistic in execution.' *The Financial Times,* London, 4 July 1978.
35. Other work being undertaken relates to the activities of MNEs in South Africa. See *The CTC Reporter,* New York: United Nations, Vol. 1, No. 2, June 1977.
36. United Nations Conference on Trade and Development, 1974.
37. For further details of this OECD work, see an excellent article by Tharp Jr, 1976. The OECD have, most recently, prepared a report on Restrictive Business Practices in Multinational Enterprises. Details are given in *The Economist,* London, 14 Jan. 1978.
38. International Chamber of Commerce, 1972b.
39. International Chamber of Commerce, 1977.
40. *The Times,* London, 1 Dec. 1977.
41. Wells Jr, 1973.
42. Ibid., pp. 178–9.
43. Penrose, 1976.
44. All of these countries are challenging IBM'S insistence on 100 per cent control of its subsidiaries. For example, Indian law requires foreign companies to divest 60 per cent of their equity to local shareholders unless they manufacture solely for export. Nigeria too wants an equity stake for locals and Indonesia is demanding that marketing must be undertaken by Indonesian-controlled companies. For details, see *The Economist,* London, 29 Oct. 1977.
45. The Coca-Cola example is an interesting one. Coca-Cola expressed willingness to form an Indian Company in which its equity would be reduced to 40 per cent. But it wanted to retain 100 per cent of a company controlling quality and guarding the secrets of its formula!
46. The list following excludes the international solution in which all governments would ban the use of tax havens, tax the firms jointly on their global earnings and share the proceeds. See Lall and Streeten, 1977, pp. 203–6.
47. The OPEC pricing system is outlined in Mabro, 1975–6.
48. The regulations of the Andean Common Market are discussed separately in later paragraphs.
49. The distinction was made in Government of Canada, 1972.

50. A 1975 Act gives the Secretary of State powers to prevent control of a British company 'of special importance to the United Kingdom', passing into foreign hands.
51. In the case of the United States, for instance, there has traditionally been a liberal attitude towards inward direct investment. However, since 1970 there have been numerous legislative proposals to regulate, control and monitor inward investment, mostly from OPEC countries. The Committee on Foreign Investment reviews investment in the US which may have implications for the United States national interest and the Department of Commerce's Office of Foreign Investment monitors individual investments and analyses the impact of inward investment on the economy and on industrial sectors.
52. Most of the information in this section was obtained from Safarian and Bell, 1973; and Rugman, 1977b.
53. This was an incorrect conclusion of the Gray Report. What should be sought is a maximisation of *net* benefits.
54. Rugman, 1977b, p. 323.
55. Ibid., p. 332.
56. This section draws heavily on a first-class article published by Ozawa in 1973.
57. The prevalence of licensing can be understood in terms of the theory of foreign direct investment. When only a few firms exist in the foreign market, a bilateral monopoly problem makes cooperation through licensing difficult. On the other hand when many potential buyers of technology exist, as in the case of Japan, the market mechanism fully appropriates the return to the seller.
58. These operated in non-restricted industries under the condition that neither income nor liquidation proceeds would be transferred abroad.
59. *The Economist,* London, 14 May 1977.
60. It is worth pointing out that Japanese policy towards outward direct investment has been equally single-minded. From 1949–69 permission was required before Japanese enterprises could invest abroad; from 1969–71 automatic approval was granted up to a ceiling limit. In July 1971 the ceiling was removed, but this does not mean that Japanese firms may invest abroad without consulting the government. Japanese companies are still highly dependent on the government for financial and other support. Therefore the government can influence the investment policies of companies in a way which meets the goals of its industrial strategy.
61. Commission of the European Communities, 1973.
62. The one exception to this principle relates to EEC policy to South Africa. The Community in 1977 agreed on a voluntary code of conduct relating to the operation of EEC companies in South Africa.
63. The proposal for worker participation derives from German experience. Currently, with the passing of the Co-Determination Act of 1976, in all organisations having 2,000 or more employees, workers' representatives in West Germany are entitled to half the seats on the supervisory board.
64. This section draws on Thompson, 1977.
65. Interestingly, the EEC are also trying to achieve some security of investment for companies investing in LDCs, by including mining ventures in the Lomé Convention.
66. The information in this section is derived from Tharp, 1976; and Furnish 1976. It should be noted that the Andean Pact has crumbled a little recently, since Chile has defected from the group.
    mean that Japanese firms may invest abroad without consulting the government,

Chapter 7

1. Apart from the original references following, this section also draws on Musgrave, 1975.
2. Keynes, 1924.
3. Jasay, 1960. Also Balogh and Streeten, 1960; Frankel, 1965; Kemp, 1962.

4. Pearce and Rowan in Dunning, 1972. Dunning, 1970, p. 100, gives a good example of the way in which different assumptions about terms of trade effects will alter the results obtained: rates of return for British companies averaged 13.5 per cent for the period 1960–64, and this was assumed also to be the marginal social product of domestic investment. The apparent social rate of return on overseas investment averaged only 8.0 per cent during these same years. Suppose however that the terms of trade were affected by overseas investment. Each 1 per cent change in the terms of trade was worth £50–60 m. per annum to the UK, so if the terms of trade improved by one per cent, the social rate of return on foreign investment would need to be increased to between 9½–10 per cent. Roughly a 3 per cent improvement in the terms of trade would thus wipe out the differential between social rates of return on domestic and foreign investment. The problem is, of course, that because of a lack of quantitative evidence regarding the parameters of the demand and supply functions, neither the sign nor the magnitude of the terms of trade effects can be established.

5. Kemp, 1964, p. 193.

6. Frankel, 1965, p. 417. This was only Frankel's starting-point. He then went on to suggest that foreign investment would lead to development benefits that would benefit the host at the expense of the home country. Therefore, overall, 'foreign investment, to be advantageous to the domestic economy, must yield a premium sufficiently in excess of what home investment would yield to compensate for the development benefits that are foregone' (p. 432).

7. In terms of world efficiency, the comparison should be made between gross returns abroad and gross returns at home.

8. Grubel, 1974.

9. Balogh and Streeten, 1960, p. 214.

10. Frankel, 1965. See note 6 above.

11. A weakness of the strict neo-classical model – which radical economists would stress – is its failure to take account of the stock-of-capital to the available-labour ratio. If the existing stock of domestic capital is under-utilised with domestic labour, then the export of capital may produce gains for labour.

12. A recent theoretical article on this subject is by Beenstock, 1977.

13. The classification is from Hawkins, 1972.

14. See Musgrave, 1975.

15. For further discussion of the issues raised in the following section, see Hawkins and Walter, 1977; and McCulloch, 1977.

16. The end result of this, it is feared, will be that the US economy will follow the pattern of the United Kingdom to become a low-growth, services-oriented economy.

17. McCulloch and Yellen, 1976.

18. The distinction was first made by H. G. Johnson, 1958, pp. 181–9.

19. Swan, 1963.

20. Snider, 1964.

21. As an interesting example of this, Zenith Radio Corporation announced in October 1977 that 5,000 of its 21,000 US workers would be made redundant during 1978, as it was intending to transfer a substantial part of its TV assembly operations to offshore locations. See The Economist, London, 1 Oct. 1977, p. 95.

22. See Litvak and Maule, 1975–76, p. 169. The authors give the example of Ford Canada which became the parent of many of Ford's Commonwealth investments.

23. Houston and Dunning, 1976, p. 359–60.

24. The IET did not apply to Canada, to the LDCs or to Japan up to a limit of $100 million a year.

25. To give an example of the quotas for one year (1973), the maximum limit for Schedule A countries is 110 per cent, for Schedule B countries 65 per cent, and for Schedule C countries 35 per cent above the average direct investment during the base period 1965–66. But the limits were placed on sums transferred, not capital outlays. This meant that companies were free to go ahead with their investment programme provided any funds above quota were raised by foreign borrowing.

26. US Department of Commerce, 1972, p. 19.
27. This figure was derived from a job-loss figure of 500,000 estimated by Ruttenberg for the 1966–69 period. See Ruttenberg, 1971.
28. The foreign tax credit was initially introduced into the US tax code in 1913. It is a system which is based on the concept of 'capital export neutrality', which means that taxation is not meant to play a role in the investor's choice between home or foreign investment. Investment projects are to be ranked in terms of their gross (pre-tax) rate of return, since this is the best comparison for allocating capital globally. Scheme 2 in Table 7.2 which favours foreign investment may be termed 'foreign neutrality'. Scheme 3 – 'national neutrality' – is based on the US national interest where the relevant comparison when selecting investment projects is between the US pre-tax rate of return and the foreign after-tax rate of return.
29. One other feature of the US tax code worth mentioning is that of the investment tax credit (ITC). This applies only to plant and equipment expenditures made in the United States and therefore represents an offset to the deferral scheme which relates to foreign investment only.
30. Stobaugh, 1974.
31. Finger, 1976.
32. Grzybowski, 1977.
33. 'Minding Other People's Business', *The Economist*, London, 20 Aug. 1977, p. 77–8.
34. Bergsten, 1976.
35. This section draws heavily on Cairncross, 1973, Ch. 4. See also Woolley, 1974.
36. It is possible that the British position may be challenged in the European Court of Justice, for the other two new member countries – Ireland and Denmark – have less stringent controls and have also agreed to some liberalisation. On the other hand, France and Italy are still being permitted to retain their exchange controls.
37. An earlier research study was that undertaken by Bell (1962). The Hufbauer-Adler work was published in 1968 (Hufbauer & Adler, 1968).
38. Reddaway in collaboration with Potter and Taylor, 1967 and 1968.
39. Ibid., 1967, p. 23.
40. See for example Dunning, 1969.
41. Stobaugh, 1971b.
42. An interesting article which is relevant to this discussion and which has been referred to in Chapters 2 and 4 is that by Kojima, 1973.
43. De la Torre, Stobaugh and Telesio, 1973.
44. Hawkins only actually calculated the job displacement figure. The 50,000 job gain is an estimate derived by the present authors. See Hawkins, 1972, p. 33.
45. From the host country viewpoint, the evidence of various studies is that some MNE investment supplements host country savings while some substitutes for it, the results being quite varied among countries and through time. Export-platform investments however seem to be largely supplemental to domestic investment. When MNE investments do not substitute for *home* country capital formation and supplement *host* country capital formation, the anti-classical assumption applies and world investment is increased. It seems likely that this has occurred in the post-war years.
46. Musgrave, 1975 p. ix.
47. Houston and Dunning, 1976, p. 367.
48. Grubel, 1974.
49. Ibid., p. 486.
50. Horst, 1977.
51. Freeman, 1976.

Chapter 8

1. *Business Week*, 19 December 1970.
2. Barratt Brown, 1974, p. 207.

3. As developed for example in Calleo and Rowland, 1973.
4. The first quotation is from Wolff, 1970, p. 225; the second is contained in Edwards, Reich and Weisskopf, 1972, p. 408.
5. Cohen, 1973, p. 15.
6. Edwards, Reich and Weisskopf, 1972, p. 435.
7. As Chapter 2 points out, of course, direct as opposed to portfolio investment could not be explained by this factor alone.
8. As outlined in Weisskopf, 1974a.
9. Baran and Sweezy, 1966.
10. Gurley, 1971, p. 56.
11. See for example Weidenbaum, 1968.
12. Tucker, 1971.
13. Schumpeter, 1919; and for more recent work see Landes, 1961.
14. For an exhaustive review of this topic see Winkler, 1976.
15. These are examined in some detail in Weisskopf, 1974b.
16. In this form the hypothesis bears some resemblance to Williamson's Managerial Discretion model. See Chapter 3.
17. Summarised from Sweezy and Magdoff, 1972, p. 41–2.
18. O'Connor in Rhodes, 1970, p. 117.
19. Frank, 1970, p. 177.
20. It should be noted that this is much wider than the 'suction-pump' explanation given on p. 333, which does not take reinvested earnings into account.
21. An issue developed in Dos Santos, 1970.
22. Ibid., p. 233.
23. Hymer, 1970.
24. Cohen, 1973, p. 215–16.
25. As for example in Moran, 1973a.
26. Head, 1974, p. 18.
27. Magdoff, 1966, Ch. 2.
28. Rosen in Rosen and Kurth, 1974, Ch. 6.
29. US Senate Committee on Foreign Relations, 1973.
30. *New York Times*, 26 Sept. 1973.
31. Odell in Rosen and Kurth, op. cit.
32. For an illustration of this type of study, see Melman, 1970.
33. Rosenstein-Rodan in Williamson, Glade and Schmitt, 1974.
34. Kobrin, 1977.
35. Barnes, 1972.
36. Moran, 1973b.
37. Emmanuel, 1972.
38. Schatz, 1969.
39. Moran in Rosen and Kurth, 1974, Ch. 8.
40. Mikesell, 1971.
41. Quoted by Vaitsos, in Williamson, Glade and Schmitt, 1974, p. 99, n. 49.
42. On ITT in Chile, see US Senate, 1973b; also Allende in Radice, 1975.
43. Department of Trade, UK, 1976.
44. Quoted in *The Economist,* London, 10 July 1976, p. 72.
45. The Tanzanian action was one of a number of setbacks Lonrho suffered in Africa subsequent to the inspectors' report on the company. In May 1977 the company was dropped from the management of a large sugar project in the Sudan, which it had pioneered, against a background of soaring costs and financing problems. Also the Kuwait Government had insisted on Arab management of Lonrho interests in its country as the annual report of the company revealed.
46. See the extensive reports and evidence in US Government, 1975.
47. Ibid., p. 17–18.
48. Quoted in Young and Hood, 1977, p. 282, which should be consulted for a comprehensive analysis of this case.
49. Bergsten, Keohane and Nye in Bergsten and Krause (eds), 1975, pp. 4–5.

Chapter 9

1. See Gilpin in Bergsten and Krause (eds), 1975, pp. 37–60.
2. Hymer in Radice, 1975.
3. Rowthorn in Radice, 1975.
4. Mandel, 1970.
5. A point developed in Bergsten and Krasner, 1976.
6. This section essentially develops what was termed in Ch. 8, 'the contemporary orthodox approach'.
7. See Ch. 2, 3 and 4 for an extended discussion of these issues.
8. Hawkins and Walters, 1977, p. 28, give an interesting example of the way in which MNEs, through their flexibility, may impose external costs on the world economy which national firms might not. Thus MNEs may move plants to locations where pollution control requirements are lenient or non-existent. If there are transfrontier effects in terms of air or water pollution, then the world as a whole may bear higher social costs.
9. See Ch. 5.
10. See Ch. 7.
11. The regulation issue is dealt with from an international and host country viewpoint in Ch. 6 and from a home country perspective in Ch. 7.
12. There is, in fact, a further dimension to the issue of conflict which derives from dissension between groups within a particular country, e.g. between labour and industry representatives.
13. See Hawkins and Walter, 1977, p. 55.
14. For a comprehensive review and appraisal of this whole question, see Sauvant and Hasenpflug, 1977, particularly Part 2, pp. 37–117.
15. Ibid., Ch. 3.
16. This section draws on T. A. Wolf in Sauvant and Lavipour, 1976, Ch. 4, pp. 79–91.
17. On the other hand, the US MNE Honeywell Inc., for example, has frequently complained that its UK affiliate is discriminated against in government and public authority contracts.
18. Chapter 6 drew attention to the case of the ANCOM code, which is so restrictive as to frighten off most prospective foreign investors.
19. Bergsten and Krasner, 1976, pp. 195–213.

Bibliography

Ady, P. (ed.), *Private Foreign Investment and the Developing World,* New York: Praeger, 1971.

Aharoni, Y., *The Foreign Investment Decision Process,* Boston: Harvard U.P., 1966.

Aliber, R. Z., 'A theory of direct foreign investment', in Kindleberger, C. P. (ed.), *The International Corporation,* Cambridge, Mass: MIT Press, 1970.

Allende, S., 'Speech to the United Nations', in Radice, H. (ed.), *International Firms and Modern Imperialism,* Harmondsworth: Penguin Books, 1975, pp. 233–47.

Ansoff, H. I., *Corporate Strategy,* New York: McGraw Hill, 1965.

Arpan, J. S., 'Multinational firm pricing in international markets', *Sloan Management Review,* **14,** no. 2, Winter 1972–3.

Arrow, K. J., 'Economic welfare and the allocation of resources for invention', in Nelson, R. R. (ed.), *The Rate and Direction of Inventive Activity: Economic and Social Factors,* Princeton, N.J.: Princeton U.P., 1962.

Baker, J. C. and **Ryans, J. K.,** 'Some aspects of international pricing', *Management Decision,* **11,** 1973, pp. 177–82.

Balassa, B., 'Trade creation and trade diversion in the European Common Market', *Economic Journal,* **77,** 1967, pp. 1–21, reprinted in Robson, P. (ed.), *International Economic Integration,* Harmondsworth: Penguin Books, 1971.

Baldwin, R. E., 'Determinants of the commodity structure of US trade', *American Economic Review,* **61,** 1971, pp. 126–46.

Ball, G., 'Cosmocorp: the importance of being stateless', *Columbia Journal of World Business,* **25,** Nov./Dec. 1967.

Balogh, T. and **Streeten, P.,** 'Domestic versus foreign investment', *Bulletin of Oxford University Institute of Statistics,* **22,** 1960, pp. 213–24.

Bank of England, Economic Intelligence Department, *Quarterly Bulletin,* London: Bank of England, **18,** no. 1, 1978 (and earlier editions).

Baran, P. A. and **Sweezy, P. M.,** *Monopoly Capital,* New York: Monthly Review Press, 1966, and Harmondsworth: Penguin Books, 1968.

Barnes, R., 'International oil companies confront governments', *International Studies Quarterly,* **16,** 4, 1972.

Barnet, R. J. and **Müller, R. E.,** *Global Reach: The Power of the Multinational Corporations,* New York: Simon & Schuster, 1974.

Barratt Brown, M., *Economics of Imperialism,* Harmondsworth: Penguin Books, 1974.

Baumol, W. J., *Business Behaviour, Value and Growth,* New York: Harcourt, Brace, Jovanovich, 1967.

Beenstock, M., 'Policies towards international direct investment: a neoclassical reappraisal', *Economic Journal,* **87,** Sept. 1977, pp. 533–42.

Behrman, J. N., *Some Patterns in the Rise of the Multinational Enterprise,* Chapel Hill: Graduate School of Business Administration, University of North Carolina, 1970.

Behrman, J. N., *Towards a New International Economic Order,* Paris: Atlantic Institute, 1974.

Bell, P. W., 'Private capital movements and the US balance of payments position', Joint Economic Committee, 87th Cong., 2nd Sess., *Factors Affecting the United States Balance of Payments,* Washington: Government Printing Office, 1962.

Bergsten, C. F., *An Analysis of US Foreign Direct Investment Policy and Economic Development,* AID Discussion Paper no. 36, Nov. 1976.

Bergsten, C. F., Horst, T. and **Moran, T. H.,** *American Multinationals and American Interests,* Washington DC: Brookings Institution, 1978.

Bergsten, C. F., Keohane, R. O. and **Nye, J. S. Jr,** 'International economics and international politics: a framework for analysis', in Bergsten, C. F. and Krause, L. B. (eds.), *World Politics and International Economics,* Washington: Brookings Institution, 1975.

Bergsten, C. F. and **Krasner, S. D.,** 'One, two, many OPECs . . . ?', in Sauvant, K. P. and Lavipour, F. G., *Controlling Multinational Enterprises,* London: Wilton House, 1976, pp. 195–213.

Bhagwati, J., 'The pure theory of international trade: a survey', *Economic Journal,* **74,** 1964.

Blackbourn, A., 'The spatial behaviour of American firms in Western Europe', in Hamilton, F. E. I., *Spatial Perspectives on Industrial Organisation and Decision Making,* London: J. Wiley & Sons, 1974.

Blackbourn, A., 'Multinational enterprises and regional development: a comment', *Regional Studies,* **12,** no. 1, 1978, pp. 125–7.

Blanpain, R., *The Badger Case,* Deventer, Netherlands: Kluwer, 1978.

Bos, H. C., Sanders, M. and **Secchi, C.,** *Private Foreign Investment in Developing Countries,* Boston: D. Reidel, 1974.

Brems, H., 'A growth model and international direct investment', *American Economic Review,* 60, 1970, pp. 320–31.

Brooke, M. Z., Black, M. and **Neville, P.,** *A Bibliography of International Business,* London: Macmillan, 1976.

Brooke, M. Z. and **Remmers, H. L.,** *The Strategy of Multinational Enterprise,* London: Longman, 1970.

Brooke, M. Z. and **Remmers, H. L.,** *The International Firm,* London: Pitman, 1977.

Brown, W. B., 'Islands of conscious power: MNEs in the theory of the firm', *MSU Business Topics,* Summer 1976, pp. 37–45.

Buckley, P. J. and **Casson, M.,** *The Future of the Multinational Enterprise,* London: Macmillan, 1976.

Buckley, P. J. and **Dunning, J. H.,** 'The industrial structure of US direct investment in the UK', *Journal of International Business Studies,* 7(2), Fall/Winter 1976, pp. 5–13.

Buckley, P. J. and **Pearce, R. D.,** *Overseas Production and Exporting by the World's Largest Enterprises – a Study in Sourcing Policy,* University of Reading Discussion Papers in International Investment and Business Studies, no. 37, Sept. 1977.

Cairncross, A., *Control of Long-Term International Capital Movements,* Washington: Brookings Institution, 1973.

Calleo, D. and **Rowland, B.,** *America and the World Political Economy,* Bloomington: Indiana U.P., 1973.

Caves, R. E., 'International corporations: the industrial economics of foreign investment', *Economica,* **38,** 1971, pp. 1–27; reprinted in Dunning, J. H. (ed.), *International Investment,* Harmondsworth: Penguin Books, 1972.

Caves, R. E., 'The causes of direct investment: foreign firms' shares in Canadian and UK manufacturing industries', *Review of Economics and Statistics,* **56,** 1974a, pp. 279–93.

Caves, R. E., 'Multinational firms, competition and productivity in host country markets', *Economica,* **41,** May 1974b, pp. 176–93.

Chang, Y. S., *The Transfer of Technology, Economics of Offshore Assembly, the Case of the Semiconductor Industry,* New York: UNITAR, 1971.

Chenery, H. B., 'Comparative advantage and development policy', *American Economic Review,* **51,** 1961, pp. 18–51.

Coase, R. H., 'The nature of the firm', *Economica,* **4,** Nov. 1937.

Cohen, B. I., *Foreign investment by US corporations as a way of reducing risk,* Economic Growth Center Discussion Paper no. 151, Yale University, 1972.

Cohen, B. J., *The Question of Imperialism: the Political Economy of Dominance and Dependence,* London: Macmillan, 1973.

Commission of the European Communities, *Multinational Undertakings and the Community,* Supplement 15/73, Brussels: EEC Commission, 1973.

Commission of the European Communities, *Survey of Multinational Enterprises,* **1,** Brussels: EEC Commission, July 1976.

Connor, J. H. and **Mueller, W. F.,** *Market Power and Profitability of Multinational Corporations in Brazil and Mexico,* Report to the Subcommittee on Foreign Economic Policy of the Committee on Foreign Relations, United States Senate, Washington: US Government Printing Office, April 1977.

Corden, W. M., 'Protection and foreign investment', *Economic Record,* **43,** 1967, pp. 209–32.

Corden, W. M., 'The theory of international trade', in Dunning, J. H. (ed.), *Economic Analysis and the Multinational Enterprise,* London: George Allen & Unwin, 1974, pp. 184–210.

Cornell, R., *Trade of Multinational Firms and Nation's Comparative Advantage,* Paper presented to a conference on Multinational Corporations and Governments, UCLA, Nov. 1973.

Courtney, W. H. and **Leipziger, D. M.,** *Multinational Corporations in LDCs: The Choice of Technology,* Washington: USAID, Oct. 1974.

Curhan, J. P., Davidson, W. H. and **Suri, R.,** *Tracing the Multinationals: A Sourcebook on US-based Enterprises,* Cambridge, Mass.: Ballinger Publishing Co., 1977.

Cyert, R. M. and **March, J. G.,** *A Behavioural Theory of the Firm,* Englewood Cliffs, NJ: Prentice Hall, 1963.

Day, R. H., 'Profits, learning and the convergence of satisficing to marginalism', *Quarterly Journal of Economics,* **81,** May 1967.

De la Torre, J., 'Exports of manufactured goods from developing countries, marketing factors and the role of foreign enterprise', unpublished DBA thesis, Harvard Graduate School of Business Administration, 1971.

De la Torre, J., Stobaugh, R. B. and **Telesio, P.,** 'US multinational enterprise and changes in the skill composition of US employment', Ch. 7 in Kujawa, D. (ed.), *American Labour and the Multinational Corporation,* New York: Praeger, 1973.

Demsetz, H., 'Information and efficiency: another viewpoint', *Journal of Law and Economics,* **12,** April 1969, pp. 1–22.

Denison, E., *Why Growth Rates Differ,* Washington: Brookings Institution, 1967.

Department of Trade (UK), *Lonrho Ltd,* Report by Alan Heyman and Sir William Slimmings, London: HMSO, July 1976.

Dernberg, T. F. and **McDougall, D. M.,** *Macroeconomics,* 4th Edition, New York: McGraw Hill, 1972.

De Vries, M. G., 'Trade and exchange policy and economic development: two decades of evolving views', *Oxford Economic Papers,* **18,** 1966, pp. 19–41.

Dicken, P. and **Lloyd, P. E.,** 'Geographical perspectives on United States investment in the United Kingdom', *Environment and Planning,* **8,** no. 6, 1976, pp. 685–705.

Donaldson, L., *Development Planning in Ireland,* New York: Praeger, 1966.

Dos Santos, J., 'The structure of dependence', *American Economic Review,* **60,** 1970, pp. 231–6.

Drèze, J., 'Quelques réflexions sereines sur l'adaptation de l'industrie belge au Marché Commun', *Comptes Rendus des Travaux de la Société Royale d'Economie Politique de Belgique,* **275,** Dec. 1960.

Dunning, J. H., 'The foreign investment controversy', *Bankers Magazine,* May, June and July, 1969: pp. 307–12; 354–60; 21–5.

Dunning, J. H., *Studies in International Investment,* London: George Allen & Unwin, 1970.

Dunning, J. H. (ed.), *International Investment,* Harmondsworth: Penguin Books, 1972.

Dunning, J. H., 'The determinants of international production', *Oxford Economic Papers,* **25,** no. 3, 1973a, pp. 289–336.

Dunning, J. H., 'The location of international firms in an enlarged EEC: an exploratory paper', *Manchester Statistical Society,* 1973b.

Dunning, J. H., (ed.), *Economic Analysis and the Multinational Enterprise,* London: George Allen & Unwin, 1974a.

Dunning, J. H., 'Multinational enterprises, market structure, economic power and industrial power', *Journal of World Trade Law,* **8,** no. 6, Nov./Dec. 1974b, pp. 575–613.

Dunning, J. H., 'The future of the multinational enterprise', *Lloyds Bank Review,* July 1974c.

Dunning, J. H., *US Industry in Britain,* EAG Business Research Study, London: Wilton House, 1976.

Dunning, J. H., *Trade, Location of Economic Activity and the Multinational Enterprise: Some Empirical Evidence,* University of Reading Discussion Papers in International Investment and Business Studies, no. 37, Oct. 1977a.

Dunning, J. H., *Trade, Location of Economic Activity and the Multinational Enterprise: A Search for an Eclectic Approach,* University of Reading Discussion Papers in International Investment and Business Studies, no. 29, 1976. Revised version published in Ohlin, B. (ed.), *The International Allocation of Economic Activity,* London: Macmillan, 1977b.

Dunning, J. H. *Ownership and Country Specific Characteristics of Britain's International Competitive Position,* University of Reading Discussion Papers in International Investment and Business Studies, no. 40, Jan. 1978a.

Dunning, J. H., 'Multinational business and the challenge of the 1980s', *Multinational Business,* London: Economist Intelligence Unit, no. 1, 1978b, pp. 2–10.

Dunning, J. H., 'How multinationals choose their locations', *Trade and Industry,* 26, May 1978c, pp. 2–3.

Dunning, J. H. and Buckley, P. J., *International Production and Alternative Models of Trade,* University of Reading Discussion Papers in International Investment and Business Studies, no. 16, Sept. 1974.

Dunning, J. H. and Gilman, M., 'Alternative policy prescriptions and the multinational enterprise', in Curzon, G., and Curzon V. (eds.), *The Multinational Enterprise in a Hostile World,* London: Macmillan, 1977.

Dunning, J. H. and Yannopoulous, G., 'The fiscal factor in the location of affiliates of multinational enterprises', in *Vers Une Politique Fiscale Européene a l'égard Des Entreprises Multinationales,* Brussels: Université Catholique de Louvain, 1973, pp. 71–114.

Eckaus, R. S., 'The factor proportions problem in underdeveloped areas', *American Economic Review,* **45,** 1955, pp. 539–65.

Edwards, R. C., Reich, M. and Weisskopf, T. E., *The Capitalist System,* Englewood Cliffs, NJ: Prentice Hall, 1972.

Ellsworth, P. T., 'The structure of American foreign trade: a new view examined', *Review of Economics and Statistics,* **36,** 1954.

Emmanuel, A., *Unequal Exchange, A Study of the Imperialism of Trade,* London: Monthly Review Press, 1972.

Findlay, R., *Trade and Specialization,* Harmondsworth: Penguin Books, 1970.

Finger, J. M., 'Tariff provisions for offshore assembly and the exports of developing countries', *Economic Journal,* **85,** 1975, pp. 365–71.

Finger, J. M., 'Trade and domestic effects of the offshore assembly provision in the US tariff', *American Economic Review,* **66,** 1976, pp. 598–611.

Forsyth, D. J. C., *US Investment in Scotland,* New York: Praeger, 1972.

Forsyth, D. J. C. and Solomon, R. F., 'Choice of technology and nationality of ownership in manufacturing in a developing country', *Oxford Economic Papers,* **29,** no. 2, July 1977, pp. 258–82.

Frank, A. G., *Capitalism and Underdevelopment in Latin America* (revised ed.), Harmondsworth: Penguin Books, 1970.

Frankel, M., 'Home versus foreign investment: a case against capital export', *Kyklos,* **18,** 1965, pp. 411–32.

Freeman, R. T., *The Optimum Foreign Investment Tax,* Working Paper no. 122, Cornell University, August 1976.

Furnish, D. B., 'The Andean Common Market's common regime for foreign investments', in Sauvant, K. P., and Lavipour, F. G. (eds.), *Controlling Multinational Enterprises: Problems, Strategies, Counterstrategies,* London: Wilton House, 1976, pp. 181–93.

Galbraith, J. K., 'The defense of the multinational company', *Harvard Business Review*, March-April 1978, pp. 83–93.

General Agreement on Tariffs and Trade, *International Trade 1976/77,* Geneva: GATT, 1977 (and earlier editions).

Gennard, J. and **Steuer, M. D.**, 'The industrial relations of foreign-owned subsidiaries in the United Kingdom', *British Journal of Industrial Relations,* **9,** 1971, pp. 143–59.

Gilpin, R., 'Three models of the future', in Bergsten, C. F., and Krause, L. B. (eds.), *World Politics and International Economics,* Washington: Brookings Institution, 1975, pp. 37–60.

Gladwin, T. N. and **Walter, I.**, *Multinationals in the Firing Line: Management of Conflict in a Hostile World,* New York: John Wiley, 1978.

Goldberg, P. M. and **Kindleberger, C. P.**, 'Toward a GATT for investment: a proposal for supervision of the international corporation', *Law and Policy in International Business,* **2,** no. 2, 1970, pp. 295–323.

Government of Canada (Gray Report), *Foreign Direct Investment in Canada,* Ottowa: Information Canada, 1972.

Greene, J. and **Duerr, M. G.**, *Intercompany Transactions in the Multinational Firm,* Managing International Business no. 6, New York: National Industrial Conference Board, 1970.

Groo, E. S., 'Choosing foreign locations: one company's experience', *Columbia Journal of World Business,* Sept.–Oct. 1972.

Grubel, H. G., 'Internationally diversified portfolios: welfare gains and capital flows', *American Economic Review,* **58,** 1968, pp. 1299–1314, reprinted in Dunning, J. H. (ed.), *International Investment,* Harmondsworth: Penguin Books, 1972, pp. 201–19.

Grubel, H. G., 'Taxation and the rates of return from some US asset holdings abroad 1960–69', *Journal of Political Economy,* **82,** 1974, pp. 469–87.

Gruber, W. D., Mehta, D. and **Vernon, R.**, 'The R & D factor in international trade and international investment of United States industries', *Journal of Political Economy,* **75,** 1967, pp. 20–37.

Grzybowski, K., 'East-west trade regulations in the United States: the 1974 US Trade Act Title IV', *Journal of World Trade Law,* Nov.–Dec. 1977, pp. 501–13.

Gurley, J. G., 'The state of political economics', *American Economic Review,* **61,** Papers and Proceedings, 1971, pp. 53–68.

Hague, D. C., *Managerial Economics,* London: Longman, 1974.

Hawkins, R. G., *Job Displacement and the Multinational Firm: A Methodological Review,* Occasional Paper no. 3, Washington: Center for Multinational Studies, June 1972.

Hawkins, R. G. and **Walter, I.**, *Challenges to a Liberal International Economic Order: International Investment and the Multinational Corporation,* paper presented at an American Enterprise Institute Conference in Washington DC, 77–86, Oct. 1977.

Hayes, J. P., *Terms of Trade Policy for Primary Commodities,* Commonwealth Economic Papers no. 4, London: Commonwealth Secretariat, 1975.

Head, I. L., 'Canada's Pacific Perspectives', *Pacific Community,* **6,** no. 1, Oct. 1974.

Heckscher, E., 'The effect of foreign trade on the distribution of income' (1919), reprinted in Ellis, H. S. and Metzler, L. A. (eds.), *Readings in the Theory of International Trade,* London: Allen & Unwin, 1950.

Helleiner, G. K., 'Manufactured exports from less developed countries and multinational firms', *Economic Journal,* **83,** 1973, pp. 21–47.

Hewitt, G. K., *The Effect of Foreign Ownership on Self-Financed Research and Development in Canadian Manufacturing Industries — a cross sectional study,* Working Paper no. 1977–3, Concordia University, Dept. of Economics, Montreal, 1977.

Hirsch, S., *Location of Industry and International Competitiveness,* London: Oxford U.P., 1967.

Hirsch, S., 'An international trade and investment theory of the firm', *Oxford Economic Papers,* **28,** 1976, pp. 258–70.

Hirschleifer, J., 'On the economics of transfer pricing', *Journal of Business,* July 1956.

Hirschman, A. O., *How to Divest in Latin America and Why,* Essays in International Finance no. 76, Princeton U.P., Nov. 1969.

Holland, S., 'Meso-economics, multinational capital and regional inequality', in Lee, R., and Ogden, P. E. (eds.), *Economy and Society in the EEC,* London: Saxon House, 1976.

Holthus, M. and **Scharrer, H. E.,** *Die Rolle der Multinationalen Unternehmen im Zusammenhang mit der Deutschen Währungspolitik,* HWWA-Institut für Wirtschafts-forschung, Hamburg, June 1974, mimeo.

Hood, N. and **Young, S.,** 'US investment in Scotland: aspects of the branch factory syndrome', *Scottish Journal of Political Economy,* **23,** 1976, pp. 279–94.

Horst, T., 'Firm and industry determinants of the decision to invest abroad: an empirical study', *Review of Economics and Statistics,* **54,** 1972a, pp. 258–66.

Horst, T., 'The industrial composition of US exports and subsidiary sales to the Canadian market', *American Economic Review,* **62,** 1972b, pp. 37–45.

Horst, T., *American Exports and Foreign Direct Investments,* Harvard Institute of Economic Research, Discussion Paper no. 362, May 1974a.

Horst, T., 'The theory of the firm', Ch. 2 in Dunning, J. H. (ed.), *Economic Analysis and the Multinational Enterprise,* London: George Allen & Unwin, 1974b, pp. 31–46.

Horst, T., *American Investments Abroad and Domestic Market Power,* Washington DC: Brookings Institution, 1975.

Horst, T., 'American taxation of multinational firms', *American Economic Review,* **67,** 1977, pp. 376–89.

Houston, T. and **Dunning, J. H.,** *UK Industry Abroad,* EAG Business Research Study, London: Financial Times, 1976.

Howard, R. S., *The Movement of Manufacturing Industry in the United Kingdom: 1945–65,* Board of Trade, London: HMSO, 1968.

Hufbauer, G. C., *Synthetic Materials and the Theory of International Trade,* London: Duckworth, 1965.

Hufbauer, G. C., 'The impact of national characteristics and technology on the commodity composition of trade in manufactured goods', in Vernon, R. (ed.), *The Technology Factor in International Trade,* New York: Columbia U.P., 1970. pp. 145–231.

Hufbauer, G. C., 'The multinational corporation and direct investment' in Kenen, P. B. (ed.), *International Trade and Finance,* London: Cambridge U.P., 1975, pp. 253–319.

Hufbauer, G. C. and **Adler, F. M.,** *Overseas Manufacturing Investment and the Balance of Payments,* Tax Policy Research Study no. 1, Washington: US Treasury Dept., 1968.

Hymer, S., *The International Operations of National Firms: A Study of Direct Investment,* doctoral dissertation, Massachusetts Institute of Technology, 1960.

Hymer, S., 'The efficiency (contradictions) of multinational corporations', *American Economic Review,* Papers and Proceedings, **60,** 1970, pp. 441–8.

Hymer, S., 'The multinational corporation and the law of uneven development', in Radice, H. (ed.), *International Firms and Modern Imperialism,* Harmondsworth: Penguin Books, 1975, pp. 37–62.

Hymer, S. and **Rowthorn, R.,** 'Multinational corporations and international oligopoly: the non-American challenge', in Kindleberger, C. P. (ed.), *The International Corporation,* Cambridge, Mass.: MIT Press, 1970.

International Chamber of Commerce, *Guidelines for International Investment,* Publ. 272, Paris: ICC, 1972a.

International Chamber of Commerce, *Guide to ICC Arbitration,* Publ. BR 72–1, Paris: ICC, 1972b.

International Chamber of Commerce, *Ethical Practices in Commerical Transactions,* Document no. 192/36, Paris: ICC, 1977.

International Confederation of Free Trade Unions, *Multinational Charter,* Brussels: IFCTU, 1975.

International Monetary Fund, *International Financial Statistics,* **XXXI,** no. 3, Washington: International Monetary Fund, 1978.

Jasay, A. E., 'The social choice between home and overseas investment', *Economic Journal,* **70,** 1960, pp. 105–13, reprinted in Dunning, J. H. (ed.), *International Investment,* Harmondsworth: Penguin Books, 1972, pp. 117–28.

Jedel, M. J. and **Kujawa, D.,** *Management and Employment Practices of Foreign Direct Investors in the United States,* Georgia State University, March 1976.

Jenkins, R., *International Oligopoly and Dependent Industrialization in the Latin American Motor Industry,* Development Studies Discussion Paper no. 13, University of East Anglia, Oct. 1976.

Johnson, H. G., *International Trade and Economic Growth,* London: George Allen & Unwin, 1958.

Johnson, H. G., 'A theoretical model of economic nationalism in new and developing states', *Political Science Quarterly,* LXXX, no. 2, June 1965, pp. 169–85.

Johnson, H. G., *Comparative Cost and Commerical Policy Theory for a Developing World Economy,* Wiksell Lectures, 1968, Stockholm: Almqvist & Wiksell, 1968a.

Johnson, H. G., 'Factor endowments, international trade and factor prices', *Manchester School of Economic and Social Studies,* XXV, 1957, pp. 270–83, reprinted in Caves, R. E., and Johnson, H. G. (eds.), *Readings in International Economics,* London: George Allen & Unwin, 1968b.

Johnson, H. G., 'The state of theory in relation to empirical analysis', in Vernon, R. (ed.), *The Technology Factor in International Trade,* New York: Columbia U.P., 1970a.

Johnson, H. G., *International Economic Questions Facing Britain, the United States and Canada in the 1970s,* London: British–North American Research Association, June 1970b.

Johnson, H. G., 'The efficiency and welfare implications of the international corporation', in Kindleberger, C. P. (ed.), *The International Corporation,* Cambridge, Mass.: MIT Press, 1970, reprinted in Dunning, J. H. (ed.), *International Investment,* Harmondsworth: Penguin Books, 1972.

Johnson, L. L. 'Problems of import substitution: the Chilean automobile industry', *Economic Development and Cultural Change,* **15,** 1967, pp. 202–16.

Jones, R. E., 'International capital movements and the theory of tariffs and trade', *Quarterly Journal of Economics,* **81,** 1967, pp. 1–38.

Jones, R. W., 'Factor proportions and the Heckscher-Ohlin theorem', *Review of Economic Studies,* XXIV, 1956–7, pp. 1–10, reprinted in Bhagwati, J. (ed.), *International Trade,* Harmondsworth: Penguin Books, 1969.

Jud, C. D., *An Empirical Study of the Industrial Composition of US Exports and Foreign Subsidiary Sales,* paper read at meeting of the Southwestern Economic Association, March 1973.

Katrak, H., 'Human skills, R & D and scale economies in the exports of the United Kingdom and the United States', *Oxford Economic Papers,* **25,** 1973, pp. 337–60.

Keesing, D. B., 'Labor skills and international trade: evaluating many trade flows with a single measuring device', *Review of Economics and Statistics,* **47,** 1965, pp. 287–94.

Keesing, D. B., 'The impact of research and development on United States trade', *Journal of Political Economy,* **75,** 1967, pp. 38–45.

Kemp, M. C., *The Pure Theory of International Trade and Investment,* Englewood Cliffs, N.J.: Prentice Hall, 1964.

Kemp, M. C., 'The benefits and costs of private investment from abroad: comment', *Economic Record,* **38,** 1962, pp. 108–10, reprinted in Dunning, J. H. (ed.), *International Investment,* Harmondsworth: Penguin Books, 1972, pp. 159–62.

Kenen, P. B., 'Nature, capital and trade', *Journal of Political Economy,* **73,** 1965, pp. 437–60.

Kenen, P. B., (ed.), *International Trade and Finance,* London: Cambridge U.P., 1975.

Keynes, J. M., 'Foreign investment and national advantage', *The Nation and Atheneum,* 1924, pp. 584–7.

Kindleberger, C. P., *American Business Abroad: Six Lectures on Direct Investment,* New Haven, Conn.: Yale U.P., 1969.

Kindleberger, C. P., *The International Corporation,* Cambridge, Mass.: MIT Press, 1970.

Kindleberger, C. P., *International Economics,* Homewood, Illinois: Irwin (5th ed.), 1973.

Klein, R. W., 'A dynamic theory of comparative advantage', *American Economic Review,* **68,** 1973, pp. 173–84.

Knickerbocker, F. T., *Oligopolistic Reaction and the Multinational Enterprise,* Boston: Harvard U.P., 1973.

Kobrin, S. J., *Multinational Corporations, Socio-Cultural Dependence and Industrialisation: Need Satisfaction or Want-Creation,* Cambridge, Mass.: Alfred P. Sloan School of Management, Massachusetts Institute of Technology, Working Paper WP907–77, March 1977.

Kojima, K., 'A macro-economic approach to foreign direct investment', *Hitotsubashi Journal of Economics,* **14,** June 1973, pp. 1–21.

Kojima, K., *Direct Foreign Investment: A Japanese Model of Multinational Business Operations,* London: Croom Helm, 1978.

Kopits, G. F., 'Dividend remittance behaviour within the international firm: a cross–country analysis', *Review of Economics and Statistics,* **54,** 1972, pp. 339–42.

Kopits, G. F., 'Intra-firm royalties crossing frontiers and transfer pricing behaviour', *Economic Journal,* **86,** 1976a, pp. 781–805.

Kopits, G. F., 'Taxation and multinational firm behaviour: a critical survey', *International Monetary Fund Staff Papers,* **23,** no. 3, Nov. 1976b, pp. 624–73.

Krasner, S. D., 'Trade in raw materials: the benefits of capitalist alliances', in Rosen, S. J. and Kurth, J. R. (eds.), *Testing Theories of Economic Imperialism,* Lexington, Mass.: D. C. Heath, 1974, pp. 183–98.

Kreinin, M., *International Economics: A Policy Approach,* New York: Harcourt, Brace and Jovanovich (2nd ed.), 1975.

Kujawa, D. (ed.), *American Labor and the Multinational Corporation,* New York: Praeger, 1973.

Lake, A. W., *Foreign Competition and the UK Pharmaceutical Industry,* Working Paper no. 155, New York: National Bureau of Economic Research, Nov. 1976.

Lall, S., 'Transfer pricing by multinational manufacturing firms', *Oxford Bulletin of Economics and Statistics,* **35,** 1973, pp. 173–95.

Lall, S., 'Less developed countries and private foreign direct investment: a review article', *World Development,* **2,** nos. 4 and 5, April–May 1974, pp. 43–8.

Lall, S., *Foreign Private Manufacturing Investment and Multinational Corporations: An Annotated Bibliography,* New York: Praeger, 1975.

Lall, S., 'The patent system and the transfer of technology to less developed countries', *Journal of World Trade Law,* Jan.–Feb. 1976, pp. 1–16.

Lall, S. and **Streeten, P.,** *Foreign Investment, Transnationals and Developing Countries,* London: Macmillan, 1977.

Landes, D. S., 'Some thoughts on the nature of economic imperialism', *Journal of Economic History,* **31,** no. 4, Dec. 1961, pp. 496–512.

Lary, H. B., *Imports of Manufactures from Less Developed Countries,* New York: National Bureau of Economic Research, 1968.

Lauterbach, A., 'Changing concepts of imperialism', *Weltwirtschaftliches Archiv,* **113,** Part 2, 1977, pp. 322–47.

Leamer, E. E., 'The commodity composition of international trade in manufactures: an empirical analysis', *Oxford Economic Papers,* **26,** 1974.

Lecraw, D., 'Direct investment by firms from less developed countries', *Oxford Economic Papers,* **29,** no. 3, 1977, pp. 442–57.

Leibenstein, H., 'Allocative efficiency vs "X-efficiency" ', *American Economic Review,* **56,** 1966.

Leontief, W. W., 'Domestic production and foreign trade: the American capital position re–examined', *Economia Internazionale,* **VII,** 1954, pp. 3–22, reprinted in Bhagwati, J. (ed.), *International Trade,* Harmondsworth: Penguin Books, 1969.

Levy, H. and **Sarnat, M.,** 'International diversification of investment portfolios', *American Economic Review,* **60,** 1970, pp. 668–75.

Linder, S B., *An Essay on Trade and Transformation,* New York: J. Wiley, 1961.

Lipsey, R. E. and **Weiss, M. Y.,** *Multinational Firms and the Factor Intensity of Trade,* New York: National Bureau of Economic Research, Working Paper no. 8, Sept. 1973.

Lipsey, R. E. and **Weiss, M. Y.**, *Exports and Foreign Investment in Manufacturing Industries*, New York: National Bureau of Economic Research, Working Paper no. 131 (Revised), May 1976.

Litvak, I. A. and **Maule, C. J.**, 'Japan's overseas investments', *Pacific Affairs*, **46**, no. 2, 1973, pp. 254–68.

Litvak, I. A. and **Maule, C. J.**, 'Canadian investment abroad: in search of a policy', *International Journal* (Canadian Institute of International Affairs), **XXXI**, no. 1, Winter 1975–6, pp. 160–79.

Mabro, R., 'OPEC after the oil revolution', *Millennium*, Winter 1975–6, pp. 191–9.

McAleese, D., 'Capital inflows and direct foreign investment in Ireland, 1952 to 1970', *Journal of the Statistical and Social Inquiry Society of Ireland*, **22**, Part 4, 1971–72, pp. 63–99.

McCulloch, R., *Trade and Direct Investment: Recent Policy Trends*, Discussion Paper no. 579, Harvard Institute of Economic Research, Oct. 1977.

McCulloch, R. and **Yellen, J. L.**, *Technology Transfer and the National Interest*, Discussion Paper no. 526, Harvard Institute of Economic Research, Dec. 1976.

MacDougall, G. D. A., 'The benefits and costs of private investment from abroad: a theoretical approach', *Economic Record*, **36**, 1960, pp. 13–35, reprinted in Dunning, J. H. (ed.), *International Investment*, Harmondsworth: Penguin Books, 1972, pp. 129–58.

McManus, J. C., 'The theory of the multinational firm', in Pacquet, G. (ed.), *The Multinational Firm and the Nation State*, Ontario: Collier-Macmillan, 1972.

Magdoff, H., *The Age of Imperialism*, New York: Monthly Review Press, 1966.

Magee, S. P., 'Information and the multinational corporation: an appropriability theory of direct foreign investment', in Bhagwati, J. N. (ed.), *The New International Economic Order*, Cambridge, Mass.: MIT Press, 1977, pp. 317–40.

Mandel, E., *Europe versus America? Contradictions of Imperialism*, London: New Left Books, 1970.

Mansfield, E., 'Technology and technological change', in Dunning, J. H. (ed.), *Economic Analysis and the Multinational Enterprise*, London: George Allen & Unwin, 1974, pp. 147–83.

Mansfield, E. et al., *Research and Innovation in the Modern Corporation*, London and New York: Macmillan, 1971.

Marris, R. L., *Economic Theory of Managerial Capitalism*, London: Macmillan, 1964.

Marris, R. L. and **Wood, A.** (eds.), *The Corporate Economy*, London: Macmillan, 1971.

Mason, R. H., *The Transfer of Technology and the Factor Proportions Problem: The Philippines and Mexico*, New York: UNITAR, 1971.

Mason, R. H., Miller, R. R. and **Weigel, D. R.**, *The Economics of International Business*, New York: Wiley, 1975.

Mekeirle, J. O. (ed.), *Multinational Corporations: The ECSIM Guide to Information Sources*, European Centre for Study and Information on Multinational Corporations, Farnborough, Hants: Saxon House, 1978.

Melman, S., *Pentagon Capitalism: the Political Economy of War*, New York: McGraw Hill, 1970.

Mikesell, R. F., *Foreign Investment in the Petroleum and Mineral Industries: Case Studies in Investor-Host Country Relations*, Baltimore: Johns Hopkins Press, 1971.

Miller, R. R. and **Weigel, D. R.**, *Factors Affecting Resource Transfer Through Direct Investment*, College of Business Administration, University of Iowa Working Paper, 1971.

Monopolies Commission, *Chlordiazepoxide and Diazepan*, London: HMSO, 1973.

Moran, T. H., 'Foreign expansion as an "institutional necessity" for US corporate capitalism: the search for a radical model', *World Politics*, **25**, no. 3, 1973a.

Moran, T. H., 'Transnational strategies of protection and defense by multinational corporations: spreading the risk and raising the cost of nationalization in natural resources', *International Organisation*, Spring 1973b.

Moran, T. H., 'The theory of international exploitation in large natural resource investments', in Rosen, S. J. and Kurth, J. R. (eds.), *Testing Theories of Economic Imperialism*, Lexington, Mass.: D. C. Heath, 1974.

Morawetz, D., 'Employment implications of industrialisation in developing countries', *Economic Journal*, **84**, 1974, pp. 491–542.

Morley, S. A. and **Smith, G. W.**, 'Limited search and the technology choices of multinational firms in Brazil', *Quarterly Journal of Economics*, **XCI**, 1977, pp. 263–87.

Mousouris, S., 'Export horizons of Greek industries', unpublished DBA thesis, Harvard University Graduate School of Business Administration, 1967.

Muller, R. and **Morgenstern, R. D.**, 'Multinational corporations and balance of payments impacts in LDCs: an econometric analysis of export pricing behaviour', *Kyklos*, **27**, Fasc. 2, 1974, pp. 304–21.

Mundell, R. A., 'International trade and factor mobility', *American Economic Review*, **47**, 1957, pp. 321–35.

Murray, R., 'Underdevelopment, international firms and the international division of labour', in *Towards a New World Economy*, Papers and Proceedings of the 5th European conference of the Society for International Development, Rotterdam: Rotterdam U.P., 1972, pp. 159–247.

Musgrave, P., *Direct Investment Abroad and the Multinationals: Effects on the United States Economy*, report prepared for the Subcommittee on Multinational Corporations of the Senate Foreign Relations Committee, Washington: US Government Printing Office, Aug. 1975.

Nayyar, D., 'Transnational corporations and manufactured exports from poor countries', *Economic Journal*, **88**, 1978, pp. 59–84.

Nelson, R. R., 'The simple economics of basic scientific research', *Journal of Political Economy*, **67**, June 1959, pp. 297–306.

Newfarmer, R. S. and **Mueller, W. F.**, *Multinational Corporations in Brazil and Mexico: Structural Sources of Economic and Non-Economic Power*, report prepared for the Subcommittee on Multinational Corporations of the Senate Foreign Relations Committee, Washington: US Government Printing Office, Aug. 1975.

Nyerere, J. K., 'The Arusha Declaration', reprinted as Ch. 2 in *Ujamaa Essays on Socialism*, London: Oxford U.P., 1968.

O'Connor, J., 'The meaning of economic imperialism', in Rhodes, R. I. (ed.), *Imperialism and Underdevelopment*, New York: Monthly Review Press, 1970.

Odell, J. S., 'Correlates of US military assistance and military intervention', in Rosen, S. J. and Kurth, J. R. (eds.), *Testing Theories of Economic Imperialism*, Lexington, Mass.: D. C. Heath, 1974.

Ohlin, B., *Interregional and International Trade*, revised ed., Cambridge, Mass.: Harvard U.P., 1967.

Organisation for Economic Co-operation and Development, *Gaps in Technology: General Report*, Paris: OECD, 1968.

Organisation for Economic Co-operation and Development, *Declaration on International Investment and Multinational Enterprises*, Paris: OECD, 1976.

Orr, D., 'Foreign control and foreign penetration in the Canadian manufacturing industries', unpublished manuscript, University of British Columbia, July 1973.

Ozawa, T., 'Technology imports and direct foreign investment in Japan', *Journal of World Trade Law*, **7**, no. 6, Nov.–Dec. 1973.

Ozawa, T., 'Peculiarities of Japan's multinationalism: facts and theories', *Banca Nazionale del Lavoro Quarterly Review*, no. 115, Dec. 1975.

Parker, J. E. S., *The Economics of Innovation: The National and International Enterprise in Technological Change*, London: Longman, 1974.

Parry, T. G., 'Trade and non-trade performance of US manufacturing industry: revealed comparative advantage', *Manchester School of Economic and Social Studies*, **43**, June 1975, pp. 158–72.

Parry, T. G., 'The product cycle and international production: UK pharmaceuticals', *Journal of Industrial Economics*, **24**, 1975–76, pp. 21–8.

Parry, T. G., *The International Location of Production: Studies in the Trade and Non-trade Servicing of International Markets by Multinational Manufacturing Enterprises*, PhD dissertation, London School of Economics, 1976.

Parry, T. G., *Multinational Manufacturing Enterprises and Imperfect Competition,* Centre for Applied Economic Research, Occasional Paper no. 1, University of New South Wales, April 1977.

Paxson, D. A., *The Territorial Diversification of Multinational Enterprises,* University of Reading Discussion Papers in International Investment and Business Studies, no. 6, 1973.

Pearce, I. F. and **Rowan, D. C.,** 'A framework for research into the real effects of international capital movements', in Bagiotti, T. (ed.), *Essays in Honour of Marco Fanno,* Padova: Cedam, 1966, pp. 505–35, reprinted in Dunning, J. H. (ed.), *International Investment,* Harmondsworth: Penguin Books, 1972, pp. 163–97.

Penrose, E. T., *The Theory of the Growth of the Firm,* Oxford: Blackwell, 1959.

Penrose, E. T., *The Large International Firm in Developing Countries: The International Petroleum Industry,* London: George Allen & Unwin, 1968.

Penrose, E. T., 'Ownership and control: multinational firms in less developed countries', in Helleiner, G. K. (ed.), *A World Divided: The Less Developed Countries in the International Economy,* London: Cambridge U.P., 1976.

Perlmutter, H. V., 'Super-giant firms in the future', *Wharton Quarterly,* Winter 1968.

Perlmutter, H. V., 'The multinational firms and the future', *Annals of the American Academy of Political and Social Science,* Sept. 1972.

Pitchford, J., 'Foreign investment and national advantage in a dynamic context', in MacDougall, I. A. and Snape, R. A. (eds.), *Studies in International Economics,* Monash Conference Papers, Amsterdam: North Holland, 1970, pp. 193–206.

Posner, M. V., 'Technical change and international trade', *Oxford Economic Papers,* 13, 1961, pp. 323–41.

Pratten, C. F., *Labour Productivity Differentials within International Companies,* University of Cambridge, Dept. of Applied Economics, Occasional Paper 50, 1976.

Radice, H., *International Firms and Modern Imperialism,* Harmondsworth: Penguin Books, 1975.

Reddaway, W. B. in collaboration with **Potter, S. J.** and **Taylor, C. T.,** *Effects of United Kingdom Direct Investment Overseas:* Interim Report (1967): Final (1968), London: Cambridge U.P., 1967 and 1968.

Reekie, W. D., *Managerial Economics,* London: Philip Allen, 1975.

Reuber, G. L. *et al., Private Foreign Investment in Development,* Oxford: Clarendon Press, 1973.

Robbins, S. M. and **Stobaugh, R. B.,** *Money in the Multinational Enterprise: A Study in Financial Policy,* New York: Basic Books, 1973.

Robertson, D., 'The multinational enterprise: trade flows and trade policy', in Dunning, J. H. (ed.), *International Investment,* Harmondsworth: Penguin Books, 1972, pp. 326–56.

Robinson, E. A. G., 'The problem of management and the size of firms', *Economic Journal,* 44, 1934, pp. 242–57.

Rosen, S. J., 'The open door imperative and US foreign policy', in Rosen, S. J. and Kurth, J. R. (eds.), *Testing Theories of Economic Imperialism,* Lexington, Mass.: D. C. Heath, 1974.

Rosen, S. J. and **Kurth, J. R.,** *Testing Theories of Economic Imperialism,* Lexington, Mass.: D. C. Heath, 1974.

Rosenstein-Rodan, P. N., 'Problems of private foreign investment and the multinational corporations', in Williamson, R. B., Glade, W. P. and Schmitt, K. M. (eds.), *Latin American—US Economic Interactions,* Washington: American Enterprise Institute for Public Policy Research, 1974.

Rowley, C. K. and **Peacock, A. T.,** *Welfare Economics: A Liberal Restatement,* London: Martin Robertson, 1975.

Rowthorn, B., 'Imperialism in the 1970s – Unity or Rivalry?', in Radice, H. (ed.), *International Firms and Modern Imperialism,* Harmondsworth: Penguin Books, 1975, pp. 158–80.

Rubin, S. J., 'Multinational enterprise and national sovereignty: a skeptic's analysis', *Law and Policy in International Business,* 3, no. 1, 1971, pp. 1–41.

Rugman, A. M., 'Risk reduction by international diversification', *Journal of International Business Studies,* Fall–Winter 1976, pp. 75–80.

Rugman, A. M., 'Risk, direct investment and international diversification', *Weltwirtschaftliches Archiv* (Review of World Economics), **113,** Part 3, 1977a, pp. 487–500.

Rugman, A. M., 'The regulation of foreign investment in Canada', *Journal of World Trade Law,* **11,** no. 4, July–Aug. 1977b, pp. 322–33.

Ruttenberg, S., *Needed: A Constructive Foreign Trade Policy,* AFL–CIO, Oct. 1971.

Sabolo, Y., 'Employment and unemployment, 1960–1990', *International Labour Review,* Dec. 1975.

Sach, I., 'Outward looking strategies: a dangerous illusion', in Streeten, P. (ed.), *Trade Strategies for Development,* London: Macmillan, 1973, pp. 51–61.

Safarian, E. A. and **Bell, J.,** 'Issues raised by national control of the multinational corporation', *Columbia Journal of World Business,* **31,** Dec. 1973.

Sauvant, K. P., 'Controlling transnational enterprises: a review and some further thoughts', in Sauvant, K. P. and Hasenpflug, H., *The New International Economic Order,* London: Wilton House, 1977, pp. 356–433.

Sauvant, K. P. and **Hasenpflug, H.,** *The New International Economic Order,* London: Wilton House, 1977.

Sauvant, K. P. and **Lavipour, F. G.** (eds.), *Controlling Multinational Enterprises,* London: Wilton House, 1976.

Scaperlanda, A. E., 'The EEC and US foreign investment: some empirical evidence', *Economic Journal,* **77,** March 1967, pp. 22–6.

Scaperlanda, A. E. and **Mauer, L. J.,** 'The determinants of US direct investment in the EEC', *American Economic Review,* **59,** Sept. 1969, pp. 558–68.

Schatz, S. P., 'Crude private neo-imperialism: a new pattern in Africa', *The Journal of Modern African Studies,* **7,** no. 4, 1969, pp. 677–88.

Schumpeter, J., *Imperialism,* New York: Meridian Books, 1959 (1st ed. 1919).

Schumpeter, J., *Capitalism, Socialism and Democracy,* New York: Harper & Row, 1947.

Severn, A., 'Investment and financial behaviour of American direct investors in manufacturing', in Machlup, F., Salant, W. and Tarshis, L. (eds.), *The International Mobility and Movement of Capital,* New York: National Bureau of Economic Research, 1972.

Sheahan, J., *Trade and Employment: Industrial Exports Compared to Import Substitution in Mexico,* Williamstown, Mass.: Williams College Center for Development Economics, Research Memorandum 43, 1971.

Sherman, R., *The Economics of Industry,* Boston: Little, Brown & Company, 1974.

Shone, R., *The Pure Theory of International Trade,* London: Macmillan, 1972.

Simon, H. A., 'New developments in the theory of the firm', *American Economic Review,* **52,** no. 2, 1962, pp. 1–15.

Snider, D. A., 'The case for capital controls to relieve the US balance of payments', *American Economic Review,* **84,** 1964, pp. 346–58, reprinted in Dunning, J. H. (ed.), *International Investment,* Harmondsworth: Penguin Books, 1972, pp. 357–74.

Sodersten, B., *International Economics,* London: Macmillan, 1971.

Solomon, R. F. and **Ingham, K. P. D.,** 'Discriminating between MNC subsidiaries and indigenous companies: a comparative analysis of the British mechanical engineering industry', *Oxford Bulletin of Economics and Statistics,* **39,** no. 2, May 1977, pp. 127–38.

Solow, R. M., 'A contribution to the theory of economic growth', *Quarterly Journal of Economics,* **70,** 1956, pp. 65–94.

Stern, R. M., 'Testing trade theories,', in Kenen, P. B. (ed.), *International Trade and Finance,* London: Cambridge U.P., 1975.

Steuer, M. D. *et al.,* *The Impact of Foreign Direct Investment on the United Kingdom,* London: HMSO, 1973.

Stevens, G. V. G., *United States Investment in Latin America: Some Economic and Political Determinants,* unpublished paper, Washington DC: Brookings Institution, 1969.

Stevens, G. V. G., 'The determinants of investment', in Dunning, J. H. (ed.), *Economic*

Analysis and the Multinational Enterprise, London: George Allen & Unwin, 1974, pp. 47–88.

Stobaugh, R. B., 'The neotechnology account of international trade: the case of petrochemicals', *Journal of International Business Studies*, Fall 1971a, pp. 41–60.

Stobaugh, R. B., 'The multinational corporation: measuring the consequences', *Columbia Journal of World Business*, Jan.–Feb. 1971b, pp. 59–64.

Stobaugh, R. B., 'More taxes on multinationals', *Financial Executive*, **42**, no. 4, April 1974, p. 12–17.

Stolper, W. F. and Samuelson, P. A., 'Protection and real wages', *Review of Economic Studies*, IX, 1941, pp. 58–73, reprinted in Bhagwati, J. (ed.), *International Trade*, Harmondsworth: Penguin Books, 1969.

Streeten, P., 'Costs and benefits of multinational enterprises in less-developed countries', in Dunning, J. H. (ed.), *The Multinational Enterprise*, London: George Allen & Unwin, 1971.

Streeten, P., 'The theory of development policy', in Dunning, J. H. (ed.), *Economic Analysis and the Multinational Enterprise*, London: George Allen & Unwin, 1974, pp. 252–79.

Strharsky, H. and Riesch, M. (eds.), *The Transnational Corporations and the Third World*, Washington: CODOC International Secretariat, 1975.

Stubenitsky, F., *American Direct Investment in the Netherlands Industry*, Rotterdam: Rotterdam U.P., 1970.

Sunkel, O., 'Big business and dependencia: a Latin American view', *Foreign Affairs*, **50**, April 1972, pp. 517–31.

Swan, T. M., 'Longer run problems of the balance of payments', in Arndt, H. W. and Corden, W. M. (eds.), *The Australian Economy: A Volume of Readings*, Melbourne: Cheshire Press, 1963, reprinted in Caves, R. E. and Johnson, H. G. (eds.), *Readings in International Economics*, London: George Allen & Unwin, 1968.

Sweezy, P. M. and Magdoff, H., *The Dynamics of US Capitalism*, New York: Monthly Review Press, 1972.

Tharp, Jr, P. A., 'Transnational enterprises and international regulation: a survey of various approaches in international organization', *International Organization*, **30**, Winter 1976, pp. 47–73.

Thompson, D., 'The competition policy of the European Community', in Curzon, G. and V. (eds.), *The Multinational Enterprise in a Hostile World*, London: Macmillan, 1977, pp. 79–88.

Thunell, L. H., *Political Risks in International Business – Investment Behaviour of Multinational Corporations*, New York: Praeger, 1977.

Tinbergen, J., *International Economic Integration*, Amsterdam: Elsevier, 1954.

Torneden, R. L., *Foreign Disinvestment by US Multinational Corporations*, New York: Praeger, 1975.

Tsurumi, Y., 'R & D factor and exports of manufactured goods of Japan', unpublished DBA thesis, Harvard University Graduate School of Business Administration, 1969.

Tucker, R. W., *The Radical Left and American Foreign Policy*, Baltimore: Johns Hopkins Press, 1971.

United Nations Centre on Transnational Corporations, *Survey of Research on Transnational Corporations*, E.77.II.A.16, New York: UN, 1977.

United Nations Conference on Trade and Development, *Restrictive Business Practices in Relation to the Trade and Development of Developing Countries*, New York: UN, 1974.

United Nations Economic and Social Council, *The Impact of Multinational Corporations on the Development Process and on International Relations: Report of the Group of Eminent Persons*, E/5500/ADDI, New York: UN, 1974.

United Nations Economic and Social Council, *Transnational Corporations: Issues Involved in the Formulation of a Code of Conduct*, Centre on Transnational Corporations, E/C.10/17, New York: UN, 1976.

United Nations Economic and Social Council, *Transnational Corporations in World Development*, Commission on Transnational Corporations, 4th Session, E/C.10/38, New York: UN, 1978.

United States Congress, Joint Economic Committee, Subcommittee on Foreign

Economic Policy, *A Foreign Economic Policy for the 1970s*, 91st Congress, 2nd Session, Washington: US Government Printing Office, 1970.

United States Department of Commerce, *US Direct Investments Abroad 1966, Part I: Balance of Payments Data,* Washington: US Government Printing Office, 1970.

United States Department of Commerce, *The Multinational Corporation, Studies on US Foreign Investment,* 1, Washington: US Government Printing Office, March 1972.

United States Department of Commerce, *Survey of Current Business,* Washington: US Government Printing Office, July 1975.

United States Government, *Multinational Report: Oil Corporations and US Foreign Policy,* Washington: US Government Printing Office, 1975.

United States Senate, Committee on Foreign Relations, *Alternatives to Bilateral Economic Aid,* report prepared by the Foreign Affairs Division of the Congressional Research Service, Washington: Library of Congress, 1973a.

United States Senate, *The ITT Co. and Chile 1970–71,* report to the Committee on Foreign Relations by the Subcommittee on Multinational Corporations of the US Senate, Washington: US Government Printing Office, 1973b.

United States Tariff Commission, *Implications of Multinational Firms for World Trade and Investment and for US Trade and Labor,* Report to the Committee of Finance of the US Senate and its Sub-Committee on International Trade, 93rd Congress, 1st Session, Washington: US Government Printing Office, 1973.

Vaitsos, C. V., 'Bargaining and the distribution of returns in the purchase of technology by the developing countries', *Bulletin of the Institute of Development Studies,* **3,** 1970, pp. 16–23.

Vaitsos, C. V., 'The changing policies of Latin American governments towards economic development and direct foreign investments', in Williamson, R. B., Glade, W. P. and Schmitt, K. M. (eds.), *Latin American–US Economic Interactions,* Washington DC: American Enterprise Institute for Public Policy Research, 1974, pp. 89–114.

Vaitsos, C. V., 'The process of commercialization of technology in the Andean Pact' (1971), in Radice, H. (ed.), *International Firms and Modern Imperialism,* Harmondsworth: Penguin Books, 1975, pp. 183–214.

Valvanis-Vail, S., 'Leontief's scarce factor paradox', *Journal of Political Economy,* **62,** 1954.

Vanek, J., 'The natural resource content of foreign trade, 1870–1955, and the relative abundance of natural resources in the United States', *Review of Economics and Statistics,* **41,** May 1959, pp. 146–53.

Vaupel, J. W., *Characteristics and Motivations of the US Corporations which Manufacture Abroad,* paper presented to a meeting of the Atlantic Institute, Paris, June 1971. Quoted in Dunning, J. H., 'The determinants of international production', *Oxford Economic Papers,* **25,** 1973, p. 317.

Vaupel, J. W. and Curhan, J., *The World's Multinational Enterprises: A Sourcebook of Tables,* Boston: Division of Research, Harvard Business School, 1973.

Vernon, R., 'International investment and international trade in the product cycle', *Quarterly Journal of Economics,* **80,** 1966, pp. 190–207, reprinted in Dunning, J. H. (ed.), *International Investment,* Harmondsworth: Penguin Books, 1972, pp. 305–25.

Vernon, R., *Sovereignty at Bay: The Multinational Spread of US Enterprises,* New York: Basic Books, 1971.

Vernon, R., *Restrictive Business Practices,* New York: UN, 1972.

Vernon, R., 'The location of economic activity', in Dunning, J. H. (ed.), *Economic Analysis and the Multinational Enterprise,* London: George Allen & Unwin, 1974, pp. 89–114.

Vernon, R., *Storm Over the Multinationals: The Real Issues,* London: Macmillan, 1977.

Viner, J., *The Customs Union Issue,* New York: Carnegie Endowment, 1950.

Wallace, Jr, D. (ed.), *International Control of Investment: The Dusseldorf Conference on Multinational Corporations,* New York: Praeger, 1974.

Wallace, Jr, D., *International Regulation of Multinational Corporations,* New York: Praeger, 1976.

407

Weidenbaum, M. L., 'Arms and the American economy: a domestic emergency hypothesis', *American Economic Review,* **58,** Papers and Proceedings, 1968, pp. 428–37.

Weisskoff, R., with **Levy, R., Nisonoff, L.** and **Wolff, E.,** *A Multi-Sector Simulation Model of Employment, Growth and Income Distribution in Puerto Rico: A re-evaluation of 'Successful' Development Strategy,* mimeo, New Haven, Conn.: Yale Economic Growth Center, 1973.

Weisskopf, T. E., 'Capitalism, socialism and the sources of imperialism', in Rosen, S. J. and Kurth, J. R. (eds.), *Testing Theories of Economic Imperialism,* Lexington, Mass.: D. C. Heath, 1974a, pp. 57–82.

Weisskopf, T. E., 'Theories of American imperialism: a critical evaluation', *Review of Radical Political Economics,* **6,** 1974b.

Wells, Jr, L. T., 'Effects of policies encouraging foreign joint ventures in developing countries', in Ayal, E B. (ed.), *Micro Aspects of Development,* New York: Praeger, 1973.

Westphal, L. E. and **Kim, K. S.,** *Industrial Policy and Development in Korea,* mimeo, Washington: Development Research Center, International Bank for Reconstruction and Development, 1973.

Wilczynski, J., *Multinationals and East–West Relations,* London: Macmillan, 1976.

Wildsmith, J. R., *Managerial Theories of the Firm,* London: Martin Robertson, 1973.

Willey, H. D., 'Direct investment controls and the balance of payments', in Kindleberger, C. P., *The International Corporation,* Cambridge Mass.: MIT Press, 1970, pp. 95–119.

Williams, M. L., 'The extent and significance of the nationalization of foreign-owned assets in developing countries, 1956–1972', *Oxford Economic Papers,* **27,** no. 2, 1975, pp. 260–73.

Williamson, O. E., *The Economics of Discretionary Behaviour: Managerial Objectives in a Theory of the Firm,* Englewood Cliffs, NJ: Prentice Hall, 1964.

Williamson, O. E., *Corporate Control and Business Behaviour,* Englewood Cliffs, NJ: Prentice Hall, 1970.

Williamson, O. E., 'Managerial discretion, organization form and the multi-division hypothesis', in Marris, R. L. and Wood, A. (eds.), *The Corporate Economy,* London: Macmillan, 1971.

Winkler, J. T., 'Corporatism', *Archives Européennes de Sociologie,* **XCII,** no. 1, 1976.

Wolf, B. M., 'Industrial diversification and internationalization: some empirical evidence', *Journal of Industrial Economics,* **26,** no. 2, 1977, pp. 177–91.

Wolf, T. A., 'East–West economic relations and the multinational corporation', in Sauvant, K. P. and Lavipour, F. G. (eds.), *Controlling Multinational Enterprises,* London: Wilton House, 1976, pp. 79–91.

Wolff, R. D., 'Modern imperialism: the view from the metropolis', *American Economic Review,* **60,** no. 2, May 1970, pp. 225–30.

Woolley, P. K., 'Britain's investment currency premium', *Lloyds Bank Review,* no. 113, July 1974, pp. 33–46.

Yannopoulos, G. N. and **Dunning, J. H.,** 'Multinational enterprises and regional development: an exploratory paper', *Regional Studies,* **10,** 1976, pp. 389–99.

Young, S. and **Hood, N.,** 'The geographical expansion of US firms in Western Europe: some survey evidence', *Journal of Common Market Studies,* **XIV,** no. 3, March 1976, pp. 223–39.

Young, S. and **Hood, N.,** *Chrysler UK: A Corporation in Transition,* New York: Praeger, 1977.

408

Index